"A revealing look at race relations from the point of view of a gifted, uncompromising military man."

—*Publishers Weekly*

# BREAKING THE SILENCE

*"Certain upper-class cadets had determined that I was getting along too well at the Academy . . . and they were going to enforce an old West Point tradition—'silencing'—to freeze me out. From that meeting on . . . no one spoke to me except in the line of duty. I was silenced for the entire four years of my stay at the Academy. But what they did not realize was that I was stubborn enough to put up with their treatment to reach the goal I had come to attain."*

In the course of his military career, Benjamin O. Davis was ostracized by his West Point classmates, passed over for long-deserved promotions, and denied admittance to racist officers' clubs. This is the singular story of a true American hero: a distinguished military man who shattered the armed forces' racially imposed barriers with this simple demand: that he be judged, not by the color of his skin, but by the content of his character.

"Throughout his achievements, General Davis has exemplified the West Point motto, 'Duty, Honor, and Country.' But more important, his life has reflected the social changes that have taken place in the United States over the last fifty years. Through the strength of his commitment to his principles and goals, he has been an inspiration to all those who have followed and served under him. . . . Indeed, Benjamin O. Davis's life is testament that we are living to see the moral reconstruction of this country."

—from the Foreword by Governor L. Douglas Wilder

*An Autobiography*

Robert —
I finally found a copy.
Happy Reading. Good luck
and God bless!

*[handwritten signature]*

# Benjamin O. Davis, Jr.

A M E R I C A N ★ ★ ★

Ⓟ
A PLUME BOOK

PLUME
Published by the Penguin Group
Penguin Books USA Inc., 375 Hudson Street,
New York, New York 10014, U.S.A.
Penguin Books Ltd, 27 Wrights Lane, London W8 5TZ, England
Penguin Books Australia Ltd, Ringwood, Victoria, Australia
Penguin Books Canada Ltd, 10 Alcorn Avenue,
Toronto, Ontario, Canada M4V 3B2
Penguin Books (N.Z.) Ltd, 182-190 Wairau Road, Auckland 10, New Zealand

Penguin Books Ltd, Registered Offices: Harmondsworth, Middlesex, England

Published by Plume, an imprint of New American Library, a division of
Penguin Books USA Inc. This is an authorized reprint of a hardcover edition
published by Smithsonian Institution Press.

First Plume Printing, January, 1992
10 9 8 7 6 5 4 3 2 1

 REGISTERED TRADEMARK—MARCA REGISTRADA

LIBRARY OF CONGRESS CATALOGING-IN-PUBLICATION DATA
Davis, Benjamin O. (Benjamin Oliver), 1912–
    Benjamin O. Davis, Jr., American : an autobiography.
      p.   cm.
    Originally published: Washington : Smithsonian Institution Press, c1991.
    Includes index.
    ISBN 0-452-26746-3
    1. Davis, Banjamin O. (Benjamin Oliver), 1912–      2. Generals—
United States—Biography.   3. United States. Air Force—Biography.
I. Title.
UG626.2.D37A3   1991b
358.4′0092—dc20
[B]                                                            91–33981
                                                                CIP

Printed in the United States of America
Original hardcover design by Alan Carter

The illustrations appearing in this book are from the collection of the author.
The Smithsonian Institution Press does not retain reproduction rights for these
illustrations individually or maintain a file of addresses for photo sources.

*To Agatha*

WITH DEEP APPRECIATION FOR HER

INNUMERABLE CONTRIBUTIONS

# ★ ★ ★ Contents

Photographs appear following pages 54 and 150.

# ★ ★ ★ Foreword

Although Reconstruction after the Civil War officially ended some 113 years ago, Gen. Benjamin O. Davis, Jr.'s autobiography reaffirms that the moral and social reconstruction of the United States has been a long, ongoing struggle that continues for minorities today. Drawing inspiration from family, friends, and his commitment to racial equality, General Davis recounts his life and career within the context of the racial prejudices and reforms of the last 50 years.

General Davis's father, Gen. Benjamin O. Davis, Sr., instilled in his son the virtues of hard work, self-discipline, and self-respect. Seeking to carry those values into life, the younger Davis began challenging the barriers of racial segregation by becoming the first black to graduate from West Point in this century. After graduating 35th in a class of 276 cadets, he attempted to gain entrance into the Army Air Corps, only to be rejected on the grounds that, at the time, the Air Corps had no plans to include blacks in their service. Although the Army's decision shocked and hurt Davis, the ruling would eventually be overturned when the United States entered World War II. Under the presidential directive of Franklin Delano Roosevelt, the first black flying squadron was created, and Benjamin Davis, Jr., became its first commander.

Although the first black pilots were forced to fight on two fronts—the German Messerschmitts on one and Pentagon officials skeptical of an all-black unit on the other—the 99th Pursuit Squadron was a ground-breaking achievement. Benjamin Davis's command broadened the role that blacks could play in America's fighting forces, and it served as a catalyst for the inevitable racial integration of the United States military. Soon after the war, President Truman initiated Executive Order 9981, which called on the armed forces to provide equal treatment and opportunity for all servicemen, and by 11 May 1949 the U.S. Air Force made the announcement in Air Force Letter 35-3 that "there shall be equality of treatment and opportunity for all persons in the Air Force." Benjamin Davis found this military ruling much more palatable than the one made 14 years earlier that had barred him entrance into the Air Corps. The Air Force's statement was the first great step toward the realization of racial integration, and it clearly showed that Davis's perseverance in the armed forces had not been in vain.

Directly following that statement, Benjamin Davis was selected to attend the prestigious Air War College, where he was trained to hold leadership positions within the Air Force hierarchy—a great honor for any officer. Davis graduated from the college to serve as a planning officer within the Air Force Directorate of Operations. From this position, he went on to command several fully integrated fighter squadrons and groups, and he reached the pinnacle of his military career in 1965 when he was chosen to serve as Chief of Staff for the United Nations Military Command in Korea.

During this period, honors and promotions came quickly. Under the Eisenhower administration, Davis was promoted to the rank of brigadier general, and by 1965, under the Johnson administration, he received his final rank of lieutenant general. Five years later General Davis retired from active service, but he continued to play a consulting role to military operations during the 1970s, and he made substantial contributions to civil aviation security policy and highway safety through his second career with the U.S. Department of Transportation.

Throughout his achievements, General Davis has exemplified the West Point motto, "Duty, Honor, and Country." But more important, his life has reflected the social changes that have taken place in the United States over the last fifty years. Through the strength of his commitment to his principles and goals, he has been an inspiration to all those who have followed and served under him, and he will continue to be so for as long as there is a United States military. Indeed, Benjamin O. Davis's life is testament that we are living to see the moral reconstruction of this country.

L. Douglas Wilder
*Governor, Commonwealth of Virginia*

**First Flight**

*Most of the details of my first flight are lost to me. About all I really remember are the takeoff and the feeling of exhilaration, looking down on the city of Washington and up at white clouds above us. And I remember a sudden surge of determination to become an aviator.*

**1.**

The family into which I was born in Washington, D.C., on 18 December 1912, was well-acquainted with pride, determination, and struggle. At that time, my father, Benjamin O. Davis, Sr., was a first lieutenant of cavalry at Fort D. A. Russell, Wyoming. My mother, Elnora Dickerson Davis, wanted me to be born in my father's home, so she made the long trip from Fort Russell to Washington for her confinement. Because my father could not get leave, she then had to make the trip back to Wyoming with me and my sister, Olive, to visit him. This kind of extra effort was typical of the Davises.

My father was all Army, through and through, and he served for 50 years before his retirement in 1948. He had always wanted to be a soldier. As a boy it had thrilled him to watch the ceremonial cavalry unit stationed across the Potomac at Fort Myer, Virginia, when they paraded by, mounted on beautiful, well-groomed horses.

How lucky I was to have a father who, in spite of formidable obstacles, would fight for his beliefs and ambitions and win! Throughout my own military career and beyond, his achievements stood as an example of what could be accomplished in the face of seemingly

1

impossible social opposition. My own career was to differ markedly from his because of the integration of the armed services in 1948, shortly before he retired. But we both suffered the pains of racial prejudice in the service and in society at large; we both fought against segregation throughout our lives; and we were both determined to help change things for the better.

Louis Patrick Henry Davis, my father's father, had spent his boyhood as a servant in the home of Gen. and Mrs. John A. Logan. General Logan, who later became a U.S. representative and a U.S. senator from Illinois, had participated actively in the effort to impeach President Andrew Johnson. My grandfather favorably impressed the Logan family and gradually became their son's companion. Later, as General Logan's protégé, he worked in the Interior Department. He thus gained a measure of economic security and was able to purchase a home at 1830 11th Street NW, where I was born.

My father's early ambition to be a soldier was nurtured by the military training he received as a cadet at Washington's M Street High School and later as a member of a black unit of the District of Columbia National Guard. My grandfather turned to General Logan and a White House aide to secure him an appointment to West Point, but he was told that for political reasons, President William McKinley could not appoint a black man to the U.S. Military Academy. Consequently, my father decided to enlist in the Army and seek a commission through competitive examination.

This plan displeased my grandfather, whose elitist view of the military held that enlisted men were of a lower order, not acceptable to his family circle. It is true that before World War II, Army enlisted people, white and black, were not accorded anywhere near the respect they enjoy today. The military budget was low, the pay was low, and the status of enlisted men was low in the estimation of the general population. As a result of this disagreement, a breach developed between my father and grandfather that lasted almost until my grandfather's death in 1921, when I believe some sort of reconciliation occurred. My father's mother, Henrietta Stewart Davis, did not actively oppose my father's enlistment, but she did express her strong desire that he seek a career as a minister. She and my father did not disagree on his career choice, however, to the extent of falling out with each other.

In spite of his parents' disapproval, my father was sworn in on 14

June 1899 and assigned to Troop I, 9th Cavalry, stationed at Fort Duchesne, Utah. The pay was $25 every two months, but neither that nor the low social status of enlistees diminished his enthusiasm for the Army. In Washington he had been known as Ollie Davis, but he enlisted as Benjamin O. Davis expressly to keep any attendant publicity from unnecessarily offending the family. Upon reporting for duty he discovered that he possessed a tremendous advantage over his fellow soldiers—he could read and write. His knowledge of Army regulations and administration and his willingness to work long hours made him an indispensable asset to his organization and enabled him to advance to sergeant-major in only a few months.

His achievements were truly awe-inspiring. How was it possible for an enlisted man in the black 9th U.S. Cavalry Regiment, at the turn of the century, to go before a regional U.S. Army board at Fort Leavenworth, Kansas, and obtain from it a solid recommendation that he be given a Regular Army commission as a second lieutenant of cavalry? And how was it possible that the War Department, in 1901, would include his name among other nominees for commission? My father never answered these questions for me, and my conclusion, very simply, is that he was a most exceptional young man, capable of convincing many in the racially unenlightened Army chain of command that he had earned and deserved a Regular Army commission. He thus joined the only other black regular line officer in the Army, Charles Young, an 1889 graduate of West Point.

My father's first duty as a second lieutenant was with Troop M, 9th Cavalry, in the Philippines. In October 1902 he returned on leave to Washington, where he renewed several years' friendship with a former schoolmate, Elnora Dickerson, who lived less than two blocks from his home. They were married on 23 October 1902, and my sister Olive was born three years later.

The Dickerson family was a large one: seven girls and two boys. Edward and Lydia, my grandparents, had moved from Virginia to Washington after the Civil War at about the same time as my father's family. My mother's father had supported his family as a driver, porter, teamster, expressman. He had no formal education, but he was able to purchase a home at 1711 11th Street NW in 1876. When he died 10 years later, his elder son took over the family business. The younger son became a piano repairman. All the girls worked as schoolteachers except my mother, who was a dressmaker.

Before I was born, my parents and Olive had been stationed at Fort Washakie, Wyoming; Fort Robinson, Nebraska; Wilberforce, Ohio; Monrovia, Liberia; and Fort D. A. Russell. After I was born the traveling continued. My father served on the Mexican border from 1912 to 1915, during the Mexican Revolution. His duties and the unsettled conditions in the area effectively cut short my mother's visit to Fort D. A. Russell and sent her, Olive, and me back to Washington, where we stayed throughout the remainder of 1913. My father visited us in December and was able to join my many aunts, uncles, and cousins for a celebration of my first birthday. By the time my father's leave was over, conditions on the border had improved sufficiently for the family to accompany him to Arizona and stay there for several months in 1914.

In February 1915 my father, now a captain, was ordered back to Wilberforce University, a black institution, as professor of military science and tactics. As a lieutenant, he had served at Wilberforce in the same capacity from 1905 to 1909. This assignment reflected the War Department's efforts to avoid assigning a black officer to a situation in which he would command white enlisted men or outrank a white officer. In each assignment my father received throughout his half-century of service, this policy remained the paramount consideration. The Army restricted him to "safe" assignments: Junior Reserve Officer Training Corps (ROTC) units at black colleges, black national guard units, military attaché to Liberia. He spent many years in such professionally disadvantageous assignments, even though his correspondence with the War Department emphasized, beyond any possible doubt, his strong preference for duty with troops. As his rank increased—he was promoted to captain in 1915 and shortly thereafter to major and lieutenant colonel—so also did the intensity of the War Department's assignment problem. My father was happiest in duty with troops, even though some of his regimental commanders expressed a dislike for mixing a black officer with white officers assigned to the same unit. When he was joined at Fort D. A. Russell by my mother, sister, and me, our family was largely ignored by the white officer families.

For these reasons, my father was always happiest overseas, where black people were treated far better than they were by most of their own countrymen at home. In later years he expressed to me many times his desire to live in retirement in southern France, leaving behind the racial discrimination that was the bane of our existence in the United States.

On 9 February 1916, nine days after the birth of my second sister, Elnora, my mother died. She had remained at Wilberforce instead of returning to Washington, as she had for her previous confinements, because the doctor anticipated no problems. She was progressing well after the birth but suddenly suffered an embolism. Two of her sisters—Mary, a schoolteacher in Washington, and Iola, a Chicago housewife—came to help my father with the family until his mother arrived. Aunt Mary died at Wilberforce only two months after my mother. I regret that I cannot remember my mother; her reputation was that of a beautiful, loving, caring person.

Shortly after her death, my father's tour at Wilberforce was terminated by orders to the Philippines, effective in June 1917. The preparation for this overseas duty was one of the most trying of his Army career. He had three motherless children and no satisfactory home for them. He particularly wanted to keep us together, and though many of the aunts volunteered to take care of one child, only my grandmother would accept all three. In May 1917, therefore, my father took us to Washington to live with our grandparents, Louis and Henrietta Davis. The three of us crowded an already full house; my grandmother's mother, Granny, was also a member of the household. My father spent two weeks with us in Washington before leaving for the Philippines, assuring himself that we were well settled and trying to make us understand his deep devotion to us and his regret in having to be separated from us. Today I continue to appreciate the wisdom of his decision to keep us together in what must have been an extremely difficult time.

My father's expected two-year tour in the Philippines turned into three years, and his request for leave was not approved. While he was there, he launched a two-year courtship-by-mail with a family friend, Sadie Overton, who had been a professor of English at Wilberforce when we lived there. At the age of five, I asked Miss Overton in front of my father whether they would get married. She turned beet red, confirming beyond question that romance was in the air. To Olive and me it was a wonderful idea, and the attention and cuddling Miss Overton habitually gave baby Nora certainly assured her a warm welcome from the Davis children.

Sadie Overton had been born in Macon, Mississippi, the same year my father was born in Washington. Her father had been a member of the Mississippi lower House in the late 1870s, at the end of Reconstruction. He later became a teacher and saw to it that his three children each received college educations. In 1916, the year after she came to Wilberforce, Sadie received her bachelor's degree from the University of Chicago. She was awarded the master of arts degree in English from Ohio State University in 1919, after taking a series of summer courses there.

When my father learned that his stay in the Philippines would be extended, he and Mother Sadie, as we came to call her, arranged her travel to the Philippines, where they were married upon her arrival on 24 December 1919. This was quite a long trip and an adventurous effort on the part of an essentially provincial woman.

Meanwhile, my grandparents coped as best they could with the three active children added to their already overpopulated household. I was five, Elnora was one, and Olive was twelve. I recall little of those days, but I do remember the pall that would settle over the house when my grandfather came home from work. Suddenly, everything would become very quiet; it was understood that no noise would be tolerated while the autocrat read his copy of the *Evening Star*. Even though my father paid for our support, I had the feeling that we were resented and not wanted.


**Early Childhood**

My memories of life at 1830 11th Street are undoubtedly a mixture of things I can actually recall and other things people have told me. I remember the icehouse directly across the street, its small buildings in which blocks of ice were stored, the big, burly iceman with a black leather pad across his back, and the tongs he used to move 25- and 50-pound blocks of ice onto his horse-drawn wagon. He delivered ice from the alley behind my grandfather's house to the backdoor pantry where our icebox stood. I remember the streetcars that passed our house going south to downtown Washington and north toward Walter Reed Hospital. I remember Katzman's Grocery on the corner of 11th and T streets, only a few doors from our house, and the excitement in the neighborhood when Mr. Katzman converted his delivery wagon to the first motor-driven truck I had seen. I remember quite well the Lincoln and Republic theaters on U Street, and the hill on 13th Street where I took my sled when we had snow.

My earliest recollection of racial problems relates to discussions I heard in my grandfather's house when I was only six or seven. I heard real fear in the voices of my cousins and my aunt when they talked about the "race riots" in progress on U Street, just one short block north of our house at 11th and T. The voices warned me not to approach U Street for any reason whatever while the riots were taking place. I do not recall just what the disturbance was about—something to do with jobs and the return of troops from overseas service during World War I—but I do know that the ominous term "race riot" was indelibly lodged in my consciousness from that time on.

My life at 1830 was certainly not all bad. Any problems I had there were relieved by the special treatment accorded me as the favorite of my many aunts and uncles down at 1711, a block away, where I was always welcome. As was frequently pointed out to me by my father's family, my mother's relatives found it easier to be nice to me because they did not have to get their hands dirty bringing me up. My Uncle Ernest regularly left money for me on the windowsill of his bedroom. He took me on long streetcar rides all over the city, and on Sundays he often took me to visit Uncle Louis, my father's elder brother, who operated his own farm far out in the country at the end of the Massachusetts Avenue streetcar line.

Uncle Louis and Aunt Ruth had nine children, all older than I. The youngest was a boy; all the others were girls who later distinguished themselves in education or in government service. Louis, Jr., died young when a defective water heater he was repairing exploded. I always looked forward to the big-family enthusiasm of Uncle Louis's household and the good times I enjoyed with my cousins. They looked down on me somewhat because I was younger and also a city boy. But the city boy quickly learned to ride a Mexican burro named Tipperary that my father had shipped from Arizona, along with a governess cart. And I did not panic when Tipperary bit me. (The family story says I bit him back.) I enjoyed swimming in the farm's swimming hole. I was intrigued by the horses, cows, pigs, chickens, and rides in the hay wagon. The city boy can still remember the painful shoulder he got when he pitched more than a small amount of hay. I always looked forward to the Sunday feast of homegrown vegetables and homemade ice cream and cake. The flies that zoomed around the dinner table bothered me a bit, but all in all Sunday at Uncle Louis's was a real treat. The farm may not have been a great financial success, but it supported a wonderful family of solid citizens.

Uncle Ernest got me my first job, a newspaper route for the *Evening Star*. He helped me load my wagon with the heavy papers, and he showed me how to fold and place them properly at the subscriber's door. His sister Lyd, the eldest Dickerson aunt, instructed me in the mysteries of making root beer and joined me in playing with her four small black Boston bulldogs. Of course, the best thing about 1711 was that I was never disciplined there.

During my last two years in Washington, 1918 and 1919, I started school. The neighborhood schools were all black, teachers and students, and in the tradition of Washington's black school system from the 1920s through the 1940s and even later, they provided an outstanding education. The classrooms were not overcrowded, the teachers were highly qualified, and an atmosphere of discipline, pride, and achievement prevailed among both teachers and students. I was given an extra push by the whole Davis family's deep respect for and interest in education, especially later by Mother Sadie.

I am grateful to all the people at 1830 for the care they gave me and my sisters, in spite of the many inconveniences three active children of three different ages must have created. When the time came to join our father and new mother, we took with us warm feelings, especially for my grandmother, who had made big sacrifices in our interest and cared closely for Elnora, who had arrived in Washington at the age of 15 months.

## A New Life at Tuskegee Institute

When my father and Mother Sadie returned to the States in May 1920, we moved to Tuskegee Institute, another all-black institution, adjacent to Tuskegee, Alabama, where the War Department temporarily solved the problem of what to do with a black lieutenant colonel by making him a professor of military science and tactics—the same assignment he had received years before as a captain. Tuskegee Institute was an island within which blacks could live and move about comfortably, surrounded by whites who handicapped themselves and poisoned their own individual and collective lives by

the virulence of their hatred of blacks. The spirit of the founder of
Tuskegee Institute, Booker T. Washington, and the concepts he had
pioneered were clearly evident in the early 1920s. All the people who
were part of the Institute—people in low positions as well as high—
believed in the vital importance of their responsibility to the mostly
young, farm-reared boys and girls who found their way to Tuskegee.
They realized that the contribution they might be able to make to
these young students could not and would not be made elsewhere by
anyone else. They knew the importance of sending graduates back to
their communities thoroughly skilled in the trades they had been
taught, instilled with the ambition to perform well and to exercise the
ethical values they had learned. In those years, Tuskegee Institute
graduates were highly respected people indeed.

My father had previously experienced serious problems with the
president and administration of Wilberforce University over the university's failure to support him in his probably ultrastrict application
of Army regulations in a civilian environment. He had no such problem with Robert R. Moton, president of Tuskegee Institute. Dr. Moton
was a big man—physically and figuratively—and he supported my
father when his positions were in the interests of the Institute. Their
one major disagreement during my father's first tour at Tuskegee,
from 1920 to 1924, involved the storage of ammunition at the Institute in quantities necessary to meet the War Department's requirements in the rifle marksmanship program. Dr. Moton believed that
the amount of ammunition to be stored—48,000 rounds—would
alarm the white citizens of Tuskegee and did not endorse the requisi-
tion. The problem went to the 4th Corps Area commander in Atlanta,
who decided that he should not support an action not approved by
the president. My father also disapproved of the less-than-firm discipline of the students as administered by the Institute's commandant
of cadets, but that matter was smoothed over. As with the ammunition problem, my father sought strict interpretation of Army regulations as they would have been applied in the 9th Cavalry, something
entirely foreign to the Institute's laissez-faire academic environment.
Many of my father's reforms and improvements were accepted, however, and the Institute benefited substantially from his presence on
the faculty. The students respected him and recognized almost unanimously his positive contributions.

For myself, I liked everything I saw in my new home, particularly the old southern custom of exchanging greetings with people I passed on the street, whether I knew them or not. I eagerly adopted this gracious gesture. We now lived in the country, in a bungalow close to the Lincoln Gates, the entrance to the campus. We had plenty of space: a living room, a dining room, and a bedroom for each of us.

Our adjustment to Mother Sadie was smooth and easy, and her emphasis on education was to benefit me for the rest of my life. She sent Olive to high school in Atlanta because she believed the Atlanta University complex would better prepare my sister for college. I went to school at the Children's House, a private elementary school in Greenwood for inhabitants of the Institute and the immediate area. Mother Sadie supplemented my formal instruction with her own curriculum. Elnora, whom we called Nora, and I were furnished a special reading light over our beds and required to spend some time reading each night. I was also given school achievement goals, and only excellence in performance was acceptable. If my grades were in the high 90s, why were they not 100? My father disciplined me; when Mother Sadie prescribed a whipping, my father took off his belt and administered it. I received only a few whippings, and those must have been well deserved. I respected both my parents and was proud of our family. We arrived on time for meals, sat up straight at the table, and ate all the food on our plates. Punctuality, neatness, and obedience were the rules; there was no such thing as talking back. Even as a child I could appreciate what was being done for us, and I never resented the decisions my parents made. I was well aware that most of my contemporaries were given considerably more latitude, but I was happy with the Davis method.

The Children's House was fine except during the coldest days of winter, when the potbellied coal stoves made it either too cold or too warm, depending upon where I sat. Mother Sadie had prepared me well, so I had no problems with my schoolwork. I liked my teachers and classmates, almost all of whom eventually left Alabama for greener fields.

It was a pleasant time for me. One of the few aggravations I remember was piano lessons. My father had purchased a piano several years earlier and took lessons, as did Mother Sadie and Elnora. The teacher was a friend of Mother Sadie's: Miss Simmons, whom I did not like. She insisted on teaching me traditional rather than "modern" music—that is, jazz. I made such a fuss about it that I was relieved of the lessons. Today I am sorry I got my way and wish I had continued with the piano. I did take trumpet lessons, but they were stopped abruptly when I played baseball one afternoon after a trumpet lesson and was late for dinner. Perhaps the noise I made on the trumpet was not entirely appreciated.

The family often walked over to the Institute to watch my father review the student body as it marched to Sunday chapel. All the students were in uniform—boys in military dress, and girls in blouses and skirts. My father would accompany Dr. Moton to chapel, but the rest of the family did not usually go. All of us would, however, attend the Sunday band concerts except on special occasions. My mother and father played bridge with members of the faculty, and Mother Sadie belonged to more than one bridge club. She also organized a Tuskegee Institute chapter of Delta Sigma Theta, a national black sorority. We frequently had house guests—my father's mother, Mother Sadie's mother, and her nephew and niece, John and Sadie Overton. We had a lively, busy, and enjoyable household.

We never went to Montgomery, even though one of the major department stores there bent the state segregation laws and let some of the Tuskegee faculty shop with a special degree of freedom from insult. We would not participate in this maneuver. Although both my father and mother made strong attempts to instill in us the beliefs that we were as good as anyone else and other people were as good as we were, and that we should treat other people the way we would want them to treat us, they could not hide the rigid segregation that existed all around Tuskegee Institute. On the rare occasions when we traveled to Washington, we saw the water fountains and toilets marked "colored" and "white." Hence, in spite of family efforts to avoid poisoning our minds about matters of race, my parents were not completely successful. The fact of racism was forced upon us whenever we left the Institute.

A particular event of a racial nature that affected all of us is sharply etched in my memory. I call it the night of the Klan. About a mile and a half from Tuskegee Institute, a new Veterans Administration Hospital for black veterans was soon to be completed. To express its preference that jobs for doctors and nurses go to whites instead of blacks, as was planned at the time, the Ku Klux Klan announced a full-scale march past the Institute. It is difficult today to appreciate fully the terror the Klan created in the minds of black people, but in the 1920s, particularly in Alabama and Mississippi, Klan lynchings still occurred frequently.

Our house and all the other houses in the immediate neighborhood were occupied by faculty and other employees of the Institute. Our official instructions were to stay indoors and turn off the lights to keep from provoking the marchers in any way. But as a Regular Army officer, my father refused to cower behind closed doors. Furthermore, he believed that the entire Davis family should make known its opinion of the Klan by staying visible and not hiding in the shadows. On the night of the Klan, therefore, Mother Sadie, my two sisters, and I sat quietly on our porch, my father resplendent in his white dress uniform, and the rest of us viewing the parade with some concern about what might happen when the Klansmen marched by. Our porch light was the only light to be seen for miles around except for the flaming torches of the Klansmen, who passed by on the street only a few feet from where we sat. Also resplendent in white—robes, masks, and hoods—they passed by without incident. In the end the Klan lost its fight, and the jobs went to blacks as originally planned. Today the hospital is staffed by both black and white doctors and nurses.

While we were at Tuskegee, my father took me with him on two trips to Washington, where he officiated as judge for the annual Dunbar High School Competitive Drill. Peculiarly enough, I cannot remember what my father and I would talk about when we were alone. In any case, it was an easy relationship for both of us. We were direct in all matters, and did not beat around the bush. My letters to him over the years were loving, but short and to the point.

When my father's tour at Tuskegee ended in late summer 1924, we departed for Cleveland. Nora and I spent a few months with our grandmother in Washington while my father and mother were settling upon a place for the family to live. They eventually purchased a house in a mainly black neighborhood of Cleveland, though a few white families had not yet moved away. The city's residential areas were mostly segregated, and though I liked Cleveland, I was always aware of being a black Clevelander.

While in Washington, I attended school until November as a member of the 7A class of the seventh grade. I then transferred to the 7A class at Cleveland's Central High, a large, racially mixed school that I was assigned to based on our residence. Although 7A was the first half of seventh grade in Washington, 7A followed 7B in Cleveland. So, by saying nothing about the whole thing I gained a full semester, and as a result graduated from Central in June 1929 at the age of 16. I probably compensated for any deficiency I may have suffered in missing a semester by extensive reading, travel, and the help I got from Mother Sadie.

My father's assignment to Cleveland was again based on the racist policies of the War Department: no black officer would be put in command of white troops or assigned to a military base where there was danger of his using a white officers' club. It was still fairly easy for the Army to avoid this situation. My father, one other black line officer, and the chaplains assigned to the black 24th and 25th Infantry regiments and the black 9th and 10th Cavalry regiments were the only officers who represented a threat to the preservation of the lily-white Army officer corps. Although my father should have been assigned to Regular Army units—he was long overdue—it was clearly his color that prevented it.

Officially, the War Department had no desire to assign my father to troops because of his rank, and disapproved in principle the idea of assigning a cavalry officer to an infantry National Guard unit. By some coincidence, a decision to federalize a black National Guard unit for Ohio finally provided an opening, and he was assigned as instructor in spite of the cavalry-infantry principle. As instructor, he was responsible to the Army chain of command as well as to the state of Ohio. He enjoyed traveling around Ohio visiting company training periods and getting to know the people assigned to the units. There were also annual maneuvers at Camp Perry on the shores of Lake Erie near Port Clinton, where field exercises, drill, and rifle practice were emphasized. I enjoyed visiting Camp Perry and learning to shoot a Springfield rifle.

Nora and I were close friends, then and now, and our parents sent us to Washington during the summer of 1926 while they toured Europe. The European trip was advertised as a graduation present for Olive, but they were the ones who were itching to go. I took typewriting at Dunbar High School that summer, and could not be convinced that minor deviations from a perfectly typed page were all that important. I also learned to swim at a public pool and suffered the embarrassment of losing my first and only pair of long trousers there.

On one of our regular Sunday trips, Uncle Ernest took me to

Bolling Field, at that time just a dirt field with no concrete runway. I suspect that Uncle Ernest had little interest in airplanes, but he had read in the *Evening Star* about the barnstormers who flew in and out of Bolling and thought I would enjoy watching the action. In my mind's eye, I can still visualize that summer day, the crowds of spectators, the airplane taking off into the clear blue sky, the thrill of seeing it climb to altitude, make its breathtaking maneuvers, and finally return to earth.

After reporting to my father on our visit to Bolling, I somehow convinced him to take me on a second visit. This time, for $5, the barnstormer took me into the air as his passenger. I cannot explain my father's motives in buying me an airplane ride. He was not a frivolous spender, and $5 was a considerable sum in 1926. I can only guess that he was looking far into the future and, seeing airplanes in that future, realized in some mysterious way that I would benefit from the experience.

Most of the details of this first flight are lost to me. I was completely overwhelmed. We flew in an open-cockpit airplane, and I had to wear goggles and a helmet. The airplane seemed to be rather frail, not solid enough to hold both the pilot and me. I can dimly recall making a few dives and steep turns that gave me some unusual sensations. I was not to experience those sensations again until my Army Air Corps indoctrination rides at Mitchell Field, Long Island, on a trip from West Point some nine years later. About all I really remember are the takeoff and the feeling of exhilaration at being in the air, looking down on the city of Washington and up at white clouds far above us. And I remember a sudden surge of determination to become an aviator.

A year later, when Charles Lindbergh flew solo across the Atlantic to Paris, I was gripped by the reports of his flight. We picked up the strong radio signal from WLW in Cincinnati, even though we were living in Cleveland at the time. I read everything I could find about Lindbergh, his reception in Paris and the rest of Europe, his trip to England, and his return to the United States aboard a Navy ship. I saw pictures of the ticker-tape parade in New York, and I read about his visit to the White House and his survey trips that so greatly advanced the development of aviation in this country. The drama of Lindbergh's contributions seized my imagination and gave me a vision of flying that I retain to this day. In May 1987, 60 years after his flight to Paris,

I delivered the annual Lindbergh Lecture at the Smithsonian Institution's National Air and Space Museum on the Mall in Washington. In 1926 I never could have dreamed that one day I would be sharing my thoughts about the great aviator with an appreciative audience.

Back in Cleveland that summer, I rented a rowboat and explored Lake Erie, discovering a derelict's decomposed body in the water and reporting it to the police. During the long winter months, I ice-skated on the lagoon at Wade Park. Cleveland had lots of snow, and at a particular stoplight near our house I could hook my sled to a car's rear bumper and get a ride to the next stoplight. Sometimes a driver would object to my piggyback and try to throw me off. The weather was usually too bad for the police to patrol the streets, so besides the gasoline exhaust smell that got into my clothes, I managed to stay out of trouble.

I had several jobs in Cleveland. On Sundays between 3:30 and 4:00 A.M. I rolled out of bed, walked to a *Cleveland Plain Dealer* distribution point, picked up as many papers as I thought I could sell, put them on my wagon or sled, and went to a likely residential selling area, where I announced repeatedly in my loudest tones, "Get your *Cleveland Plain Dealer!*" This job certainly developed my voice, and I always sold all my papers. I also worked in a corner drugstore during my first two summers, and at Christmas I worked downtown at the May Company delivery room, where the pay was 75 cents a day. I was 15 when I got a full-time job working in the mail room of the Cleveland Electric Illuminating Company, where I was paid $15 per week. At the end of summer, before I returned to school, I took the whole family to Luna Park and insisted that they enjoy all the rides. In partnership with my close friend Lawrence Schumake, I also bought my first car, an ancient Ford. Unfortunately, we failed to keep enough oil in the crankcase, and one day the engine froze, effectively eliminating our means of transportation. The car had cost us $25— $12.50 each.

My school, like those in Washington, was a fine one. Central High still had a healthy cross section of Cleveland's population in attendance—white, black, Italian, Polish, and several other nationalities. The teachers were mostly white, and the historical background of the school inspired them to maintain an excellent learning environment. I remember warmly my first homeroom teacher, a Miss Chesnutt, who came from a distinguished black family. I also remember Ethel Weimer, a white teacher who gave her students small, leath-erbound editions of Shakespeare's plays as prizes for scholarship. I still have four of these books, and I treasure them. I wrote to Miss Weimer during the early part of my stay at West Point to thank her for the inspiration and encouragement she had given me. The letter was found among her effects shortly after her untimely death, and it was published in a Cleveland newspaper.

Just before graduation I had a crisis: the civics teacher announced that I would not be permitted to graduate unless I turned in a current events notebook that I should have been bringing up to date each week during the semester. After negotiating a new deadline for com-pliance, I spent several days clipping news items from old newspapers and pasting them in a looseleaf notebook. My next-door neighbor and friend Lynn Coleman, a boy with an artistic bent, copied a color picture of a prominent historical figure (Louis XIII, I believe) that I put on the cover. I submitted it and was permitted to graduate.

I had done well at Central, being elected president of the student council and finishing at the very top of my class. I received a student council award, and at graduation exercises I played the character Public Trust in a morality play entitled *Every Youth*. After graduation Mother Sadie sent me to summer school at Fisk University in Nashville, to take courses in mathematics and learn what it was like to attend a black college. Fisk was a black oasis in a traditional, rigidly segregated, mid-sized southern city. I went to the segregated down-town theaters and became fully acquainted with the ugly details of southern segregationism.

## Marking Time

In the fall of 1929 I enrolled at Western Reserve University. By this time my sister Olive had married, having met her husband, George Streator, while she was teaching at Bluefield State College in West Virginia. They were living in Cleveland and both seeking master's degrees at Western Reserve. I was a paying guest in their home. George, who was studying mathematics, tried to explain to me the theory of the functions of a complex variable. He and Olive also tried to get me in the middle of their erudite discussions, which some people call family fights, but I was fleet of foot and avoided getting caught.

On the whole, I felt that I was merely marking time. I had no clear objective in going to college, and no particular interest in my studies or my intended major, mathematics. Perhaps the atmosphere at Western Reserve had something to do with it; perhaps I was not attuned to college life. Then, too, I did not really enjoy living with Olive and George. So probably a large part of my unhappiness was my own fault. I had not even considered how I was going to support myself. My father paid all my expenses and gave me any money I truly needed (though he required a strict accounting, down to every penny).

By the end of the school year I was frustrated, filled with indecision and concern about my future. My life was brightened somewhat by my father's decision to take me to France with him while he escorted a group of Gold Star Mothers and Widows visiting the graves of loved ones who had fallen during World War I. On my return, however, I had to face up to the problems I had left behind. A major element of my concern was that my parents had always held high hopes for their three children. Olive, now 23, was well on her way toward a career in social work. Nora was in high school in Xenia, Ohio, and excelling in all her subjects. Father and mother had insisted that she attend the white high school in the city district where our house was located, and she encountered some resentment among the white teachers. The situation eased after a short time, and though it remained uncomfortable for her, she did not let it get in the way of her education.

As for me, now 17, I still wanted to fly airplanes, but the harsh reality was that there was no way for a black man to become a professional pilot. The United States then offered few career opportunities of any kind to black people. Blacks took many jobs that whites did not want: redcaps in railroad stations, waiters, Pullman porters, dishwashers, street cleaners, garbage handlers, elevator operators, car washers. If educationally qualified, they could become doctors, lawyers, ministers, businessmen, and teachers, but only where there was little or no mixing with whites. I thought that perhaps I could become an engineer and move to South America, as some blacks were doing, seeking careers not available to them in the United States.

The upshot of it all was that I was not interested in any of the available careers for blacks, and I could not think of any realistic way to get into flying. The lesson of my father's assignments in the Army was all too clear to me, and even in the unlikely event that I could get appointed to West Point, I had no reason to believe that the Army would train me to be a pilot. It was only after I had completed more than two years as a West Point cadet that I naively began to believe that the Army Air Corps might accept me for pilot training.

There was no question that my father secretly wanted me to go to West Point. He had wanted to go himself, and it was only natural that he wanted opportunities for me that he had been denied. But he had never urged me to seek admission, nor did he even suggest it. So I continued to drift along, undecided and frustrated, until April 1931, when suddenly everything became clear to me: no matter what obstacles might present themselves, I was determined to attend West Point and pursue the career my father had chosen.

Unknown to me at the time, events had already been moving me toward West Point. My father had learned through the black press that a young black Chicagoan, Alonzo Parham, had entered West Point in July 1929. Parham had been appointed by the one black representative in Congress, Oscar De Priest, a Republican from Illinois. Black America was proud of Parham, and the black press frequently reported on his progress at the Academy. My mother and father discussed his appointment and, aware of my lack of interest in any specific career, wondered whether West Point might appeal to me. I was in the eligible age bracket, I was in excellent physical condition, and I could be depended upon to succeed academically. Meanwhile, in December 1929, Parham was discharged for academic deficiency along with the usual one-third of the plebe class. My father, a prolific and convincing letter writer, was spurred by this news to write in his beautiful penmanship to De Priest, expressing his regrets that Parham had not been continued and his hope that the young man would qualify for reentry through the reexamination option open to discharged cadets. De Priest replied in a cordial letter, expressing his determination to continue appointing blacks to West Point and also to appoint the first black to the Naval Academy.

My father believed strongly in America despite all its deficiencies. A serious student of American history, he was proud of the performance of blacks in America's wars from the Revolution on. He believed that only through the full integration of blacks into society could American life be fully representative of the democratic principles so clearly enunciated by our Constitution but so poorly observed in practice. In another letter to De Priest, he pointed out that his Army service was approaching an end, but he was reluctant to retire because the Army's active list would be left without a single black regular officer. He also named me as a possible appointee.

Congressman De Priest then offered me an alternate appointment, which I had to decline because I could not meet the requirement of Illinois residency. At this point, my father and mother made a major decision: I was to move to Chicago, thereby becoming eligible to be appointed to West Point by De Priest. In addition, I was to enter the University of Chicago in the fall of 1930.

It took several months for the details of the West Point idea to develop, but eventually I agreed with my parents to seek a De Priest appointment and enter the Academy in July 1931. Meanwhile I attended classes at the University of Chicago and rented a small room from the Gibson family for $16 a month. The Gibsons had two sons about my age, Truman and Harry, and a much younger daughter, Alberta. Then as now, Chicago was one of the most rigidly segregated cities in the United States, and racism abounded. I ate my meals in restaurants, even though the Gibsons invited me to take all my meals with them, because I felt I had more freedom with this arrangement. Downtown restaurants were off limits to blacks, and it was dangerous to go into certain areas away from the all-black South Side.

On 9 February 1931 I received a principal appointment to West Point. Elated, I reported to Fort Sheridan, Illinois, on 4 March 1931 for three days of examinations. Unfortunately, because I had completed more than a year and a half of college with good grades, I had mistakenly assumed that I would not have to take the academic part of the examination, given only once each year. I had to take it without preparation. To receive an overall passing grade, one had to pass every subject, and regardless of how I did on the rest of the examination, it would have taken considerable preparation on my part to pass English history and European history, which I had never studied.

On 7 April 1931 I wrote my father to tell him I had failed. It was an extremely difficult letter for me. Failing the examination was worse than an embarrassment; it was mortification. I apologized for letting the family down and confessed that I was not the man I had considered myself to be. I asked that he renew his faith in me and give me another chance. He must have been as thoroughly embarrassed and disappointed as I was, but his reply was a classic letter of support, indicating his continued faith in me. It was just what I needed at the time, and it certainly was an admirable act on his part.

On 14 April 1931 I received official notification that I had failed, but seeing it in writing only made me more determined than ever. It was on this day that I fully resolved to go to West Point, graduate, and seek a career in the Army Air Corps. I never had further doubts of any kind about my future, which I was completely convinced lay in the military service.

I finished the spring quarter at the University of Chicago, and because my father and mother were going to Europe again, I was left to my own devices. Mother Sadie believed I should spend the summer profitably by attending Ohio State University, so I took three mathematics courses there. Then I returned to the University of Chicago and completed the fall quarter in 1931. All my college work after Western Reserve was at the A level. Through hard experience, I had learned how to study effectively.

I dropped out of the University of Chicago at the end of the fall quarter to study intensively for the 1932 West Point entrance examinations. The Academy had furnished applicants with copies of examinations from the previous five years, covering the same subjects I had been examined in the year before. My approach was ridiculously simple. I worked on all five examinations in each subject until I could pass each year's examination with a high grade. I did not have to prepare for the algebra examination, but the crash courses in English and European history and the reviews of American history, plane geometry, English grammar, literature, and composition required many hours of concentrated effort. I gave it all my best for two months until I was positive there would be no repetition of the previous year's fiasco. When I reported to Fort Sheridan in March, the examination was an anticlimax, and I immediately told my father that I had passed. War Department notification and orders to report to West Point on 1 July 1932 arrived in early May.

**Silence**

**2.** *I was silenced solely because cadets did not want blacks at West Point. Their only purpose was to freeze me out. What they did not realize was that I was stubborn enough to put up with their treatment to reach the goal I had come to attain.*

Everyone in our family had been taught the value of a dollar, and the depression years made us even more careful in the handling of money. As children and teenagers, my sisters and I were always expected to turn in any extra change after a purchase, and we often joked about how the leftover nickels and pennies had to be returned to "the Colonel." But my father was so thrilled when he received my letter telling him I was going to be in West Point's class of 1936 that he sent me a check for $25, saying, "I am adding an extra five." He meant that I could spend the "extra five" without having to account for it.

With his letter came a few words of advice. Normally he was cautious of making suggestions to me or my sisters. He wanted us to learn how to think and make decisions for ourselves. At this point, however, he must have wanted to help guide me over the big changes I would have to make in entering the Academy:

Now just understand that I am very happy. I feel you have the makings of a good cadet and officer. Just have patience, concentrate all you have got and who knows you may lead your class, or certainly, at least make the

[Army Corps of] Engineers. If you do that you have the world waiting for you. Remember twelve million people [the black population of the United States] will be pulling for you with all we have. Let me have your notice and any other official papers you receive. I will put them with some of my own. Somebody, some day, may wish to write something about us and we will have the original papers. Two hours before I found your letter I was talking to a group of colored reserve officers. I was asked if I thought a young colored man could get into West Point. I told them I felt that when a colored person passed the exam, he would be admitted, that I knew one young man who I was sure had passed and would go to West Point July 1. So you see how I felt about you. When I got your letter I felt like shouting. I shall save this letter of yours. To me it is great. . . . I am indeed proud of you, am honored to be,

Your loving Dad

In climbing through the Army's ranks from 1898 to 1932, my father had overcome what seemed almost impossible odds. In spite of the attitudes of whites in the United States toward all people of color, he had managed to buck the system and accomplish his goals. He had made life easier for me. Now it was my turn to make things better for those who would come after me. I was determined to succeed.

I had to ask my father for $100 to live on during the four weeks before I left Chicago—with the understanding, of course, that I would return what I did not spend! I hoped this would be the last time I would have to ask my father or anyone else for money, because cadets were paid $65 a month, deposited to their West Point account. Our family's kind of discipline certainly helped me in keeping my finances straight, although at the time I thought it was funny. An incident involving Henry O. Flipper, who in 1877 was the first black cadet to graduate from the Academy, must have had something to do with my father's demand for strict financial accounting. Flipper had been court-martialed and dismissed from the service for allegedly mishandling government funds. It was not until President Carter's administration in 1976 that pressure from concerned citizens and politicians resulted in a review of the case, and Flipper was given an honorable discharge decades after his death.

Once I got to the Academy on 1 July 1932, I would have no leave until December 1933, so I wrote to my parents suggesting I visit them at Tuskegee before going into "confinement." But they were leaving shortly for Paris, where they traveled as often as they could, and my visit did not work out. My father was studying French, and both he and Mother Sadie loved the freedom and warmth with which the French people had always received them. In Europe, they moved about without restriction and encountered no discrimination of any kind. It seemed ridiculous and totally unnecessary that, for non-whites, life outside the United States could be equal and free for all, while at home it was so frequently painful.

Because I would be in uniform until June 1936 and had no use for my civilian clothes, I gave away everything except what I would wear on my way to West Point. Chicago was full of people who had no homes, no jobs, and no prospects for bettering their livelihood. While at the University of Chicago, I wrote a term paper called "Living Conditions of the Poor in Chicago" for a course in sociology. I wanted my paper to be accurate, so I frequently visited some families in their humble homes on the South Side, close to the Loop, and talked with them about their day-to-day lives. These were some of the people to whom I gave my civilian clothing.

When the big day finally arrived, I was so excited that the train ride to West Point seemed to take forever. I marveled at the blue sky and the green forests, shimmering in the summer sunshine, that covered the domed hills of northern New York. The scenery was spectacular, and I felt lucky to be alive and at the beginning of what promised to be the greatest adventure of my life so far. My admiration for West Point was unbounded. During my last hours on the train, I dreamed about the four wonderful years that lay ahead. I wondered about the new friends I would make and how I would adjust to taking orders and living the Academy motto, "Duty, Honor, Country." After four years of training, those of us who had survived would all react to the same orders in the same way, think the same thoughts, and dress the same way, but each of us would retain something unique to contribute toward improving the lot of our fellow soldiers. From the attrition statistics I had seen, I realized that many of us were destined to drop by the wayside. I was positive, however, that failure was not in my scheme of things, that I would perform at West Point exactly as I had performed in my life up to this time—with considerable routine and expected success. I had no way of anticipating how hard won that success would be.

## Special Treatment

I distinctly remember my first day at the Academy—the picturesque highlands above the Hudson, and West Point's mammoth, fortresslike stone buildings. We were met in a civil manner and driven by bus to the central barracks, where all civility promptly disappeared. There we were greeted by the raucous voices of handsome young men who sought, successfully, to convince us that they were God's chosen creatures and that we were the lowest possible dregs. Later I learned they were "yearlings" (sophomores), men who less than a month before had been plebes, and only a year before had been in the same position we found ourselves in now. For our first month, the yearlings of the so-called Beast Detail (from BCT, Basic Cadet Training) were to be our masters in every respect, responsible for our development from the low status of "new cadet" to the exalted position of "cadet."

The Beast Detail seemed to be composed mostly of men from the South, perhaps bearing out the popular notion that southerners held a particularly high belief and pride in military tradition. We new cadets were not permitted to walk; unless in military formation, we were required to double-time everywhere. Several times on that first day I felt as if I could not take another step. The roughest part of it all was standing at an exaggerated position of attention for long periods. On my second day, one man gave me all his attention for the entire day. He did not exactly haze me—hazing was against regulations— but the "training" he dispensed was rigorous, to say the least. I thought at the time that he was testing me as he would have tested any other new cadet.

At first, the only indication that I was being singled out for special treatment was the fact that I was rooming alone in a large room designed for at least two cadets. But shortly after I arrived at West Point, the commandant of cadets told me in what he obviously considered to be an act of kindness that, officially, I was to be "treated like a white man." Of course, I was thoroughly disgusted by this condescending attitude. He also explained that, in accordance with Academy tradition, roommates were voluntary, and no white boy could be asked to room with me. It was hard for me to believe that West Point could take such a stand. Even at this early stage in my career as a cadet, it did not seem consistent with the "Duty, Honor, Country" creed I had read about.

Recently I read the original orders from the commandant's office, dated 12 August 1932, confirming my "beast barracks" solo room assignment. The next-to-last paragraph states, "Room 1844 will be occupied by only (1) cadet." I do not know why the order was issued so late—I had reported to "beast barracks" on 1 July. Similarly, a 12 September order gave me sole occupancy of Room 2744, into which I had moved at least several days earlier. It seems clear that my rooming alone had been planned, in fact directed, and that no white cadet had even been given the opportunity to refuse to room with me. Some of the senior officers who issued the orders must have had considerable doubt about the legality of their actions, but I will never know the details of the conversations that must have taken place.

I obviously had much to learn about the Academy. Many years later I learned that in 1925, seven years before I went to West Point, the Army War College had determined in a study forwarded to the Army Chief of Staff that blacks were decidedly inferior to whites and should be relegated to a special status within the Army. The commandant of the War College stated that this report, entitled "The Use of Negro Manpower in War," was the product of "several years study by the faculty and the student body of the Army War College." It concluded that the intelligence of black people was lower than that of whites, that blacks lacked courage, that they were superstitious, and that they were dominated by moral and character weaknesses. It also stated that the "social inequality" of blacks made the close association of whites and blacks in military organizations "inimicable to harmony and efficiency." The Army had approved this "study" and used it as the basis for its discrimination against blacks.

My plebe classmates were too busy coping with the Beast Detail to be hostile toward me. A cadet from Tennessee wanted to know all about me, and a couple of cadets who lived across the hall were friendly for the first two days. They seemed to be as overwhelmed by their new environment as I was. A yearling from Wichita, Kansas, Warren S. Everett, "recognized" me, told me he was my friend, and said he was "going to look out for me," which made me feel better at least temporarily. "Recognition," which implied a friendly and personal relationship, could be bestowed by any upperclassman upon any plebe, but it was usually reserved for the en masse recognition ceremony at the end of plebe year. Everett was the first and only cadet to recognize me until graduation week a year later.

Our company commander in beast barracks, also a yearling, was Charlie Rich, later Lt. Gen. Charles W. Rich. He let me know in an indirect way that he was from West Virginia by asking me whether I had ever heard of Bluefield Institute and West Virginia State College, black educational institutions. Then, as a test, he asked me where he was from. I said West Virginia. A couple of days later I met him in "the sinks" (that is, the toilet). He told me that if I acted in the future as I had during those first few days, I would get along all right. His and Everett's were some of the few kind words ever spoken to me at West Point, so I remember them well. Rich and I were in M Company together for three years, and although we were not friends—I never had any friend at West Point—he seemed to be at least neutral in his attitude toward me. I wish there had been more like him.

We plebes were routinely forced to stand at extreme attention, among the many forms of physical torture that fell short of actual violence: shoulder blades touching, buttocks rolled forward, back flat, gut sucked up, chest up, chin tightly back and in. Standing at attention for 30 minutes or more at a time made my feet go to sleep and my arms ache, and the constriction of blood vessels produced a pronounced dimness of vision. On my fifth day at West Point, the captain of my company pronounced my room and equipment the best in the company. At that moment, one of his assistants put the finger of his white glove on the woodwork and found some dust. Suddenly commands came from everywhere: "Pull your chin in, mister." "Keep your shiny, green eyes straight to the front." "Roll your buttocks under you." "Get the sway out of your back." "Get some blood in those ears." "Break out in a sweat, mister."

In the mess hall, though the food was excellent, the eating was difficult. We had to keep our eyes on the floor while we double-timed into the dining hall, and then we had to sit on the front 3 inches of our chairs and keep our eyes strictly on our plates. We were required to serve the upperclassmen first, with special attention to the senior cadet, the table commandant, who sat at the head of the table. We spoke only in prescribed phrases when performing our duties, and in addition, we were required to recite pieces of "poop," that is, information we had memorized. After the upperclassmen were served, the serving dishes were passed down to the plebes at the other end of the table. Sometimes we were kept so busy "sitting up" and answering questions that we did not have time to eat as much as we liked.

These practices, while tough, actually gave me no problem whatsoever. However, just when I thought that I was getting along extremely well—that life at West Point, even for plebes, was a piece of
cake—the roof fell in. I was in my room shining my shoes and brass
when I heard a knock on the door announcing a meeting in the sinks
(the basement) in 10 minutes. As I approached the assembly where
the meeting was in progress, I heard someone ask, "What are we
going to do about the nigger?" I realized then that the meeting was
*about* me, and I was not supposed to attend. I turned on my heel and
double-timed back to my room.

From that meeting on, the cadets who roomed across the hall, who
had been friendly earlier, no longer spoke to me. In fact, no one spoke
to me except in the line of duty. Apparently, certain upperclass cadets
had determined that I was getting along too well at the Academy to
suit them, and they were going to enforce an old West Point
tradition—"silencing"—with the object of making my life so unhappy that I would resign. Silencing had been applied in the past to
certain cadets who were considered to have violated the honor code
and refused to resign. In my case there was no question of such a
violation, which would have been formally cited by the Honor Committee; I was to be silenced solely because cadets did not want blacks
at West Point. Their only purpose was to freeze me out. What they did
not realize was that I was stubborn enough to put up with their
treatment to reach the goal I had come to attain.

## An Invisible Man

Except for the recognition ceremony at the end of plebe year, I was
silenced for the entire four years of my stay at the Academy. Even
though West Point officialdom could maintain that this silence had no
official basis, they knew precisely how I was being treated and that I
was the only cadet in the corps treated in this manner. When we
traveled to football games on buses or trains, I had a seat to myself;
even as a first classman (senior), when we traveled to Fort Benning,
Georgia, and Fort Monroe, Virginia, I lived alone in whatever quarters were provided, usually large enough for two or more cadets.
Except for tutoring some underclassmen after my plebe year, I had no
conversations with other cadets. The situation was ridiculous, but in

no way was it funny. To this day I cannot understand how the officials at West Point and the individual cadets, with their continually and vociferously stated belief in "Duty, Honor, Country" as a way of life, could rationalize their treatment of me.

It also amazed me that in later years many officers stated publicly that I had *not* been silenced during my stay at the Academy. A letter from Col. Jack Rudolph to *Newsweek*, dated 22 October 1973, stated flatly that I had not been silenced. Gen. Albert ("Bub") Clark, a classmate of mine, and Gen. Milt Summerfelt, commander of his and my Company M, said the same. Also in 1973, I received a note from Gen. William ("Bozo") McKee, West Point class of 1929 and former Air Force Vice Chief of Staff, in which he referred to a newspaper report alleging that I had been silenced at West Point. "I just don't believe this," he wrote. "If this is an outright lie, I don't think you should let it go by." I never answered General McKee's note. My last recollection of him was of a conversation he once had with my wife, Agatha, in which he said he had been responsible for my being promoted to a general officer. Agatha replied rather pointedly that I had earned all my promotions.

It is true that at the end of plebe year, at the recognition ceremony at Company M, large numbers of upperclass cadets from all over the corps came up to me, recognized me, and congratulated me. But after that I reverted to my status as an invisible man. Many of my classmates refuse to recognize that I was silenced—and from a narrow, official standpoint, they are correct. From the standpoint of basic humanity and justice, however, they were grossly lacking in their handling of the situation. Perhaps the absence of a "legal" silencing in my case eased their consciences. But the fact remains that the great majority of the Corps of Cadets silenced me absolutely for four years, some going along with the program quietly, others with considerable enthusiasm based on blind racial hatred.

This cruel treatment was designed to make me buckle, but I refused to buckle in any way. I maintained my self-respect. First, I did not mention my troubles in letters to my mother and father. Second, I made my mind up that I would continue to hold my head high. At no time did I consciously show that I was hurt; even at this early date, I took solace in the fact that I was mature enough to live through anything other people might submit me to, particularly people I considered to be misguided. I kept telling myself that I was *superior* in character to them, even to the point of feeling sorry for them. Certainly I was not missing anything by not associating with them; instead, I bolstered my feelings by thinking that they were missing a great deal by not knowing me.

I received other forms of special treatment. The commandant called me in three times to ask how I was getting along. My answer was that I intended to graduate, regardless of how I was treated. We did not discuss the particulars of that treatment. Similarly, after the cadet captain of my company had told the company tactical officer that I was a good worker, the tactical officer called me in and asked me whether I was getting proper instruction in tactics and whether I was being treated all right generally. Like the commandant, he said that I was to come to him in case any difficult situation arose. I was well aware that neither of them had any intention to correct or even alleviate the silencing. They quite obviously knew what was going on, and they must have had their own personal reasons for not saying anything more about it.

But I was in no mood to trust anyone, and I had enough intelligence to know that complaints about my situation would not help me. I kept my letters to my parents cheerful and took encouragement from theirs. I asked them for a number of things, just to get mail. For some obscure psychological reason, I ate a prodigious amount of candy. I also read many, many books and magazines, and regardless of the weather, I ran lots of solo cross-country in the hills, after which I always felt better when I returned to my empty room. I never felt sorry for myself. I knew I could push aside any obstacle in my path. My father had taught me to be strong; he had endured adversity, and so could I.

Only on one occasion during my four years at West Point, in the fall of 1932, did I initiate a call on the commandant. Some of the cadets seemed to enjoy creating a situation in the mess hall that embarrassed and infuriated me. Ordinarily cadets were assigned tables and seats, but on Sunday mornings, when the Catholics were at mass, several tables were broken up and the cadets who regularly sat there had to find seats at other tables. The approved procedure was to ask the table commandant's permission to sit at his table, but on many occasions I was denied a seat with the excuse, obviously untrue, that the table was filled up. One Sunday the Cadet Choir went to New York City and, as usual, several tables were closed. At every meal

I had trouble finding a seat. It was more embarrassing than usual to have to double-time around the mess hall looking for a seat when the rest of the corps was seated and settled, and I made up my mind that if I could help it this would not happen again.

I went to the commandant of cadets at seven o'clock the next morning and told him my story. He thanked me for telling him about it and promptly expressed his opinion that the way I had been treated was plain bad manners. Cadets were like sheep, he said, and most of them followed where a few led. He wanted to know the names of the cadets who had refused to let me sit at their tables. I thought that reporting them would not do much good, and then, too, that I might have been mistaken in one or two cases. I decided, however, that if I ran into a sure case in the future, I would take it up without delay.

After my interview with the commandant, I immediately noticed results. Of course, he had asked the same old question: "How are you getting along otherwise?" I could have told him how every month table assignments were posted on the company bulletin board one day and changed again the next because some cadets objected to eating at the same table with me. But even if I did, what could he do about it? He had as little say in the matter as he had over my living alone for four years without a roommate. The Academy believed that it could not require a cadet to eat with me if he did not want to. My feelings about this type of treatment oscillated between embarrassment, anger, hate, and pity. Pity was the emotion that sustained me.

New cadets were presented with a little volume entitled *Bugle Notes, 1933, United States Corps of Cadets,* which we were required to study. We even had to memorize parts of it, and to this day I can recite Gen. Winfield Scott's "Fixed Opinion" on the contribution West Point cadets had made during the Mexican War. When challenged by an upperclassman with the question, "What do plebes rank?" we would give the prescribed answer from *Bugle Notes:* "Sir, the Superintendent's dog, the Commandant's cat, the waiters in the Mess Hall, the Hell Cats, and all the Admirals in the whole blamed Navy."

I was struck in particular by the hypocrisy of one section of *Bugle Notes,* "Advice from the First Captain': "Everyone [at West Point] begins on the same basis for there is no distinction except merit. Money is nothing; character, conduct, and capacity everything. In this respect West Point is truly the greatest democratic institution in existence." In my idealism I respected these principles and believed they were worth striving for, even though they apparently did not extend to blacks.

Also included was a section on honor, in which the "Guiding Principles" of the West Point honor system were enumerated. For the most part, besides familiarizing myself with these principles, I followed the dictates of my own conscience. The kind of honor spelled out in the "Guiding Principles" referred to a legal system with which every cadet was required to comply. In practice, it was painfully apparent that the system overlooked another and more basic kind of honor: the simple respect of one human being for another. Throughout my career at West Point and beyond, it was often difficult to reconcile the principles of Duty, Honor, and Country with the Army's inhuman and unjust treatment of individuals on the basis of race.

All that first month at West Point I had to work harder than anybody else to avoid getting demerits, which would be written into my permanent record after 1 August. As one first classman remarked, they could always find something to give a plebe demerits for. We had to do punishment tours for every demerit over 14 per month— walking at "quick" time, talking to no one except officially, saluting officers, and carrying a rifle. These tours were served on Wednesday and Saturday afternoons, normally free time. Demerits were a factor in the appointment of cadet officers, and in spite of what I had already learned about how things worked at the Academy, I was still naive enough to believe that I had a chance to be a cadet officer if my performance merited the appointment.

The end of July marked the end of my first period of training. We started our practice parades and wore our white trousers for the first time. On 6 August we ceased to be "new cadets" and became simply "cadets." We dressed all in white—white uniforms, gloves, cross belts and waist belts with brass plates, and white caps with the black and gold braid. On our coats we wore the brass "U.S." and the emblem of the U.S. Military Academy. We carried rifles and wore bayonets, and even though we still marched pretty badly, anyone would have been impressed to see us pass in review. At almost every parade, men fell out (fainted) and had to be carried off the field and taken to the hospital in an ambulance—I suppose from the heat and the intense physical effort of standing at attention for long periods. I never had any problem; in spite of the silencing, I was feeling physically good and believed that I could stand anything, including carrying a pack and rifle 20 miles a day on the plebe hike, scheduled for the end of August. After the parade we camped on the Hudson River side of the Plain, away from the barracks, where we were assigned places in our regular companies. We were assigned to companies by height, and the tallest cadets, in A and M companies, would march on the outside of parade formations. I was 6 feet 2 inches, so I was assigned to M Company, which carried a streamer on its guidon marking it as the best in the corps. My quarters in this camp was a large pyramidal tent—for me alone.

Cadet life was hard, particularly guard duty, to which I was assigned during the first week of August. I had a 24-hour tour—two hours to walk post and four hours off. My main problem was staying awake at night while walking post; I found that I could fall asleep while I was walking. Guard duty put a lot of men in the hospital, and while I managed well physically, it indirectly caused me to get two demerits. This was not a bad total for the week, and demerits were never a significant problem for me during the entire four years.

The commandant inspected us on Saturday after a practice march, and I came through triumphantly without any demerits. He ordered me to see him after inspection and repeated everything he had said when I arrived at West Point. Again he insisted that I come to see him if any situation arose I could not handle, told me he could not make personal friends for me but would do all he could officially, that he regretted the racial situation in America, and so on and so forth.

After plebe hike, the last exercise of the summer, we moved into our permanent quarters in the M Company barracks. Although rigorous, the hike had provided a much-needed week of relaxation and relief from the strict upperclass-plebe relationship, and all of us benefited from spirit of the operation. The entire summer had been trying, both mentally and physically. Once it was over I was a little shocked to realize that those two months had been the greatest of my life. I was proud of the way I had reacted to the difficulties of the situation, and my pride was enhanced by the fact that I alone understood my feelings. A couple of our classmates had elected to resign in August, but the rest of us slogged along with the system, proud that we were West Point cadets.

## Plebe Year Continues

Our lives as plebes were dominated by the routine of the Blue Book, which told us in clipped and precise language all the things we were supposed to do and when we were supposed to do them, and also the things we were forbidden to do. I enjoyed much of the routine— there was something to be said for being told what was expected, so that one could do it. On Sunday mornings we marched to chapel, where battle flags from the Civil War, the Spanish-American War, and the Philippine Insurrection hung from the triforium. The rest of Sunday was free. Having no one to talk to, I kept up correspondence with my mother, father, and sisters.

My initial grades were not as good as I thought they should be, but they improved as time went on. I liked the method of "teaching"— mostly memorization and regurgitation—and the system of daily grading. Weekly grades were posted each Saturday, so each cadet could find out just how he was doing compared to his classmates. The big problem was finding time to study, what with drill, intramural athletics ("Every man an athlete"), and parade. The old statement was basically true: "You've got time for everything at West Point." I frequently got up before reveille to study.

I won a monogram on our championship lacrosse team, qualified in swimming, and received a perfect grade on my boxing test. I fought a cadet who was about equal to me in ability. He hit me twice where I could feel it, once in the eye, then in the center of my body, where my ribs separated, but I paid him back with a fast blow to the chin as the second round ended. My grade probably reflected effort more than skill. We had been warned that we had to fight as hard as we could; otherwise we would be marked down.

In early October my father wrote Maj. Gen. William D. Connor, the Superintendent, stating his intention to visit me at West Point. General Connor replied immediately to make arrangements, adding, "The good work that Cadet Davis is doing must be evident from the academic reports. In his Conduct he has been a model cadet." The visit went better than either of us expected, and I was proud of the hospitality shown my father by the Corps of Cadets and the Academy. He, too, was pleased with the treatment he received; although he was in civilian clothes, many cadets saluted him. He dined with me on the balcony of the mess hall, usually reserved for distinguished visitors, and he visited with me in my room. Among other things we discussed, he gave me some pointers on military tactics. Although he must have noticed that I was rooming alone, the subject of my silencing never came up. I could think of no way in which my father could appreciably improve my situation, so there was no use in saying anything about it. In the last analysis, only time—precisely, the passage of four years—could solve my problems at West Point.

Soon it was football season. Before the Harvard game I had received a written invitation to visit the 3d Battalion of the black 372d Infantry Regiment of the Massachusetts National Guard. My request to dine separately from the Corps of Cadets was approved, and after we staged a review for the distinguished citizens of Boston, cadets going on dining permits were allowed to fall out of ranks. I was met by two National Guard officers who showed me historic Boston and then took me to lunch with two young women. I was seated between them at lunch—a good looker on my right and a personality queen on my left. This was the closest I had been to a female for several months. I was able to stifle the personality queen and enjoy chatting with the attractive one on my right.

After the game we had the usual breath inspection before boarding the train, but the tactical officers really did not look or smell too closely. Several of the cadets had been drinking—a dismissal offense—but we all got back safely on this trip. After we boarded the train we had dinner and went to bed. All the time I thought about the lovely girl at the National Guard luncheon, whose name I did not remember. The whole experience in Boston—the girls, the good food, the entertainment, the conversation, and the break from the tightly controlled routine of West Point—had a disintegrating effect upon me. The 17 days until New York, the traditional site of the Army–Notre Dame game, seemed like a year, and the 25 days until Philadelphia and Navy seemed like forever.

Time passed slowly indeed after the football season and the trips. I had a series of sore throats, and the doctors thought I should have my tonsils removed. With nothing to do during the Christmas break, and preferring not to spend time in the hospital during classes, I elected to have them out forthwith. While the upper classes were away on Christmas leave, the fourth class enjoyed freedom from their customary subservience and could attend fourth-class hops and pursue other forms of entertainment. Fourth classmen could accept invitations to one meal on weekends at the homes of officers living on the post. Nobody ever told me not to attend hops, but I never went to one because I realized that I was not welcome, and I never received any dinner invitations. So I spent Christmas in the hospital. I still remember the hours immediately after my tonsils had been removed, while I was still pleasantly anaesthetized with morphine, lying in my hospital bed three-quarters conscious of all that was going on about me.

We entered the annual gloom period after Christmas. Sixty-five cadets were found (dismissed): 52 plebes out of the 435 who entered with me, and 13 yearlings. All except the several dismissed for discipline had the option to be "turned back" to the next class, but few took advantage of it. We had courses in the function of the Engineers, which brought to my mind my father's observation that if I did well at West Point, I might qualify for that branch of the service. But I was not truly attracted to the Engineers; my goal was still to be a pilot in the Army Air Corps. Not until after graduating was I to learn that racial segregation limited my choice of service to the Infantry, with its black 24th and 25th Infantry regiments, and the Cavalry, with its black 9th and 10th Cavalry regiments.

Because I had nobody to talk to, I resorted to listening to a radio that I had received in the mail from my mother. Radios were against regulations. I kept mine in a special place in my locker and used it during "release from quarters" because the company tactical officer inspected the lockers only during "call to quarters." By attaching a wire from the radio to the radiator, I could pick up Chicago, Cleveland, and Boston. In March an upperclassman "skinned" (reported) me for "radio in room," and I was given five demerits and five punishment tours.

Demerits could get out of hand, particularly if upperclassmen got the idea that a cadet was bucking the system. I had to be especially careful to keep my demerits down, because even if they could not freeze me out I could still be found for discipline. While I was still in the corps, Felix Kirkpatrick, a black plebe who had also been appointed to West Point by Congressman De Priest, was awarded an excessive number of demerits and found for discipline. I do not know for sure that he was railroaded out of the Academy. It was a fact, however, that at nearly any time a plebe could be skinned for offenses that would have been overlooked in someone else. I thought many of the demerits I got were unjustified, but then again, I am sure that most cadets felt the same way.

In July 1933, toward the end of my plebe year, I received a friendly letter from Alonzo Parham, the black ex-cadet who had been dismissed from the Academy in 1929. His letter was of great interest to me, primarily because it described the prejudicial treatment Parham had received at West Point, very similar to what I was living through. Uncanny in his perceptiveness, he concluded by writing, "Cadets do not take kindly to change of any kind." My way of dealing with the situation was to keep up my nerve and, as much as possible, to forget my feelings. My classmates were beginning to get better acquainted with each other, but I, having no roommate or genuine friends, was left out in the cold. I felt it for a while, but soon I found myself adjusting to the situation and able to concentrate on doing my work well.

Maj. Gen. John F. Preston, the Army inspector general, made an official visit to the Academy and observed many cadet activities during his stay, including our formation as we entered chapel for services. As usual, I got stared at; the "brown curiosity" always attracted lots of attention. People seemed to think that because I was black I was different from the other cadets, so I constantly had to endure their stares.

My silence was broken by a visit from Mother Sadie and Nora, and I enjoyed showing them around the Academy. I shared my knowledge of *Bugle Notes* with them as we toured the campus—knowledge that I had carefully armed myself with against the constant questioning of upperclassmen. At the end of the day they watched our parade, in which no fewer than 34 cadets fell out, and then they drove back to New York. I hoped they had enjoyed their visit as much as I had.

Recognition, on the eve of graduation day, constituted a major milestone in my four years at West Point and an acknowledgment of success in itself. But I wondered what would happen at the ceremony itself—if people would continue to look right through me, as they had all year long or if, for once, I would be seen and recognized. I had completed a whole year, filled with training and indoctrination, and I had received another unofficial kind of training that would stay with me throughout my military career and for the rest of my life. Besides learning to withstand physical hardships, I had become hardened to personal abuse. When people hurt me, either by ignoring me or outright maltreatment, I gave no indication that I had been hurt, and an impassive look in response to insult became one of my most useful strategies. On this day, at least, the look was not necessary, for a large number of upperclass cadets came up to me, shook my hand, and told me I had done a good job. I appreciated their unaccustomed generosity and felt happy about my achievements. Academically, I was 12th in my class. I had only three more years to go. I was a *yearling!*

That summer our class trained in field artillery, coast artillery, signal corps, and riding. The riding instruction was the best thing I had been exposed to at the Academy. A detachment of black cavalrymen took care of the horses. Again I was stared at—they must have been amazed to see a black cadet—but in a manner quite different from the usual staring I got from strangers. I saw the cavalrymen only in the riding hall and had no opportunity to talk to them, but I believe they were proud that a member of their race was a cadet, and they saw to it that I got good horses. Up to that point, even though my father had been in the Cavalry, I had never been taught to ride. After more instruction cadets would be permitted to take horses out on their own, and I eagerly looked forward to that day. Eventually, riding turned out to be one of the few joys I experienced at West Point.

We also went on a five-day practice march, during which we got dirty, tired, and mosquito-bitten. We were told by our new commandant, Col. Simon Bolivar Buckner, that we would be part of a tactical situation from the moment we left camp until we returned, meaning we might be fired upon at any time, whether we were marching or camping at night. Colonel Buckner's reputation as a tough field soldier had been made known to us, so we expected the worst. On the second day we all got sick from bad food and vomited all over the camp. It never stopped raining during the maneuvers, and we slept in 3 inches of water every night. For five days I never removed my shirt or breeches. Contrary to orders, at least half of us had carried extra blankets. Colonel Buckner saw to it that these were all sent back to camp, explaining that if a man could not be comfortable with one blanket and one poncho, he was soft. He got a Bronx cheer for this statement. The last day we made a forced march of 20 miles over a mountain range in a driving rain. On the whole, I had no ill effects from the practice march, except that my feet got badly swollen. But after fighting the mud and mosquitos for five days as a field soldier, I wanted more than ever to fly airplanes.

Congressman De Priest visited West Point before the summer ended. He brought with him Col. Spencer Dickerson, commander of the black 8th Illinois National Guard Regiment. I had met Colonel Dickerson before, and I was glad to see him in this setting. We dined at the cavalry detachment barracks. I enjoyed seeing Congressman De Priest, and expressed to him my sincere thanks for the appointment he had given me to West Point—especially after I had failed the first entrance examination.

During this period I had an unusual experience in a history class. While studying the Civil War period, we reviewed a chapter on plantation life. Two of my classmates were required to deliver 10-minute speeches on slavery and slave life. Their speeches were full of "nigras" and the like, and I was struck by the absolutely blind racial prejudice that existed in the minds of these supposedly intelligent men. One of them told a story of a "nigress" who had triplets and named them after three different men because she did not know who the father was. Of course, this cadet would have been shocked to learn that such things also happened among the lily-white women of the South. The instructor, also from the Deep South, was not quite as prejudiced as some of his students and tried to convince them that some blacks were not depraved. When he said there was no comparison between the highly educated black and the poor white, quite a bit of shock registered on the faces of my classmates.

## Family Reunions and New Relationships

Some people at West Point said that leaves and furlough were a snare and a delusion, and by the time I got back from Christmas leave in my second year, I was inclined to agree with them. I set out hoping to find a lady I could fall in love with. I met many attractive women, and my uniform seemed to get their attention, but I was afraid to isolate myself too much with any one of them. My leave ended with me high and dry, with lots of glorious times of such variety that nothing tangible remained—only memories, sweet memories. On New Year's Eve I had three dates, at 6:00, 9:00, and 12:30. I never made the 12:30 date, and naturally I conjectured on what I had missed. Anyway, though a number of women had other ideas, I remained a free agent, which was actually what I had wanted all the time.

I had always told Mother Sadie that I did not plan to marry. I meant it every time I said it. But there *was* one lady who really impressed me during Christmas leave. She had poured confetti down the back of my full-dress coat during our attendance at a formal New Year's Eve dance, and that, along with the tilt of her head, her fingers, her shoes, got my attention. In my frantic haste at that time, I did not get her name or address right, but I was sufficiently smitten to write a rather long letter to her on 23 January 1934—the first of several hundred. It was a rather silly letter; I was groping. I did not know her first name (I thought I had heard someone call her "Boots"), so I addressed the envelope "Miss (?) Scott." I wrote that though I had seen her on one night only, a few glimpses convinced me "beyond a doubt of the perfect rapport that could exist between us—incredible, isn't it, considering that I know nothing of you."

The persistent gloom of my silencing got to me in late January and early February, but I was consoled by the facts of where I was and what I was doing. I began to think about graduation, realizing that my class standing would qualify me for any Army branch but that I would probably be restricted to the black Infantry or Cavalry, unless I could get into the Army Air Corps. Sometimes I even imagined that when I became a first lieutenant I could be reassigned as an instructor at West Point.

Meanwhile, my father badly wanted a change of assignment for himself. He had called on Gen. Guy V. Henry, the Chief of Cavalry, in Washington and clearly expressed his desire for an assignment with troops. Although General Henry had been cordial and sympathetic, he had not encouraged my father to believe that such an assignment would be made. It did seem that because he had been at Tuskegee Institute for four years and asked for a change, an effort should have been made to find him another assignment. But it was the same old question of a black colonel's being assigned to a position that would put him in command of white officers. I tried to console my father about his current assignment to Tuskegee Institute: there he could see the results of his work, and the Institute meant a great deal to southern blacks. I also conjectured, after hearing a lecture called the "Far

East Question," that we would undoubtedly have to keep the world safe from the Japanese before his service was up.

Furlough passed rapidly—too rapidly. I enjoyed the reunion with my family and old friends in all the places I visited. Most of all, and I cannot say it too emphatically, I enjoyed my freedom. My social isolation during the first two years at West Point, even with all the satisfaction of success, had not been easy. In Tuskegee my father and I often rode in the morning. We played bridge, and we sat around a lot and talked. I basked in the sunshine of my parents' admiration, and I savored being among people who liked me.

While on furlough I unwittingly defied the local segregation laws. Without thinking about where I was, I ordered a Coke in a white drugstore on the public square in Tuskegee. Apparently the man at the soda fountain was so startled by my breach of southern custom that he served me without question. I drank the Coke before realizing what I had done, then turned on my heel and left the store. I did not look back to see whether the man broke the glass I had used. When I got home I described the incident to my father. He told me to forget it, and fortunately I heard nothing more about it. Otherwise, my temporary forgetfulness might have disturbed the already fragile black-white relations that existed between the town and the Institute.

In late August I left Tuskegee and traveled to Chicago to visit old friends. There I also saw the well-remembered young woman I had written to the previous January. This time I learned her name: she was Agatha Scott of New Haven, Connecticut, a student in residence at the Art Institute for the summer who had taken courses at Yale. We both attended a party given by a mutual friend; I was alone, but unfortunately Agatha was with someone else. She reminds me now that I permitted myself to be presented to her. It was not convenient at the time to discuss future plans, but I knew it was inevitable that we would meet in New York during the Christmas holidays. She was as attractive as ever, just as I remembered her, and just as I see her today, 56 years later.

I had made some arrangements to meet an attractive Chicago acquaintance, Maudelle Bousfield, in New York and be her escort for the Christmas holidays. I liked Maudelle's appearance and manner, and apparently she was satisfied to have me for an escort, but that was about as far as it went on either side. When I encountered Agatha on 137th Street in New York (completely by chance, but with a lot of fate thrown in), I found that she had committed herself to a similar arrangement for the holidays with Paul Binford, a dentist from York, Pennsylvania. I had known Paul for several years, having met him when we were both students at Fisk University in 1929. Unfortunately for our friendship, he stood between me and Agatha, just as my commitment to Maudelle (and the mother who had brought her to New York for the holidays) was an impediment to the relationship I now deeply desired to develop with Agatha Scott. I never found out how Agatha solved her part of the problem, but I am ashamed to admit that I solved mine ruthlessly.

Agatha and I spent as much time together as we possibly could during the holidays. I learned a lot about her, and was enchanted by everything I learned. A schoolteacher with a pronounced artistic bent, she lived with her parents in New Haven, was a nonsmoker and a nondrinker, and was very sociable and popular. Upon my return to West Point I wrote my father that I was very much in love with her and was considering giving her an engagement ring, a miniature of the class ring I would receive the following October.

When I wrote Mother Sadie, I had to disclaim all my previous statements that I would never marry. If not for the Academy regulation prohibiting marriage, I told her, Agatha and I would already be married. (Each time a cadet left the Academy, he was required, upon return, to sign a paper stating that he was not married; marriage was equivalent to resignation. About half of each class married soon after graduation.) The small problem of how to survive on a second lieutenant's pay did not phase me. If all those other recent graduates could marry and make it financially, I rationalized, so could I. The Army promoted the notion that single lieutenants could devote all their time to their profession and hence perform better. But when I told my father that I intended to marry Agatha at the earliest possible time, he concurred quite clearly that if that was what I wanted to do, I should do it.

Agatha drove over from New Haven to see me nearly every Saturday, which made my silencing much easier to bear. Her visits never lasted long, but when she left I always felt as if my batteries had been recharged. She experienced the same silence I did on these afternoons, but we were happy despite our isolation and did not need anyone else. Throughout all her numerous trips to West Point, she never met another cadet.

My relationship with Agatha has remained the central part of my life since I met her. I have depended on her fully, confiding my innermost thoughts and realizing with regret that all the suffering I endured I also imposed on her. Even during these early days at West Point, I realized that our lives together would be largely restricted to each other. But I consoled myself with the knowledge that Agatha is a person of great character and resilience who can make the best of any situation, immersing herself in her myriad interests. Indeed, I have never had to worry about her. She has the indispensable facility of enjoying life in spite of its difficulties, and she has given me an invaluable base of self-assurance in all my struggles.

## The Air Corps Declines

My classmates and I undertook many tactical exercises in the spring of 1935 to prepare us for our summer trips to Mitchell Field (where we would be introduced to flying), Fort Monroe, and Fort Benning. My ambition to fly in the Air Corps had remained uppermost in my mind. It did occur to me that it would be something new for a black cadet to be assigned to the Air Corps, but I had already met all sorts of difficulties and overcome them, so I saw no reason that the lack of a precedent for such an assignment could not be overcome too.

We had a course in aerodynamics that would help us at Mitchell, and we studied the infantry intensively. My comment to my father was, "The more I see of the infantry, the more I'm convinced that I don't care much for it." But I liked field and coast artillery, and after a five-day cavalry exercise, I went out alone on privileged riding in the hills. Riding remained one activity at West Point I truly enjoyed. With spring in the air, it was a great time to be alive, especially with all the good things we had to look forward to during the summer.

President Franklin D. Roosevelt gave the graduation speech for the class of 1935. It was short and snappy, and when it was over, the realization hit me hard that I had completed three years at West Point, that I was now a first classman, and that exactly a year later I would be graduating. It was sobering to ponder the responsibilities entailed in becoming a second lieutenant and actually beginning a career in the Army.

We spent five days at Mitchell Field that summer, an experience that once again reinforced my desire to be a pilot. We flew 20 hours as passengers in bombers and observation planes. Most of the time we flew in single aircraft, but we also did some formation flying and learned about interplane radio communications and the control of individual aircraft within the formation. I enjoyed every minute of it, and there was no doubt in my mind that the Air Corps was for me.

My parents sailed again for Europe on 30 April for what my father later said was the best trip he had ever made. In a letter, my mother mentioned that they particularly enjoyed the company of a French couple with two attractive daughters. She said she regretted that I was not with them to meet these pretty girls, but that Agatha would not take lightly to my giving them any attention. I kept getting these little digs from Mother Sadie about my former independence from women and my present state of being so far gone on Agatha.

My parents drove to Brussels, Liège, and Aix-la-Chapelle, and took the beautiful route along the Rhine from Cologne to Frankfurt. My father had his military/foreign affairs eyes wide open, and he observed the glaring examples of German militarism that were there for the entire world to see: all men under 30 wore some kind of uniform, with swastikas on their left sleeves. My parents also saw sentinels walking post with shovels on their shoulders, and they passed many groups of marching men with full pack but no weapons, some singing, some maintaining a rhythmic cadence with the clatter of their hobnailed shoes. After visiting Montreux, Lausanne, Geneva, and Grenoble, they proceeded to Nice, Toulon, and Marseilles, the gateway to France's African colonies. My father was thrilled by the thought that he was following the same route Napoleon had taken when he escaped from Elba. Upon seeing the vast variety of races and cultures mingling in Marseilles, he wrote to me, "I am enjoying freedom and find it hard to think that I have to return to the place [the United States] where before I try to enter [any white establishment], I've got to be sure I'll be accepted, even though I have the price." In another letter, he wrote, "After the freedom I've enjoyed here American restrictions will be hard for a time." He must have been thinking about the long drive from Washington to Tuskegee Institute, with no public accommodations available to him and Mother Sadie along the way, and the indignities they would have to suffer in "the place" after being treated like human beings in Europe.

West Point's end-of-summer hike was tame that year compared to the one of two years before—we had only a half hour of rain the entire five days. The end of this hike was another milestone: I had pitched my last pup tent and eaten out of my last mess kit. The move back to barracks and the start of academics firmly entrenched me in the last phase of my stay at the Academy. It was the beginning of the end.

Felix Kirkpatrick, a plebe, came to see me one evening after parade. Like me, he was living alone, and he had little opportunity for social relationships with anyone. We had never really gotten acquainted because his barracks were distant from mine. He seemed to be having an especially bad time. Academically, he was above the middle of his class, but his difficulties with the other cadets seemed to be unbalancing him. He told me that more than one cadet in his company was determined to push him over the limit in demerits and have him dismissed. Some were hazing him a great deal, while others seemed to ignore him. He had a pew to himself in chapel, and one upperclassman had told him that he would walk the area as long as he was at the Academy. Clearly West Point attitudes toward blacks had not changed in the short time I had been there. I sympathized with him and could see myself as I had been three years before. But by that time he was already on the verge of being expelled for conduct demerits, and the situation had deteriorated beyond the point where I might have been helpful.

Not long after this meeting, he came to see me again. The commandant had just informed him of his discharge, and he wanted to know if anything could be done. I had never seen nor heard anything about him except in his favor, and everyone at West Point understood the real reason for his discharge—that he was black. Unfortunately, however, the expulsion due to demerits was entirely legal, and nothing could be done.

I applied for the U.S. Army Air Corps in October 1935. Early that month we were given a thorough physical examination, which I passed. In November General Connor called me in to discuss my plans. When I arrived at his office, I was handed my application and a letter from Brig. Gen. Oscar Westover, the Assistant Chief of the Air Corps, saying that I had been rejected because no black units were to be included in the Air Corps. The letter had been approved by the Chief of the Air Corps.

This decision, which came as a complete shock to me, was shameful. Unworthy of the great democratic nation in which we lived, it was another manifestation of the Army's long-standing position that no black officer should ever command white troops. In my father's case, the Army had already demonstrated the intractibility of this policy, but I still thought it possible and reasonable that under different conditions, in a future no one could confidently forecast, I might command white troops and fly an Army airplane. Of course I was angry and hurt, but at the same time philosophical and hopeful that in some way the policy could be overcome. After the initial disappointment, I refused to believe that my career was over, and I was determined to remain available for whatever opportunities might come my way.

General Connor told me quite frankly that my rejection was "only the beginning" of what I would encounter in the Army because of my race, and that perhaps it would be best for me to obtain a detail permitting me to attend law school with a view to entering politics and pursuing a congressional career. It was not "logical" for a black officer to command white troops, he said. Consequently, he intended to suggest to the Chief of Infantry that the Army send me to law school, thereby solving both my "problem" and theirs.

I replied that I intended to stay in the Army. In the first place, I knew that upon graduation I would stand high enough in my class to choose the branch of the service I desired. Second, my physical examination rated me high among all applicants. It was patently unfair to deny me the opportunity to be trained as a pilot, whether the Air Corps was going to have black units or not. Even the great U.S. Army—and it surely was not so very great in 1935—could not afford to turn down the services of a highly qualified West Point graduate who was eager to serve his country in the Air Corps.

General Connor's subsequent actions left no doubt in my mind that he was being completely honest and truly believed everything he suggested was in my interest. The decision to stay in the Army was mine alone. I had no interest in law school; I was still determined to fly airplanes. In my mind, the decision to stay in the Army was equivalent to the decision to stay at West Point. General Connor and others would have advised me not to submit myself to the bigotry and maltreatment that had been an inevitable part of my life as a West Point cadet. I would not have taken any such advice to go easy on myself and leave the Academy, and especially considering what I had already been through, I was not about to resign my commission now. Still optimistic, and perhaps a little conceited, I thought that I had enough to offer that the Army might, under certain conditions, change its ridiculous policies and open its ranks to all who could contribute.

Since then I have often thought that General Connor did me a favor by suggesting I seek a career outside the military. He brought out my stubborn streak. My decision to continue on my chosen course was largely based on pure obstinacy—a determination to prove my worth in comparison with the other officers. This determination remained a central part of my psyche, and it governed my behavior throughout my service.

With the official action on my application for the Air Corps still reverberating loudly in my consciousness, I went to Philadelphia for the Army-Navy game. Agatha and I were sitting in the railroad station before the game when I happened to see our former commandant of cadets, Lt. Col. Robert C. Richardson, in civilian clothing. He also recognized me and immediately came over to speak. He complimented me on my work at the Academy and asked what I intended to do the following year. Upon learning that I was somewhat undecided, he mentioned that he was commanding the 5th Cavalry in Texas and would be pleased to have me join his regiment. The 5th was a white unit. I appreciated the spirit of the invitation, but he and I both realized that if I went into the Cavalry, my assignment would be to the black 9th or 10th Cavalry regiments and not to Colonel Richardson's command. I resolved then and there that, having stated my preference for the Air Corps and been refused, I would let the Army decide what to do with me, even though my class standing alone should have given me the right to choose any branch of the service.

At Christmas Agatha and I traveled to Washington to see my grandmother and other relatives. Although Agatha and I had maintained a lively correspondence and an awareness of each other's activities and thinking, it was scintillating to be in her company for longer than a weekend visit. Among her other talents, she was a brilliant conversationalist, not only with strangers but also with me. One call, on my birth mother's sisters, did not go well. They had always regarded me as their own and felt they should have been able to select the girl I would marry. Their most important criterion was that she should be a Washingtonian, from a family that met with their approval. They did not approve of my intention to marry an "outsider" like Agatha, so we had a rift that was never genuinely healed. I regretted it because they had been extremely kind to me in my childhood, but all my priorities were with Agatha.

Early in January the Superintendent of the Academy told me he had called on the Chief of Infantry in Washington to discuss my future. He gave me this handwritten note:

> For Mr. Davis:
>
> 1. Apply for commission in the Infantry, 2. Apply for Fort Benning as station, 3. You will be sent there and ordered to take the Company Officers' Course as soon as practicable, 4. After taking that course, you can be stationed in Chicago with the 8th Illinois Inf, or Cleveland, Boston, or Washington with the 372nd Inf, or New York with the 369th Inf. You could be attached to one of these organizations and authorized to take a course in college while on duty in the city. This opens up Chicago U., Western Reserve U., Harvard, George Washington, not a bad choice. Or you could add to these duty, with a Reserve Unit at Baltimore, when Johns Hopkins would be available. Harvard and Columbia are doubtless the best Law Schools, but Chicago is your home.

Of course all the units mentioned in this note were black National Guard units. I was astounded that the Army would go to all this trouble to rid itself of the problem of a black second lieutenant. Amazing!

My parents traveled to New York to see my sister, Olive, in early March, and they took advantage of the trip to visit me. I very much wanted them to meet Agatha. We all met at West Point, and Agatha and my parents took to each other immediately. The chemistry continued to work as long as my parents lived, without any in-law problems of the smallest kind.

About the middle of March, only three months before graduation, I learned that West Point administrators were still having trouble finding nine other cadets who did not object to sitting at the same table with me in the mess hall. The situation had improved after I complained to the commandant as a fourth classman, but table assignments continued to change after they were published. The subject had not been made much of in the recent past (at least it had not come to my attention), but it was embarrassing to me and for that reason troublesome.

My father also experienced a problem about the same time. He had found it necessary to suspend a Tuskegee Institute cadet for assaulting a cadet officer. Unfortunately, the suspended student happened to be a star basketball player. Not only did Dr. Frederick Patterson, the president of the Institute, reverse my father's decision; he went on to state that he disapproved of military training in colleges. My father had no alternative but to resign his position as commandant of cadets. About a month later, he was informed that he might be transferred to Wilberforce the next year, perhaps as result of this incident.

## Graduation

I had the knotty problem of deciding what to do with the eight tickets to graduation exercises allotted to each cadet. Many friends and acquaintances had written to me asking for tickets, telling me how proud they would be to attend. Whatever I did, it would turn out to be wrong; there were more people than tickets. I sent two to Congressman De Priest, three to my parents and Elnora, and two to Agatha and her mother; I do not remember who got the other ticket. The few days in June before graduation, called June Week, were filled with horse shows, recitals, and various ceremonies for the first classmen and their families. There were also nightly hops at Cullum Hall and the Thayer Hotel. I was interested to learn from a black cadet who graduated a few years later that he was told not to attend any of the hops. I received no such instruction, but I was well aware that I would not be welcome. I passed June Week quietly, reading and contemplating the details of graduation and the days immediately following. Agatha and I were to be married on 20 June at West Point. After 90 days' leave, I would report as a second lieutenant to the 24th Infantry Regiment at Fort Benning, Georgia, on 12 September.

My feelings as I approached graduation were bittersweet. I was extremely proud that I had withstood the forces that opposed me so actively for my entire four years as a cadet, and that I would be the first black in the 20th century to graduate from West Point. My father had hoped that I would do well enough to join the Engineers, and I had, ranking 35 in a class of 276. Nevertheless, I still had my heart set on being a pilot. My father had also said more than once that he did not want to leave active duty without at least one black Regular Army line officer on the active list. It was somewhat reassuring to know that when I graduated, there would be two. I had become stronger and healthier, and I had acquired many valuable skills. I had learned to live with myself and by myself. Living as a prisoner in solitary confinement for four years had not destroyed my personality, nor poisoned my attitude toward other people. I had even managed to keep a sense of humor about the situation; when my father told me of my many supporters, the many people who were pulling for me, I said, "It's a pity none of them were at West Point."

All these positive aspects held great meaning for me that would help sustain me for the rest of my life. But there was no denying the very substantial negatives. I had spent many miserable days, weeks, months, and years at West Point. My problems were not in any way related to basic military training. I believed in the Academy and its educational approach; I actually enjoyed the rigid discipline that was designed to produce leaders who could endure the hardships of war. The silencing imposed on me, however, was an entirely different matter. Upon entering West Point, I had looked forward to making lifelong friends who would endure the Academy experience along with me and with whom I would be closely and sympathetically associated throughout our service. It did not turn out that way; I left West Point without any genuine friends and with only the most distant of acquaintances.

Graduation went well. Gen. John J. Pershing spoke, and though I was too preoccupied to notice, many of those present told me later of the prolonged applause that occurred when he presented me with my commission and degree. Newspapers all over the United States, both black and white, carried articles about the graduation of the first black cadet from West Point in this century, and a prominent black magazine, *The Crisis,* pictured me on its cover as the "Number One Graduate of the Nation." I received many telegrams and letters from people who had read these articles.

I was subdued after the ceremony. My overriding emotion was one of relief; at last I would be leaving West Point, having accomplished the goal that I had set for myself. I think I had the presence of mind to thank my parents for all the support they had given me. A few of my classmates came up and exchanged congratulations; most of them I

have never seen again. Then I was ready to go. I went back to my
room, got out of my cadet uniform for the last time, and dressed in
the civilian clothes I would wear for the next three months. None too
soon, I left behind the orders, the routine, and the silence I had
endured for four years.

# The Real World

## 3.

*I believed that I might well end up teaching at
Wilberforce and Tuskegee for years, as my father had.
More than anything else, I wanted to be regarded with
the respect due a Regular Army officer. And I wanted
to earn that respect through performance and
demonstrated ability.*

Silencing at West Point received national publicity in the early 1970s,
when the Honor Committee found Cadet James Pelosi guilty of completing an answer on an examination after the order to cease work
had been given. Claiming to be innocent of the charges, he refused to
resign and appealed to a board of officers. The case was dismissed on
the order of Lt. Gen. William Knowlton, the Superintendent, when it
was revealed that the Honor Committee had seen a note from a high-
ranking officer stating that Pelosi was clearly guilty of an honor violation and his case should therefore go forward without delay. Although his case was dismissed, Pelosi was officially silenced by the
student body. Many of the articles on the case referred to the silencing
I had undergone 40 years earlier, even though my experience was in
no way related to an honor infraction, and mentioned that I had
chosen not to talk to the press about it. In June 1973, Agatha wrote
to Pelosi to express her feelings on the subject:

Dear Lt. Pelosi:

Congratulations upon your graduation from West Point. You have proven
your true worth as a man to your classmates after a year and a half of

51

being officially silenced. Now your classmates will have to prove their true worth to you. I am sure it will take more than a year and a half. In some cases, it can't be done in a lifetime. I know you will forgive them but never forget. They will forget but never forgive you for being man enough to succeed in spite of all the obstacles that were surreptitiously or openly thrown in your path.

I write to you because I think I know what your life at the Academy must have been. My best friend spent four years of silence at the Point. You were given a reason for your silence, invalid though it may have been. You were also accepted on face value when you entered the Academy. My friend was given no reason and was never accepted on face value because the face happened to be black. However, under every possible handicap a human could be given, he succeeded in showing his classmates and all those persons with whom he ever came in contact through all the years since 1932 that he never veered from his goal he had set for himself in spite of his many bigoted detractors. He was and is a born optimist, and believes that all are good until proven evil. As a result of his high ideals and principles, he has earned the respect of men at home and abroad. He understands the foibles of man, as no man is without them. He respects only those who have earned his respect. It must be earned. Race, color, creed, national origin, money, position in life, and all the other frivolous attributes have nothing to do with respect. This is a quality no man is born with.

From 1936, when I married that best friend of mine, until 1949, I, too, was silenced by his classmates and their wives. It was in that year that attitudes started to change and are still changing. I did meet the Captain of his Company recently and questioned him about the treatment and lack of fairness for no reason to one lonely cadet that was allowed to be acceptable to the whole Corps. After all these years, he still saw nothing wrong in the persecution and concerted effort to belittle the life of a brilliant (35th in the Class of 1936), outstanding human being.

You may not have to spend as many years being an outsider as my friend did, but there will always be those who will stand in your way. Don't resent them; just feel sorry for them. They are not worthy of your friendship or respect. Hold your head high and look up to no man. Your conscience is clear, and you can live with yourself. The best of all that is good in life is my wish for you.

Sincerely,
Agatha S. Davis

It was the custom in the Army for silenced cadets to bear the mantle of silence throughout their careers as officers, and according to Pelosi, his classmates continued to silence him long after his graduation. I had heard about this custom when I was at West Point, but I could not believe that it would be applied to me because of the fundamental differences between my case and those that had occurred before. Hence, I felt that my graduation represented a watershed in my career and that the worst was over. Because of the prevailing attitudes toward blacks in the military and society at large, I was not expecting the officer corps to welcome me with open arms. But I did think I would be treated with the respect I was due as an officer. Subsequent events proved me to be wrong.

## Good Times in Chicago and Tuskegee

Agatha and I were married in the Cadet Chapel at West Point two weeks after graduation. The huge chapel was empty except for us, the chaplain, and three family members: Elnora; Agatha's mother, Sarah Josephine Scott; and her sister, Mildred. But the occasion was full of the love, happiness, and serenity that we knew would last for the rest of our lives. After the ceremony we drove to New York, where I became acquainted with Agatha's parents. They both followed the New England custom of calling friends and acquaintances by their surnames, but from the first time I met them I was "Ben." We became great friends. Once Agatha had completed the school year, we felt at liberty to leave. She said a teary goodbye to her family, and we took off for Chicago.

We made a conscious decision to spend our money having a good time in the big city before leaving for Fort Benning. Racial segregation and discrimination were still actively practiced in the North, but in the South our activities would be even more severely restricted. We would be living near Columbus, Georgia, and Phenix City, Alabama, a notoriously rough town on the Chattahoochee River, where we would certainly not be welcome. Knowing we were headed for the worst of the worst, we wanted to enjoy ourselves as best we could beforehand. Agatha had never been farther south than Washington, D.C., but she had heard many ugly stories about the treatment of blacks and Jews by southern white people of all stations of life: the lynchings, the illegal arrests, the restrictions on places to live, to eat, to go to school and church, to be born and to die. She considered it all cruel and disgraceful, yet she showed no trepidation about entering this wasteland.

Our marriage was off to a wonderful start. We spent a month going to the races, being entertained by our many friends at dances and picnics, sightseeing, visiting the museums and stores, and eating in restaurants where blacks were welcomed. During this visit I revealed again my unfamiliarity with life in the real world. One day we went to a matinee in the Loop, and after dropping Agatha off, I parked our convertible Buick with the top down on one of the main streets, neglecting to turn off the ignition or remove the key. Luckily, the car was there when we got back, with the motor still running.

One Sunday I visited six churches in the company of Congressman Oscar De Priest. He introduced me to each congregation, and in turn I told them how he had made it possible for me to go to West Point and how his energy and enthusiasm had always been an inspiration to me. It seemed that I was to be the main plank in his campaign for reelection. I visited the Third Ward Republican Club one night and made another speech describing what a fine man Mr. De Priest was. I did believe he was the outstanding black leader in public life, and I will ever be grateful to him for giving me the opportunity to prepare for an honorable career and a respectable life.

In early August 1936 we left Chicago with wonderful memories and headed south for a visit with my parents. Traveling in the South was in itself a big problem: no places to stay, no places to eat, and no rest rooms to use unless we were willing to go into a room with a door marked "colored." It was better to find a spot behind a tree in the woods than to use the filthy toilets reserved for blacks. In those days, roadside accommodations were few and far between even for whites. Unless a black person knew someone along the route to his destination, he would pull his car off the road and sleep in it. It took us three days and two nights to make the trip from Chicago to Tuskegee. Sleeping in a car was not much fun, but it helped us avoid the worst aspects of segregation, and we consoled ourselves with the knowledge that the Davis home awaited us at the end of the road.

I spent the rest of August and early September with my parents, seeing old friends and schoolmates from my days at the Children's House, showing off my bride, and meeting new people. It was an exhilarating period. The people of Tuskegee Institute welcomed us with such warmth that we felt immediately at home. They were extremely proud of my accomplishments at West Point, pointing out that my struggle would make it easier for the next black man at the Academy, and happy that all the obstacles I had met had not destroyed my spirit or deterred me from reaching my goal. It was truly

Benjamin O. Davis, my father, as a first lieutenant of cavalry in the U.S. Army in 1907.

Elnora Dickerson Davis, my mother, in 1910.

At age 20 months, in 1914.

The Davis children in 1917: Olive, 12; Elnora, 2; and me, 5.

Astride Tipperary at my Uncle Louis's farm in 1917.

My stepmother, Sadie Overton Davis, in 1920.

The Davis family at the National Guard Encampment at Camp Perry, Ohio, in the late 1920s: me, Benjamin Davis, Sr., Olive, Mother Sadie, and Elnora.

Herman A. Scott, Agatha's father.

Sarah J. Scott and her daughters Edith and baby Agatha.

Father and son, on the occasion of the senior Davis's visit to West Point in 1933.

Agatha, me, and sister Elnora in New York in 1936, shortly after my graduation from West Point. Agatha and I were married a week later.

Second Lieutenant Davis of the 24th
Infantry Regiment at Fort Benning,
Georgia, in September 1936.

Members of the first class of Tuskegee
Army Air Field graduates in 1942:
George "Spanky" Roberts, me, Charles H.
DeBow, Lt. R. M. Long (an instructor in
advanced flying), Mac Ross, and Lemuel
R. Custis.

This photograph of Secretary of War Henry Stimson inspecting the 99th Pursuit Squadron in 1942 was modified on Pentagon orders by superimposing my photograph. I did not, in fact, meet the Secretary during his visit (see chapter 4).

Climbing into my advanced training AT-6 at Tuskegee Army Air Field in the spring of 1942.

Agatha and the family dog, Major, outside our home in Tuskegee in the summer of 1942.

A group of Air Corps wives (husbands overseas) gathers on base at Tuskegee Army Air Field for bowling in 1943: Luwanna Knighton (standing) and Blanche Lawrence, Frankie Jones, Rose Lane, and Agatha (sitting).

Colonel Davis, commander of the 332d Fighter Group, in Italy in 1944, with P-51, "By Request."

Returning to Ramitelli from enemy radar strafing in southern France in August 1944.

Father pins the Distinguished Flying Cross on me at Ramitelli in September 1944. The others awaiting their turn to be decorated are Capt. Joseph D. Elsberry, 1st Lt. Jack D. Holsclaw, and 1st Lt. Clarence D. Lester.

The senior staff of the 332d surrounds me at Ramitelli.

pleasant to live in an atmosphere where both friends and strangers spoke to us and sought our company. We enjoyed this kind of treatment, however, only within the confines of the Tuskegee Institute community grounds and at the black Veterans Administration Hospital. The adjacent town of Tuskegee, mostly white, was still as hostile as it had been when I lived there as a child.

Mother Sadie and my father gave a huge reception for Agatha and me at their home. Among the guests were George Washington Carver, the world-famous scientist, and Monroe N. Work, the archivist at the school library, whose claim to fame was keeping annual statistics on lynchings of blacks in the United States, as well as many studies by black scholars on progress and hindrances in race relations. Mother Sadie had invited people of all ages, nearly all of them associated with the Institute. Many of them extended southern hospitality to us and became our friends for life. We had a jubilant time, establishing ourselves in the social life of this small community, and for many years it remained our home away from home.

Although Tuskegee Institute was a "hick town," there was always something going on. In those days, contract bridge was a favorite pastime. Agatha did not know how to play bridge; in New Haven, it was considered a game for old people. To please me and my parents, however, she agreed to learn. The first lesson turned out to be a disaster; it was a case of too many teachers who seemed to take delight in criticizing each of her mistakes. Before long she folded her cards, threw them across the bridge table, and said, "I've never met such egotistical men in my life." She then got up from the table and went upstairs. I had never seen her so angry before, and I realized too late that by joining in on the criticism of her bridge playing, I had contributed to her embarrassment. I followed her upstairs and begged her to play again. She agreed under the condition that neither I nor my father expect her to be a super bridge player. From that time on, we dared not give her a bad time. She did learn how to play bridge—an acceptable game—and the rest of us learned that she was a person to be reckoned with.

## The Silence Continues

After these two happy months of freedom, it was time to get on with my career, our first home, and a new way of life. We were looking forward to becoming an active couple in the 24th Infantry Regiment as residents of the nation's largest military post. Fort Benning was about an hour's drive from Tuskegee Institute. On the way to Columbus, the red Georgia clay road was hazardous, hilly, and full of holes and ruts. We passed horse-drawn carts, road scrapers, farm machinery, and people walking, some barefoot. On both sides of the road stood lean-to shacks, shanties, cabins, shotgun houses, a few antebellum homes, ramshackle buildings and barns, poorly kept gardens, and farms. It was shocking and disturbing to see people living in such poverty and squalor.

Before graduation, all first classmen had been issued orders on the "Customs of the Service." Included in these orders, a paper called "Hints of Behavior" told us how to behave militarily and socially as second lieutenants. On the way to Fort Benning, Agatha and I studied this paper carefully. The Army was very particular about etiquette, and we wanted to do everything correctly at my first station. While in Chicago, we had purchased our engraved calling cards—an absolute must—at Marshall Fields. Some of the customs, rules, and regulations in "Hints of Behavior" followed Emily Post; some were strictly Army; and some were just strange.

I was expected to call on my commanding officer as soon as possible after arriving. After presenting my orders, I would enter the room correctly, salute, and remain standing, unless invited to sit. The commanding officer would indicate when the interview was over by standing. We were also to make a social call on him and his family in his quarters within 48 hours after signing in, preferably on the evening of my arrival. Everything would be arranged by the adjutant, the equivalent of a protocol officer. We had to be sure to "drop" the proper number of calling cards, one for each adult in the household. The "Hints" cautioned: Be prompt, and do not stay longer than 20 minutes. We would also call on the battalion and company commanders, in order of rank. Other officers would call on us, the new arrivals, and we were expected to return their calls. We were also expected to join the officers' club, a good way to become acquainted with other officers and their families. It was taboo to associate socially with enlisted personnel; we were instructed to treat enlisted men with consideration but to avoid familiarity. Agatha and I planned to go by all the rules.

I reported in on 11 September to Capt. Victor Phasey, the assistant adjutant, who told me when Agatha and I could make our official call on Col. Ellery Farmer, commander of the 24th Infantry, and Mrs. Farmer. When we arrived at the Farmers' quarters, the lights were on, the front door was open, and the screen door was locked. They were obviously at home. I rang the bell; no one responded. I waited a few minutes and rang again. We waited again for a longer time and concluded we were not to be allowed to make our official call that night. Disappointed, we left our calling cards at the door and went home. It was the custom to return an official call within 48 hours, which meant that if protocol were followed, the Farmers would call upon us. We were not told by the adjutant's office to expect a call, however, so we were surprised to find their calling cards at our front door when I left for work a day or so later. We must have been at home when the cards were slipped under the door, so it was obvious that we were being avoided.

We pitied the Farmers for the smallness of their actions. This intentional personal insult and blatant disregard for time-honored military tradition would have done no credit to anyone, much less a senior officer in a position of high responsibility. Colonel Farmer, like so many other whites, probably rationalized his behavior in terms of prevailing attitudes; when dealing with blacks, it was acceptable to ignore the usual standards of human decency. After a while, I arrived at the conclusion that, by leaving his card, he had actually intended to maintain the fiction of military etiquette. Captain Phasey did not suggest that we call on any other senior officers, and he apparently did not suggest to those officers, who were already members of the 24th, that they call on us—another breach of tradition. Not a single white officer extended us a welcome to the 24th. It was West Point all over again.

Agatha and I felt even more deeply our rejection by the Fort Benning Officers' Club. When Captain Phasey suggested I apply for membership, I immediately filled out a form, enclosed a check, and mailed it. By *return mail,* I received a letter from the club secretary stating that, because I had not used the club, it was assumed that I was not interested and he was therefore returning my check to me. This was one of the most insulting actions taken against me during my military service: the letter was a deliberate falsification of the facts of the matter and an action unworthy of any officer of the U.S. Army. The whole masquerade had been arranged in advance by Captain Phasey and the club secretary to make it appear that I had been offered membership. I felt nothing but contempt for both of them and regretted that we had to associate at all with such small-minded, bigoted people. To this day I have not seen the inside of the Fort Benning Officers' Club.

Segregation was complete and absolute at Fort Benning. The only exception seemed to be the fact that our quarters were not in a black area. One day Agatha was walking down our sidewalk to the car when Mrs. Alton Denton, whose husband was a student at the Infantry School, was coming out of her quarters, the other half of the building in which we lived. They greeted each other warmly—a good sign, but it only lasted about one day. Agatha is fair, and apparently Mrs. Denton took her for white. When I came home from work the next day, Mrs. Denton was going into her house. I looked at her, smiled, and said hello. She turned her head and said nothing. During the seven months we lived in the duplex the Dentons never looked at nor spoke to us. In their favor, I could say that their behavior was not unique. I never saw nor spoke to any of my nine West Point classmates at Fort Benning either, and we were consistently snubbed by all the other white officers and their wives.

I was the only second lieutenant in the 24th and the only black officer except for Maj. Alexander W. Thomas, the chaplain. While I was still at West Point, a report had been distributed to our class by the United States Infantry Association on "stations of infantry organizations and vacancies available." Second lieutenants of infantry were "recommended for assignment to all infantry regiments in the United States and foreign possessions, except tank regiments and the 24th Infantry." No one told me why the 24th Infantry was excluded, but it was easy for me to guess.

The first day at work I was assigned to duty with Company F, all black except for our commanding officer, Capt. Truman C. Thorson. My duty was not even slightly interesting. In those days, black troops were trained not for combat but for "service"—maintaining equipment and grounds, janitorial service for officers' quarters, cleaning stables—in short, the kind of work relegated to black people in the rest of American society. It quickly became obvious to me that the Army was not taking advantage of my talents and training. During my one year with the 24th, we performed only two very short maneuvers in connection with an Infantry School exercise.

Although I had been denied membership in the officers' club, in October I mistakenly received a memo announcing the annual "Infantry School Hunt." All members and their families and guests were invited to participate in the hunts, but Agatha and I chose to go hunting with two particularly pleasant people—ourselves. We enjoyed doing things together, just the two of us. We were so happy to have each other and our own home that we did not permit the stones and brickbats thrown our way to detract from our happiness.

A letter I received that October from a West Point cadet, J. P. Conner, came as a great surprise to me. He was in my Company M and therefore aware of the silent treatment I had received at the Point:

> I wanted to sit down and shoot the bull with you for a while June Week, but you were pretty damn busy, what with your Poppa there. All I wanted to tell you was what a hell of a lot I thought of you and how nice it had been to know you the three years we were both here. The narrow mindedness of some people is astounding and I believe that this place instead of diminishing that quality in men, increases it. Some of the things I heard said and done against yourself lead me in part to that conclusion. But also by the same process I found how you can take it; and what a damned fine model you would make in that respect. Whatever the reaction towards you where you are now and whomever from, I am sure you are accepting it in the same manner that you accepted the bumps here, i.e. with poise and grace and like a man. No fooling, you are so big that some of the resentment and ill will which is felt by some for you drops harmlessly at your feet instead of hurting you.

I appreciated the sentiments expressed in this letter. Through the years of my service I would receive many such letters and apologies from classmates who had allowed me to be invisible during my four years at West Point.

Frequently Agatha would walk to the post exchange and commissary. One day as she was walking along the road, a lady driving a car stopped and offered her a lift. They had a very pleasant conversation. That was the first and last time Agatha saw the woman, but she did see a picture of her in the local newspaper. The accompanying article gave her name as Mrs. John Moreland, the president of the Infantry School Women's Club, which had been organized in 1923 to bring together the officers' wives and promote a spirit of friendliness and comradeship. Agatha had never been told there was a women's club, and I am sure she was not expected to join, especially because it was affiliated with the Columbus Federation of Women's Clubs. Mrs. Moreland was the only woman who had recognized Agatha as a new officer's wife and was thoughtful enough to offer a kind word.

Agatha and I were unofficially silenced by our peers at Benning exactly as I had been silenced at West Point. Diagonally across the backyard from our quarters lived the Weeks family, mother and daughter. Mrs. Weeks, the widow of Colonel Weeks, had been given a job as manager of the post exchange craft shop. She was cordial as craft shop manager, but as our neighbors neither she, her daughter, nor her daughter's boyfriend, a classmate of mine, bothered to speak to us. Agatha passed this off as she did all the slights we endured at Fort Benning: "We haven't missed anything by not knowing them, but they are missing a very great deal by not knowing us."

We led what might be called a weekend social life. Chaplain Thomas was the only officer of the 24th Infantry to call on us. He invited us and some of his civilian friends to his house in Columbus for dinner. There we met an outstanding couple, Dr. Tom Brewer and his wife, Billy, with whom we became close friends, exchanging dinners, picnics, sightseeing trips, and bridge games. They and their friends extended to us southern hospitality in its most relaxed and kindest form. My parents were still living at Tuskegee Institute, and we also exchanged visits with them and the many friends we had made during our month's stay there.

After a Christmas holiday in New York, I was ready to go back to work, with the hope that in 1937 I would be assigned more worthwhile work. Things did pick up when I was made officer in charge of recruits. There had been little turnover in the 24th Infantry in previous years. Most of the enlisted men, known as "old soldiers," went from payday to payday, eagerly awaiting the retirement promotion routinely awarded for 30 years' honorable service. I was to train a new breed of enlistees—younger, with more education, and interested in being trained. Although my relationship with them was short, it was a pleasure to be associated with these eager and receptive young men. They had abundant potential, and it was a shame they were relegated to essentially nonmilitary duties after their initial recruit training. At least I was getting the opportunity to apply some of my West Point training; working with them made me feel I was in the military again, and I was pleased to see them develop from volunteer recruits into effective soldiers.

It was at Fort Benning that I began to learn a valuable principle of leadership: you must genuinely like and respect those who are performing under your command, for neither the liking nor the respect can be successfully faked. Early in my service in the 24th, I made a mistake that was overlooked because of the genuine respect between the people involved. William Smith, a first sergeant, ran the orderly room and was the main point of contact between me, the other enlisted men, and Captain Thorson. In an effort to be friendly, I called the first sergeant "Smith"—not a respectful way for a shavetail second lieutenant to address an old soldier. Both First Sergeant Smith and the supply sergeant, Joe Lay, forgave me for my errors and in reserved fashion educated me in matters that every second lieutenant should have in his repertoire.

In February I received a letter from Major General Connor at West Point. He had not forgotten me and our talk about my career, and he congratulated me for reports he had received on my work at Benning. He informed me that I would be detailed to the Infantry School at Fort Benning for 1938–39 after having served only two years—one year earlier than usually required. He also suggested that before graduating from the Infantry School, I apply for the National Guard or an ROTC detail in Chicago. I was greatly impressed by the letter, primarily because General Connor had followed through on the suggestion he made to me when my application to the Air Corps had been rejected. He could properly have considered that his participation in my Army career had been satisfactorily concluded. Instead, he pursued the matter in a commendable manner, demonstrating a loyalty downward that is rare among most senior people.

In June Agatha and I obtained Georgia drivers' licenses. Under "color," the motor vehicle people typed "white" for Agatha and "colored" for me. Under "color hair," they put "black" for both of us, though we both had brown hair. We laughed about it and wondered what would happen if the police stopped our car and wanted to see our licenses. In most southern states, intermarriage was a crime.

Traveling in the South was full of difficulties. In some areas, signs in big letters read, "Coloreds not allowed after sundown," and segregation laws were rigidly enforced by state and local authorities. If someone—particularly a black person—parked too close to the lines separating parking spaces, he was subject to arrest and a fine. When Agatha took a train to visit her family for two weeks in August, however, she had no problems; she sat where the conductor told her to sit. When a person's race was questionable, southern whites would never hazard insulting one of their own, and Agatha never did have to ride in a Jim Crow car.

I saw no future in my assignment to the 24th Infantry. Because of the nature of the work assigned to the regiment—primarily menial tasks and little genuine training—I could expect few challenging projects to be assigned to me. So I was happy and surprised to receive orders in July relieving me from duty with the 24th and assigning me to the Infantry School for the 1937–38 school year, even earlier than General Connor had indicated. I felt as if I were moving up.

Because we were already living in student quarters, we would not have to move. We did get new neighbors, though. When Lieutenant Denton graduated, Lt. Seymour Madison and his family moved in next door. The Madisons turned out to be "hello" people. Apparently they discussed us with their young son, who called us names. Prejudice and bigotry are taught to children by their parents. We felt sorry for this small child, who did not realize that what he was saying was offensive to us.

At the end of my tour with the 24th Infantry I received an efficiency report signed by Captain Thorson with an endorsement by Colonel Farmer. My duties were listed, and I was rated "excellent" for duty with Company F and "superior" for handling officers and men, performance and field duties, physical activity, and attention to duty. Captain Thorson stated that he knew me "very well," that with more experience and service I would be well qualified for duty with "colored civilian components," and that I was one of the most conscientious and efficient officers of my grade he had ever observed. Finally, Captain Thorson stated that I was "potentially an excellent officer and of great value to the service." Colonel Farmer did not wholly concur. His comments: "Lt. Davis, a colored officer, has used tact, sound judgment and common sense in all his duties and relationships, official and unofficial. In civil life, due to his exceptional ability and intelligence, I believe he would achieve great success." In the printed efficiency report form, a category for race was not included, but the buzzwords "colored" or "Negro" always appeared some place in my record. This meant: Do not assign to white troops or units.

Meanwhile, my father suffered the humiliation of being transferred to Wilberforce University as a professor for a third time. This

assignment should have been embarrassing to the Army, but I suppose it was not. It seemed that he would spend the remainder of his
military career shuttling back and forth between Wilberforce and
Tuskegee Institute. He had repeatedly requested duty with troops, but
each time he had been denied. He did believe that living at Wilberforce in Ohio was better than being stashed away in the Deep South
with all its restrictions and general hatefulness. My father was a
senior colonel by then and saw no genuine future in the Army; this
would probably be the best and last assignment he would get. His
transfer should also have been the handwriting on the wall for me,
but I had not reached the point of thinking about future assignments.
My assignment to the Infantry School also gave me hope because I
was to attend after being in active service only one year with troops.
This action put me one to two years ahead of other officers who had
been commissioned in 1936.

## A Year in the Infantry School

On 10 September the Infantry School opened the Regular Course for
the class of 1938. Brig. Gen. Asa L. Singleton welcomed the 178
students and told us about the good relations between the school and
the citizens of Columbus, who would receive us hospitably. Needless
to say, I was skeptical. In our course in tactics and techniques, each
student was required to write a monograph on a subject of his choosing. I chose to write about two British rear guard actions that took
place in August 1914, two or three days after the battle of Mons in
World War I. This was my main project for the course. In May I
lectured on the subject before the class, and I was pleased with my
performance. To give credit where credit is due, my own rear guard,
Agatha, made the maps for the lecture, and the quality of the visual
aids made the presentation.

By the end of March 1938 most of my classmates had already
received their orders, and I impatiently waited for mine. On 30 March
Agatha and I learned from friends at Tuskegee Institute that my orders to report there as professor of military science and tactics, effective 16 June, had been published in the *Atlanta Constitution*. Even
though we would be living among friends at Tuskegee, the news
came as a major letdown from a professional standpoint. The job was

currently held by Sgt. John Patton, who had succeeded my father when he had been reassigned to Wilberforce. It seemed as if history were repeating itself. I had spent four years at West Point, another year with the 24th Infantry, and was about to complete the Regular Course at the Infantry School. All logic and customary Army procedure pointed to my reassignment to an active Regular Army infantry regiment. It appeared that General Connor had been correct in his judgment that there would be no real career for me in the Army.

Agatha cried on the way back to Benning. She knew how disappointed I was, and both of us guessed that as long as I stayed in the Army, I would probably be shuttled back and forth between Tuskegee and Wilberforce. Like it or not, however, I decided to do my very best. Dr. Patterson gave me the impression that the ROTC program at Tuskegee would be upgraded. If this upgrading occurred, the job of professor of military science and tactics would become more respectable. Agatha and I would also be living in the big house my family had lived in during their last tour.

In the wake of this disappointment, we had some of the best news in years. My father was reassigned to command the black 369th National Guard Regiment in New York City. At last he would be on duty with troops. On 5 May the governor of New York, Herbert H. Lehman, released a statement to that effect, referring to my father as "an officer of long and honorable service in the Regular Army" and pointing out that he was scheduled to retire in 1941, giving him three years as commander of the regiment.

Col. Joseph A. Mundy invited me and Agatha to the review that would be held in my father's honor on 3 June. He requested that I not tell "the old man" we were coming, as they wanted to surprise him. Traveling by train to New York, we arrived at the armory in time to greet my parents before the review. It was a happy, memorable, and triumphant occasion. Thousands cheered as my father, with me as his aide, reviewed the regiment at its full peacetime strength of more than 1,100 men. We were very proud of this tribute.

My father's reassignment did not affect my thinking about my career in any way; I was unable to foresee the opportunities that would come my way later. At the time, I believed that I might well end up teaching at Wilberforce and Tuskegee for years, as he had. More than anything else, I wanted to be regarded with the respect due a Regular Army officer, a position that then carried considerable prestige. And I wanted to earn that respect through performance and demonstrated ability.

My studies at the Infantry School entered their most interesting phase that spring, involving much work in supply and administration. In our field exercises I played every part from colonel to lieutenant and even dreamed that after eight or ten years of study I might become eligible for the Command and General Staff School at Fort Leavenworth. But the Army's misguided underrating of black people in general intruded on those dreams once again after graduation, this time in an efficiency report prepared by Col. C. F. Thompson, the assistant commandant, and signed by General Singleton. It read as follows: "In frequent observation, academic ratings, Graduate Regular Course, his academic rating is 'Excellent.' No special aptitude noted for any particular class of duty. Suited for training for high Command and General Staff duties. He is well mannered, dignified, serious, resolute, discerning, well informed, zealous, and efficient. By dignified exercise of discretion and good judgment, *he overcame any handicap on account of his race* [emphasis added]. He has a high present and potential value."'

## Back to Tuskegee

I approached the move to Tuskegee with mixed feelings, looking forward to living among friends once again after two years of silence at Fort Benning, but concerned about the lack of a professional challenge. When I arrived, I was a second lieutenant; a year later I was a first lieutenant with a large increase in pay and allowances; and just a year after that, in September 1940, I was promoted to captain of infantry. But I performed no daring deeds, nor did I accomplish anything outstanding enough to merit these promotions. They resulted quite simply from the facts that I had graduated from West Point, and that the armed forces of the United States were expanding and preparing themselves for active operations in the European war.

My job at Tuskegee Institute was as close to nothing as it could be and still be called a job. The Army had created Senior ROTC units at various colleges and schools to provide trained officers commissioned as second lieutenants upon college graduation. These new lieutenants had spent four years in training, but I was to administer Junior

ROTC or Section 55c units—so named from the paragraph in the law creating ROTC. The Army provided these units with only limited support. For a few months after we arrived at Tuskegee, I served as commandant of cadets. This arrangement did not continue, however, because of a basic conflict between me and the dean of men, whose ideas of discipline in the student body were radically different from my own. He played favorites with popular campus students, particularly athletes, on matters of discipline. These individuals could do no wrong, and if I punished them for infractions of discipline the dean would let them off. My contribution to the program for the 30 months of my stay therefore consisted of three 45-minute lectures per week from September through early May. I had no official duties from May until the opening of the next school year in September, during which time I was entitled to one month's leave. It irked me that for the rest of the summer I had to remain at Tuskegee with absolutely nothing to do.

Even though I derived no pleasure from my paltry duties, both Agatha and I participated actively in the community, and we valued our associations with the residents of the Institute and the employees of the Veterans Administration Hospital. We rode horses, played cards and golf, and Agatha imported clothing from New York and sold it at a nominal profit to women who could not find comparable merchandise in Alabama. (Blacks could not try on clothing, hats, or shoes in the white-owned stores in our area.)

Agatha also participated in an effort to desegregate the theater in Tuskegee town. Rich Harris, a relative of a friend with whom we regularly associated, was waiting in line at the Tuskegee post office one day when the postmaster asked him to step out of line and let a white person go ahead of him. When Rich refused to move, the postmaster came out from behind the counter and slapped him. The news of this incident spread like wildfire, enraging the citizens of Tuskegee Institute and the civilian workers at the Veterans Administration Hospital.

Agatha and a group of our friends wanted to take a course of action that would express their outrage and discourage such violent assaults in the future. Boycott was prohibited by Alabama law, so without actually using the word and thereby being vulnerable to legal action, they decided to stop patronizing the theater and other white-owned businesses. The theater had a single ticket booth and two side-by-side sections, one for blacks and one for whites. After the "boycott" began, the theater was forced to close because of low attendance, and it remained closed for two years. At this point an attempt was made to reopen the theater, but the organizers of the boycott, realizing that with a single ticket booth black customers would be forced to wait in line until all white customers had been taken care of, demanded construction of a second ticket booth for blacks. When this demand was met, the boycott was lifted. Whites had learned that they could not afford to lose black patronage, and racial relations improved somewhat as a result.

Agatha and I tolerated the essentially nonproductive, even useless existence we lived at Tuskegee partly because there was so little opportunity elsewhere. A deep worldwide depression was in progress, and even in good times only limited opportunities existed for blacks in the starkly and rigidly separate white and black societies of the United States. Fortunately, events conspired to make my career vastly different, and our 2½ idle years at Tuskegee Institute turned out to be the only time in our lives when we were not challenged to perform and produce in vitally important and intensely interesting assignments.

Opportunity knocked in the fall of 1940. At the advanced age of 63, nine months short of the statutory retirement age of 64, my father was nominated by President Roosevelt for promotion to the rank of brigadier general. Although the promotion was motivated primarily by the hope of winning black votes in the 1940 presidential election, my father had richly deserved it for many years. After confirmation by the Senate, he was ordered to command the 4th Cavalry Brigade, composed of the 9th and 10th Cavalry regiments—all black except for the officers, who were white.

When my father received his orders, he requested my reassignment as his aide. General officers had considerable latitude in the selection and appointment of aides. Having spent many years at Tuskegee, he was well aware that my current assignment was inadequate, and he also needed someone he could trust to do a good job. When the War Department approved his request and transferred me from Tuskegee Institute to Fort Riley, Kansas, Agatha and I felt that things were definitely changing for the better.

# ★ ★ ★ The Experiment

**4.** *The attitude of blacks nationwide toward the Tuskegee Army Air Field can only be described as mixed. Those looking upon it with optimism and favor believed that the U.S. caste system could be broken down only in times of great social upheaval; the war would give participating blacks more opportunities to learn skills than they had in the past, and they could keep alive what they had achieved and pass it on to others.*

When Agatha and I and all our worldly possessions arrived at Fort Riley in February 1941, we were assigned quarters on the post, as were my parents. The war in Europe and Asia had created an air of urgency at 4th Brigade Headquarters. The U.S. government was still maintaining a stance of neutrality at this time, but many informed people believed that we could not stay out of the war much longer.

I enjoyed meeting the newly assigned officers who reported in, presenting them to my mother and father when they made their formal calls, and receiving many of them when they called upon us. People seemed to come and go rapidly. Several officers stayed in the brigade for only a short time before being called to fill quotas in the Philippines. Many of them must have been part of the Bataan Death March or died on the Japanese prison ships we sank on their way to Japan from the Philippines. When we met them, they had just been commissioned, either from ROTC or Officers Candidate School. They were uniformly good-looking, enthusiastic officers.

During the four short months we lived at Fort Riley, Agatha and I were much happier than we had been at Benning. I cannot say that a warm feeling existed toward us on the post, but it was at least luke-warm, probably because of my father's position as commanding general of the brigade and my position as his aide. The atmosphere was certainly different from the deep freeze of Fort Benning. But we could not use the all-white officers' club, and we attended movies at the theater the Army had, in what it considered a generous gesture, provided its black personnel. In 1941 the Army still regarded all blacks as totally inferior to whites—somewhat less than human, and certainly incapable of contributing positively to its combat mission. But we were only months away from war with Japan, Germany, and their allies, and events in the approaching conflict would prove once and for all the fallacy of that position.

I had been at Riley only a few weeks when my father received a letter from the office of the Chief of the Air Corps suggesting that I be released for pilot training. The news came as a complete surprise. After my application had been rejected in 1935, it seemed clear that the Air Corps viewed as insurmountable the problems that would inevitably arise between black officer pilots and white, noncommissioned officer mechanics and other enlisted men. As part of the Army, the Air Corps also thought it was only reasonable and proper to comply with the Army's regulations on segregation. There was another major consideration: it was obvious that the nation was going to be involved in the war in the immediate future, and no upsettingly radical social changes in the corps were to be permitted to interfere with its rapid mobilization.

The explanation for the Air Corps's sudden about-face was to be found in a Roosevelt administration directive to the War Department to create a black flying unit. Before the 1940 presidential election, the administration had responded to political pressures for broadened black participation in mobilization plans. The War Department's target was the all-white Army Air Corps, and the objective was a black flying unit, later to be known as the 99th Pursuit Squadron. Once I had satisfactorily completed pilot training, I was to command this squadron. Naturally, I was elated, and my father immediately approved of the Air Corps's suggestion. For the first time I saw vague possibilities for a military career that could go far beyond assignments as a professor of military science and tactics at black colleges.

The decision to create a black flying unit was a major step in the struggle for equal opportunity in the armed services, but to the best of my knowledge the concept of racial integration was not even a gleam in the eye of any War Department planner in 1941. Even people like William Hastie, the civilian aide to Secretary of War Henry L. Stimson on issues concerning blacks, limited their efforts to reducing the most overt and unpleasant aspects of segregation. In 1941, as the Governor of Alabama, George Wallace, would remark many years later, it was segregation today, tomorrow, and forever.

Shortly after my father notified Headquarters, Army Air Corps, in Washington of his willingness to release me, I was ordered to report for a flight physical at Fort Riley. I regarded the examination as a mere formality because I had passed easily at West Point. The flight surgeon at Fort Riley, however, did not know that the Air Corps had changed its policy of not accepting black applicants and unhesitatingly failed me by reporting a falsified history of epilepsy. Considering that Air Corps Headquarters was in no way mystified or deterred by this report, it is reasonable to assume that the corps had told flight surgeon examiners to fail black applicants for pilot training. Headquarters immediately understood why I had failed the physical and flew me to Maxwell Field in Montgomery, Alabama, for another, which I passed with no difficulty, my epilepsy having miraculously disappeared in a few days. The failure of a good many other black pilot training applicants to qualify must have been based on similar policy directives to examining flight surgeons, who manufactured phony "deficiencies."

I had orders to report in the late spring of 1941 to what later became Tuskegee Army Air Field (TAAF) and the first black pilot training class. At first, because of a housing shortage, Agatha and I moved into a school dormitory that housed other trainees. The dormitory was also to be used for administration and classrooms for ground-school training in navigation, meteorology, communications, aircraft and engines, and intelligence. Tuskegee Institute seemed to be full of people trying to rent living space. Fortunately, an energetic minister in the community, Rev. Theodore Newman, was building a new house with his own hands, apparently planning to live in it himself. When the house was completed, he was kind enough to rent it to us for $40 a month.

A white officer, Maj. James Ellison, had been assigned as commander of this training effort by the Southeast Air Corps Training Center at Maxwell Field. He was also responsible for the development of the airfield, several miles distant, and primary flight training at Moton Field, near the town of Tuskegee. Basic and advanced flight training were to be conducted at TAAF, which was scheduled to be in the first stages of readiness by late fall.

Both Agatha and I were aware of the high-stakes game we were about to be involved in. Even at that early date it was apparent to us that the lot of blacks in the postwar military and particularly in the postwar Air Corps would be largely determined by black combat performance during the war. Fortunately, the combat performance of the 99th Fighter Squadron and later that of the 332d Fighter Group demonstrated the professional capabilities of black airmen and effectively secured for them a respect that up to that time had been given to very few black people.

## Racial Problems at TAAF

From the time it was conceived until its closing after the end of World War II, TAAF was plagued by racial problems. Hindsight points out the crucial and basic mistake of consolidating the flight training of all black pilots there. In the eyes of Air Corps planners, however, to do otherwise would have set the stage for the deployment of black pilot graduates in white Air Corps squadrons—a completely unheard-of and undesirable idea. In January 1941 the National Association for the Advancement of Colored People (NAACP), which had long campaigned for the participation of blacks in military aviation, staged a National Defense Day protest throughout the nation against discrimination in the defense program. NAACP leaders registered strong complaints in four areas: the separation of white and black Army units, the use of white officers for black troops, assignment of black units to noncombat duties, and delays in the Army program to attain its 10 percent quota of blacks. In reply, the Army stated its desire "to avoid the segregation question" by setting up an all-black unit. Four hundred blacks would be placed in training at Chanute Field, Rantoul, Illinois, for 22 weeks under white instructors, then moved to Tuskegee, where a "special" field would have been established. Concurrently, 35 black candidates would be chosen under the Civil Aeronautics Authority (CAA) from the Civilian Pilot Training Program, established by Congress in 1939 to train civilians while they were going to college, and given 30 weeks of flight training under white instructors. The Army did not say whether more black groups would be trained before this "experimental" unit had completed training, nor whether the unit would have a black commander.

Tuskegee Institute was delighted with the Army plan. Its president, Dr. Patterson, secured enough money from the Rosenwald Fund to purchase land for the primary pilot training field about $2\frac{1}{2}$ miles northeast of white Tuskegee. This field was later named Moton Field after an earlier president of the Institute. It was inaugurated by President Patterson on 19 July 1941 at the Booker T. Washington monument. Maj. Gen. Walter R. Weaver, commander of the Southeast Training Center, participated in the ceremony.

Moton Field later became a contract flying school for the Army Air Corps. At that time, black instructors provided primary training, and a few of them later became instructors for basic and advanced training at TAAF. Charles Anderson, affectionately known as Chief, headed this exceptionally capable group of black civilian flying instructors, whose mission was to train black pilots and send those who satisfactorily completed the primary course on to basic and advanced. Chief was assisted by Charles Foxx, Perry Young, and others who saw to it that Moton Field performed in exemplary fashion throughout the war.

I had met Chief Anderson in the late 1930s when I was stationed at Tuskegee Institute, and had taken an immediate liking to him. As a favor he had given me two rides in his own Piper Cub, which he operated at a small field near Tuskegee. Because he was in the flying training business, he may have thought that I was interested in obtaining a private pilot's license. Chief offered the opinion that I had a strong aptitude for flying, but at the time it still seemed far removed from practical career considerations.

Major Ellison busily supervised the development of TAAF. The Air Corps had to move rapidly because it was behind in its preparation for the coming war, and the pressure was on to reach deployment readiness and strength. It let contracts with a black Nashville building contracting firm, McKissack and McKissack, which hired a black architect, Hilyard Robinson, from Washington, D.C. The Air Corps well understood the political mine fields that stood in the way of the airfield's development: the attitude of the white citizens of Tuskegee; the attitude of the white officers and enlisted men assigned to the base; the War Department's segregation policies; and the basic question posed by the TAAF "experiment," as it came to be known in the popular press. Could blacks fly airplanes to the standards required by the Army Air Corps?

In 1941 these problems were very real indeed. The selection of a site was important enough to require the personal attention of the Chief of the Air Corps, Gen. George Brett. As soon as rumors reached Tuskegee's white citizens that a black-manned airfield was to be created in the vicinity, a detailed letter of protest and petition signed by a lifelong and influential resident, Judge William Varner, and more than 100 other white Tuskegeeans was dispatched to Alabama Senators John Bankhead and Lister Hill. Complaining about the placement of a "colored aviation camp" on the boundary of Tuskegee, Senator Hill asked General Brett to look into the matter. The letter complained that the field would block "the only direction for white people to expand," but upon investigation General Brett discovered that it was to be built a full 6½ miles northwest of Tuskegee and would not interfere with the town's expansion. Hence that complaint was easily disposed of.

There were other objections. William Hastie complained about building separate barracks for white and black officers, arguing that whites must live in the same building with blacks. He also criticized plans to install separate drinking fountains and rest rooms for black and white personnel. In his discussion with Senator Hill's secretary, General Brett expressed the view that Hastie was demanding desegregation and that he, Brett, "did not think this is going to work in the South." Hill's secretary responded that he "did not think it would work anywhere." Eventually, the segregated facilities were built, but they continued to be a major bone of contention throughout the base's existence.

The negative attitudes toward blacks of the white officers and enlisted personnel assigned to TAAF—attitudes that prevailed in the United States in 1941—were reinforced and supported by Army segregation regulations. The physical location of TAAF in the Deep South exacerbated the situation. All the white personnel worked with blacks during the day and retreated to the exclusively white environment of a small southern town at night, creating severe problems on both sides. Tuskegee's local whites felt threatened. Blacks on the base resented all forms of segregation and believed that the white administrators and flying instructors had aligned themselves with Tuskegee whites to the detriment of all black people. A confrontational atmosphere developed early on and never fully relaxed itself to permit wholesome man-to-man, friend-to-friend relationships.

The antagonistic white-black relationships, official segregation practices, and the hateful racism that prevailed in the Deep South at the time plagued our everyday lives and could easily have sabotaged our mission. Was this tension by design? Was it all just an unfortunate mistake? Looking back, I have to state my unhappy conclusion that Air Corps Headquarters, determined to maintain its policy of segregation at all costs, was solely to blame for the situation. The initial basis for the plan was preparation for war: "not to hobble the war effort with desegregation." Under these conditions, there had to be a TAAF. In the opinion of the Air Corps, it would have been ruinous to spread black pilots and support personnel throughout the white training establishment because the next step would inevitably have been to integrate blacks into white tactical units, a change that would presumably have prevented the Air Corps from attaining its combat capability goals. The decision to support TAAF, therefore, was followed by another decision to confine the "black problem" as much as possible within the airfield's geographical limits, resulting in the equivalent of a prison camp for black servicemen and their families. All of TAAF's operations were dedicated to a segregated structure, one that would prevent dilution of the Air Corps's white establishment.

The attitudes of blacks nationwide toward TAAF can only be described as mixed. The NAACP criticized TAAF because of its implied perpetuation of segregation, and later fired a member of its staff who praised the 99th. Some black editors ranted against Uncle Toms—blacks who were willing to serve in black units and seeemed to tacitly support segregation. Fortunately, the view was also expressed that the new black pilots of TAAF would contribute to the prestige of their race and that TAAF offered a significant step toward equal opportunity in a vital part of American democracy. Those looking upon TAAF with optimism and favor believed that the U.S. caste system could be broken down only in times of great social upheaval; the war would give participating blacks more opportunities to learn skills than they had in the past, and they could keep alive what they had learned and achieved and pass it on to others.

My own opinion was that blacks could best overcome racist attitudes through their achievements, even though those achievements
had to take place within the hateful environment of segregation. I
believed that TAAF should move ahead rapidly and prove for all to
see, especially within the Army Air Corps, that we were a military
asset. The coming war represented a golden opportunity for blacks,
one that could not be missed, and our future in the Air Corps would
be determined by the account we gave of ourselves. At that moment,
years before the integration of the armed services became a possibility, it seemed as if we had made a number of gains. We owned a
fighter squadron—something that would have been unthinkable
only a short time earlier. It was all ours. The airplane would be the
center of our squadron's existence. Furthermore, we would be required to analyze our own problems and solve them with our own
skills. And although we might be confronted with problems on the
ground by racists who would seek to divert us from our primary
mission, I was confident that we could meet all challenges.

With my limited knowledge of the administrative situation, I
thought Major Ellison made good progress in his difficult and complicated mission of developing TAAF. After operations began, the
townspeople of Tuskegee continued to watch all action at TAAF with
considerable apprehension. Apparently, it was not so much the existence of the base that disturbed them as the large number of blacks
stationed there. In the fall Major Ellison was transferred, reportedly
because he was not administering TAAF in a way that took into
consideration the concerns of the local white population. In his place,
Col. Frederick von Kimble, a West Point graduate, was assigned as
base commander.

Colonel Kimble arrived with large numbers of base support personnel and set about strengthening command administration. He also
took certain actions that immediately antagonized TAAF's black population. According to black newspapers of the time, these actions
included creating segregated sections in the mess hall for commissioned officers; posting signs that read "For Colored Officers" and
"For White Officers" on washroom doors; cooperating with townspeople to have black noncommissioned officers humiliated through
unnecessary curfew laws; ordering white officers "not to socialize
with black officers"; barring all white officers from the officers' club
and the post theater because blacks were admitted; stating that no

black officers would be promoted above the rank of captain as long as he was in command; and perhaps worst of all, refusing to assign high-ranking black officers to jobs for which they were qualified. Many examples of the improper assignment of capable and qualified black officers were printed in the black press, which initiated a campaign to have Colonel Kimble removed from his command. Clearly, race relations were dominating every aspect of what went on at TAAF, and the conflict was having considerable adverse effects on our mission.

While Colonel Kimble was considered cold and aloof, eager to keep blacks in the subordinate position decreed by the Army's segregation policies, another senior white officer, Maj. Noel Parrish, won the respect and liking of many blacks at TAAF. Major Parrish, a southerner, had been assigned as director of training several months before Kimble's arrival. Acting as a combination of psychologist and sociologist, he was eager to understand blacks and treat them on an equal, man-to-man basis. He made it his business to ask black personnel what effect racial tensions were having upon them as individuals, leaving them with the feeling that he understood their problems and was sympathetic to them.

In the early 1940s it was unheard-of for blacks to be recognized as equally capable as whites in just about any field of endeavor, and for a long time the Army Air Corps did not believe that blacks trained by TAAF to fly military airplanes were generally within the same range of ability as white pilots trained at other Air Corps bases. In fact, the general belief within the Air Corps that blacks could fly to required standards did not develop until years after World War II. Parrish's professional attitude toward the training of black pilots and his application of reason to the problem—his ability to overcome any prejudices he may have brought to Tuskegee by recognizing the abilities of black pilots—enabled him to support black military aviation at a time when its future hung in the balance. As director of training, he was in an influential position to advise those above him whether blacks could be trained to fly to Air Corps standards, so his goodwill was of major importance. Just as significant, his personality and his willingness to talk to blacks softened their reaction to the continued segregation and the complete control of all activities by white officers, from the commander down to the flying instructors.

It would be fair to say that most blacks at TAAF transferred their hatred of segregation to Colonel Kimble and the other white administrative officers in the command structure. Much of this hatred was based on what they considered the unfair utilization of black officers and discrimination in the promotion system. Many black aviation cadets were also "washed out," that is, cut from the program—eight out of my class of thirteen trainees. Given that all the basic and advanced instructors were white, and given our collective experience of racial discrimination both inside and outside the military service, it was only human nature for some of those who were washed out to blame not their inability to fly, but rather racism.

Kimble's strict adherence to segregation as it was practiced in the Deep South roused further resentments. Black military police (MPs) from the airfield were frequently harrassed by the white police of Tuskegee. Pat Evans, the town sheriff, complained to Colonel Kimble that black MPs were driving jeeps through Tuskegee with side arms strapped to their legs. The issue came to a head one night when a black airman was arrested by town police and held in the town jail. Following standard procedure, black MPs entered the jail and asked that the prisoner be released to them for transfer to the TAAF guardhouse. When one MP became belligerent, the town police reacted with their customary brutality and relieved the MPs of their weapons. Much to the dismay of Capt. George Webb, the commander of the guard squadron, Colonel Kimble acceded to the sheriff's demand that MPs not carry weapons in Tuskegee or anywhere else in Macon County. Captain Webb, who considered the entire situation degrading to him and his men, protested this action to Colonel Kimble, but to no avail.

The following poem written by Agatha is a valid description of life at TAAF and the attitudes of many of the men who trained there:

### Dear Mom, This Is a Hell of a Hole

Dear Mom, this is a Hell of a hole.
To Tuskegee Army Flying School you are to report,
From Headquarters was the message they sent me, sweet and short.
At last I would go to the field that had been my first choice,
Again I could feel like a man, a real man with a voice.
"Goodbye and good luck," to me my old pals happily said.
They knew where I was going, Jim Crow would surely be dead.
I paid my debts, packed my bags, signed the book, and took my leave,
Glad to go to a good place, where no longer I would grieve.

"Chehaw," the conductor called from the rear of the car,
As the slow train came to a stop with an awful jar.
Much we had heard of this one and only Negro air post,
Here was one place of which officers and soldiers could boast.
"Reporting, sir," were the words I used as I entered camp,
And I had a strange feeling then that things were cold and damp.

Dear Mom, this is a Hell of a hole.
Well, it really didn't take very long for us all to see
That the morale and place were not what they're supposed to be.
The Air Corps officers seemed to be a mighty fine bunch,
I thought when I talked to a group of them after a light lunch.
The tales they told of the feeling of hate were sad but true;
In the South, they said, that was the lot that all black men drew.
It makes them ever so bitter, angry, and hateful, too,
Because about it, there's not a single thing they can do.
To tell of the awful treatment that the colored man took
Honestly would fill page after page and book after book.
He's neither man nor American in this State you know,
He's a nigger or a coon, a darky, or something low.
He has no rights, no peace, no voice, no, not even a vote.
The crackers in this area on the race issue dote.
In other words, their law says please do all and what you can
To make a Negro feel small, down, and much less of a man.

Dear Mom, this a Hell of a hole.
The blacks have their own mess and the whites have theirs.
They sort of look down on us like we're big, ugly black bears.
They don't seem to know we feel, we hope, we love, and we hate;
In some things our plans and our actions might well seal their fate.
They want us to appear unfit, weak, stupid and so lame
That at a superior rating, we dare not aim.
Tuskegee, the small town nearest the post, is really frail.
It started many years ago, but it is truly stale.
Prejudice and jealousy are the two things that have grown;
They have developed well ever since the day they were sown.
It's a crime for a Negro to walk on the street after ten.
The only place wide open is the vile city jail pen.
There they will throw you, beat you, fine you without any cause
If in this unjust southern village too long you should pause.

Dear Mom, this is a Hell of a hole.
It seems to me a great pity this old, old State should be
A place where Americans and Southerners can't agree.
They have rules, and their interpretations are fair to none;
And thus, true justice and fairness are ever on the run.
It's the whites against the blacks and the blacks against the whites,

One just fighting and the other fighting for his rights.
Neither can ever win as long as there is racial hate;
True religion in this area simply doesn't rate.
We are very thankful there are a few who are quite sane,
Who talk and think and even act like they might be humane.
They try to be fair and just and hear both sides of a tale,
Before they pass judgment on whom they are to send to jail.
I mean whites at the base when I say they, but let me see,
I don't believe if I tried very hard, I could find three.

Dear Mom, this a Hell of a hole.
There's Colonel Parrish, he's the new C.O. on this air post.
Perhaps he's the one the officers and soldiers like most.
Now Parrish, he's short, he's thin, he's fair with hair that is blonde.
Sometimes, of the colored chap, I think he is rather fond.
He will form an opinion after he has thought a while,
And if he agrees with you, he will start with a smile.
"I think you have something there," he will very often say,
And then convincingly tell you why he thinks your way.
If he disagrees, he will talk to you as man to man
And tell you quite frankly why he hasn't taken that stand.
It is refreshing and pleasing when you are sure you know
That there is one open mind to which any man can go
To discuss his own problems whether they be large or small
And get an answer, free from hate, in a true Southern drawl.
You can tell he's from Texas as soon as you hear him speak,
But he is one Southerner who thinks of you strong, not weak.
He has a fine sense of values no one can ever change,
And so some white men think of him as being very strange.

Dear Mom, this is a Hell of a hole.
Say, just the other day, some fellows bet me half my pay,
That Parrish may be O.K. now, but there will come a day
When I will find out how sincere a guy he really is
And if he's still the way he was last year or just a fizz.
Ten to one, I made the bet, because it is my belief
That to this rotten post he can and will bring some relief,
And make each man feel there are some things good left in this life,
That for the black man, there isn't always heartache and strife.
I asked the men who else they would honestly say was fair.
Do you know, Mom, not one other fellow would they call square?
Now there is one officer, the Hatchet Man, I am told,
Who swears and rants and rants and swears 'til he is clammy cold.
A cracker from Mississippi is he, who bears no love.
In days of old, he would surely have gotten the left glove
Across his sickly looking face, which shows contempt and hate
For everything that means that Negroes can do, and must rate.

Dear Mom, this is a Hell of a hole.
One officer, a major, must be very low and bad,
Because 'tis said that no friend has he got nor ever had.
He lies and cheats to make a point he thinks will help his cause,
But then when the truth comes out he always tears his drawers.
His greatest pleasure and fond delight is Form Two O One.
He thinks to keep a good man's rating down is heaps of fun.
Have you any idea how he got in this U.S. Army?
Whoever let this sad guy in must have been halfway barmy.
There is the matter of promotion that always comes up;
Now here's a special subject that is everybody's cup,
A white face and a few months' service is what it requires.
To go to the next grade they just have to pull a few wires.
He's a failure if he doesn't go up twice every year;
The white boy rises fast in his military career.
The black officer stays right where he was when he began.
To up him at this post was not the original plan.

Dear Mom, this is a Hell of a hole.
Surely, I say, there must be something good about this place,
Something besides Negro rank and the great stress laid on race.
The man who is more black than white, he has an awful time
When one step up the ladder of success he tries to climb.
He tries his best to bear a lot of knocks and insults too,
So that he can have added courage to follow it through.
There is one mulatto to whom everyone points with pride.
To us he stands out as our correct military guide.
On his judgment, the pilots of the 99th depend,
At this flying field he is our faithful high-ranking friend.
To him we go for advice because he will help us to grow,
When we feel down and out and our spirits are very low.
He tells us the way and gives us the will to be on top.
In his famous air squadron there never could be a flop.
His fairness and knowledge have made him an example to all;
He is not guilty of things that are cheap, petty, and small.

Dear Mom, this is a Hell of a hole.
It's guys like our colonel who give us the reason to stay
And hope that things soon will be run the democratic way.
He knows all the answers to difficult questions we ask;
To lighten our worries, he makes our problems his own task.
From the officers and men, he gets honor and respect;
On all of us he has an invigorating effect.
He praises when good we do and asks us to do better;
No man has done his best 'til he's perfect to the letter.
In his command, he tries to call each man by his right name.
Be they good or bad, you know that he treats them all the same.

When he asks you questions, he expects you to be sincere,
And if you are not, you will find his manner quite severe.
He has the feeling, if you do your best from day to day,
You will find that for you, honesty and hard work do pay.
He does his job well and expects you to do yours as fine;
The highest standards have been set for dear old 99.

Dear Mom, this is a Hell of a hole.
I've tried to tell you some things, Mom, of how this place is run.
You know there are always those, who out of life do take the fun.
In spite of all, we aim to prove to all the world at war,
That we of T.A.F.S., United States Army Air Corps,
Are doing a patriotic job on the side of right
In an effort to win the Double V for which we fight.
We hope that after war will come a fair and lasting peace
And all hostility between the blacks and whites will cease.
It always makes me glow to think of the day there will be
A world of brother-loving men, all men equal and free.
Hate and force will be gone and tolerance will take their place,
'Twill matter not if you belong to the black or white race.
A home where you want it and the right to vote if you choose,
A job you are fit for and no reason to sing the blues.
Until that glorious day, dear God, give me control,
So for my Mom's sweet sake, I can stand this Hell of a hole.

My own attitude toward the racial situation at TAAF was influenced by an incident that occurred after a visit to the base in 1942 by Secretary of War Stimson, when I was a lieutenant colonel. The usual photographs of the occasion were taken, but when he returned to the Pentagon, someone asked for a photograph of him being greeted by me. I had not been asked to participate in the Secretary's visit in any way, and no such picture existed. Nevertheless, the word came down from Washington to furnish them with one. It was a case of "what the Secretary wants, the Secretary gets." I was called in to TAAF Headquarters and given a raincoat to put on, because it had been raining on the day of the Secretary's visit. They took my picture, superimposed it on a photograph that had actually been taken during the visit, and sent it to Washington. This phony photograph was mailed to the Pentagon to prove beyond a doubt that Lieutenant Colonel Davis had met Secretary Stimson at TAAF. It appeared in many newspapers.

The resentment toward Colonel Kimble, which continued to accelerate, was exemplified by an unsigned letter addressed to Secretary

⌐.imson and sent to Claude Barnett, head of the Associated Negro Press. Barnett received the letter shortly after Stimson visited TAAF and reported favorably on conditions there:

> On your visit to TAAF your commendation of Kimble was based on your inability to peer beneath the surface in so brief a visit. We are vitally interested in the success of the Tuskegee venture. Tuskegee has a fine group of flyers doing a fine technical job, but Kimble does not have the sympathetic approach to problems that men need solved to lift their morale. They are exalted with flying but dispirited over conditions which surround them. Two or three of Kimble's officers (Southern) bear down on Negro officers. These three are hated (cordially disliked?). Kimble maintains rigorous segregation of officers—separate mess and quarters, a condition not true at nearby Fort McClellan. MP's from TAAF patrolling Tuskegee are not armed and are forced to use sticks due to protests of towns people. . . . Kimble's attitude is difficult to put on paper—there are countless examples of it in small happenings according to TAAF officers. Suggest you send your personal investigator. . . . Purpose of this letter is in the interest of truth and morale of 99th men whose success means so much to an entire group of people who will, if given full opportunity, write a worthy chapter in our country's military history.

Barnett viewed the letter as too weak to force Colonel Kimble's transfer and declined to send it to Secretary Stimson, but in his reply to the letter, he indicated his continued strong support of Parrish as a much-preferred replacement for Kimble. Eventually, Kimble became a casualty of all the controversy that had surrounded his command from the start, and he was transferred. In his place, Parrish was assigned as commander of TAAF and successfully discharged his responsibilities in a most creditable manner throughout the war. The basic problems at TAAF under Kimble did not change with Parrish's assumption of command, but Parrish's personal approach to the situation and his demonstrated goodwill toward the airmen and their families made a tremendous difference.

## Forming the 99th

In organizing the 99th Pursuit Squadron, the Air Corps made a positive effort to avoid the worst aspects of segregation by creating an authentic and highly professional flying unit, similar in all respects to white pursuit squadrons except for the color of its personnel. In

March 1941 the Army called for volunteers on a first-come, first-served basis for the squadron, which was to be composed of 35 pilots and a ground crew of 278 men. The selection system was the same as for white pursuit squadrons. Preference would be given to pilot recruits who had CAA training, and in fact the final 35 candidates were chosen from CAA secondary course graduates. Maintenance crews were required to have at least a high school education, and pilot applicants had to have completed at least two years of college. Maintenance crews would be trained at Chanute Field. Men qualifying as pilots would be commissioned in the Air Corps as second lieutenants and trained at TAAF, initially by white instructors.

Looking back, it seems clear to me that the Air Corps set and maintained high qualification requirements for the 99th. The corps made a conscious effort to select the best black aircraft maintenance, armament, communications, and supply people that the basic training centers could produce. Black enlisted people already in the service were undoubtedly selected because of their high qualifications and expressed desire. The cream of the crop of black enlisted personnel was available at the time, and from personal experience I can attest that the people assigned to the squadron were highly qualified. The requirement for two years of college was later eased as we approached Pearl Harbor and the Air Corps tried to find qualified applicants for pilot training who had not been to college.

I was convinced that my professional future in the Air Corps would have to be based upon my own qualification as a pilot and assuming command of the 99th. On 19 July 1941, General Weaver addressed us at a ceremony at Tuskegee Institute inaugurating the flying training of blacks. "The eyes of your country and the eyes of your people are upon you," he said. "The success of the venture depends upon you. . . . You cannot be inoculated with the ability to fly. . . . The life of a flying student is no bed of roses." Contrary to the general's predictions, I found the life of a flying student completely agreeable, especially compared with the life of a professor. From my entry into flying school until graduation in March 1942, I was mostly free of administrative duties and able to devote myself to my almost forgotten first love—flying.

Late in July 1941, I and 12 aviation cadets, the first of many classes to be trained at TAAF, started ground training in a barrack at Tuskegee Institute. I was appointed commandant of cadets, but that job was easy because my fellow students were so willing and eager. We had no discipline problems of any kind. Five of us went on to win our wings, and each washout was an unhappy experience for those who remained.

My classmates were an especially fine group of young Americans, selected after rigid examinations at military bases all over the United States. The backgrounds of this first group bore evidence of the careful criteria that had been applied to them. Marion Carter and Charles Brown came from active artillery units. John Anderson, an all-American from Toledo University, was a 16-letter man and a straight-A student. Theodore Brown had bachelor's and master's degrees from Northwestern University and was one course short of a doctorate. Several of the cadets had participated in the Civilian Pilot Training Program. Lemuel Custis, a policeman from Hartford and a Howard University graduate, won his wings and became an outstanding combat pilot. Mac Ross, an inspector at an iron works in Ohio; George ("Spanky") Roberts, a graduate of West Virginia State College and CAA; and Charles DeBow, a graduate in business administration from Hampton Institute, were also commissioned as rated pilots after completing their training. My relationship with these cadets was informal and good. As the first group of black trainees with a serious chance of being accepted by the Army Air Corps, we had an exceptional sense of unity and mutual respect.

In August we started flying. Primary training took place under white instructors at Moton Field. Throughout our training, our instructors were exclusively white commissioned Army Air Corps officers. Chief Anderson and his corps of black flying instructors took over primary training for all succeeding classes, after my class had moved on to TAAF for basic and advanced training. Then as now, most washouts in military flying training occurred in primary. All over the nation, flying schools like Moton operated under contract with the Air Corps and eliminated students who demonstrated less than the desired potential.

For me flying was a complete, unadulterated joy. It was summer in Alabama, and flying over the green trees, the streams, and the orderly plots of brown farmland below was more exhilarating than anything I could have imagined. During my first few flights, the instructor occupied the back seat. He was completely in control, and I had to comply with his every wish. Soon he had me control the movement of the plane, putting it in the various attitudes he had demonstrated. We were flying a primary trainer (PT-17), a rugged biplane with a radial engine that I could manhandle and horse around with in the air to my heart's content.

After I had logged six hours of dual flights, I was ready for my first solo flight. On the morning of 2 September, my instructor went up with me and gave me some simulated forced landings. In case of engine failure, a pilot has to be aware at all times of his options to land. Sitting in the back seat, the instructor suddenly retarded the throttle to idle, and I had to glide the airplane to a position in the air that would enable me to land. If I let my nose get too high, or if my airspeed got dangerously low in the process, I would have failed the test, but all indications were that we would have walked away from an emergency landing.

Then I completed a few "touch-and-go" landings, putting the wheels on the ground, applying the throttle, and taking the plane back up for a "go around" in the traffic pattern. After the last landing, the instructor took his parachute, got out of the rear cockpit, and told me to take it up alone. This was what I had been waiting for. Up until this moment, he had watched my every move, but I had not received any real indication about how I was doing. Now I knew that he approved. I took it up and went over some of the maneuvers I had performed under his instruction. It was my airplane.

For the next seven months I immersed myself in the miracle of flight. In September, after we had flown the required number of hours in primary and filled in all the boxes on the training chart, we and our instructors transferred to basic at TAAF. There I flew the BT-13, a rather lumbering airplane that was much less maneuverable than the PT-17, although more powerful. The BT-13 did have landing flaps, but its landing gear was no more retractable than that of the PT-17, and the pilot had to crank down the flaps. I loved it all—stalls, practice landings, forced landings, pins, inverted flight, loops, slow rolls, snap rolls, and vertical reverses. We also did chandelles— abrupt, steep, climbing turns that had to be smoothly executed to gain maximum altitude and change of direction at the expense of airspeed. It is a beautiful and satisfying maneuver, requiring precision flying.

In basic we were also introduced to formation and night flying. For the first time, I had the feeling that someday I was going to fly an airplane on a real mission and not just for fun. We traveled to Maxwell Field and Gunter Field, near Montgomery, for night flying because TAAF did not have facilities for taking off and landing at night. I did not particularly like the dark Alabama night, and it was a relief to be able to read the next beacon and know I was on course. I recall a night cross-country from Maxwell to Atlanta to Birmingham and back to Maxwell, during which I was extremely impressed with the size of the state of Alabama and just how dark the hazy night sky could get.

In December we got the news that the Japanese had bombed Pearl Harbor. It was a Sunday afternoon. Agatha was in New Haven, and I was at Tuskegee Institute having a quiet dinner in a restaurant. Everyone was mystified how the Japanese could have avoided observation up to the point of attack. But the declaration of war did not noticeably increase the pressure on us, and we continued to focus on airplanes and flying.

Not even the fact that we were about to go off and fight for our country saved us from the abuses of racism. In advanced training, we flew air gunnery and bombing missions at Dale Mabry Field in Tallahassee, Florida. We had not been expecting much in the way of hospitality at Dale Mabry, but it sent a chill through us to learn we were to stay in a building that had been used as a guardhouse for black prisoners.

During this phase of our training we moved from the BT-13 into the AT-6, a great airplane with landing flaps, retractable landing gear, and a 650-horsepower engine. Later it was called the T-6, and for many years it was used all over the world as a training airplane. It is still actively flying today. In the AT-6 we fine-tuned the maneuvers we had learned in basic and again filled in the boxes on the training chart.

At this point, we had completed all the prescribed requirements for graduation, and the five of us who had stayed the course received our wings at a ceremony at the TAAF base theater on 7 March 1942. Of course, all the doubts concerning the ability of blacks to fly airplanes remained; we needed a great deal more proof to convince the Army Air Forces (AAF) that blacks could fly as well as whites. (Until 1941 the Air Corps was merely one branch of the Army, but thereafter it became the Army Air Forces, reflecting a change of organization and its increased stature in the War Department. As a result of this reorganization, AAF achieved parity with the Army Ground Forces and the Army Service Forces.) We needed to prove that the 99th could go to war and demonstrate proficiency in an active combat theater.

After graduation I flew with instructors I had never flown with before. Robert ("Dick") Rowland, a fine officer who many years later was assigned to a key position in Vietnam's Military Assistance Advisory Group, loved to demonstrate whip stalls. He would put the AT-6 in a vertical attitude and let the airspeed bleed off to zero. The aircraft would stall and slide back on its tail, and the nose would drop so that the plane was pointing downward toward the earth. Some thought the tail might snap off, but that possibility did not bother Dick a bit.

I also flew with another instructor who slightly overdemonstrated a short-field landing maneuver every pilot should have in his repertoire: slipping with full flaps. This technique enables the pilot to lose altitude rapidly and put the airplane on the ground in the landing position at the near end of the field. When the wheels touch the ground, the plane will have a much shorter roll than it would in a normal landing. On a bad day for both of us, this instructor overdid it at TAAF's auxiliary field at Shorter, Alabama. The AT-6 stalled completely several feet above the ground. Fortunately, the left wing hit the ground first, crumpling and therefore absorbing most of the shock. The nose then hit, and the plane went over on its back. There was no fire, and with some difficulty we were able to get out. I cut my forehead when my head went through the glass canopy, and my neck was compressed from landing on my head—an injury that causes me considerable pain to this day. The instructor's pride was hurt, but the accident did not diminish my enthusiasm, and in a few days I was flying again. At least I had learned how not to slip with full flaps!

I continued to fly the AT-6 and exercised the privileges of a rated pilot by checking out in the P-40, the pursuit aircraft that was to be the 99th's equipment. Rated pilots were permitted to take an airplane on weekend cross-country flights as long as we stayed within 300 miles of the TAAF flagpole. I took full advantage of this opportunity to increase my flying hours and improve my proficiency, sometimes flying solo and sometimes carrying nonrated military passengers in the backseat. Some of these cross-country flights took me to Savannah, Nashville, and New Orleans.

Several war-weary P-40s were delivered to TAAF, each a slightly different model, but every one of them leaking oil. Most and perhaps all of them had fought the undeclared war in China with the Flying Tigers, and they still had dirty, mottled green camouflage paint on their oily fuselages. The overall appearance and condition of these P-40s were not exactly encouraging for the pilots who flew them. But after carefully reading the technical orders and pilot guides that came with the airplanes, fly them we did. The long nose and low seat of the P-40 prevented the pilot from seeing objects directly in front of him when he was taxiing. Thus, he had to "ess" the aircraft to the right and left to avoid the unforgivable sin of a taxi accident. Takeoff required a strong right leg because of the engine's torque. At first I was disappointed with the P-40 because I expected the airspeed indicator to show much higher numbers than it did. But after a few flights I began to feel at home in it and even began to like its maneuverability. From the war stories I had heard from P-40 combat pilots, the airplane had three important virtues: turn, turn, and turn. It was vitally important that I and all the other pilots like the P-40; it was the airplane we were going to war in.

But we did not go to war quite as soon as TAAF's rumor mill had suggested. In mid-May I received two sets of orders. The first promoted me to major, and the second, to everyone's surprise including my own, promoted me to lieutenant colonel. Both promotions were effective more than two months earlier on 1 March 1942. This was the date all AAF officers in the West Point class of 1936 were promoted to lieutenant colonel, the objective being to help meet expansion and mobilization requirements. My new rank caused some problems in the TAAF white-black hierarchy, so my assignment was changed to a newly created position, executive for troops. I am not sure how this solved the problem, but apparently the new assignment was thought to be more in keeping with my new rank. Soon after this assignment, I received orders designating me commander, 99th Pursuit Squadron.

During this time, an old friend, Rev. Harry Richardson, the chaplain of Tuskegee Institute, had given me and Agatha a dog who had been making a nuisance of himself by chasing the Reverend's chickens. Agatha, who was afraid of dogs because of a bad childhood experience, was reluctant to take him at first, but she agreed on a trial basis. Because he was coming into a military family, she named him

"Major." Shortly after he came to live with us, the dog got sick and turned to Agatha for sympathy, putting his head pitifully on her lap. She fell in love with him, and he stayed. When I was promoted to major, Agatha immediately named him "Colonel," just to keep me in my place. But a few days later, when I received my second promotion to lieutenant colonel, we demoted him back to "Major" because we could not have two colonels around the house. Major was our dog for almost seven years thereafter, spending the war years in New Haven and New York with Agatha.

## Waiting for Deployment

Successive classes of pilot graduates were assigned to the 99th until the squadron reached its full strength in all personnel specialties in July 1942. I spoke at the graduation that month of the fourth and largest class yet. By this time, blacks had been flying Army airplanes for almost a year. I emphasized our success in proving that, to the surprise of many, blacks could fly military aircraft within AAF standards. I also cautioned, however, that the job had barely been begun. Tuskegee had done its job. We had ours yet to do in the air against the enemy.

Within the bounds of segregation and racial prejudice, AAF did a good job of preparing the 99th and assigning it to combat operations in an active theatre. We took in stride the 25-mile hike that was part of the POM (preparation for overseas movement) inspection. The inspectors from 3d Air Force Headquarters, to which we as a tactical pursuit unit were assigned, pronounced us ready for deployment in September 1942, and most of them believed we would move in late October.

I thought we were about as ready as we were ever going to be within the still tense environment of TAAF. Antagonism between airfield personnel and white Tuskegee continued. In one incident, a race riot could have developed when town police attempted to seize the weapons of black MPs guarding a government warehouse in Tuskegee. Rumors about the near riot spread quickly, and some people were saying that a black woman had been a prime mover in a confrontation with white townspeople. I was asked to go to the scene

of the disturbance and try to defuse the situation, but first I tele-
phoned home to see whether Agatha, who was always quick to
respond to provocative behavior, was involved. There was no answer
and I began to fear the worst, but when I arrived at the scene I
discovered that the situation had been exaggerated and matters were
relatively quiet. Agatha had not been involved in the incident, which
became just another footnote in TAAF's troubled history.

False rumors could have the same adverse effect as real cases because many blacks had good reason to believe the worst. Under these
conditions, I believed that the squadron's morale could deteriorate
badly unless we were moved quickly. The strategic situation in the
war, however, changed in a manner that essentially invalidated plans
for early deployment of the 99th.

AAF had dodged the deployment decision for many months. Under
the original plan, the 99th would have been sent to Roberts Field,
Liberia, as part of a task force providing air defense to an important
point on our line of communications to North Africa, the Middle East,
and China. Apparently, AAF thought it would be appropriate to assign
its black fighter squadron to black Liberia to minimize racial troubles.
This task force would be all black except for some white officers in key
positions. An aircraft control and warning unit would have accompanied us, as would other supporting units comprising the self-
sufficient task force. But with the success of the Allied landings in
North Africa in November 1942, the need for the air defense of Roberts
Field was eliminated. Another plan was developed that would deploy
the 99th to India and Burma, where again AAF thought racial and
political factors would make the presence of a black fighter squadron
less objectionable. This plan was also scrapped, perhaps because the
theater commander refused to accept the unit, perhaps because of
logistic factors of which I had no knowledge. Finally, but also within
the bounds of segregation, it was decided to move the 99th to North
Africa in the spring of 1943 as a separate squadron in the Mediterranean theater. AAF units had been operating in North Africa since the
November 1942 landings, and the 99th would join these units. But the
precise date for our deployment remained in doubt throughout the
winter of 1943.

The waiting got tiresome. We had only a casual interest in the war
news. The Tuskegee area had no good newspaper, so what little we

heard about the war came to us over the radio and in *Time* magazine. The on-again, off-again deployment situation created confusion and inconvenience. Members of the squadron made family plans, cancelled them, changed them into new plans to fit our delays, and then changed them again. While we were living from one overseas movement alert to the next, Agatha raised $500 to buy a piano for the service club; she had one contribution of $50, but she had to collect the rest in small change.

In the meantime, however, men in the squadron got to know each other better, and the pilots became much more closely associated with ground crews. Our sense of unity improved considerably. We used the time getting ready and keeping ready. The unit lived and worked together as a team, flying the ancient, beat-up P-40s, which our ground crews maintained as well as they could, considering the planes' age and the limited availability of parts. I was confident of the abilities of both our pilots and technicians, and although we were on the brink of what could only be a monumental adventure, I had no qualms about the combat operations that lay ahead of us. Above all, we needed theater indoctrination and the seasoning of real combat experience, which no amount of rear-echelon simulation could provide.

Finally, late in March 1943, I learned that within a matter of days the 99th would move to a port of embarkation and be deployed to an active theater of operations. We started getting ready to leave on the morning of 1 April. This was it. After many false starts, we were finally about to leave the racial turmoil of TAAF behind and enter the air war.

Every airman and government worker who served at TAAF could tell many stories about the unfairness, demeaning insults, and raw discrimination that were inflicted upon them, even though they were doing their best to contribute to the war effort and prove that they were patriotic Americans who deserved to be treated as such. Some good, fair white people had been with us at TAAF, but the Army's segregation policies and unfriendly attitudes had set the stage for the unhappy tension that had been played out there. As we said our goodbyes, we pushed far back and away the ugliness that we had endured. After all, we had successfully passed the first obstacle standing in the way of a better life for all of us—learning to fly airplanes.

We were now eager for the second step—learning to fly in combat as legitimate members of Uncle Sam's Army Air Corps. We did not regret leaving TAAF. We knew there were many decent human beings elsewhere in the world, and we looked forward to associating with them.

★ ★ ★   **Under Fire**

**5.** *All those who wished to denigrate the quality of the 99th's operations were silenced once and for all by its aerial victories over Anzio on two successive days in January 1944. There would be no more talk of lack of aggressiveness, absence of teamwork, or disintegrating under fire.*

The men of the 99th Fighter Squadron boarded the train in Chehaw, Alabama, on 2 April 1943. We were leaving our loved ones, and there was always the possibility that we would never see them again. My separation from Agatha, on whom I depended in so many ways, was a serious loss. It would be months before I saw her again. Preoccupied as I was with this thought, I probably did not do much deep thinking about what lay ahead. I did realize that I was embarking on a highly important mission, the outcome of which would affect the lives of all the men in my unit and possibly the future of millions of other black people in the United States. All the members of the 99th were beginning to understand the significance of our assignment, which went far beyond purely military considerations. If a black fighter squadron could give a good account of itself in combat, its success might lead the way to greater opportunities for black people throughout the armed services.

The train took us to Camp Shanks, New York, to await a call to board the SS *Mariposa*, a luxury liner detached from the Pacific cruise trade and converted into a military transport. We had been reminded many times that "loose lips sink ships," so I was surprised that we were allowed to visit New York City and call home without restrictions. The *Mariposa* had once been a beautiful ship, but most of it was now covered with dull gray camouflage paint to make it blend into its new and frequently colorless environment, the waters of the Atlantic Ocean. We were informed that the *Mariposa*'s speed would enable her to outrun the U-boats and deliver us within 10 days to a debarkation point somewhere in the Mediterranean.

The 99th turned out to be more than just passengers aboard the *Mariposa*. Several days before we sailed, I was requested to come aboard with a small staff prepared to act as troop commander, meaning I would be the senior officer among all the troops being transported. This appointment, contrasted with the anonymity and facelessness of the segregated treatment we had endured at TAAF, caused the members of our squadron to feel that, for the first time, we were being recognized as an important cog in the vast U.S. war machine.

Not until boarding the *Mariposa* in Brooklyn did I learn our destination: North Africa, which probably meant Casablanca. Our people, the only AAF personnel on board, stood out beautifully from the thousands of Army troops. In uniform we were truly resplendent, and the insignia of rank on the sleeves of a large number of those uniforms obviously impressed the other Army troops who watched us embark. Of the approximately 4,000 troops aboard, only 15 percent were black, yet I and my staff were occupying a key position in ship administration. As we left the shores of the United States on the morning of 15 April, we felt as if we were separating ourselves, at least for the moment, from the evils of racial discrimination. Perhaps in combat overseas, we would have more freedom and respect than we had experienced at home.

The first 23 pilots of the 99th to go to war were all outstanding Americans who served their country unselfishly. Despite treatment that would have demoralized men of lesser strength and character, they persisted through humiliations and dangers to earn the respect of their fellows and others who learned of their accomplishments. I will mention only a few of this illustrious group; the others are no less deserving, and the same is true of our outstanding technicians, who kept us flying day after day.

My operations officer, George Roberts, later succeeded me as com-

mander of the 99th and the 332d Fighter Group. He retired as an Air
Force colonel in 1968. The first aviation cadets in communications,
logistics, and armament—Dudley Stevenson, Elmer Jones, and
William Thompson—rendered indispensable service to the 99th and
elsewhere in the Air Force later. Our mess officer, Bernard Proctor, a
Wilberforce University graduate, served with the 99th until August
1945. John ("Jack") Rogers was one of our pilot mainstays. Today he is
a judge in Chicago. Big, imposing Willie Fuller, who flew 76 fighter
pilot combat missions with the 99th, is now district executive of the
South Florida Council, Boy Scouts of America. James Wiley, another
of our outstanding pilots, continued in aviation in the Wind Tunnel
Branch of the Air Force Laboratory at Wright-Paterson Air Force Base
and as a commercial airline pilot. Today he is engaged in real estate and
civic work in Seattle. Herbert Carter, my engineering officer and a pilot
in the early days of the 99th, served in both jobs with enthusiasm and
dedication. He later became professor of aerospace studies at Tuskegee
Institute. Willie Ashley, Jr., who flew 77 combat missions and destroyed three German planes, went on to earn a doctorate degree in
zoology.

I developed close relationships with the officers and especially
with the technicians of the 99th. The squadron was small and tightly
knit, and it is inevitable for such closeness to grow among people
who go to war together. We were that much closer because we were
racially isolated—lonely blacks in a sea of hostile whites. I had the
greatest respect for all our people, because of their dedication to the
mission and their understanding of its importance. I also had great
affection for them, although as their commander I consciously tem-
pered the warmth I felt for each of them with an insistence on high
standards of performance. There were very few occasions when any
of them gave me less than our organization deserved.

My duties as troop commander kept me and my staff busy for the
first two or three days, and then we settled down to the dull routine
of a troop ship. We had one submarine alert as we approached the
Mediterranean, but we arrived at Casablanca on schedule, moved to a
bivouac area for a couple of days, and then boarded an extremely
slow train that took us to our indoctrination training base at Oued
N'ja, an uninhabited area about halfway between the towns of
Meknès and Fez.

## Preparations in North Africa

We arrived at Oued N'ja about 1 May. Several miles from nowhere, a dirt strip had been cleared for our use. The ground in the area appeared to have been worn by trampling footsteps over the ages. We set up a tent camp as soon as we arrived, sleeping on the hard ground for the first days because we had no cots. Our cooks prepared food out of mess kits as best they could; there was considerable truth in the statement that military cooks could massacre perfectly good food in such a way that it became almost inedible. Many men stopped shaving and grew beards, but the pilots shaved every day. We used slit-trench latrines without any tarpaulin cover because we had no tarps. Straddling the trench in the open, we soon got used to the lack of privacy, and to the phlegmatic faces of the Arab women who wandered in and around our camp. These women were popularly considered faceless, sexless, and less than human. They did laundry, however, and sold fresh eggs, which relieved us from the monotony of the powdered eggs that were our breakfast mainstay. The whites of our men's eyes turned yellow and their ears rang from atabrine, which was supposed to ward off malaria. Fortunately, our flight surgeon, Capt. Maurice Johnson, gave the pilots quinine instead.

On 7 April the U.S. 1st Army and the British 8th Army had joined lines near Gafsa, Tunisia, surrounding the Axis forces in North Africa. But when we arrived at our training base, the enemy had not yet been driven out, and our participation in the air war was eagerly anticipated. The arrival of the 99th in the theater was already well known through the *Stars and Stripes* and Armed Forces Radio, and our ferry pilots were pleased to be recognized as members of the squadron. They picked up 27 brand-new P-40Ls at Casablanca and Oran and delivered them to us at Oued N'ja.

In record time, we had our new P-40s flying and dogfighting with pilots of the 27th Fighter Group, based at nearby Ras el Ma, the largest American base in the area. The 27th flew A-36s, a distinctive airplane that looked something like a P-51. The dogfighting was impromptu; we prepared ourselves for combat by remaining ever alert for any craft in our airspace. If we observed a flight of A-36s, we attempted to achieve an advantageous position and attack the "enemy" aircraft. It was a serious game; each side tried to demonstate its superior flying ability by getting on the tail of the opponent in a position to fire.

A strong bond exists among those who fly regardless of race, and we got along well with the men of the 27th. Col. Philip Cochran, a famous veteran of the winter air battles following the North African landings and the real-life prototype of Flip Corkin in "Terry and the Pirates," the comic strip by Milt Caniff, flew several training missions with the 99th. We all caught his remarkable fighting spirit and learned a great deal from him about the fine points of aerial combat. Maj. Robert Fackler and Maj. Ralph Keyes, both experienced combat pilots, also advised us during this phase of our preparation and alleviated our vague anxieties about the job we were about to undertake.

While we worked hard to prepare for war, we also explored the area. The beauty of North Africa impressed us, particularly away from the odors and filth of the crowded cities. Our relations with the other troop units in the area were excellent, and it was easy to enjoy the free and open customs of this region and forget the hateful attitudes that dominated our lives in the United States. The foreigners we met did not seem to stereotype all blacks the way white Americans did. Although obviously proud of their heritage, they did not give the impression that they harbored feelings of superiority.

At a troop show in Ras el Ma we saw the expatriate American and darling of Paris, Josephine Baker. This talented and remarkable woman completely captivated her audience. Widely known among black people, the double-V campaign—victory at home and abroad—may have originated with the *Pittsburgh Courier.* Josephine Baker had her own double-V campaign, and she worked at it. At her home in southern France she cared for 17 adopted children of several different nationalities and races. In her public life she entertained Allied troops. She thoroughly understood the uneasy relationships between black and white military personnel and, realizing that the 99th needed all the help it could get, she went out of her way to welcome us to Morocco and introduce us to the French and Arab people of Fez. A series of elaborate dinner parties culminated in an emotional victory celebration on 8 May, the day the Axis left North Africa in defeat, just before Miss Baker left for France. I saw her 30 years later, as beautiful as ever, when she made her last appearance on the stage in Paris; she died only a few days after that performance.

Our training and general theater indoctrination accelerated. After almost exactly a month in Morocco, the squadron flew east to Fard-jouna, on the Cap Bon Peninsula near Tunis. The field, dominated by the azure Mediterranean sky, looked stripped and naked. It had been a German airfield, and much discarded material was scattered about. Many of our men picked up souvenirs of German weaponry, but they had to be careful because some of it had been booby-trapped. I inspected a crashed German Me-109, one of the planes we would be fighting, and was impressed with its smallness and the efficiency of its cockpit design. I reported to Col. William ("Spike") Momyer, commander of the three P-40 squadrons of the 33d Fighter Group, from whom we would receive our operations orders. He received me as a colonel would a lieutenant colonel—not in a friendly manner, but quietly official.

### The 99th Enters Combat

While no AAF unit had gone into combat better trained or better equipped than the 99th Fighter Squadron, we lacked actual combat experience. So as we approached our first missions, my own inexperience and that of my flight commanders was a major source of concern. On the other hand, we had averaged about 250 hours per man in a P-40 (quite a lot for pilots who had not yet flown their first missions), and we possessed an unusually strong sense of purpose and solidarity.

I assigned Lts. William Campbell and Charles Hall to fly element for the 33d on 2 June, our first day of combat. They flew a strafing mission against the island of Pantelleria, still held by the enemy, as part of a wider effort to gain control of the shipping lanes to Sicily and Italy. In these early missions, we dive-bombed gun positions that intelligence had pinponted along the island's coast. We were carrying small, 500-pound bombs, so only a direct hit—extemely hard to achieve—could be effective in destroying these positions.

The campaign against Pantelleria was short and not substantially different from dropping bombs on the range. Our pilots averaged about two missions a day, and they and our ground crews benefited greatly from the experience. All the members of the squadron participated, and I was proud of the quality of their performance.

For the first week we saw no enemy aircraft. In addition to our strafing missions, which were unexciting for the most part, we began to fly bomber escort missions. American A-20, B-25, and B-26 bombers were infrequently attacked by enemy fighters diving in from high altitude and quickly zooming up out of range. Our heavy bombers, B-17s and B-24s, also bombed Pantelleria, and after several days, on 11 June, the enemy garrison surrendered. It was the first defended position in the history of warfare to be defeated by the application of air power alone.

Our first encounter with enemy fighters occurred on 9 June. We were escorting a flight of 12 A-20s on a routine bombing mission. As the A-20s came off the bomb run at 3,000 feet, they were attacked by four German Me-109s, which had just taken off from an airfield near the target. Eight of our P-40s stayed with the bombers and escorted them home. The other four turned into the Me-109s, and Willie Ashley damaged one as they quickly departed the area.

Combat flying was of course far more stressful than flying in a friendly area, and certain types of mistakes could be fatal. You had to work as a team with the other pilots in the formation and keep turning your head and eyes to areas of the sky where enemy fighters were likely to appear. Most of the enemy fighters were Me-109s and FW-190s, which could fly higher and faster than our P-40s. This capability gave the Germans the initiative and the ability to engage or not engage at times of their own choosing. They usually made a high-speed pass from high altitude out of the sun. Their primary targets were the bombers, but enemy fighter pilots, like our own, were eager to shoot down any legitimate aerial target they saw.

Combat flying became less stressful as we gained experience, confidence, and the ability to keep turning our heads and eyes to our rear quadrants with a minimum expenditure of energy. We did not worry too much about antiaircraft artillery. We thought the flak could not hit us, but the slight possibility that it might always lurked in the back of our minds. We were uncomfortably conscious of the distance that had to be flown across the water from North Africa to Sicily. And the airfield at Fardjouna was so dusty that sometimes we had to take off 12 P-40s abreast, each plane maintaining its heading and position by reference to the plane on its right. Fortunately, we never had an abort during these hazardous takeoffs. Everything ballooned into a deep cloud of dust after the maneuver, obscuring the field and making it unusable for some time.

From 11 to 16 June things were relatively quiet. We all sensed that the invasion of Sicily was next on our agenda. We flew four missions on 15 June, covering friendly shipping in the Mediterranean; all pilots returned. We encountered enemy aircraft again on 18 June. Six of our pilots, led by Lt. Charles Dryden, encountered a formation of 12 German bombers—twin-engine Dorniers—and 22 escort fighters above Pantelleria. In a dogfight that lasted 15 or 20 minutes, two of the German fighters were damaged. The bombers departed the target area without scoring effective hits.

On 2 July I led a 12-plane escort of 12 B-25s to Castelvetrano in southwest Sicily. It was on this mission that I saw my first enemy aircraft, an element of two FW-190s and a flight of four Me-109s, far above my part of our formation, which was flying close escort to the B-25s. When the enemy planes dove on the bombers, our top cover turned into them and kept them out of range. During this mission we had our first pilot losses: Lts. Sherman White and James McCullin. We believed at the time that both these pilots had made forced landings along the Sicilian coast, but regrettably, it did not turn out that way. The loss of fighter pilots was like a loss in the family. On each combat mission, members of the squadron watched the takeoff and were always on hand in large numbers to count the planes as they returned and greet the pilots. On the brighter side of that mission, Lieutenant Hall shot down an FW-190, the first time a black pilot had downed an Axis plane, and damaged an Me-109. All our other pilots returned to base.

On the afternoon of the same day, Gens. Dwight D. Eisenhower, Carl Spaatz, James H. Doolittle, and John Cannon visited our squadron base to congratulate us on our first victory and spur us on. Air Vice Marshal Arthur Coningham, commander of the Northwest African Tactical Air Force and an eminent tactician, visited us on 6 July and talked with us for more than an hour—all about strategy and tactics of the air war. He gave us his views on the war in North Africa before the surrender of the Axis forces. The practice of establishing defensive air umbrellas had been a popular tactic during the late stages of the campaign, but he eliminated them after arriving in the theater, pointing out their wasteful, defensive nature and emphasizing offensive operations. He pointed out, correctly, I think, that an air force on the offensive automatically protects the ground forces.

At the time of Coningham's visit, we were between campaigns. Pantelleria had surrendered, and although we did not know it at the time, we would invade Sicily within a week. We had no perspective on the conduct of the war and could not be given any because we were engaged in combat operations and subject to capture and interrogation. Our mission was to fly and fight; we had no knowledge of the bigger picture.

After the surrender of Pantelleria, Col. J. R. Hawkins, the area commander, wrote to me as follows: "I wish to extend to you and the members of the squadron my heartiest congratulations for the splendid part you played in the Pantelleria show. You have met the challenge of the enemy and have come out of your initial christening into battle stronger qualified than ever. Your people have borne up well under battle conditions and there is every reason to believe that with more experience you will take your place in the battle line along with the best of them."

The long-awaited invasion of Sicily began on 10 July. We were off at first light to cover our troops landing at Licata on the southern coast. All our pilots returned. On 11 July Lt. George Bolling was shot down by antiaircraft fire. He spent 24 hours in a dinghy before being picked up by an Allied destroyer. The overall mission was typical of those few in which we encountered enemy aircraft. Twelve FW-190s attempted to attack friendly naval vessels discharging troops to the beach. When we intercepted them, they made a single pass at us that did no damage to our forces, then scattered in two ship elements. We made no claims.

We left North Africa permanently on 19 July. Twenty-nine C-47s took our air echelon to Sicily—enough people and supplies to enable us to operate in combat—until the remainder of the squadron joined us at our new base at Licata. In contrast to Cap Bon Peninsula, Sicily was lush in vegetation. Throughout our stay in Sicily, we enjoyed living conditions that were markedly superior to those we had left in North Africa. The melons, corn, and other fruit and vegetables we picked in the fields came as a welcome addition to our rations. We were also able to keep ourselves and our clothing much cleaner in Sicily.

On 21 July we flew our first missions from Licata, a grueling total of 13 from early in the morning until last light, and on 26 July we flew 12. On 28 July I flew to Tunis with Lt. Herbert Carter, our squadron engineering officer, to meet Secretary of War Stimson—this time for real. I suppose the meeting was cooked up by the War Department or AAF's public relations department.

We welcomed the remainder of our squadron, the ground echelon, on 29 July. They had come by boat from Bizerte to Palermo and then by truck convoy to Licata. With our squadron base at Licata, we were only minutes from the bomb line. Thus we were able to deliver ordnance on target, return to base quickly, rearm, and proceed posthaste on another mission. These missions consisted of fighter sweeps, strafing, patrol, and escort. They continued through July and most of August until the end of the Sicilian campaign and the departure of the Axis forces from the island.

I was called home unexpectedly from Sicily on 3 September 1943 to assume command of the 332d Fighter Group, which had been activated on 13 October 1942, and prepare it for combat. The group consisted of three squadrons and several support units, giving it a degree of self-sufficiency that was not to be found in a squadron. Except for its white commander, Col. Robert R. Selway, Jr., and his white training personnel, the 332d was an all-black fighter group. Having commanded a squadron in combat, it was logical for me to command the 332d if it had been specified that the unit was to have a black commander. These orders, however, took me completely by surprise. Colonel Selway was probably expecting to accompany the unit overseas, so he may have been equally surprised when he learned that I had been chosen as the group's new commander.


## Hostile Criticism

I had no qualms about leaving the 99th in the hands of my operations officer, Lt. George Roberts. Roberts was a solid pilot and an officer who could be depended upon to carry out assigned missions. His subordinate officers, people like Lts. Lemuel Custis, Clarence Jamison, Herbert Clark, Louis Purnell, Charles Dryden, William Campbell, James Wylie, and many others, were also capable pilots and men of character. There was no doubt in my mind that the squadron would continue to develop and improve its performance, and subsequent events proved me to be correct.

Unfortunately, certain officers in the 33d Fighter Group did not agree with me. On my arrival in the States, I discovered that adverse criticism had been made of the 99th's operations and the capabilities of our pilots. Colonel Momyer had submitted a letter stating that the 99th had demonstrated insufficient air discipline and had not operated satisfactorily as a team; that its formations had disintegrated under fire; and that its pilots lacked aggressiveness. Judging from this letter, AAF officials were skeptical about how a black pilot in a P-40 would react when antiaircraft fire burst about his ship or when an enemy was strewing cannon shells and machine gun bullets around his cockpit. The courage of our pilots and their ability to maintain their composure under fire were being called into question.

The major thrust of Momyer's report was that the unit should be removed from combat operations and relegated to the sterile and monotonous mission of coastal patrol. This recommendation was endorsed through channels by Maj. Gen. Edwin J. House, Major General Cannon, and Lieutenant General Spaatz. General Spaatz's endorsement stated that the 99th had been given a fair test in combat. Another endorsement remarked, "The Negro type has not the proper reflexes to make a first-class fighter pilot," a definite throwback to the 1925 War College report, which had referred to anthropological literature placing blacks lower on the scale of human evolution than whites because of their "smaller cranium, lighter brain, [and] cowardly and immoral character."

Upon receipt of Momyer's report, the commanding general of the AAF, Henry H. ("Hap") Arnold, recommended to Gen. George C. Marshall, the Army Chief of Staff, that the 99th be removed from tactical operations; that the 332d Fighter Group, when ready for deployment, be sent to a noncombat area; and that the then-current AAF plan to activate a black bombardment group, the 477th, be abandoned. In the minds of the commanders of the Mediterranean theater and the AAF, the "experiment" was over, and blacks had demonstrated their expected inability to perform in combat at the required level of proficiency.

I was furious. Momyer's criticism was completely unwarranted and unreasonable, and surely the details should have been brought to my attention at the time the alleged deficiencies were observed. By mid-September, I had quieted down sufficiently to hold a press conference at the Pentagon, where I went to some length to tell the story of the 99th from the time I had assumed command until my return to the States. I stressed that the Army Air Corps had looked upon the 99th as an experiment that would have to prove that blacks could be taught to fly airplanes to its standards, and that blacks could operate effectively as a team in combat. In retrospect, it seems ridiculous that as late as 1943, the AAF still believed that the utilization of black men as pilots had to be regarded as an experiment. But the same kind of backward thinking had inspired the racist 1925 War College report, and many otherwise capable and reasonable senior AAF leaders continued to believe that blacks could not possibly qualify as combat pilots, in spite of what the 99th had already accomplished.

Shortly after the press conference, on 20 September, *Time* magazine published an article entitled, "Experiment Proved?" The article further angered me, not only because it cast aspersions on the 99th's combat performance, but also because classified information about the squadron's future role in the war had been leaked to the press:

> So little operational data on the 99th had reached Washington that it was impossible to form a conclusive opinion about its pilots. It has apparently seen little action, compared to many other units and seems to have done fairly well, that is as far as anyone would go. But unofficial reports from the Mediterranean theater have suggested that the top air command was not altogether satisfied with the 99th's performance: there was said to be a plan some weeks ago to attach it to the Coastal Air Command, in which it would be assigned to routine convoy cover.

When AAF Headquarters was questioned about the discrepancies between my account and the *Time* article, Col. William Westlake stated on more than one occasion that they stood by my report. Agatha responded to the article in the following letter, which *Time* printed in its 18 October edition:

> *Time* has made some definite statements about the 99th Fighter Squadron and unashamedly admitted these statements to be based on "unofficial reports. . . ."
>
> Are you justified in saying that the record of the 99th Fighter Squadron is only fair? My husband tells me that his judgment, based on comparison with the work done by six veteran P40 squadrons in the same area on the same types of missions over the same period of time, is that the record of the 99th Fighter Squadron is at least worthy of favorable comment.
>
> My indictment is that by publishing an article based on "unofficial

reports" you have created unfavorable public opinion about an organization to which all Negroes point with pride. You should realize that those few
printed words in *Time*—words which may be creating a false impression—
have struck at one of the strongest pillars upholding Negroes' morale in
their effort to contribute to the winning of the War.

On 16 October I was ordered to the Pentagon to meet with the War
Department Committee on Special Troop Policies, headed by Assistant Secretary of State John J. McCloy. The McCloy Committee, established in August 1942 as a "clearing house for staff ideas on the
employment of Negro troops," had studied General House's endorsement of Colonel Momyer's letter and wanted to hear what I had to
say about it. Serving on the committee at this time were Truman
Gibson, whose family I had lived with before I entered West Point;
my father, a member of the Office of the Inspector General; and Gen.
Ray Porter of the Operations Division of the War Department.

In my rebuttal of Colonel Momyer's letter, I argued that during the
actions against Pantelleria and Sicily, the 99th had performed as well
as any new fighter squadron, black or white, could be expected to
perform in an unfamiliar environment. I painted a vivid picture of the
growth of our combat team from inexperienced fliers to seasoned
veterans, giving the example of the bomber escort mission I had led
on 2 July and describing how we had stayed right with our bombers
and absorbed the attacks of the enemy planes. The squadron's training had been entirely adequate, but our lack of combat experience
had inevitably led to some mistakes in the first missions. This would
have been true of any squadron handicapped by a lack of experienced
pilots. I told the committee that if there had been any lack of aggres-
sive spirit in the 99th at first, we had soon made up for it as our pilots
gained confidence and began to work successfully as a team. I also
pointed out that the squadron had been at a manpower disadvantage;
we had only 26 pilots, compared to between 30 and 35 in other
squadrons, because expected replacements had not come through
until we had been in combat for two months.

My presentation at the Pentagon did not come near to expressing
the depth of the rage I felt about Colonel Momyer's letter, which,
after all, was only a reflection of the prevailing AAF attitude toward
blacks. I have no way of knowing how the letter originated at 33d
Fighter Group Headquarters—whether Momyer himself or one of the
racists on his staff wrote it. I do know, however, that it was written

behind my back. The letter could have expressed heartfelt beliefs, or it could have been written at the direction of AAF Headquarters with the express intention of removing black pilots from the combat program. In any case, it created an unwarranted situation for me that had to be handled with the utmost discretion. It would have been hopeless for me to stress the hostility and racism of whites as the motive behind the letter, although that was clearly the case. Instead, I had to adopt a quiet, reasoned approach, presenting the facts about the 99th in a way that would appeal to fairness and win out over ignorance and racism.

During my defense, I pointed out that what the AAF considered an experiment was a serious challenge to me and every man in the 99th, and that we would go through any ordeal that came our way, be it in garrison existence or in combat, to prove our worth. Everybody in the 99th was constantly aware that the future of blacks in the AAF depended largely on the manner in which they carried out their combat mission. Our airmen considered themselves pioneers in every sense of the word, and every one of them was stared at when he landed at a new field because of the novelty of seeing a black pilot. And yet nothing mattered to them as long as no bad mark was registered against our squadron.

My presentation raised the question: "If black and white soldiers can work and fight together in a common cause on the battlefront, why can they not be trained together in this country?" I pointed out that the minute we stepped on board the *Mariposa*, segregation and discrimination had ceased. Why did they have to be perpetuated in the armed services at home? As the article in *Time* reported, the 99th was "only a single facet of the Army's problem to train and use black troops," and "most thoughtful Army officers probably would agree that blacks would never develop potentialities as an airman or other soldier under the system of segregation in training."

Shortly after my presentation, queries were made about reports that the AAF was going to reassign the 99th to coastal patrol duties. General Arnold's office stated through a spokesman that these reports had no basis in fact. When further queried about the inconsistencies in press reports about the performance of the 99th in combat, the same spokesman made it clear that my defense of the squadron was valid, and General Arnold's office stood by my report.

Colonel Momyer's letter and the endorsement by General House had come within inches of destroying the future of black pilots forever. Fortunately for the 99th and other blacks in the Air Forces, General Marshall directed that before the final decision was made on the fate of the 99th, the Army conduct a G-3 (operations office) study on the role of blacks in combat, both in the air and on the ground. I am fairly certain that AAF Headquarters had made its recommendation to General Marshall before the McCloy Committee met, and I believe that his decision to conduct the G-3 study was based on their review. Perhaps my testimony favorably influenced this decision; the matter was classified at the time and did not become known to me until much later.

The G-3 study, "Operations of the 99th Fighter Squadron Compared with Other P-40 Squadrons in the Mediterrean Theatre of Operations," examined our combat experience from July 1943 through February 1944. It rated the 99th according to readiness, squadron missions, friendly losses versus enemy losses, and sorties dispatched. The opening statement in the report was the clincher: "An examination of the record of the 99th Fighter Squadron reveals no significant general difference between this squadron and the balance of the P-40 squadrons in the Mediterranean Theatre Operations." The study also recommended that the endorsements of Momyer's report by Generals House, Cannon, and Spaatz "be studied in connection with the attached statistical report, since it sheds light on the comparison [with other P-40 squadrons] from a qualitative and theatre point of view."

Even now, I do not know exactly what "sheds light on the comparison from a qualitative and theatre point of view" was supposed to mean. I do know that the G-3 evaluation stated irrefutably that the 99th's operations for the eight-month period of the study were as good as or, by my reading of the statistics, better than those of any other P-40 squadron in the theater. Some casual observers had deplored the small number of 99th aerial victories and the fact that the 2 July victory was the last one for a period of several months. These observers neglected to understand the nature of most of the P-40 squadron missions—dive bombing and support of ground troops—during a period when encounters with enemy aircraft were practically nonexistent.

All those who wished to denigrate the quality of the 99th's operations were silenced once and for all by its aerial victories over Anzio on two successive days in January 1944. Eight enemy fighters were

downed on 27 January, and four more were destroyed the next day.
There would be no more talk of lack of aggressiveness, absence of
teamwork, or disintegrating under fire. The 99th was finally achieving recognition as a superb tactical fighter unit, an expert in putting
bombs on designated targets, and a unit of acknowledged superiority
in aerial combat with the Luftwaffe.

# ★ ★ ★ The Red Tails

**6.** *We were embarking upon an adventure that could make an enormous difference for the future of black airmen, and I knew I had to impress this fact on the officers and men of the 332d, just as I had impressed it earlier on the officers and men of the 99th.*

Agatha's letters sustained me through the lonely days and nights overseas just as they had at West Point. We had been married almost seven years when I boarded the train at Chehaw. It was a long five months before I saw her again in Washington, when I returned to defend the 99th at the Pentagon and assume command of the 332d Fighter Group.

Agatha is not the type to sit and twiddle her thumbs. Once I had left, she felt very much at loose ends. She seriously considered going into the Women's Army Corps but decided against it, primarily because she did not want to be prevented from joining me if I were to return to the States. Instead, wanting to contribute to the war effort, she applied for a job at the Sperry Gyroscope Company in Brooklyn and was immediately hired. Her eyesight was especially good, and she was employed as an inspector of naval gunsights. She lived in the Bronx with her sister Vivienne and her family, sleeping on a sofa in the living room and riding the subway to work. She had not been at Sperry's long when articles appeared in the papers about me and the 99th, then fighting the war in North Africa. Some of the articles mentioned Agatha and her job at Sperry's, and one story about her was distributed nationwide.

Sperry kept all its windows sealed tightly shut to prevent dust from getting into the gunsights. It was midsummer, there were no fans or coolers, and the heat was unbearable. Agatha joined the other workers to request that the windows be opened. When Sperry refused, they announced that they would have to walk out. Their supervisor told Agatha that she should be ashamed to leave work with a husband fighting a war overseas. She replied that she was fighting a war at home, too. The crisis eased when Sperry decided to open enough windows to permit a small amount of ventilation into the work area. Agatha greatly enjoyed her association with her fellow workers—men and women of all classes, ages, and many different races and religions. Her letters spoke of their eagerness to work and contribute as best they could to the war effort.

I assumed command of the 332d Fighter Group at Selfridge Air Force Base, near Detroit, on 7 October 1943. Agatha stopped work temporarily and stayed with me until I returned to Europe at the end of December. Katherine and Ivan Harris welcomed us as paying guests in their home in Mt. Clemens, and through their generosity we enjoyed a short time together.

## Tensions at Selfridge

Ever since I learned that I was to command the 332d, I had been looking forward to the challenge. I knew from press reports that the base had a history of racial turbulence and discrimination. The command at Selfridge erred grievously in not permitting black officers to use the officers' club, in direct violation of Army Regulation 210-10, published in December 1940, which stated, "No officer clubs, messes, or similar organization of officers will be permitted to occupy any part of any public building . . . unless such club, mess, or other organization extends to all officers on the post the right to full membership." The base commander, Col. William Boyd, denied entry of black officers to the club and almost caused a riot. He was backed up by Selfridge's parent command, the 1st Air Force. Its commander, Brig. Gen. Frank O. D. Hunter, took the position that blacks would have to await the construction of their own club. Considerable sympathy for this position was expressed verbally by telephone to 1st Air Force Headquarters by AAF headquarters in Washington.

Locally, the installation of the 332d had met with mixed reaction. The black citizens of Detroit welcomed the newly arrived group on 1 May 1943, with the mayor of the city as the guest of honor. After initial opposition by local whites, the 332d was also welcomed to Oscoda, Michigan, a subbase of Selfridge. In response to a recommendation made by the Board of Supervisors of Iosco County (the parent county of Oscoda) demanding that the 332d be moved elsewhere because blacks would "create social and racial problems," citizens of Detroit joined together to entertain members of the group stationed in Oscoda. The Governor of Michigan and its two U.S. Senators vigorously denounced the Board of Supervisors, stating that under no circumstances would such a move be supported. Nothing came of the board's recommendation, but it left resentment among 332d people.

The 332d was composed of the 100th, 301st, and 302d fighter squadrons. I had known some of its officers at TAAF, and I looked forward to serving with them in combat. Many of them had become seasoned combat veterans and completed full overseas tours. The 332d had been activated at TAAF a year before my return to the United States and moved to Selfridge in late March 1943 under the command of Lt. Col. Sam Westbrook, who was white. This period had been marked by a great deal of personnel turbulence, with numerous transfers of officers among the three squadrons, the dispatch of officers to technical schools, and the arrival of several hundred enlisted men who had been trained by the AAF Technical Training Command—airplane mechanics from Chanute Field, radio personnel from Fort Monmouth, New Jersey, armorers from Buckley Field, Colorado, and many other technical graduates in all the specialties required by a fighter group. When the group headquarters was established at Selfridge, however, it was a fighter group in name only. Most of its pilots were recent flying school graduates, and they had not flown together enough to identify themselves as members of a team. The enlisted men in the three squadrons, which had gradually grown to authorized strength at Oscoda, hardly knew each other.

In early June 1943 Colonel Selway, Jr., succeeded Westbrook in command of the 332d. He immediately initiated an intensive training program to whip the unit into shape and prepare it for overseas deployment. At this time the 332d was assigned a new plane, the P-39, and training aids were furnished for aircraft recognition. A rigid training schedule was published—flight and ground training for pilots, and ground training for nonflyers. A bomb and gunnery detachment was established at Oscoda, composed of white supervisory personnel, with two pilots and enlisted men as training specialists. This detachment was part of the white supervisory squadron, the 403d, based at Selfridge. Gradually the new arrivals from technical schools were absorbed into the squadrons, and the pilots began to fly together as well-organized teams. In spite of the continuing low morale, Colonel Selway and his staff deserved credit for having developed the 332d into the predeployment posture I found when I took over the command in October.

Unfortunately, no cadres had been established in any of the group units, and personnel turbulence continued: transfers to, from, and between squadrons. As the squadrons were activated, a nucleus of experienced airmen, or cadres, should have been assigned to each one in the various career fields. Thereafter, the various staff sections would have grown around the cadres, facilitating the indoctrination and training of new arrivals and allowing team spirit to build. At this relatively late date in the development of segregated units, the cadre system should have been recognized as the only successful way of achieving rapid, solid, and effective squadron capability.

When I arrived, the situation was still far from hopeful. Nobody seemed to be minding the store. The officers' club dispute had rankled the relationships among whites and blacks. The prevailing attitude was, "We're all boys together." The squadron commander was just another one of the boys, the flight commanders exerted no authority, and the senior noncommissioned officers were not carrying out the responsibilities of their ranking positions. The mission was not being properly emphasized, and nobody had been able to resolve the problems that had arisen. The lack of discipline had a great deal to do with the polarization between Colonel Selway and his white supervisory personnel on one side, and black personnel on the other.

Interestingly enough, shortly after Agatha and I arrived, we were honored by a reception at the club that had earlier been off limits to all black officers. Maj. James Ramsey, the senior black officer at Selfridge, organized the event. I renewed acquaintance with many people

I had known at Tuskegee and met others who were soon to distinguish themselves in combat in Italy.

When I arrived, the group was already equipped with P-39s, a beautiful, small-looking fighter-bomber with a tight, crowded cockpit—especially tight when it was flown by a six-footer. My head rubbed against the canopy, and I had to keep my back bowed. Although the Russians had used the P-39 successfully on the eastern front and it was doing well in the war in the Pacific, it could not fly as high as the FW-190s and Me-109s we were likely to encounter in Europe. I liked the four .50-caliber machine guns mounted in the wing toe to concentrate fire and the 37-mm cannon that extended through the hollow propeller hub in its nose. The pilot could use all the guns or any combination of them by flipping a selector switch in the cockpit. I actually would have preferred another airplane, but because the P-39 had already been chosen for the unit, I declared it to be the best airplane we could possibly have and belittled all criticism of it, such as its rumored tendency to tumble. This rumor arose from the fact that the engine sat behind the pilot in the center of the aircraft, and its nose was not as heavily weighted as those of most other planes. After my first flights in the P-39, I flew up to our gunnery camp at Oscoda, where I flew the strafing, dive-bombing, and skip-bombing maneuvers I supposed would be our bread and butter in Europe.

The primary difficulties I met upon assuming command were lack of experience and maturity in the squadron and flight commanders. These difficulties persisted for several months. The commanders had to be carefully chosen, and thereafter I had to meet with them frequently in private and with peers to offer encouragement and talk over any problems that had arisen. Charles DeBow, my flying school classmate and a fine young man, became a squadron commander by seniority, but the position was beyond his ability; acting on the evaluation of the flight surgeon, I had to make a change shortly after we arrived in Italy. I did have some outstanding squadron commanders—William Campbell, Melvin ("Red") Jackson, Edward Gleed, Lee Rayford, and others. They ran their squadrons on the ground and in the air, choosing their own flight commanders, and I could depend on them to carry out the responsibilities of the group on combat missions.

On 17 October General Hunter visited Selfridge and addressed all officers at the base theater, stressing the need for strict discipline among officers and enlisted men, and improved cooperation between the base personnel and the trainees. I did not hold a high opinion of General Hunter, who was notorious for his racist attitudes, but his speech was necessary. He emphasized the important role that base personnel played in our deployment preparations. He also promised that everything possible would be done to ready the 332d for combat, and that everyone in the 1st Air Force would carefully follow the group's activities.

By 28 October all training at Oscoda had been completed, and the bombing and gunnery detachment disbanded. Most of our pilots completed their operational training requirements by the end of November. The preparation requirements for overseas movement were met in early December, and after a gala farewell party in downtown Detroit on 20 December, we boarded trains for Camp Patrick Henry, Virginia.

While we were at Patrick Henry waiting for further orders, I visited the post headquarters to convince the post commander that an integrated post motion picture theater was far preferable to the unrest that was certain to develop if it remained closed to blacks. The matter was settled forthwith. All concerned recognized the fact that men about to go overseas to fight for their country were not submissive targets who should be subjected to discrimination.

### Action in Italy

On 3 January 1944 we departed for Italy. The trip was long and boring except for one submarine alert at the entrance to the Mediterranean. When we disembarked at the port of Taranto, we knew we had a job to do, so we were glad to set foot on land. We immediately received news of the 99th's aerial victories over the Anzio beachhead on 27 and 28 January, just days before our landing. This came as a tremendous shot in the arm. The glamour of a quick succession of aerial victories immediately produced a wave of recognition for the 99th and other black airmen in the theater. No number of bombs expertly placed on ground targets or in support of ground troops could have produced comparable acclaim. A few days later, *Time* magazine stated that the 99th experiment had been successfully completed: "Any outfit would have been proud of the 99th's record. Its victories stamped the final seal of combat excellence on one of the most controversial outfits in the Army. . . . They had finally got their big chance flying cover for the Allies' Nettuno beachhead and they knew what to do with it. . . . The squadron was veteran, well-led, sure of itself. . . . [T]he Air Corps regards its experiment proven, [and] is taking all the qualified Negro cadets it can get."

My elation over the 99th's victories was short-lived. Soon after landing in Italy in early February 1944, I was thoroughly disgusted and angered to learn that the 332d had been assigned to coastal patrol. The assignment was a direct result of the initial Mediterranean theater assessment and the evaluation of the 99th Fighter Squadron's performance during its first three months in the theater, since the G-3 reassessment was not completed until March. To assign the group to a noncombat role at a critical juncture in the war seemed a betrayal of everything we had been working for, and an intentional insult to me and my men. I expressed my feelings to no one, however. I had to show to all concerned an attitude that what we were doing was vitally important to the theater mission, whether I believed it or not.

The 332d was assigned to the 62nd Fighter Wing, 12th Air Force, under the command of Col. Robert Israel. We were to replace the 81st Fighter Group on 15 February, when that group moved out of the theater. Our mission would be convoy escort, harbor protection, scrambles, point patrol, reconnaissance, and strafing. Harbor and convoy protection were significant missions because of the large quantities of war materiel that were coming in daily for all units in the theater. The protection of convoys traveling from Naples to Anzio, the only line of supply for our forces operating there, was of vital importance. We were to patrol the area from Cape Palenuro and the Gulf of Felicastro to the Ponsiano Islands, assuring our ground forces a continuous flow of supplies.

I was fortunate to have Capt. Robert Tresville, Jr., West Point class of 1943, in my fighter group. Bob was the son of a warrant officer who had also served with me in the 24th Infantry at Fort Benning. He was a fine officer, and I put him in command of the 100th Fighter Squadron when a vacancy developed in that position. The 100th began operations from Montecorvino, near Salerno, on 5 February, and had a permanent change of station to Capodichino, near Naples, on 21 February. It was joined at Capodichino by the 302d Fighter Squadron, under Lt. Red Jackson, on 6 March. The 301st Fighter Squadron began operating at Montecorvino on 15 February under the command of Capt. Charles DeBow. DeBow was hospitalized shortly thereafter, and I turned his command over to Capt. Lee Rayford. By late February we were settling down fairly well. We had our airplanes; we had ground transportation; we were flying missions regularly. When we first arrived in Italy we had lived in tents and were constantly fighting the mud, but by now we had set up headquarters in a not-too-unattractive building on the Montecorvino airfield. We had our own mess, a good enlisted men's club, and a good officers' club. For the first time, I was personally comfortable. I had an electric light and a stove made out of a five-gallon gasoline can with a hole cut in it for draft and four or five bricks piled inside. Another can dripped gasoline from a petcock for fuel. I could put a basin of water on my stove and have a hot bath, and naturally the world looked a lot better when I was warm and clean.

During the three months we were assigned to the 62d Fighter Wing, our operations were largely uneventful. We had only three encounters with Ju-88 reconnaissance planes (light bombers), two of which we damaged. Shortly after our arrival, on 18 February, Lt. Lawrence Wilkins of the 302d sighted a Ju-88 near Ponza Island, off Gaeta Point in the Tyrrhenian Sea. He chased it as far as the Anzio beachhead, getting several bursts into the ship before his guns jammed. Just as low fuel forced him to return to base, he saw metal parts fly from the enemy plane, which then went out of control and fell several hundred feet before the German pilot recovered and limped out of sight into the sea mist. Because an airplane must be seen to crash or disintegrate, or its pilot bail out, for a victory to be credited, Lieutenant Wilkins missed that distinction, but it was doubtful that the Ju-88 got home safely.

All of us were encouraged by the thought that our mission might be more action-filled than we had anticipated. Unfortunately, during our assignment to the 62d, our P-39s damaged only one other enemy aircraft. In this encounter, Lt. Roy Spencer spotted a Ju-88 off Ponza Point, due west of the Volturno River line. Spencer called Lt. William Melton to join in the chase, spraying it with machine-gun bullets until his guns jammed. Melton closed in and expended all his am-

munition, observing smoke from the right engine of the target airplane. They followed the Ju-88 for some 60 miles and saw him lose
speed, but they were unable to fire and complete the kill.

The flying experience gained by our pilots and the development of
all other personnel from working under the pressure of combat operations were the main benefits to the group during this period. We had
some pilot- error and operational accidents resulting from landings
and takeoffs with restricted visibility, but we suffered no losses of
aircraft or pilots. From time to time, usually about two in the morning, we had bomb alerts and had to move to our foxholes. I doubt
there was any bombing; it was probably only an enemy reconnaissance ("bed-check charlie") aircraft intruding at night to avoid interception by our fighters.

In late March Vesuvius showered the territory for miles around
with volcanic ash. The fine texture of the ash particles made them
particularly dangerous. Many of our men wore gas masks; others
wore eye masks. A nearby group of B-25s was temporarily grounded
by hot ash particles that destroyed aircraft fabric surfaces.

I received word in March that I had been recommended for the
Legion of Merit for my service with the 99th. It was interesting that
the recommendation was made at this late date and not when I had
departed the 99th six months earlier. I suspect that the AAF felt guilty
about its attempt to take the 99th out of combat after the Sicilian
campaign, and the Legion of Merit constituted a sort of apology. But I
was happy because of the tacit official recognition of the 99th's combat performance.

Agatha wrote that she was doing volunteer work, helping raise
money for educational scholarships for the United Negro College
Fund. She also passed the civil service examination for a job with the
New York State Railway Mail, near Penn Station in Manhattan.
When she was on the night shift, she found herself walking Manhattan's streets and riding the subway in the middle of the night and the
very early morning, something unheard of in today's New York. She
was one of 25 workers on the civil service list, which included the
first women to be given this job. She became one of the prime movers
seeking to honor the seniority of her fellow civil service workers over
those who had been hired as replacements for their drafted spouses.
(These replacements had not been required to take the civil service

examination.) Seniority for Agatha and her fellow workers assumed considerable importance, because it determined their exact civil service rank.

Early in March Gen. Ira Eaker, commander, Mediterranean Allied Air Force, requested that I report to his headquarters at Caserta. He described a plan to transfer the 332d from its coastal patrol mission to bomber escort with the 306th Wing, 15th Fighter Command. This decision must have been based in part on the G-3 reassessment of the 99th's performance, which had just been completed. General Eaker pointed out the contribution the 332d could make to reducing heavy losses of B-17s and B-24s (the command had lost 114 planes the previous month). Under this plan, we would be reequipped with P-47s and join the escort mission now being performed by the other fighter groups in the 15th Fighter Command. Needless to say, I leaped at the opportunity. The escort mission was vitally important to the war, and our new aircraft would enable us to meet the Germans with the same altitude and speed capability that previously had given them definite advantages over our P-40s.

On 29 May 1944, shortly after the 332d was transferred to the 306th Wing in Brig. Gen. Dean C. ("Doc") Strother's 15th Fighter Command, I was promoted to colonel. Unlike the 62d Wing, the 15th Fighter Command (the fighter arm of the 15th Strategic Air Force) had an offensive mission. Composed of several groups equipped with P-47s, P-51s, and P-38s, the command escorted the heavy bombers of the 15th Air Force—B-17s and B-24s—on their far-ranging missions to the Balkans, Romania, Austria, Czechoslovakia, Germany, France, Spain, Yugoslavia, northern Italy, Bulgaria, and Greece. It was also able to carry out offensive fighter missions, usually strafing attacks on suitable targets in the 15th's area of operations.

On 20 April I had accompanied General Eaker on a visit to the 99th at Cercola, where the squadron was attached to the 324th Fighter Group under Col. John Lydon. It occurred to me that the sand, dust, and scattered trees at Cercola were quite similar to the topography of Fardjouna in North Africa, where the 99th and I had been the year before. The 99th had a new commander, Capt. Erwin B. Lawrence. The enlisted men I had left the previous September were still in the unit, now seasoned veterans. Spanky Roberts had completed his tour and was back in the States, as were Lemuel Custis, Charlie Dryden, Lou Purnell, and all the others who had traveled with me to North Africa the previous April. They had been replaced by later TAAF graduates, among them Lts. Elwood Driver, Howard Baugh, Henry Perry, Lewis Smith, and Edward Toppins. These new men were also veterans by now, masters at dive-bombing techniques, laying 500-pound bombs on motor transports, railyards, supply lines, and gun emplacements. They had also become adept at aerial gunnery. Over Anzio on 27 January, they had caught the enemy coming out of a dive-bombing run and destroyed eight FW-190s, probably destroyed another two, and damaged four. The next day they had attacked more German planes as they approached our ships in the assault beach area, and shot down four more fighters. General Arnold had sent a congratulatory message, and General Cannon had visited the squadron in person.

During our April visit, General Eaker alluded to the upcoming change in our mission in a short speech to a group of 99th personnel. "By the magnificent showing your flyers have made since coming to this theater," he said, "and especially in the Anzio beachhead operation, you have not only won the plaudits of the Air Forces, but you have earned the opportunity to do much more advanced work than was at one time planned for you." Later I was to learn that the 99th would not join the 332d until an intensive 12th Air Force tactical operation had been completed in May. General Cannon wanted to retain the 99th's tactical expertise until the May operation had been completed. He regarded the 99th as his most hardened and experienced P-40 unit and wanted it for pinpoint dive-bombing missions close to our frontline troops.

The 99th already had 17 enemy planes to its credit, but it continued to execute vital dive-bombing missions against strategic and tactical targets in the Italian campaign. Early in May, when the 332d was flying patrol, every 99th ship on the mission made a direct hit on an important target south of Rome, relieving the pressure in a small but significant way on the Anzio-Nettuno beachhead area. Two days later, six of eight 99th planes laid their bombs precisely into a concentration of supplies at a road junction just north of Cassino, making possible a further Allied advance in that key sector. For weeks the focus of action in Italy, Cassino had absorbed the most concentrated bombing on a small area in history. The mission briefing stressed that no bombs could be short because our troops had just withdrawn from the area. The 99th complied, accurately hitting a factory area with bombs and clusters of incendiaries and destroying six buildings, fuel dumps, and one huge fuel tank, which burst into a spectacular, massive fireball.

Shortly before the 99th joined the 332d, it experienced a humorous yet dangerous incident. For a long time, a ranking enlisted mechanic, T. Sgt. Henry Cornell, had wanted to fly a P-40. One memorable day he warmed up a P-40, bent forward in the tiny cockpit, attached a sheet of instructions to the instrument panel, taxied to the end of the takeoff strip, and with a green light from the control tower, roared down the runway and leaped into the air in a steep climb. The news spread like wildfire among the mechanics, pilots who happened to be on the flying line, and others, none of whom could take their eyes off the crew chief. In the plane, Sergeant Cornell referred to the instructions on the panel to remind himself of the sequence of actions he must perform to get the P-40 back on the ground. When he opened the canopy as part of the prelanding procedure, however, the wind blew his instructions away, and the daring sergeant was at a loss as to his next move. He did recall reading that he should lower the landing flaps, but when he did, he lost so much airspeed that the plane stalled and crashed nose first on the approach to the runway. The humor of the incident was lost on those in the chain of command, because of the loss of a combat airplane. Sergeant Cornell never achieved his heartfelt desire for flight training in the Army Air Forces, but he had experienced the flight of his life and satisfied once and for all his belief that he really could fly a P-40. Fortunately, only his feelings were hurt.

On 2 June 1944, the anniversary of the first combat mission flown by the 99th from Fardjouna to Pantelleria, the 99th celebrated by flying seven combat missions for a total of 26 sorties. At this point, the squadron had flown 298 missions in the Italian theater and 500 cumulative missions for a total of 3,277 sorties. Members of the 99th could take full credit for proving the skill of black airmen in combat, enabling AAF Headquarters to reverse its previous decision to remove black air units from tactical combat operations and relegate them to an essentially noncombat role in an inactive theater of operations. The combat performance of the 99th was directly responsible for the continuation of the 477th Bombardment Group and the reversal of the earlier decision to deactivate that unit. But by far the most important result of the 99th's performance was a satisfactory role for blacks in the postwar Air Force.

The officers and men of the 332d had followed the 99th in training at TAAF, but their experience there and elsewhere was entirely different. The 99th was an isolated squadron, the first black flying unit, and not affiliated with any fighter group. It trained and operated as a squadron at TAAF for many months prior to its deployment to North Africa, and it experienced little or no personnel turbulence. All its people were deeply aware of the necessity to demonstrate their abilities in ways that would reflect favorably upon their proud unit. The squadrons of the 332d, on the other hand, had moved from TAAF to Selfridge to Oscoda and back to Selfridge, each seeking to develop an identity and sense of unity. Each squadron had a succession of commanders and numerous transfers in and out of officers and men. The 100th and 302d squadrons developed their personality early on; the 301st's leadership came along somewhat later. The 332d thus learned to operate effectively under the pressures of overseas operations, converting to P-47s and readying itself for a new and important assignment. For these reasons, the coastal patrol mission during the 332d's first three months was not a total loss.

From the time that General Eaker forecast the future role of the 332d, I was deeply involved in preparing for our move to Ramitelli, our new base on the Adriatic, and our new offensive mission in the 15th Air Force, which would put us in direct contact with the Luftwaffe. We were embarking upon an adventure that could make an enormous difference for the future of black airmen, and I knew that I had to impress this fact on the officers and men of the 332d, just as I had impressed it earlier on the officers and men of the 99th. The indoctrination of the 332d had to be much faster; it had to be compressed into a few weeks, whereas the 99th had come to appreciate its importance over a period of several months at TAAF.

The 332d established itself at Ramitelli, an agricultural area on the Adriatic, in June 1944. It had a pierced-steel plank for a runway, and we set up our operations complex in the largest of several buildings. The 332d was soon to be joined by the 99th Squadron, making it a four-squadron fighter group, the largest fighter group in the theater. The group would switch over to P-47s and begin its initial escort missions with this aircraft. I started flying the P-47, affectionately known as "the Jug," in late May and early June. It was much larger and more rugged than the P-39, and its eight .50-caliber machine guns and its altitude and speed capabilities were real luxuries for pilots who had engaged the enemy in P-40s. On my first flight I far exceeded any altitude I had previously experienced, and I was delighted with the P-47's maneuverability. Its wing tanks would give us plenty of escort range from our base in Italy to all 15th Air Force targets. It had front and rear armor protection for the pilot and bullet-proof glass. Its fuel tanks were leak-proof. For fighter-bomber missions, it could carry 500-pound bombs. We believed that no other fighter of the time could outfight, outclimb, or outdistance it.

I habitually led the combat missions I participated in, including our first 15th Air Force combat mission on 7 June, the day after the invasion of Normandy. We observed no airborne enemy aircraft on this mission, a fighter sweep by 32 aircraft of the Ferrara-Bologna area. We flew a similarly uneventful mission on 8 June, while escorting the B-17s of the 5th Bomb Wing on penetration and withdrawal from Pola, Italy.

Our third P-47 mission was penetration escort for B-17s and B-24s to the heavily defended Munich area. As the formation leader I was responsible for the takeoff from Ramitelli and joining up in a way that would enable us to rendezvous with the bombers. We had to position ourselves carefully so that we could react to the radio calls announcing the presence and location of enemy fighters. We also had to accommodate the bombers: sometimes they were early, sometimes late; sometimes they changed direction and altitude because of cloud cover. The B-17s usually flew higher than the B-24s, but we had to maintain an altitude that would enable us to take care of the entire force. Bombers dropping to the rear of the formation because of battle damage were also our responsibility. Our pilots had to stay in a position to attack enemy fighters as they made their passes at the friendly formations, and they had to protect our own formation at the same time, so our eyes had to be everywhere. As we approached Munich, I dispatched Capt. Red Jackson's 302d Squadron to meet a threat developing at the high right rear side. Simultaneously, two Me-109s flew through the squadron I was leading. We took our best possible defensive maneuver, turning into them. In the turn, I fired a wide deflection shot at the closest enemy fighter without visible results. Captain Jackson gave this report in his debriefing: "An Me-109 came in on my tail . . . out of the clouds behind me; a dogfight ensued until I shot the Me-109 down. Metal flew off his left side as the door flew off. The Nazi pilot bailed out over a German airfield. I hit the deck and came home. Flak was everywhere." Including Captain Jackson's kill, we destroyed a total of five enemy fighters. Over the Udine area enemy fighters attacked the B-24s, and we were able to damage one Me-109. Upon our return to Ramitelli we received the following message from one of the bombardment wing commanders: "Your formation flying and escort work is the best we have ever seen." I was later awarded the Distinguished Flying Cross for leading this mission.

In June we flew bomber escorts to Munich, Budapest, Bratislava, Bucharest, and Sofia, and strafing missions to Airasca-Pinerale Landing Ground, Italy, and to troops on roads in Yugoslavia and Albania. We did not encounter enemy aircraft on any of these missions. This dry spell continued until 12 July, when on a B-24 escort mission to Toulon our pilots destroyed four of the FW-190s that flew through our bomber formation.

After about a month in the P-47s, we converted to P-51 Mustangs, which had a longer escort range and performed better at the higher altitudes where we flew with the B-17s. Many of our pilots developed a distinct preference for the P-51, but all of us had loved the Jug, and I never heard any adverse criticism of this great fighter.

We flew our last P-47 mission on 30 June and our first P-51 bomber escort mission on 6 July. I led a seven-hour, four-squadron group mission to Spain via Rome, Toulon, and Marseilles, and landed in Corsica to refuel. On 16 July we destroyed two Macchi 205s on a fighter sweep to Vienna, and on 17 July three Me-109s on a bomber escort mission to Avignon. Our best day of the month came on 18 July, when the 99th flew its first long-range escort with the group as a complete unit. On this day we flew a four-squadron escort of the bombing of Memmingen Airdrome by the B-17s of the 5th Wing. We destroyed two FW-190s in the Memmingen area and nine Me-109s over Udine and Treviso. Between 20 and 30 July our pilots destroyed 19 enemy fighters, making a total of 39 aerial victories in nine missions between 12 and 30 July. We received many promotions to captain in July.

August and September were also busy months. We flew 28 group missions in August, most notable for the destruction of radar stations in southern France in preparation for the 15 August invasion; three long escort missions to the Ploeşti, Romania, oil refineries; destruction of 22 aircraft on the ground at enemy airdromes after providing cover for the two B-24 wings that bombed the Blechammer, Germany, oil refinery; and finally, a field day strafing Grosswardein Airdrome, during which we destroyed 83 aircraft on the ground. Because of bad weather, we flew only 16 missions in September, mostly routine bomber escorts. A strafing mission to Ilandza Airdrome, Yugoslavia, did destroy 30 aircraft on the ground, all left burning.

In early September the 99th celebrated the first anniversary of the Salerno invasion. A few of the pilots who had participated in the mission supporting the invasion were still present; others, including Spanky Roberts, Bill Campbell, and Herbert Clark, had returned to the 332d after a rest in the States. We had also received 25 pilot replacements, which gave a lift to all four squadrons. When these replacements arrived, some of the old-timers could go home. In other fighter groups, 50 combat missions completed a combat tour; in the 332d, with our sole replacement training capability at Tuskegee and Walterboro Air Base, South Carolina, our replacement requirements were not always met in a timely fashion, and many of our pilots flew as many as 70 missions before being sent home. The situation was not a happy one. The more missions a pilot flew, the greater the chance he would never go home at all.

S. Sgt. Joe Louis, heavyweight champion of the world and an inspiration to all black Americans, visited us in August. Several of our men had their pictures made with the champ. He was mobbed by hundreds of admirers who were thrilled to be in his presence, shake his hand, and explain to him what we were doing in Italy.

## Recognition at Last

Morale was soaring in the group and in all its squadrons. We took deep pride in our mission performance. Our pilots had become experts in bomber escort, and they knew it. Complimentary remarks from pilots, navigators, and other bomber crew members came to us by teletype or telephone. As consciousness of the job we were doing grew, crews were quick to voice their praise of the Red Tails, as we had come to be known from the painted tails of our P-51s. They appreciated our practice of sticking with them through the roughest spots over the target, where the dangers of attack were greatest, and covering them through the flak and fighters until they were able to regroup. They particularly liked our practice of detaching fighters to escort crippled bombers that were straggling because of battle damage.

The Allies were gaining momentum throughout the European theater, which also contributed to morale. After the invasion of France and the fall of Rome, many were forecasting an early end to the European war. Our officers and enlisted men were visiting rest camps in Rome, Naples, and Montenero, where the food was generally good. Even at Ramitelli, we had movies, plays, chorus, lectures, ping pong, softball, and touch football, and we were getting ready for basketball.

The 332d was honored by a visit on 10 September by General Eaker; Gen. Nathan Twining, commander, 15th Air Force; General Strother, commander, 15th Fighter Command; and my father. It was good to see Dad again. During this visit he presented the Distinguished Flying Cross to Capt. Joseph Elsberry, Lts. Jack Holsclaw and Clarence ("Lucky") Lester, and me. Elsberry received the decoration for destroying three FW-190s in a single mission on 12 July 1944 while escorting B-17s on a bombing mission to Toulon; Holsclaw for two victories on the 18 July escort of B-17s to Memmingen Airdrome; and Lester for a triple victory he scored in minutes on the 18 July mission over Udine and Treviso.

This visit by our top commanders constituted a significant recognition of the 332d's contributions. I appreciated the gesture the AAF made in arranging the decoration ceremony. Surely it exhibited a far different attitude from that of the previous year, when it had been in the process of recommending the removal of black pilots from combat operations. Also during September, I presented 31 Air Medals and 127 Oak Leaf Clusters to the Air Medal. Many of our men were promoted, and even more important to everyone's morale was the return of two officers who had been shot down while strafing in France and Romania.

We were fortunate to be visited frequently by black war correspondents stationed in Italy. Thomas Young of the *Norfolk Journal and Guide* covered the 99th's entry into the war in North Africa and the beginnings of the Italian campaign. After six months in the theater, he was replaced by Lemuel Graves. Lem traveled to Italy with the

332d and landed with us at Taranto. Much later he was replaced by John Jordan. Other black war correspondents also covered our operations: Art Carter of the *Baltimore Afro-American* and Ollie Harrington of the *Pittsburgh Courier*. All these men encouraged our men in combat, as well as our families back in the States, during these trying times.

Black correspondents on the front asked for no special privileges. They endured the heat and cold. They lived with us in tents, along with the snakes and lizards. They ate C-rations and K-rations; they endured the mud and the dust. The malaria-bearing mosquitos bit them as well as us. They attended our numerous awards ceremonies and dutifully reported on them. When we asked complicated questions about AAF progress in manning TAAF with black officers in key positions, they got the information for us. And when a group came home from the day's mission, the correspondents were standing on the side of the runway to count the number of planes that had returned. They joined us, too, when the Red Cross girls met us with doughnuts and coffee to top off the mission. The theater's military daily, the *Stars and Stripes*, covered us too, and we read it avidly. But the black correspondents filled our needs in a special way, and it would have been a lonelier and less confident war for us without them.

These correspondents played a positive role in keeping blacks throughout the United States informed about the activities of blacks in the military. Since 1940 black publishers had exerted considerable pressure in the interest of creating a role for blacks in the Army Air Corps. They chided the War Department for slow progress in the overall utilization of blacks. They harped on the shame of segregation, reluctantly tolerating the existence of segregated black units during the war while looking forward to integration in the postwar period. They presented detailed reports on a weekly basis to their readers. Because we did not see black newspapers firsthand, we looked forward to letters from our families congratulating us upon our accomplishments and informing us of activities on the home front.

Black reporters covered all our most productive combat missions in detail, recounting the exploits of the pilots who had distinguished themselves. Articles were written about Capt. Edward Toppins and his 130 missions; Capts. Wendell Pruitt, Gwynne Pierson, and Joseph

Elsberry, who strafed an enemy destroyer, causing it to blow up and sink in the Adriatic near Trieste; and Capt. Lucky Lester, a native of Chicago, who flew a P-51 purchased for $75,000 by the students and teachers of the Sisters of Notre Dame's Alphonsius School in Chicago. George Bolling, who was shot down over Sicily into the cold waters of the Mediterranean before being picked up the next day, spent three months in a hospital with a broken ankle. After being grounded by the flight surgeon because of a prolonged cold, Bolling served overseas for 16 months before finally going home after 70 missions to a happy family reunion. The black press also covered the tragedies: Captain Tresville and Captain Lawrence, both squadron commanders, were killed on low-level combat missions. And they told how Elwood Driver won the Distinguished Flying Cross. Driver, an expert in low-level strafing, was determined to disprove all the antiquated racist theories that dictated our segregated status. On a single mission, though low on fuel, he made repeated passes on an enemy column, destroying 35 trucks resupplying enemy forces in Anzio. Black correspondents did not disregard the efforts of the 332d's ground personnel, particularly the mechanics, armorers, and communications people who kept our aircraft operational. These largely unsung people contributed greatly to our efforts.

The black press performed another vitally important service in reporting what was going on at TAAF, Selfridge, Oscoda, and Walterboro, our replacement training base toward the latter part of the war. Lots of things were going on at home that we learned about secondhand. Our families and friends read stories about these events in the black press, then retold them to us in V-Mail letters.

One subject of major interest to us was the experience of black veterans after they returned to the States. I recall one long newspaper story about Lemuel Custis and his new stateside assignment training new AAF pilots at TAAF. The AAF had started using a few black instructors in late 1943. Lem had been a member of my class in flying school and served with distinction as operations officer in the 99th. He believed strongly that, as a combat veteran, he was able to inspire new men learning to fly combat airplanes. Genuinely happy in this new assignment, Lem understood that he contributed to the morale of younger pilots and increased their personal confidence in a way that TAAF's white instructors could not, simply because they had not flown combat missions.

Other black combat returnees, however, were unhappy with their assignments after returning to the States. The AAF reassigned most of them to TAAF or Walterboro, and they felt that their experience, rank, and talents were being neglected or misused. Colonel Parrish later cited the surplus of black officers at TAAF and his inability to use them effectively; AAF Headquarters, which preferred to confine its black officer problem to as few bases as possible, continued reassigning black combat returnees to TAAF and Walterboro. Some of these returnees, notably Lee Rayford, Herbert Clark, Bill Campbell, and Louis Purnell, after having completed one combat tour with the 99th, were so dissatisfied with their status as returnees that they joined the 332d for a second tour and the "easier" job of combat flying. The fact that they preferred risking their lives overseas to the uselessness of their jobs in the States gives some idea of how little genuine responsibility they were given.

I recall the case of Capt. Wendell Pruitt, one of our best flight leaders. After he completed his 70 combat missions he went home and was reassigned as a flying instructor at TAAF. Shortly thereafter I received a rather agitated letter from him asking that I request his immediate reassignment to Italy. The day after I had answered his letter assuring him that I had already requested him, I received a letter from Agatha informing me that she had read in the *Pittsburgh Courier* of Pruitt's death in an aircraft accident.

Throughout our stay in Europe, we followed the story of the 477th Bombardment Group and its racial troubles at Selfridge, Godman, and Freeman fields. Selfridge was one of the bases of the 1st Air Force under the command of Major General Hunter. General Hunter visited Selfridge in April 1944 in response to black grievances and a War Department investigation of conditions at the base. At a meeting of the black officers of the 477th, he was quoted as saying, "This country is not ready to accept a colored officer as the equal of a white one. You are not in the Army to advance your race. Your prime purpose should be in taking your training and fighting for your country and winning the war. In that way you can do a great deal for both your race and your country. As for racial agitators, they shall be weeded out and dealt with." Stating in no uncertain terms this prevailing attitude of white AAF officialdom toward blacks, General Hunter showed complete disregard for the chilling effect these remarks were certain to have on his troops.

We also learned that segregation had been eliminated at the TAAF post restaurant. On 19 August 1944, 14 black officers at TAAF, armed with copies of a 1940 War Department directive outlawing segregation in Army post exchanges and restaurants, walked into the section of the restaurant previously reserved for white officers, demanded service, and got it. White officers protested, but after a few days of temporizing, including an attempt to persuade the black officers not to disturb the status quo, Colonel Parrish informed all concerned that he had no alternative but to comply with the directive and desegregate the restaurant. From our vantage point thousands of miles away, we could not understand why this action had not been taken much sooner.

## The European War's Final Months

After 6 June 1944 Rome became a resting place for war-weary GIs. Late in July nine of our most deserving airmen spent a three-day leave amid the beauties of the ancient city. Upon their return to Ramitelli, I learned how impressed they were with the democratic spirit that seemed to permeate the former fascist capital. They were surprised to find relatively large numbers of blacks integrated into the civilian population. Rome was a pleasant place to visit, not only because of the opportunity to visit its cultural centers, but also because of the close association between black airmen and other members of the armed forces who were also there on leave. Everywhere they went, they were greeted with enthusiasm. They found that both the civilian population and the ground forces were familiar with the vital role the 332d had played in capturing Rome for the Allies. It was also widely acknowledged that the 332d's destruction of German radar used to detect approaching aircraft and surface ships had contributed greatly to the relatively light losses incurred during the invasion of southern France.

During October 1944 the 332d was stricken by the loss of 15 pilots. Captain Lawrence died when his aircraft hit a trip wire while strafing Athens Tatoi Airdrome. His wingman, Lt. Kenneth Williams, was observed to crash on the same mission. Lt. Joe Lewis also crashed after strafing. Lts. Shelby Westbrook and Robert Chandler were lost strafing, following an escort mission to Regensburg. Capt. Alfonza

Davis, one of our most effective leaders on the ground and in the air, did not return from an escort of a P-38 reconnaissance aircraft to Munich. Lts. Carrol Woods and Andrew Marshall crash-landed following strafing of Athens Kalamaki Airdrome; we were elated to see Marshall when he came back about two weeks later. I personally observed Lt. Fred Hutchins strafe an ammunition dump and go down in the resulting explosion. To my surprise, Freddie returned unhurt to our base a few days later. Lt. William Green crash-landed in Yugoslavia but avoided capture, joined up with Tito's partisans, and returned to us seven days later. Lt. Walter Westmoreland crash-landed at Tapolca Airdrome. The effect of these October losses was somewhat eased by the return of several pilots only days after the missions on which they had been lost. The Greek airfield targets we strafed did not seem worthwhile in terms of what we were able to destroy, especially when measured against such losses. On the other hand, I led one highly productive mission to Budapest and Vienna on 12 October, in which we destroyed nine aircraft in the air, 26 on the ground, and some locomotives, barges, and trucks.

Many visitors came to Ramitelli during October. General Strother and the commander of the 306th Fighter Wing, Col. Y. A. ("Buck") Taylor, inspected our installation and troops. After the inspection, General Strother spoke informally to our officers. He warned against the optimism many of us were feeling for a quick German collapse and the winning of the war, accurately forecasting many more months of hard fighting. General Strother and Colonel Taylor were fully aware of our October losses, and I appreciated their positive leadership in visiting us when we needed some encouragement.

With flying increasingly limited by poor weather in the target or base areas, we ordered textbooks and began an intensive orientation effort. Eager though they were for combat, replacement pilots were learning that they might fly many missions without seeing enemy aircraft. On 16 November, while escorting a crippled "big fellow" of the 304th Bomb Wing, three of our P-51s engaged eight Me-109s at 24,000 feet in the Udine area. Capt. Luke Weathers shot down two, the only victories that month, thus enabling the crippled bomber to return to base. On 19 November we strafed railway, highway, and river traffic in the Györ, Vienna, and Esztergom areas in direct support of the Russians, who were hammering in from the east. We were commended for our "untiring efforts," and our ground maintenance

crews were cited "for keeping the maximum number of aircraft operational." During November we lost seven pilots—fewer than half of
our October losses. We received 15 pilot replacements during November, and 14 veterans completed their tours and went home. Lts. Westbrook and Chandler, shot down strafing on 30 October, evaded capture in Yugoslavia, worked their way through enemy territory, and
after 37 days were back for an enthusiastic welcome.

We redoubled our winterization efforts. Ramitelli had a notoriously bad winter climate: heavy winds off the Adriatic, rain, and
mud. We moved our tents closer together and made all-weather
walkways to keep out of the mud as much as possible. The war went
on, but it moved at a slower pace. We were 50 miles from nowhere,
and there was now little for us to do except fly the long missions to
targets in enemy territory. The entire 15th Air Force was concentrat-
ing on preparing our winter quarters and maintaining a disciplined
approach to our mission. My own home continued to be snug and
comfortable; I had a constant-flow gasoline stove in my fireplace that
gave off no odor and no smoke. Nevertheless, it was a long and dreary
winter.

In December, a month marked by the first appearance of German
jets, we flew 22 missions. If Hitler had concentrated on building and
manning these jet fighters, he could have effectively stopped our
bombing operations. The jets were a frightening development, and
their advantage over our prop fighters could have been overwhelming. We saw 13 Me-262s on 9 December; two of them attacked our
formation. On Christmas Day, beside celebrating with decorated
trees, fruitcakes, and assorted nuts, we flew an escort mission to
provide cover for a bomber formation attacking Brux, Germany. We
saw four Me-109s but did not engage them.

On 30 December 20 B-24s landed at Ramitelli because of bad
weather at their home base. Suddenly we had more than 200 white
visitors scattered throughout our camp, living, eating, and sleeping as
best they could under the severely crowded circumstances. Such a
mixing of the races would never have been allowed to occur in the
United States. Freddie Hutchins, from Waycross, Georgia, and a white
B-24 pilot from Atlanta were obliged to share a pup tent, and Freddie
gave him a liberal education. The B-24 pilots were grounded for
several days. They enjoyed their stay and learned that, in matters of
humanity, we were not any different from them.

I provided a case of Johnny Walker for my New Year's Eve party. We drank, ate cheese, crackers, and nuts, sang the New Year in, and played poker. General Strother visited us on New Year's Day and presented the Distinguished Flying Cross to Maj. Lee Rayford and Capts. Andrew Turner, William Campbell, Melvin Jackson, Vernon Haywood, Dudley Watson, and George Gray. Bronze Stars were awarded to T. Sgt. Raymond Washington and S. Sgt. Professor Anderson. Following the ceremony General Strother delivered a brief resume of the 332d's accomplishments since coming to his command. He said we had done well and that he was communicating this fact to higher authority. He also gave me a plug, saying that I was of great value to the group. Our bomber friends were still weathered in with us, and took communion with us at the Sunday service.

We flew only 11 missions in January—photo reconnaissance escort and bomber escort missions to communications and oil targets in Vienna, Munich, Prague, Stuttgart, Regensburg, and Linz—although we briefed many others that never got off the ground. It was a month of frequent rains, snow flurries, freezing temperatures, and curtailed operations. Our basketball team won the fighter command tournament. Two pilots failed to return during the month. On 22 January 1945 I presented the Distinguished Flying Cross to Maj. George Roberts, Capts. Woodrow Crockett, Samuel Curtis, Claude Govan, Freddie Hutchins, William Mattison, Gwynne Pierson, Lowell Steward, Alva Temple, Luke Weathers, Jr., and 1st Lt. Frank Roberts, and the Bronze Star to S. Sgt. Marshall Jones. I closed the ceremony by citing the group's superior performance of its important mission and my deep personal appreciation of the efforts of all who had made our success possible.

The weather improved considerably in February, and we flew 39 missions in 28 days. Only one mission, flown on 25 February and led by Capt. Edward Gleed, group operations officer, produced any genuine damage to the enemy. (The bombing of oil targets by the 15th Air Force seemed to have reduced enemy oil production.) On that date, our mission was to strafe rail traffic that might be carrying oil in the area bounded by Ingolstadt, Linz, and Salzburg. Captain Gleed led 45 P-51s to the area, where the 99th, 100th, and 301st squadrons destroyed a variety of targets. Sighting a target of opportunity, Captain Gleed directed the 100th Squadron to strafe an airdrome. There the 100th destroyed two He-111s and damaged one He-111 and one Me-109. We sustained five combat losses in February.

Colonel Taylor visited us on 26 February and commented on the 332d's continuing splendid record. He presented seven Distinguished Flying Crosses and thirteen Air Medals to our pilots, and four Bronze Stars to M. Sgt. Nathaniel Wade, T. Sgt. Roland L Poindexter, S. Sgt. Elliot Lucas, and Cpl. John Fields.

I closed out the month by leading the group on its 200th mission on 28 February, providing target cover over Verona for the B-17s of the 5th Bomb Wing. Early in March the 302d Fighter Squadron was inactivated, and on 12 March the unit convoy departed. I greatly regretted the loss of the 302d. Developing a traditional AAF fighter pilot spirit quite early in its existence, it had made a tremendous contribution to the 332d's mission and produced many of the group's most outstanding stars. I suppose its inactivation was inevitable because of the limited flow of black fighter pilot replacements being trained at Tuskegee. Perhaps the segregated pilot training system could produce only enough pilots for the 477th Bombardment Group. Obviously the segregated system was at least indirectly responsible for this loss of a combat-capable fighter squadron. I was given no reason for the 302d's deactivation, but I was happy to be invited to Luke Air Force Base in 1987 to attend the 302ds reactivation as an Air Force Reserve fighter squadron. Thus, the 302d lives on.

Replacements and pilots from the 302d were assigned to our remaining three squadrons, and during March we flew 50 missions—bomber escort, photo reconnaissance escort, and strafing. Especially notable was a 24 March mission escorting the 5th Bomb Wing's B-17s to Berlin—a 1,600-mile round trip from Ramitelli, the longest 15th Air Force mission of the war. Within 50 miles of the Daimler-Benz target, 30 Me-262 and Me-163 jet fighters dived into our formation to attack the bombers. Our P-51s fought back, destroying three Me-262s and probably destroying two Me-262s and one Me-163 in a five-minute encounter; we then conducted a fighter sweep over Berlin. The 332d was awarded the coveted Distinguished Unit Citation for this outstanding accomplishment. We finished March in a blaze of glory: on the last day of the month, I led a fighter sweep of the Munich area, during which we encountered 17 German aircraft conducting a low patrol above an enemy airdrome 30 miles east of Munich. Not one escaped unharmed. We destroyed 13, probably destroyed three, and damaged one—our largest number of enemy aircraft destroyed in the air on any single day. Reflecting the high number and dangerous nature of the missions flown during March, we sustained the loss of 11 pilots.

We had many promotions in March, and I presented the Distinguished Flying Cross to Capts. Clarence Bradford, Robert Friend, Stanley Harris, Armour McDaniel, and Alton Ballard, and to 1st Lts. Roscoe Brown and Marion Rogers. I presented M. Sgt. Ellsworth H. Dansby with the Bronze Star. These promotions and awards, and the beautiful spring weather, boosted group morale. Our Red Tails won the 15th Air Force basketball championship, only to be beaten in the Adriatic finals by the fast-breaking Bulldozers from an Engineer battalion.

Two distinguished visitors arrived on 9 March: Truman Gibson and Maj. Gen. James Bevans, deputy commander of the Mediterranean Air Force. We made every attempt to acquaint these gentlemen with our mission, our performance, and our problems—mainly finding pilot replacements and properly utilizing our veterans after they went home. We realized that both men occupied a position in which clear understanding of the 332d would undoubtedly be helpful to the AAF. I had known Truman before entering West Point, when I lived with the Gibsons, and he and I attended the University of Chicago.

Although the world now knows that the war in Europe ended in early May 1945, even as late as April those of us fighting that war could not visualize such an early end. We flew 54 combat missions in April, the most in any single month. In the course of strafing, fighter sweeps, bomber escort, and armed reconnaissance missions, we destroyed 17 enemy aircraft in three encounters. On 1 April eight of our pilots engaged 16 FW-190s and Me-109s while escorting bombers over southern Austria. We destroyed eight FW-190s and four Me-109s. (On two successive days, 31 March and 1 April, we destroyed a grand total of 25 enemy fighters!) On 5 April Lt. Jimmy Lanham shot down a lone low-flying Me-109 in an assigned strafing area. On 12 April we escorted the B-24s of the 49th Bomb Wing when they bombed a railroad bridge at Saint-Vith, Germany, losing two pilots when they collided during withdrawal. A third pilot was lost on 15 April when his aircraft was hit over Munich; except for his loss, this strafing mission to Munich, Salzburg, Linz, and Regensburg was highly successful, resulting in extensive destruction of railroad transportation materiel. On 23 April we lost another pilot who was hit by flak, but who was observed to climb to 4,500 feet and bail out. On 26 April six P-51s escorted a P-38 reconnaissance aircraft to Linz, Prague, and Amstetten: our pilots observed five Me-109s over Linz, destroyed four, and probably destroyed the fifth. At the end of the month I pinned on nine Distinguished Flying Crosses and presented the Soldier's Medal for bravery to Woodrow Crockett.

These victories would be our last ones of the war. The entire group took sad note of the death of President Roosevelt, and along with many others, regretted that he did not live to see the end of the war; most of us regarded him as a war casualty. We began to feel and believe that the war in Italy, if not in the rest of Europe, was just about over. I should have known it was over when I received new living quarters at Ramitelli—a trailer that had a genuine bed with springs, lots of drawer space, running water, a washstand, and a built-in mirror—but I had not moved into it because it had no heat. There had been talk and conjecture about our going directly to the Pacific without going home. I hoped this would not happen; by April 1945 the 332d was composed mainly of replacement pilots, few flight leaders, and no experienced squadron commanders, all the result of our segregation within the AAF. Segregation had once again robbed us of the flexibility needed to manage our manpower and maintain our supply of high-quality pilots.

During the last days of April, I sent an advance party headed by Lt. Col. Nelson Brooks north to establish a new base at Cattolica, a better location for meeting operational requirements. By this time, Venice and almost all of northern Italy had fallen into Allied hands. On 1 May I flew up to see the results of the advance work and was pleased to find that Cattolica, a former Italian air force base, surpassed by far any of our previous bases. Our stunning headquarters building looked like an expensive villa in a travel magazine. A sign extending across its facade announced, "Home of the Red Tails, Hq 332d Fighter Group." Red was clearly the dominant design motif: the ends of two whitewashed walkways were painted red, and a green iron fence in front of the headquarters had red gates opening to the building's entrance. Within days we completely evacuated Ramitelli, and all our aircraft, materiel, and people moved to Cattolica Airdrome. Spotless white buildings welcomed their new occupants, and almost immediately neat tents and houses surrounded these buildings in each squadron area. Though our future was still unknown to us, we embarked happily on the new era of peace.

We were fortunate to have a Red Cross Clubmobile unit based with us. Roger Gordon, a Red Cross field director and a friend of long standing, administered a large area of Red Cross responsibility in Italy. The Red Cross had served us well throughout the war, supporting us in personal emergencies and offering routine Clubmobile service. Some of the Red Cross girls attended our dances, as did the local Italian girls, who were more respectable than those we had encountered near other Italian bases; there were very few prostitutes near Cattolica. Many British and East Indian nurses from a nearby hospital habitually visited our officers' club, a building occupied by the Germans, British, and Canadians before we renovated it. We had plenty of whiskey, so the club was popular.

On 2 May Berlin fell and, as we had been expecting for months, the German forces in Italy surrendered. A few days later a group flight of the 332d participated in the 15th Air Force review over Caserta and Bari, and on 8 May, the formal end of the war in Europe, we celebrated a solemn but eventful V-E Day with a colorful ceremony. Colonel Taylor reviewed the massed personnel of the 332d and awarded Distinguished Flying Crosses and Air Medals to pilots, and Bronze Stars to key support personnel. Our basketball team also received medals for their showing in the 15th Air Force championship and the Adriatic Zone finals. Everyone looked impressive in their uniforms, and their marching in review was fine, even to the critical eye of a West Point graduate. Although the ceremonies expressed the group's pride and high morale, most of us felt that V-E Day was an anticlimactic ending to the slowdown that had been inevitable for many days.

Just three days later we again had visitors—Major General Twining, Brigadier General Strother, and Colonel Taylor. I realized intuitively that this was a farewell visit by Generals Twining and Strother. Another group review went off well, and we had an especially good dinner with a rare treat—chocolate ice cream. In a letter of commendation to me, Buck Taylor remarked that ours was a fine military organization; among our accomplishments, we had achieved the distinction of never losing a single bomber to enemy fighters on an escort mission.

Some of our pilots who had been missing in action returned to the group. Missing since 16 August 1944, 1st Lt. Herbert Clark returned to the 99th on 7 May 45. He had evaded capture for more than eight months and continued to fight as leader of a partisan band that had conducted raids against the Germans in northern Italy. Clark looked well; apparently the rough life had agreed with him. Also from the 99th, 1st Lt. Hugh White returned from northern Italy, and 2d Lt. James Hall, Jr., was repatriated from Romania. Flight Officers James Mitchell and Lem Spears rejoined the 301st from Poland.

## Loose Ends

At this point we were simply awaiting orders to go home, and I was at loose ends. I visited Rimini on the east coast, southeast of Bologna, and found it completely bombed out. I visited our rest camp in the Posilipo section of Naples, with its magnificent view of the Tyrrhenian Sea. On days that were not fogged in, one could see Naples harbor, Capri, and the comings and goings of military and civilian shipping along the coast. Capt. William Womack, the officer primarily responsible for establishing the rest camp, had done a consistently fine job for our fighter pilots, who visited there at least a few times during their combat tours. It had contributed significantly to our mission.

I could have driven to Venice, Milan, and Turin, but my letdown feeling prevented me from being interested in sightseeing. Italy *was* beautiful—just like Alabama in May, and I looked back to May 1941, when Agatha and I had left Fort Riley and were driving to Tuskegee. It had been four years of hard work, including one year of the toughest kind of air combat. In spite of our many troubles, I felt that the 332d's contributions had been recognized by AAF officially in war records and personally in the testimony of our commanders and the men who had fought and died alongside us for our common goal.

I was extremely proud, gratified, and surprised to receive a certificate "in recognition of Courageous Service in Aerial Combat" for 35 combat missions over enemy territory, signed by Colonel Taylor and General Strother and issued by the direction of Major General Twining. As gratified as I was to receive this personal recognition, I understood that it was truly a recognition for the men of the 332d Fighter Group, and that my success as their commander had depended entirely on their support and conscientious efforts.

After a few days of waiting for some news of our future, I finally relaxed, taking each day at a time and joining in the happiness of accomplishment that now characterized the group's mood. I walked around the base and out into the country. I visited San Marino, a tiny landlocked nation untouched by the war that had been fought all around and over it. I finally drove to Venice with Maj. Vance Marchbanks, our flight surgeon. Venice had not been bombed, only occupied by the Germans. There were no other Americans there at the time. Vance and I stayed in the best hotel in town, which the British had taken over. We rode gondolas, went shopping, listened to the band concerts in the Piazza San Marco, drank at the bar in the hotel, and talked with a couple of British nurses who were on their way to Austria. Everything remained as it had been before the war, even the prices.

Toward the end of May, we changed completely to peacetime status and concentrated on our training program for pilots and ground personnel. We continued training flights and launched into classes on Japanese aircraft recognition, Pacific orientation and topography, and tropical medicine and weather. I declared Sundays, Wednesday afternoons, and Saturday afternoons as holidays, so the men had plenty of time to play. Swimming in the warm waters of the Adriatic was a favorite, and they took tours to Venice, Genoa, Milan, and Bologna in addition to the regular rest periods in Naples and Rome. The anticipation of going home kept morale high.

Memorial Day called attention to the bitter cost of war. Assembled at Cattolica Airdrome on an incomparably lovely day, fanned by breezes from the beautiful blue Adriatic, we remembered the valiant airmen who had ventured forth across its broad expanse, never to return. All of us felt the magnitude of their sacrifices and a debt of gratitude for their service to our country.

On 8 June 1945 my service in Italy came to an end. Colonel Taylor presented the final combat awards to pilots and enlisted men of the 332d. I was awarded the Silver Star for gallantry in action on 15 April 1945, when I had led a group formation to strafe enemy targets in Austria. Distinguished Flying Crosses were awarded to Lts. Jimmy

Lanham, Gentry Barnes, Bertram Wilson, Robert Williams, and Carl Cary. Air Medals were awarded to Lt. Charles Lane, Jr., Samuel Matthews, Felix McCrory, and Frank Jackson, Jr. The Bronze Star was awarded to 1st Sgt. Samuel Henderson, 99th Fighter Squadron. The group then passed in review to close the ceremony and bid farewell to me as commander of the 332d. A few hours later, 15 officers, 25 enlisted men, and I stepped into two B-17s to depart for the United States.

It was my intention that the officers and men of the 332d returning with me to the United States from Italy would occupy key positions in my next command. To those who did not, I wrote the following farewell letter:

> In parting I would like to say that it has been a signal honor to be a part of such a fine organization as the 332d Fighter Group. It is with regret that I leave you with whom I have been so closely associated during the past many months. We have been through much together, and the many common experiences we share make it most difficult for me to tear away so abruptly. However, the war is but half won, and we cannot let up until Japan is defeated. In the words of Brigadier General D. C. Strother, who recently commanded our Fighter Command, the 332d has been a credit to itself and to the Army Air Forces. All of us who have been connected with the 332d know this to be a fact. I am proud to have been associated with you, and I am certain that even if we do not serve together in war time, we will meet again in peace. I wish all of you Godspeed, and may all of us carry on in the future as nobly as we have in the past.

★  ★  ★  **Integration**

**7.**

*To almost everyone's surprise, but not mine, the integration of blacks in the Air Force soon began to take on a life of its own. I knew the high standards and performance of the Lockbourne people; I was positive that after the initial shock of reassigning blacks to white units, they would be recognized as important assets.*

My new orders were to assume command of the 477th Bombardment Group at Godman Field, Kentucky. On 21 June 1945 I flew from Washington to Godman with General Eaker, deputy commander, Army Air Forces. Truman Gibson and my father, both members of the McCloy Committee, were also on board. I do not remember the flight, but my thoughts must have concentrated on the 477th Bombardment Group and the challenging job I would have as commander.

I was greatly pleased to be chosen for this assignment. Everything I had read or heard about the 477th indicated that the unit had traveled a rocky road since its activation in January 1944. There had to be a good reason that the unit was not ready and eagerly awaiting shipment overseas, and in the days after our arrival at Godman I learned that there were indeed many reasons. General Eaker helped me considerably by attending the change of command ceremony. His presence demonstrated the AAF's confidence in me and my ability to solve the extremely difficult problems associated with the 477th. Agatha traveled separately from Washington to attend the ceremony.

I do not remember any of the speeches, but when I bid General Eaker, Truman, and my father farewell, I was ready to tackle my new challenges.

Challenges I had, both in magnitude and number. Seventeen months after activation, the 477th still had not achieved combat readiness, and we were scheduled for deployment in the Far East by 1 October 1945, just three months away. At the root of all the problems was, of course, racial conflict between black trainees and white supervisors. The morale of the 477th had started at a low ebb and hit bottom two months before my arrival with accusations of mutiny and the pending court-martial of several of its officers. Like the 332d, the 477th had had difficulties finding a permanent home because of the opposition of local whites. The unit had been shuttled from base to base: first Selfridge; then Godman; then Freeman Field, near Seymour, Indiana; and finally back to Godman. Had combat readiness been the overriding objective, the unit would have stayed at Selfridge, where the weather was relatively good and there were ample gunnery ranges for crew qualification. Instead, the first move to Godman had been intended to remove the 477th from the troubled racial environment that supposedly existed in nearby Detroit. The move to Freeman was an attempt to escape Godman's bad winter flying weather, its lack of hangar and apron space, and the absence of an air-to-ground gunnery range. The move back to Godman from Freeman resulted from the cold reception of Seymour townspeople and the accusations of mutiny. Added to all these group moves were dozens of squadron moves, ostensibly made to chase better flying weather, better air base facilities, and an air-to-ground gunnery range.

White-black command arrangements contributed heavily to the problems. Colonel Selway was white; all his senior staff and his squadron commanders were white. Black airmen could be trained and assigned as mechanics, but they could never become B-25 crew chiefs. Colonel Selway's white officers had come from the European and Pacific war theaters and from the Zone of the Interior (ZI)—mainly the United States. His black officers had come from Tuskegee, Walterboro, and Italy. No black officer could occupy a position that would put him over a white officer, and black officer combat returnees were frequently made subordinate to white officers with no combat experience. When white officers were promoted and moved to other positions, thereby creating new promotion vacancies, they were replaced by other white officers, who also became eligible for promotion. Under this discriminatory system, almost all black officers were denied promotion. The end result was a sour white-black relationship, which soon had developed into outright enmity.

## A "Conspiracy to Revolt"

As had been the case at Selfridge before I assumed command of the 332d, segregated officers' clubs were one of the foremost grievances of the black officers. As Alan L. Gropman writes in *The Air Force Integrates: 1945–1964:*

> Godman officials sought to avoid the problem by having whites join the all-white officers' club at Fort Knox, leaving the Godman club all black. Since Fort Knox could extend membership to whomever it wished, and since no Negro officers were assigned to Fort Knox it was suggested that there were no grounds for Negro complaints. Colonel Selway notified the blacks before the move to Freeman Field that there would be two separate (but equal) officers' clubs. Race was supposedly not involved: one club was for supervisors and the other for trainees. But all supervisors were white and all trainees black.

Colonel Selway's pretense of maintaining separate facilities on the basis of personnel function rather than race did not hold water with the black trainees, who saw the order as a clear violation of Army Regulation 210-10. They decided to organize a protest. On the night of 5 April 1945, groups of black officers repeatedly tried to enter the officers' club at Freeman Field and were told that it was not open to trainee personnel. Some left when they were refused entrance. Sixty-one others entered anyway and were arrested. On legal advice, Selway released all the men who had been arrested except for three who had used force to gain entrance. A few days later, however, when he ordered all personnel to sign a regulation on the policy of separate facilities, about 100 black officers refused and were arrested.

General Hunter interpreted these actions as a "conspiracy to revolt." He maintained the position that segregated facilities were legal—in the words of an opinion written by the judge advocate of the AAF, Brig. Gen. L. H. Hedrick, "where circumstances make such division necessary or desirable from a practical, disciplinary, or morale standpoint." The opinion was largely based on War Department Pamphlet 20-6, which seemed to give commanders the option of maintaining racially segregated facilities.

The Freeman Field affair immediately came to the attention of the McCloy Committee. Early in May the committee received a summary of official opinion favoring continued segregation in the AAF. Truman Gibson strongly opposed these recommendations, arguing that the policies of Colonel Selway and General Hunter were based primarily on racial, not practical, considerations. Later that month the committee issued its report, finding that Selway "had acted within his administrative police powers in arresting the blacks, but his other actions were in conflict with Army regulations" *(The Air Force Integrates)*.

When I arrived at Godman, about a month after the McCloy Committee report was published, the case against the indicted officers had not yet been decided. The furor created by the case was still a major obstacle to achieving combat readiness, and I hoped it could be resolved quickly. The racist attitudes and actions of Colonel Selway and General Hunter were wrong because they were based on wrong interpretations of War Department regulations. I was amazed that General Hunter, who had been made aware of the details of those regulations in connection with an official reprimand to Col. William Boyd, his Selfridge field commander, continued to violate them. I understood the Deep South mindset that underlay General Hunter's statements and decisions; but I could not understand putting the issue of segregated facilities ahead of the need to prepare the group for war; nor the decisions to move the 477th from one airfield to another, which halted progress toward combat readiness for several months.

The conduct of the scores of black officers who challenged Colonel Selway's denial of the use of the officers' club at Freeman had been carefully planned and executed. Although the AAF had intended to try all the officers who tried to enter the club and refused to sign the regulation, only the three who used force were charged. The government's case against two of them collapsed. The third officer was found guilty of "shoving a provost marshal" and fined; with the exception of this single incident, the demonstration had been proper in every respect. The crisis blew over, and at last the 477th could prepare to enter the war in the Pacific.

The 477th had an outstanding flying safety record except for the three months following the Freeman Field affair, when five accidents resulted in eleven deaths. After the court-martial capable black officers took over the positions of responsibility that had been denied them so long, and morale began to recover. I had brought with me many veterans of the Italian campaign: Bill Campbell, Andrew Turner, Elmer Jones, Herbert Carter, Lee Rayford, Vance Marchbanks, Ed Gleed, and Thomas Money. In addition, many strong, capable 477th officers provided leadership: C. I. Williams, Elmore Kennedy, George Knox, Lott Carter, John Beverly, William Edelin, James Redden, Charles Stanton, George Webb, and Carl Taylor.

I had to deal with the problem of finding family housing for the officers and airmen who had returned with me from Italy. Although the mayor of Louisville, Wilson Wyatt, had presented me the key to the city, I did not receive any such welcome from the commanding general of Fort Knox. Colonel Selway's command and other supervisory officers and airmen had been given family quarters at adjacent Fort Knox, and these quarters were soon to be vacated. When I asked Fort Knox to provide quarters for my unit as they had for the 477th's white personnel, my request was denied entirely for racial reasons. "I don't know whether you are familiar with Fort Knox or not," the post commander complained to 1st Air Force Headquarters, "but this is an old cavalry post, we have four General Officers living here . . . by God, they just don't want a bunch of coons moving in next door to them" *(The Air Force Integrates)*. The subject was discussed by Fort Knox officials with General Eaker, who did not support my request.

As a result of this decision, all our married people, about 60 couples, were housed under extremely crowded conditions in two barracks buildings at Godman. The building Agatha and I lived in had two bathrooms, one for men and one for women, but the other building had only one bathroom for two floors full of people, and they had to devise a guard system to indicate whether the bathroom was being used by men or by women at any particular time. In both buildings the rooms, which had been designed for single occupancy, were more like cells. In the other building they had been partitioned off from one another with wooden panels that went only halfway to the ceiling, so there was no privacy. It was an absolutely disgraceful situation, and a terrible way to treat combat veterans who had fought one war and were soon to be on their way to fight another. I shall never forget nor forgive this shameful treatment of our veterans and their families by officers of the U.S. Army, who were fully aware of the situation and yet allowed it to continue. To add insult to injury, our palatial quarters were adjacent to barracks occupied by Italian prisoners of war under the control of the Fort Knox command.

Racism victimized our families in other ways also. Lucille Gleed, wife of Ed Gleed, my deputy commander, took the long train ride from St. Louis to Louisville with their two young daughters to join Ed at Godman. Lucille and the girls were fair-skinned, and they rode the coach reserved for whites. When the girls went to sleep, Lucille went to take a nap on a bench in the ladies' room. While she was gone, the children were rudely awakened by the conductor, who asked, "Are you niggers?" They replied that they did not know. The conductor then went to the ladies' room looking for Lucille, threw open the door without knocking, and asked her the same question. "What do you think?" she answered succinctly. This rocked the conductor back on his heels, and as he left, he remarked, "You just can't tell who is and who isn't a nigger these days."

The Gleeds' troubles did not end there. Lucille took her six-year-old, Bettye, to school at Fort Knox the morning of the fall opening, where she was cordially received by the principal. About noon, the principal called Lucille back to the school, where she was informed that only the children of families stationed at Fort Knox could attend the post school. Undoubtedly, word had come down from Fort Knox command that blacks were not welcome. Ed had no choice but to send Lucille and the girls back home to Kansas so that Bettye could start school.

It took me a long time to absorb the effects of how the Fort Knox command treated our people. I remained livid with anger and frustration because of a situation that was beyond my ability to correct. I was responsible for the welfare of the unit, but we were living under appalling conditions I could not improve. I was mad at the world, and particularly mad at the U.S. Army. After Lucille's experience, I requested that our children be allowed to attend the Fort Knox school, but I was denied, just as I had been denied in my request for family housing. Two things helped me through this difficult time. First, I had a mission to perform, and I distracted myself by dealing with the myriad technical problems associated with getting the 477th ready for deployment. Second, I took some consolation from the fact that our recently arrived families were so happy to be reunited that they tolerated the insulting housing situation. The last commander I had in the military service, Gen. John Throckmorton, had been stationed at Fort Knox at this time. When I served under him, I never brought up the subject of what had happened 25 years before. I did not want to know whether he had played any part in the decision to deny us quarters at Fort Knox—a decision we lived with uncomfortably from June 1945 until we moved to Lockbourne in March 1946.

## Demobilization

In early August 1945, in response to an invitation from Colonel Parrish, I visited TAAF for the first time since my departure overseas in April 1943. Speaking at TAAF's fourth anniversary celebration, I summarized its history and described its lasting problems, the solutions of which were so important to the AAF and the 99th. I told the story of the 99th's combat record before and after it joined the 332d and mentioned the planned deployment of the 477th to the Far East. In closing, I commended the people at TAAF for their vitally important contribution to the black combat units of the AAF.

Soon after my return to Godman from TAAF, we learned of the bombing of Hiroshima and Nagasaki. It was apparent that the Pacific war was soon to be over and our lives were to be radically changed once again. Most of our people were suddenly asking themselves how soon they could expect to get out of uniform and move back into a civilian life that only a few days before had seemed far in the future. Nobody had any way of knowing what the postwar Air Force would do with its black veterans. I assumed that the 99th would be retained along with a B-25 unit, but there had to be a massive demobilization that would require most of our people to leave the military service. The postwar Air Force was certain to be much larger than the prewar Air Corps, but I had no knowledge of plans for a separate Air Force or regular commissions for black officers, and at this early date none of my thoughts even vaguely touched upon the possibility of integrating blacks into white units.

The 477th remained at Godman through V-J Day, marking the end of the Pacific war, and beyond. We became a composite group, consisting of the 99th Fighter Squadron and two B-25 squadrons. My own mission eased considerably: I was to facilitate the discharge of all eligible personnel, train on a peacetime basis, and reorganize. We were to remain at Godman until a suitable permanent ZI base could be found for our organization. Gen. Edward ("Ted") Timberlake, AAF Headquarters, and I visited several likely bases, but only one would willingly accept us: TAAF. Dr. Patterson, the president of Tuskegee Institute, extended an invitation to us for peacetime utilization of TAAF by the Air Forces.

From our standpoint, TAAF was not satisfactory, although the Veterans Administration Hospital had survived in Tuskegee, and Tuskegee Institute was a pleasant place for its faculty, students, and native inhabitants as long as they did not venture forth into the hostile Alabama environment. One of Colonel Parrish's "proposed solutions" to the many white-black problems he had encountered during his tenure as commander was to suggest that only blacks with a "southern background" be assigned to TAAF. He believed that black southerners would "understand" southern customs and be less likely to challenge them than blacks who had grown up in the North.

When I relayed Dr. Patterson's invitation to General Timberlake with my recommendation ("Thanks, but no thanks"), he did not even take time to discuss the matter. Apparently, AAF Headquarters did not want to buy unnecessarily into the problems of day-to-day strife between TAAF's black airmen and Alabama whites. Granted, the South did not have a monopoly on racial discrimination, but the existence of laws mandating segregation made life there far more difficult than it was in other parts of the nation.

General Timberlake and I therefore continued to consider alternatives. We inspected Bradley Field, near Hartford, Connecticut, and Lockbourne Air Base, near Columbus, Ohio. In each case we found we were not wanted by the local community. I recalled the resolution by the Iosco County Board of Supervisors raising objections to aerial gunnery training by the 332d's fighter squadrons at Oscoda. This objection had been voiced at the height of World War II, in the spring of 1943; one might have expected that the importance of the war effort would have caused people to relax their prejudices, but that was not the case. I also recalled the chilly reception by the citizens of Seymour when the 477th moved into Freeman Field in early 1945.

Apparently there was no room at the inn for the 477th. With this realization, AAF Headquarters finally twisted the arm of the Ohio congressional delegation and decided to move us to Lockbourne, despite the loud objections of the *Citizen*, one of Columbus's two major newspapers. The AAF's all-weather flying school, headed by Gen. Benjamin S. Kelsey, had become the sole occupant of Lockbourne after V-J Day had eliminated the need for the wartime B-17 combat crew training center. This unit was of great importance to the AAF because of the need for improved all-weather flying proficiency throughout the service. It was moved over General Kelsey's vehement objections because of the difficulties associated with locating the 477th on a satisfactory permanent base.

The move to Lockbourne constituted a milestone in the struggle of blacks to gain an equal footing in the armed services. For the first time, blacks were to administer an AAF base in the continental United States without the immediate supervision of white officers. Many doubted our ability to develop a successful operation, but in spite of chronic personnel shortages Lockbourne became one of the best bases in the Air Force.

## Settling in at Lockbourne

When we first arrived in March 1946 we found an empty base, but were favorably impressed with its ample facilities and overall appearance. All our people eagerly applied themselves to making improvements to our new home and developing our operations capability as rapidly as possible. We were happy to have a place to live away from the South, where we had experienced so much unhappiness in the months before the deployment of the 99th.

My staff immediately went to work converting existing barracks into family housing. Meanwhile, everyone—Agatha and I included—had trouble finding a place to live. After many false starts, the Urban League suggested we get in touch with Lena and Charles Johnson. Lena was a native Ohioan from Marysville, a small town near Columbus, and Charlie had lived in Columbus all his life. They took us in, and we immediately became fast friends. The Johnsons also helped many other 477th people find housing. We remain friends of Lena to this day; Charlie died recently.

The 477th was now a Tactical Air Command (TAC) installation with a threefold mission of demobilization, recruitment of military personnel, and maintenance of combat readiness. We participated in TAC's air indoctrination courses for students at Army schools and colleges. Gen. Elwood R. Quesada, the TAC commander, devoted considerable effort to teaching a new generation of ground officers the air-to-ground doctrine and tactics he had developed during the war in Europe. We perfected our gunnery, bombing, and rocketry at Myrtle Beach, South Carolina, and at Eglin Field in Florida, and we flew firepower demonstations and air shows.

We ceased being a composite group in July 1947. Our B-25s were deactivated after participating in combat exercises in Georgia conducted by our parent headquarters, the 9th Air Force, commanded by Maj. Gen. Paul Williams. I was particularly gratified to hear General Williams's complimentary remarks on this occasion, because we had been given little in the way of encouragement from senior people since the move to Lockbourne.

With the loss of our B-25s we again became the 332d Fighter Group, and later, reflecting the wing-base organization adopted by the AAF in 1947, the 332d Fighter Wing. The 332d Fighter Wing now closely resembled the wartime 332d Fighter Group, and the names of our three squadrons stayed the same. After TAAF was closed in 1946, its pilots who wanted to stay in the Air Forces were reassigned to Lockbourne, which now had more than 10 percent of all black airmen in the AAF and 75 percent of its black officers.

One major difference between the wartime group and the 332d Fighter Wing was the size and mission of our medical group. When we arrived at Lockbourne, there was no hospital, only an empty hospital building. Under the expert supervision of Col. Vance Marchbanks, our base surgeon, the group developed complete medical services, fully staffed with capable doctors, dentists, nurses, and technicians.

Although I was assisted by a capable and experienced team of officers, and Lockbourne was well organized under the wing-base concept, we were handicapped by personnel losses throughout my command. We had 83 P-47s to keep flying, as well as training requirements arising from our need to convert B-25 pilots into fighter pilots. We remained short of qualified pilots until all three squadrons had qualified at Eglin Field in dive-bombing, rocket firing, napalm dropping, and smoke laying. In addition, the temporary loss of several of our most capable officers to air tactical school and a heavy load of missions assigned by higher headquarters stretched our capabilities to the limit.

In the early days at Lockbourne, much of my job consisted of solving the public relations problems associated with the influx of black personnel into the Columbus area. The base was eight miles out of town in the country, but the people of Columbus objected to our being stationed even that close. In time, however, their attitude began to change. The governor of Ohio, the mayor of Columbus, and representatives of prominent civic organizations ultimately came to view Lockbourne as their base. The Ohio National Guard was a tenant at the base, reserve pilots flew proficiency flights in our aircraft, and the Ohio Civil Air Patrol held its encampments at Lockbourne. Important political, civic, and military figures visited us whenever we invited them to Army Day celebrations or other public relations events. We also hosted the Eastern Area Air Track and Field Meet, which Lockbourne won with the assistance of a 1948 Olympic gold medal winner, S. Sgt. Mal Whitfield, a member of our 100th Fighter Squadron, thereby putting Lockbourne and Columbus on the national sports pages. Such events certainly helped improve our image with the local population.

After the war, married women did not hold jobs nearly as commonly as they do today, and Lockbourne wives were active in all of these public relations events. With good reason, I developed great pride in them. Not only were they a hard-working group, but they were perceptive in recognizing needs and problems, and prompt in taking steps on their own to address them. Lockbourne families were scattered all over the Columbus area; we had no family housing. If our base was ever to have cohesive feeling and spirit, the women believed they had to create a way for people to meet under unofficial conditions. And they knew that if wives were to get together as a group, their children would have to be provided for. Consequently, they organized the Lockbourne Officers' Wives' Club. Agatha called the first meeting and served as president for the first two years. Although progress was initially hampered by the constant turnover of our men, plans for establishing a nursery—one of the first on an Air Force base—were rapidly put into motion. The men of the base band gave a benefit concert, the officers' club donated money each month, and the women conducted frequent fund-raising activities. The base

# 99ᵀᴴ SQUADRON CITED FOR DOWNING 3 PLANES

Story on
Page 3

SQUADRON COMMANDER—Benjamin O. Davis, Jr., Lieutenant-Colonel in the Air Force, one of whose flyers, Fl Lt. Charles Hall, was personally commended by Gene Eisenhower for knocking out three German planes.

## 99th Fliers Score First Air Victory; Gen. Eisenhower Brings Thanks in Person

ALLIED HEADQUARTERS IN NORTH AFRICA—The boys of the 99th Pursuit Squadron who wanted a "chance to show the world what we can do," roared into the skies over Sicily, July 2, and when they returned to the home field they found General D. Eisenhower waiting to commend them for giving a fair show of what to expect in the future.

The PRICE OF THE AFRO IS
**7 CENTS**
IN D. C.
PAY NO MORE!

# WASHINGTON AFRO AMERICAN

### Ten Per Cent of Tan Yanks to Stay in Germany

PARIS—ETO headquarters revealed on June 13 that the U.S. Army will try to have 10.4 per cent of colored troops in the total American occupation force in Germany, and apply the same ratio to troops sent home for eventual discharge. That is the standard percentage used by the War Department wherever possible in fixing the proportion of colored troops.

53rd Year. No. 45 · Contents of This Newspaper Copyrighted 1945 by The AFRO-AMERICAN Company · WASHINGTON, D.C., JUNE 23, 1945 · Entered at the Postoffice at Washington, D. C., as Second-Class Matter, under Act of March 3, 1879 · 24 PAGES

# Davis Heads 477th

New Commander of Air Group

Colonel B. O. Davis Jr., the nation's top ranking colored air officer and commanding officer of the 332nd Fighter Group in Italy, is shown relaxing following his return to Washington, where he will remain for about five days before returning to duty. Colonel Davis, holder of the Silver Star, the Legion of Merit and the Distinguished Flying Cross, was on Thursday inducted as head of the 477th Bombardment Group and may be promoted eventually to a brigadier general, the same rank as that held by his father.

Headlines such as these kept readers of the black press in the States informed of the achievements of the 99th and the 332d.

With the senior staff of the 447th
Bombardment Group at Godman Field,
Kentucky, in the summer of 1945.

Agatha enjoys a visit from her sister
Vivienne Melville at Godman Field
in 1945.

With senior staff of the 332d Fighter
Wing at Lockbourne Air Base near
Columbus, Ohio, in 1947.

Agatha at home in the Davis quarters at
Lockbourne in 1948.

Maj. Gen. Elwood Quesada, commander, Tactical Air Command, on inspection with me at Lockbourne in 1948.

Dad admires a photograph of mine in 1950. The other photos on the shelf are of my sister Elnora, her husband James McLendon, and John Overton, Mother Sadie's nephew.

One of my happiest duties as commander of the 51st Fighter Interceptor Wing in Korea was visiting the 51st's orphanage, which provided a home for 450 children.

At a December 1953 office briefing in Suwon, Korea, Col. Harry Young, the 51st's Deputy Wing Commander; Major Berner, the adjutant; and I discuss personnel matters.

Climbing aboard an F-86 for a training mission in Korea in 1954.

Briefing a patrol of the Korean west coast in 1954.

Gen. Earle E. Partridge, FEAF commander, pins my brigadier general stars in Tokyo in October 1954.

WELCOME Gen. Davis
First General in
Seijo Machi

Our neighbors in Seijo Machi made this sign for a spontaneous congratulations party upon my promotion in 1954.

Agatha's Japanese language teacher, Arakawasan, describes for us the scene depicted on a traditional scroll painting in Tokyo, 1954.

Gen. Wang Shu Ming, commander, Chinese Air Force, in 1955–57. General Wang was a superb colleague and close friend.

Gen. Chiang Kai-shek greets me soon after my arrival in Taiwan in 1955 as vice commander, 13th Air Force, and commander, Air Task Force Provisional 13.

Agatha and I blow out the candles on my 43rd birthday cake, at a party hosted by General Wang and his wife Linda.

Planning a gunnery training mission with an expert—Capt. John Giordano—at Wheelus Air Base in Libya, 1957.

Preparing to fly an F-100 gunnery
training mission at Wheelus in 1958.

Gen. Gabriel P. Disosway pins on my
second star at Ramstein in 1958.

Agatha and I relax in our quarters at Ramstein Air Base in Germany in 1958.

Gen. James McGee, commander of Dhahran Air Base in Saudi Arabia, greets Agatha and me on our way to Washington from Germany the "long way around" in June 1961.

In June 1963 I received an honorary LL.D. degree from Morgan State College in Baltimore.

Gen. J. P. McConnell, Chief of Staff, U.S. Air Force, pins on my third star, with Agatha's assistance, at the Pentagon in 1965.

With two golf buddies at Yongsan, Korea, in 1966: Maj. Gen. Edward Burba, Chief, Korean Military Advisory Group, and General Kim, Chief of Staff, Republic of Korea Army.

Gen. Dwight Beach of the Army briefed former Vice President Nixon during his 1966 visit to Korea. Army Major General Schlanser and I were also in attendance.

Trooping the line of the United Nations Command Honor Guard in Seoul in 1967. The host for this farewell ceremony was Army Gen. Charles H. Bonesteel III, left, Commander in Chief, UNC, for whom I had served as Chief of Staff.

Shortly before my departure from Korea in 1967, Agatha and I met Vice President Humphrey during his visit to attend the inauguration of President Chung Hee Park.

During a 1967 return visit to Taiwan, Agatha was able to spend time with her friend Deh Fong Lai, a composer and wife of Gen. Lai Ming Tang.

President Se-Se Mobutu of Zaire was one of many African leaders I met during the course of my duties in 1968–70 as Deputy Commander in Chief of the U.S. Strike Command, which conducted peacetime military activities in the Middle East/Southern Asia and Africa South of the Sahara command area.

Four members of West Point's class of 1936 reunited during an exercise at the Supreme Headquarters Allied Powers Europe (SHAPE), Belgium, in 1969: Lt. Gen. J. A. Heintges, Gen. H. M. Estes, Jr., Gen. William Westmoreland, and me.

Talking with cadets and an Academy tactical officer during a 1972 visit to the U.S. Air Force Academy.

At a 1977 White House meeting with President Carter and Secretary of Defense Harold Brown of the Presidential Commission on Military Compensation.

provided a building, and day care was initially made available for 36 children for half a day, Monday through Friday. The first supervisor was Rosalyn Fairfax, the wife of M. Sgt. Augustus Fairfax. She had experience in nursery operations and turned out to be an outstanding asset. Believing firmly that children derive some of the most important lessons of their lives not from books but from people and experiences, she emphasized social and personal development.

Among its many other activities, the wives' club raised money for the Red Cross and the Public Employees Division of the Community Chest. Fund-raising efforts for the Red Cross were especially well supported by Lockbourne people because of the popularity of Edward and Nancy Zimmerman, a white couple. An experienced Red Cross field director, Ed had been assigned to the Columbus area with responsibility for our base and nearby Fort Hayes, an Army post. Both the Zimmermans integrated themselves into Lockbourne life, inviting many of our officers and their wives to their home for dinner and bridge. On one occasion, Nancy Zimmerman created a stir at the Fort Hayes Wives' Club when she invited Agatha to the monthly club luncheon. The Fort Hayes women initially questioned the propriety of Agatha's presence, but after heated discussion welcomed her at the luncheon. Agatha was not aware of the debate her attendance had caused until Nancy told her about it driving back to Lockbourne. Many years later, long after Lockbourne had been closed and we and the Zimmermans were living in the Washington area, Nancy told Agatha that, incredibly, she and Ed had been investigated by the FBI because of their associations and friendships with Lockbourne Air Force Base people. Presumably, they had been suspected of communist leanings and questionable loyalty to the United States. Agatha's attendance at the Fort Hayes luncheon had been part of the "reason" for the investigation.

The attitudes of the Fort Hayes Officers' Wives' Club were in no way surprising. In the late 1940s, Columbus was still a segregated city with racial divisions, customs, and practices similar to those in the Deep South. Some of the men's and women's clothing and shoe stores preferrednot to have black customers, no black needing a haircut dared to walk into a white barber shop, and the YMCA and YWCA maintained separate white and black facilities. In general, the attitude of whites toward blacks, while not actively hostile, was definitely cool.

Lockbourne Air Force Base made a big difference in these relationships. The predominantly white civilian work force that had been
working at the base before we came upon the scene quickly decided
their jobs were worth keeping. They welcomed us and performed
their mission satisfactorily. These employees had never been subordinate to black officers before, and at first their cooperation may have
been motivated mostly by a desire to keep their jobs. Soon, however,
they joined us in a spirit of mission accomplishment. More slowly,
Lockbourne became understood as a major asset in the minds of all
Columbus's residents, whites as well as blacks. Undoubtedly, the
base's payroll contributed to the changing attitudes.

These changes were also reflected in the attitudes of senior AAF
officers, who began to realize that blacks possessed hitherto unrecog-
nized administrative abilities. In the 1940s, most whites either in or
out of the military simply did not believe that blacks could perform
on a par with whites in any area of endeavor. Our success at Lockbourne, which came as a surprise to many Air Force policymakers,
undoubtedly contributed to the coming move toward integration.

When the barracks had been converted to family housing, many of
the married officers and airmen who had been living in Columbus
moved onto the base. Adequate family housing completely changed
the base's personality. Of the 110 sets of family quarters converted
from barracks, I allocated 56 to the families of airmen and 54 to the
families of officers. Agatha and I moved into what had originally been
a farmhouse, then a club, before it was renovated into living quarters.
We put in a large garden, which Agatha planted and harvested, yield-
ing all kinds of fresh vegetables. The original owner had planted
horseradish and asparagus that were still producing; I have not tasted
asparagus of that quality since. Our garden produced such large
quantities of food that we were able to share much of it with the base
mess. I contributed to the base beautification program by planting a
large circular bed of flaming salvia in front of our quarters that could
be seen from a considerable distance on the ground as well as from
the traffic pattern in the air.

Shortly after our arrival at Lockbourne, Lt. Alvin Downing, my
special services officer, conceived the idea of organizing on-base entertainment for our troops and planned a series of talent shows after
the regular Friday movies. Each week a different squadron was
charged with the responsibility of entertaining the entire base. Lieu-

tenant Downing eventually chose the best talent from these unit revues and put together a gigantic three-hour show, Operation Enjoyment. I invited Col. Joseph Goetz, chief of the Entertainment Section, Special Services Branch, Air Force Headquarters, to see it. Colonel Goetz was extremely enthusiastic about Lieutenant Downing's work and suggested that he develop the idea into a "soldier show," hoping it could travel to other Air Force bases. I did not take to this idea initially; we had a great deal to do that was more closely related to our basic mission. Colonel Goetz had been closely associated with show business, however, and he had contacts that turned out to be of great value in creating such a show. T. Sgt. George B. Pugh trained our Women of the Air Force (WAF) chorus girls, the Rockettes. Pfc. Calvin Manuel was a major star of the show, and Chappie James, later a four-star Air Force general, was also a member of the cast. After a few performances at Lockbourne, Operation Happiness, as it was renamed, was booked at Air Force bases all over the world. The troupe enjoyed its travels and raised the morale of servicemen wherever it performed. In spite of a widely advertised shortage of Air Force funds, there always seemed to be enough money for the costumes, staging, and travel of Operation Happiness. Lockbourne became famous all over the world, and its people in the show were admirable representatives.

## The Shift toward Integration

In June 1947 I joined my father, who had been designated President Harry Truman's ambassador plenipotentiary and special representative to Liberia, for that country's 100th anniversary celebration. I was assigned by the Department of State to make the trip as aide to my father. We traveled on an aircraft carrier, the USS *Palau*, and I was favorably impressed with the Navy people on board. It came as a surprise to me that white and black personnel were integrated, and even more of a surprise that sailors and marines were assigned according to their abilities, not their race. Official and unofficial opposition to integration was so entrenched in the AAF at this time that it had hardly even occurred to me as a real possibility; on board the *Palau*, however, integration even seemed to carry over to off-duty activities. The ship's band, an impromptu organization composed of two officers and seven enlisted men, two of whom were black, regularly played concerts before the evening movies. In every respect, there seemed to be a fine spirit among officers and men.

The Navy's record in the utilization of blacks was not necessarily superior to the AAF's. In the Navy the number of black officers had increased from 12 at the beginning of World War II to 52 at the end of the war, and the senior black officer was a reserve lieutenant commander. During the same period, the number of black officers in the AAF had increased from none to 1,191, with one colonel, two lieutenant colonels, and many majors. The Navy had no black pilots. The Navy assigned most of its black sailors to the Stewards Branch, which remained segregated into the 1950s, and relatively few blacks were integrated into the General Service Branch, where most of the fighting was done. Still, on 28 February 1946, the Navy had issued a truly remarkable directive: "Effective immediately, all restrictions governing the types of assignments for which Negro naval personnel are eligible are lifted. Henceforth, they shall be eligible for all types of assignments in all ratings in all activities and all ships in the naval service. . . . In the utilization of housing, messing, and other facilities, no special or unusual provisions will be made for the accommodation of Negroes."

Obviously there were many shortfalls between the issuance of this historic directive and its implementation. All the services encountered major obstacles in arriving at an integrated posture. But because of its relatively large number of blacks and its failure to promote interracial cooperation, the AAF had an especially difficult time.

The effective integration of blacks did not become my problem until much later. When I returned to Lockbourne on 18 August, matters were going well. During my absence, the base had been inspected. The report remarked that Lockbourne was "the best-managed base in the Air Corps and could well be a model for other bases." This statement represented a genuine tribute to the fine officers and enlisted people who were assigned to the 332d. A month after my return, the Army Air Forces became a separate branch of the military service—the U.S. Air Force.

The change required me to log long hours on administrative decisions. One major subject was the integration of our people into the Regular Air Force. In October I was disappointed to learn that some of our best officers had not been selected and, conversely, others had been selected who, in my view, did not merit it. A glaring omission from the list, Tom Money, was one of our most knowledgeable and capable officers. Tom later served a full career in the U.S. Air Force as a reserve officer, retiring as a colonel, and it was indeed fortunate to have had his services. Many officers who did not receive Regular Air Force commissions were faced with the choice of dropping in rank to the grade of master sergeant or being separated from the service. It was not unusua to see an officer wearing pilot or navigator wings one day and a day or so later with the same wings, but with the stripes of a master sergeant.

Opinion at Lockbourne on the desirability and method of integration covered a wide range. Some approved of integration under certain conditions, suggesting that the Air Force should retain the 99th Fighter Squadron with the understanding that it would be manned with black and white pilots. Those defending this position held that the squadron's commander should be a black officer. Others at Lockbourne were opposed to integration because they did not trust the all-white top echelon of the Air Force and thought that whites would get preferential treatment in an integrated unit. Within this group, some believed their careers would have much better opportunities for promotion and general career advancement within the segregated environment we had known up until then. Some maintained close touch with people in the Pentagon and, in what I considered a sneaky manner, tried to market their ideas and manage the integration movement through the black press. Fortunately, their efforts were thwarted by sincere black leaders who realized that the integration movement should not be weakened by a few individuals acting out of what they believed to be self-interest.

My own views on integration grew out of my personal experience and the teachings I had received as a child. It had been indelibly impressed on me that racial discrimination was morally wrong. Furthermore, it was a cancer on the military. It continues to constitute the major problem facing our nation, and one that must be dealt with at the earliest possible time. It will not go away on its own.

I did not attempt to quiet the voices at Lockbourne opposing integration. Some of these opponents were senior officers immediately subordinate to me in the 332d Fighter Wing. I strongly disagreed with their attitudes, but I recognized their right to their personal opinions. I could understand how their individual experiences had led them to oppose a clean integration solution that would treat blacks and whites evenhandedly with respect to all operational and administrative actions. First, few could accept that integration as it finally came into being was a real possibility. I had started to believe that it was, but I did not anticipate that change would come as soon or as rapidly as it did. Second, their experience growing up in the separate and unequal institutions of black America inevitably and reasonably created their negative attitudes toward whites. And third, from 1941 on they had endured segregation in the Army Air Corps, the Army Air Forces, and now the U.S. Air Force.

In September 1947, shortly after the U.S. Air Force became a separate service, Lt. Gen. Idwal Edwards, the deputy chief of staff for personnel, ordered Lt. Col. Jack Marr, a member of his staff, to study the racial policy and practices of the Air Force. General Edwards had been a member of the McCloy Committee during the war, and he believed that the policy of racial segregation promoted wasteful uses of manpower. The ultimate objective of the study was to improve military efficiency and manpower utilization with resulting budgetary savings, but it also led the way to more profound social changes throughout the military services. Thus, almost two years before President Truman's Executive Order 9981 ordered the integration of the armed forces, the Air Force was already taking some initiative in that direction.

Initially, I was surprised to learn of the study, but I welcomed any Air Force action that might lead to a solution of racial problems. Until the end of 1948, I was mostly an interested observer. Lieutenant Colonel Marr did discuss certain aspects of his plan with me, perhaps more as a matter of courtesy than to learn anything valuable. I got the impression that he needed me mainly as a sounding board for policies that were already in the process of being formulated. He had a full understanding of conditions affecting blacks in the Air Force, and he did his work so thoroughly that he avoided many pitfalls that might have doomed the plan, if not to failure, at least to delays that could have enabled internal opposition to build.

Stuart Symington, the Secretary of the Air Force; General Spaatz, the Chief of Staff; and General Edwards all played vitally important roles in evading the mine fields that threatened reform. General Edwards, intensely aware of the explosive nature of the study, bypassed normal channels of staff coordination at the field-grade officer level and insisted on coordination only at the three-star deputy chief of staff level. This was a dangerous course of action, because the plan in its final form might have suffered from the lack of full consideration by knowledgeable staff officers. I suspect that Jack Marr, a brilliant staff officer, covered all the bases by consulting a wide range of people.

## Under Fire Again

In late January 1948 I was shocked to receive a letter from my commander, Maj. Gen. William D. Old, 9th Air Force, which described allegations of grossly unsatisfactory conditions at Lockbourne uncovered by a TAC logistics staff inspection. It mentioned the inability of the inspection team members to contact key Lockbourne logistics officers, commercial radios in offices during duty hours, and worst of all, a sit-down strike in progress in the 99th Fighter Squadron. The clincher, however, was the accusation that numerous events in the preceding months indicated I had not been carrying out my duties as wing commander.

I replied to General Old that the officers sought by the TAC inspection team must have been unit supply officers (pilots) of the fighter group, because all officers of the airdrome group and the maintenance and supply group sought by the inspecting party had been contacted. Our records of the day in question showed that the unit supply officers had been flying, and the inspecting party had been so informed. My investigation also revealed that there had never been a revolt or threat of revolt against constituted authority by the 99th Fighter Squadron, and I presented detailed information on actions taken to correct reported logistics deficiencies. I closed my report by saying that the TAC inspection report did not paint an accurate picture, that the statement about the sit-down strike should be further investigated within the TAC inspecting party, and that an unannounced inspection of the 332d Fighter Wing should be made for the specific purpose of determining my qualifications for command. If I were found unqualified, I wrote, then I should be relieved from command and the reasons for this action be placed in my permanent record. In choosing to believe my own people rather than the inspection team, I was putting myself at considerable risk professionally, but I was not about to let an inspection team come in and throw its weight around without justification.

General Old's reply stated that his concern had been based on the theft of some $5,000 worth of food, the general condition of our warehouses, and the conditions in our WAF squadron. There would be no further investigation, he wrote, and he wanted to assist the 332d Fighter Wing in every way possible. At this point I considered the matter officially closed, although I would never know all the facts and I suspected chicanery. The impossibility of the accusations in the report suggested that, for reasons known only to them, members of the TAC inspecting party were trying to make trouble for the 332d.

Immediately after the war, a board made up of Lt. Gen. Alvin C. Gillem and three other generals had recommended limited racial integration in War Department Circular 124, dated 27 April 1946, but the idea had almost no support and it had not been implemented. Throughout 1948 we paid close attention to the struggles of the military services to comply with the recommendations of the Gillem Board, which I considered the first government entity to point the way to eventual integration. At the time its report was published, most careful readers recognized that the board was proposing the eventual utilization of all people on the basis of their individual abilities. A manpower policy of this kind would surely eliminate segregation. The only adverse criticism to be leveled against the board from my point of view was that it did not go far enough, failing to state that the armed services were headed for total integration.

The first clear statement of the Air Force's intention to integrate was made by General Spaatz in March 1948: "It is the feeling of this Headquarters that the ultimate Air Force objective must be to eliminate segregation among its personnel by the unrestricted use of Negro personnel in free competition for any duty within the Air Force for which they may qualify." As Alan Gropman describes in detail in *The Air Force Integrates*, most senior Air Force people and many of the rank and file opposed integration and took steps to let their personal views be known. General Spaatz, General Edwards, and Secretary Symington steadfastly faced this opposition, citing President Truman's executive order and pointing out that integration would increase efficiency, economy, and increased effectiveness. They were men of great vision who, at a time when the Air Force was still the baby of the armed services, risked their careers to further the cause of racial equality.

The strongest impetus for the proposed changes came that summer from the Commander in Chief. On 26 July 1948 President Truman signed Executive Order 9981, calling on the armed forces to provide equal treatment and opportunity for black servicemen. I do not understand fully, even today, the series of events that led to the signing of this order. The President's Committee on Civil Rights, established in January 1947, had recommended integration of the armed forces, but Truman had not taken any steps in that direction. On the other hand, he needed every vote he could get to win the 1948 election, and by signing the order he was certainly trying to appeal to black voters. The military services had also independently recognized the manpower inefficiences of their segregated system, and integration would have come to the armed forces at some time, probably much later, if the services had been left to their individual courses. Among these imponderables, one overriding fact stands out: once the executive order had been signed, the Air Force integrated blacks throughout its structure in a highly effective and efficient manner.

Late in December 1948 I was vacationing in the Caribbean with Agatha when I received a message directing me to report to Washington to work on the integration problem. There I had discussions with Jack Marr and the Assistant Secretary of the Air Force, Eugene Zuchert. Jack reviewed the progress he had made since I last saw him and brought me up to date on Air Force plans for integration. Things were happening that could not have been foreseen even a short time earlier. The Marr study became the basis for the integration plan submitted by the Air Force to the Secretary of Defense in January 1949.

On 23 February 1949 I wrote to my father, "I am fairly certain the new Air Force policy (desegregation) is bogged down in politics, but I feel budget problems will force it into the open before 1 July." In April the *Army Navy Journal* reported that the President's Committee for Equality of Opportunity and Treatment in the Armed Forces, chaired by Charles Fahy, had heard plans to abolish segregation in the Air Force and reassign black airmen on an Air Force–wide basis. As I had guessed, the Air Force was anxious to inaugurate desegregation for budgetary reasons. The article reported that the 332d Fighter Wing and Lockbourne Air Force Base were to be deactivated, and I was to be reassigned to the Air War College in August. On 19 April I again wrote to my father: "I have my orders to the Air War College, but other changes for Lockbourne will be delayed until Congress adjourns, so that Air Force actions will not have an adverse effect on certain Dixiecrat congressmen."

On 11 May 1949 the Air Force made a momentous announcement in Air Force Letter 35-3: "It is the policy of the United States Air Force that there shall be equality of treatment and opportunity for all persons in the Air Force without regard to race, color, religion, or national origin." Integration was planned in two phases: the reassignment of black personnel throughout the Air Force worldwide, and concurrent changes in the remaining all-black units. As base commander and someone who was trusted to make impartial decisions, I was appointed president of a screening board, which met at Lockbourne on 17 May to review the qualifications of Lockbourne officers and airmen for reassignment. As General Edwards had stated, "skilled and qualified individuals" were to be assigned to white units "just like any other officer or airmen of similar skills and qualifications."

Many blacks at Lockbourne were angered by the mere existence of screening boards, and I sympathized with them. Considering the far greater good of discontinuing the existing system and integrating, however, I thought the critical initial stages of the program warranted caution. Basically, the Pentagon's idea was to carefully observe the effects of the Lockbourne reassignment action first and then proceed with similar actions in other commands. The screening board concept was weak in that the Air Force wanted the board to recommend reassignment to white units only when the individual was "first, of such temperament, judgment, and common sense that he can get along smoothly . . . in a white unit, and secondly, that his ability is such as to warrant respect of personnel of the unit to which he is transferred." These stipulations emphasized personality over qualifications. General Edwards and I agreed, however, that this vitally important and revolutionary change should not be jeopardized by incidents that could flair up between mutually hostile whites and blacks.

The second phase of integration dealt with the continued existence of some black Air Force units. No strength quotas would be observed for minority groups, and "qualified Negro personnel" could be assigned to fill "any position vacancy in any Air Force organization . . . without regard to race." Finally, the Air Force placed full responsibility for implementation of its new personnel policies on its commanders. As I would discover, my new station, Maxwell Air Force Base, near Montgomery, Alabama, was guilty of some of the worst foot-dragging.

## The Fahy Committee's Report

The Fahy Committee reported progress toward the implementation of Executive Order 9981 to President Truman on 22 May 1950. Although the committee was deeply interested in justice for blacks, its overriding interests were the making of a better armed service and the development of increased military efficiency. When I worked with the committee's permanent staff, I was impressed with the practical approaches they took toward tremendously complicated problems. At Lockbourne, I was concerned mainly with implementing changes, and my problems were simple compared to those they addressed. Aware that the military services were old institutions with long-established customs and habits, the committee conferred with the services frequently while conducting its study. By taking a sympathetic approach, it convinced senior officers that the proposed reforms were sound in principle and, when initiated, would improve military efficiency.

Committee discussions delved deeply into philosophical questions. Because of differences in skills and education in black units, some people believed they could not perform the complete range of functions required of white units or provide the same opportunity for building diverse individual skills. Yet segregation required that highly qualified blacks be assigned to black units where there might be no use for their skills. Thus segregation not only deprived blacks of the opportunity to practice their skills, it also deprived the services of black talent. In spite of these factors, many senior service leaders persisted in believing it was preferable to suffer the loss of individual black talent than to face up to the problems of mixed units.

The Fahy Committee was highly energetic and thorough. It heard testimony from each service; visited many Army posts, Navy ships and stations, and Air Force bases; and held more than 40 formal committee meetings. Its report to President Truman described the state of implementation of the executive order in each service.

The Army's policy changes had yet to be implemented in May 1950. On 30 September 1949 the Army had directed that all its jobs and school courses be opened to blacks. In January 1950 three additional changes were made: blacks would be assigned to any Army unit according to their qualifications, and not just to black units; blacks in mixed units would be integrated on the job, in barracks, and in messes; and the 10-percent limit on black strength and enlistment quotas would be eliminated.

When the executive order was first issued, the Navy argued that blacks were not as adaptable or efficient as whites and hence should not be assigned to the general service. The Navy senior staff also believed integration on shipboard was not feasible. They used the usual kind of excuses: a lower level of skills among blacks and a consequent loss of efficiency and morale on board ship. But experience showed that blacks could be trained and deployed in as wide a range of skills as whites and that failure to use them resulted in manpower waste that neither the Navy nor the United States could afford. After a short trial period, the Navy became proud of its black manpower and integrated ship efficiency. In five years, it moved from a policy of complete exclusion of blacks from its general service to complete integration, opening all jobs and ratings in the naval general service to all enlisted men. It also opened all courses in all Navy technical schools to qualified people without regard to race or color, and without racial quotas. Blacks were already attending most advanced technical schools and serving in their ratings in the fleet and ashore. The committee's sole suggestion in 1950 was to increase the number of blacks in the general service (then only 2 percent) and the number of black officers throughout the Navy (then only 17, including two Waves).

Except for the 99th Fighter Squadron, the 332d Fighter Group, and the 477th Bombardment Group, the Air Force had used blacks only in service capacities and heavy-duty work: air cargo resupply, military police, ammunition companies, air base security battalions, and medical detachments. In 1945 8 percent of the Air Force was black— 140,000 men and women. At that time, many senior Air Force officers realized that segregation deprived the Air Force of skilled workers. I had more navigators than I could use at Lockbourne, but even though the Strategic Air Command needed navigators, the rules of segregation prohibited them from finding jobs in SAC. For white units, ability was the sole criterion for job qualification; in black units, there was an additional requirement—color. If a black officer or specialist were not available, a second- or third-rater had to be used or the position left vacant.

The Air Force recognized the problem in 1945, but it did not realize until later that the solution was to abandon its segregation policy. At the time of the blanket policy change of May 1949, almost all Air Force commanders preferred segregation and feared that the new policy would have dire results. In less than six months, however, they reported to the Chief of Staff that their fears had not been borne out. Only a short time after integration they recognized that many of the Air Force's earlier problems and troubles had been eliminated.

The Fahy Committee report showed that Air Force implementation had progressed further and more rapidly than that of any of the other services. In May 1949 the 332d Fighter Wing comprised about 75 percent of all the blacks in the Air Force. After the 332d was inactivated on 30 June 1949, all of Lockbourne's people were integrated into the Air Force worldwide, some to bases in the continental United States, some overseas, depending on their specialties and Air Force manpower requirements. Lockbourne Air Force Base was then closed. Black personnel began to serve in previously white units in their military specialties, or to attend technical schools in specialties that in some cases had previously been reserved for whites. All Air Force jobs and schools had been immediately opened to all qualified people without restriction or quotas. At the time of the committee's report, 74 percent of the 25,000 blacks in the Air Force were serving in integrated units; 26 percent still served in black units.

The Fahy Committee arrived at conclusions that were surprising and educational to its readers in 1950, but which are universally accepted today. The most important findings were that the range of abilities of black servicemen was much wider than the services believed prior to the opening of all jobs to blacks; that with sufficiently high enlistment standards, many blacks would be able to compete with whites; that the potential skills of blacks were wasted under segregation because black units probably would be unable to use all the available skills of their members; and that neither the services nor

the United States could afford to continue losing the services of
skilled blacks under a segregated system. Perhaps most significant of
all, enlisted men were far more willing to accept the integration than
senior generals had believed, and the integration of blacks and whites
at work, in school, and in living quarters did not present the insurmountable difficulties that had been predicted.

To almost everyone's surprise, but not mine, the integration of
blacks in the Air Force soon began to take on a life of its own. I knew
the high standards and performance of the Lockbourne people; I was
positive that after the initial shock of reassigning blacks to white
units, they would be recognized as important assets. That is exactly
the way it turned out. The large number of black units in the Air
Force—more than 100 in June 1949—was reduced to nine by the
end of December 1950. By that time, 95 percent of the black airmen
in the Air Force were serving in integrated units. Shortly thereafter,
all black units had disappeared. In law, if not in spirit, integration had
been achieved.

These policy changes in the Air Force placed it far out in front of
existing social relationships in the United States. They were implemented in spite of the strongly voiced objections and misgivings of
senior generals. Prior to and in the initial phases of implementation,
there were two major hurdles: the widespread belief that blacks did
not possess adequate skills and technical qualifications for the full
range of military jobs, and the force of the custom of utilizing blacks
only in black units. Finally, there was the deep fear that moving
ahead of the nation's practices in racial relationships would almost
certainly adversely affect morale and efficiency.

Considering how firmly ingrained these attitudes were in the national and the military consciousness, the integration of the U.S. Air
Force amounted to an act of faith in the people who made up this
great military service. I found myself in the middle of some critical
situations during my military career, some of which involved national
security, but none of them approached the magnitude of the problem
confronted by the Air Force in the late 1940s. The other services took
years to comply with the President's executive order. The Air Force
acted in 1949.

Without a doubt, the wartime performance of the black fighter
units I had commanded and the success of Lockbourne Air Force
Base both influenced the Air Force's decision to integrate. Although

President Truman may have issued his order for political reasons more than for any abiding concern for the welfare of blacks, and although Secretary Symington and General Spaatz may have been deeply convinced of the moral rightness of the new policy, they could not have supported its immediate and forthright implementation without the backdrop of the 332d Fighter Group's record in the war. It became my fixed belief that the Air Force had led the way in integratating the armed forces because of the basic professionalism in air operations that had been demonstrated by black units during World War II, moving the cause of integration forward to a much earlier date than could have been achieved otherwise. Similarly, at Lockbourne we proved that blacks possessed administrative abilities never before recognized—abilities that still go widely unacknowledged today.

Most people now agree that the Air Force became a far more effective organization as a result of integration. For the first time, it was able to train, assign, and deploy its black manpower with complete flexibility. Had we achieved utopia? Hardly. Most whites in the Air Force had grown up with segregation and had never even known any black people; racist attitudes were far from extinguished. The Air Force's new policy was a first and important step, but it would take many years before it was fully implemented throughout the armed services. And even today a wide gap continues to exist between the ideals of integration and the realities of daily life in the armed services and in American society at large.

# ★ ★ ★ Indoctrination

**8.** *Before the Air War College, I had never had the chance to associate with my white peers—not at the University of Chicago, not at West Point, and not during World War II in North Africa, Sicily, or Italy.*

Cars were extremely hard to come by after the war, and Agatha and I were lucky to get one of the first postwar models, the 1947 Studebaker, known primarily for its compact beauty and the confusion its design created: where was the front of the car, and hence, which way was it headed? When we left Lockbourne, we drove to visit relatives in Washington, New York, and New Haven. My father and mother were always glad to see us, and they filled us full of good food during our stay.

Keeping himself busy writing the strong views he held about his life in the Army and as a black citizen of the United States, my father particularly resented the favorable treatment white Americans reserved for black foreigners visiting the United States, compared with the treatment the same white Americans accorded American blacks. I had always admired his sense of humor and his ability to deal calmly with such unpleasant subjects as segregation without getting incensed. He often illustrated a point he was making with something he had personally experienced. I was in my late thirties at this time, and I appreciated my parents' accomplishments more than ever.

My father kept a diary and made entries every day, probably with the idea of writing the story of his life when he retired from the Army. He realized that his retirement would in all likelihood be the end of his working days, because there were so few decent jobs for blacks. He did start writing after he retired but apparently became discouraged and gave it up, hoping that I or someone else would finish the book. Marvin Fletcher, professor of history at the University of Ohio, completed the biography, and it was published by the University Press of Kansas in 1989 as *America's First Black General.*

As always, we enjoyed our reunion with Agatha's sisters, brother, and parents. Her father, Herman A. Scott, had owned and operated a successful dyeing and cleaning business in New Haven for many years. Scott's Dyers and Cleaners was well known in the city and all the nearby towns and suburbs; it had been one of the first businesses in New Haven to operate a motor delivery truck. Mr. Scott had survived the Great Depression—no small accomplishment. Agatha's mother, a beautiful woman, had grown up in Savannah, Georgia, moved to New York, and met Mr. Scott at a dance in Hartford. They married shortly thereafter and lived happily in New Haven until Mr. Scott's death in 1968. Mrs. Scott was the life of any gathering she attended, a true matriarch. Over the decades I knew her, I never saw her angry or displeased, nor did she ever say or do anything inconsiderate. I always thought Mr. Scott was the boss, but Agatha says it was her mother, which tells a story in itself.

## Life at Maxwell

After leaving Lockbourne, Agatha and I both felt that a phase of our lives was over. We had enjoyed the comforts of Lockbourne, yet while we had lived in comfortable surroundings and associated with friendly people, the cloud of segregation, with all its demeaning features, had always remained in the background. At this point—August 1949—we were putting legal military segregation behind us, and our day-to-day lives would certainly be better for it. For the first time since I had started my career in the military, we would be protected, to a degree, by the Air Force policy mandating equality of treatment and opportunity for all its people. We were not naive, however. We well understood that the attitudes of white Air Force people toward us would continue to be the attitudes they had learned as children and nurtured throughout their lives in the vast segregated structure of the United States, maintained through more than two centuries of government-supported racism. Nevertheless, we were proud of the contributions we had made that had accelerated the Air Force toward its improved personnel policies. We were eager to put the past behind us and embark upon a future that was certain to be a great improvement over our previous 13 years in the military.

As we drove into the Deep South from Washington, Agatha's thoughts and mine drifted back to the woundings we had received at Fort Benning, and even further back, to the slights and downright hatred I had experienced at West Point. We did not seek out these thoughts; they forced themselves on us the moment we left Washington for Maxwell Air Force Base. On the way, we had no rest-room accommodations and no place but the car to spend the night until we arrived at the home of our old friends, Apple and Lottie Waddell, at Tuskegee Institute. We also knew we were returning to the heart of the Confederacy. The Air Force was introducing integration throughout the United States, wherever it had military installations. In practically all cases, the civilian population at and near these bases responded adversely to the example being set by the military. Fortunately, Agatha is a strong person with a sense of self-worth that had carried her through the racial insults blacks had learned to expect just about anywhere in the United States. She always held her head high and invariably made it a point to return in kind the treatment she received.

As Agatha and I approached Montgomery on the last leg of our trip to Maxwell, we discussed the education Air Force integration was giving white Air Force members by placing blacks in Air Force units, schools, barracks, dining halls, and recreational facilities. We realized that few whites in the Air Force had in any substantial way previously associated with blacks. We knew that most whites viewed blacks as inferiors and not as equals with the same qualities, talents, faults, preferences, and dislikes that they themselves possessed. In putting itself socially so far out in front of the rest of the nation's institutions, the Air Force had created a new way of life for itself and all its members—white and black. We entered that new life when we were waved through the Maxwell Air Force Base gate.

It was a distinct honor to be selected as a student at the Air War

College. Attendance at Air Force schools constituted recognition that the student was being prepared for promotion to top positions in the service. I was determined to justify the Air Force's decision to send me there. Gen. George Kenny, Gen. Douglas MacArthur's airman during the Pacific war, commanded the Air University, a major command including the Air War College and the Air Command and Staff College at Maxwell, and the Air Tactical School at Tyndall Air Force Base, Florida. Most Air Force officers were not selected to attend Air University schools, and those who were certainly benefited. Some Air Force officers attended the schools of other services; a few, particularly in the early years of the Air Force, moved successively from one assignment to another without formal schooling. Among the advantages of attending Air University schools was the opportunity to learn from the experience of others and to associate for several months with men whom one would be certain to encounter officially in future assignments. Attendance was an asset to each officer's career and increased the likelihood that he would be considered for later promotions.

When Agatha and I arrived at Maxwell, we moved into students' quarters, within walking distance of the Air War College building and the flight line. In those years, Air War College students maintained flying proficiency locally or on weekend cross-country flights to various Air Force bases in C-45s, C-47s, B-25s, or B-26s. We were authorized to take off Friday afternoon and required to be back in class on Monday morning.

In the few days before school started, we spent most of the time rehabilitating our quarters. Because I was the only black officer stationed at Maxwell, we were curious about how we would be received. Our neighbors welcomed us cordially, and a few of them invited us to their quarters shortly after we arrived. Not until the first get-acquainted cocktail party for our class were we made to feel uncomfortable. When we walked into the gathering, which was held at the previously segregated officers' club, we were stared at like monkeys in a cage. Scott Hall, who had been at West Point during my stay there, brought his wife, Ann, over to greet us, which made it all right for some of the other guests to relax and welcome us as they had welcomed other newcomers.

For years after integration became part of Air Force life, we remained "the only ones." Agatha and I had always believed that to make friends, one has to meet the other person half way. Fortunately, our parents had taught us to be outgoing, and neither of us had any trouble meeting people and developing friendly relationships as long as we stayed within the military environment. Outside that environment, it was a different story. At Maxwell, we had no social life of any kind off base, and Montgomery was like a foreign country.

## The Air War College

The mission of the Air War College aimed directly at the individual student. In brief, that mission was to increase the scope and breadth of the student's thinking and to contribute to his understanding of problem solving. All the instruction and exercises were designed to develop a capacity to solve problems with facility, clarity of thought, and competence. At the same time, the student was to learn to recognize, appraise, and reject dogmatic military authority and be prepared to present his ideas in an effective manner.

During the 10 months of instruction we were appraised by our colleagues and compared with our fellow students on the bases of breadth and scope of thinking, critical ability, projection of ideas, competency in problem solving, and overall leadership. Seminar advisers also evaluated each student to determine his potential for various high command and staff assignments, and, equally important, to measure the effectiveness of the Air War College in meeting its educational objectives.

My class included officers from the Air Force, Army, Navy, Marine Corps, Royal Air Force, and Royal Canadian Air Force. The course encompassed academic, military science, and planning phases. Morning lectures were followed by question-and-answer periods for the rest of the morning and seminar meetings during the afternoon. Each student was required to write a term paper on a subject of his own choosing. I chose manpower utilization because I thought it would be of critical importance in any future war. In those days, Strategic Air Command planners were advocating the concept of a massive nuclear strike or "short war," but I did not believe in it to the exclusion of conventional warfare. I believed strongly that the use of the bomb against Japan in August 1945 had been necessary, but that our nuclear superiority over the Soviet Union was sure to be short-lived and we had to prepare ourselves for other eventualities. Consequently, my paper stressed the importance of full manpower utilization, a need that was clearly demonstrated in Vietnam in the 1960s after we had ruled out the use of nuclear weapons. In 1986, during a visit to Maxwell, I took another look at the paper, but I was not very impressed. It no longer seemed persuasive, and I was bothered by its tone of theoretical smugness.

The student appraisal forms that we received at the end of the year, however, were complimentary to me without exception. One read, "A reasonable, logical, constructive, serious, and dependable officer, articulate to a very high degree. His cooperation and intelligent participation in the discussion of the group left small room for improvement. His sense of responsibility and of proportion were excellent, as was his basic reasoning. His contribution to the solution of the seminar problem was of material value." Another, "An impressive officer with a calm, pleasing manner which commands the respect of all who know him. He is sincere, frank, natural." And another, "A thoroughly cooperative and productive officer. Polite, considerate, and congenial. . . . A gentleman in all respects." I was bowled over by these and many other similar appraisals. The forms were not signed, indicating that they expressed sincere beliefs; and, unlike some of the effectiveness reports I had received in the past, none said that I was capable for a Negro officer and well suited for duty with black troop units or civilian components.

The Air War College had all sorts of favorable features that made the 10 months I spent at Maxwell among the best I spent in the service. Dozens of lecturers, all authoritative in their areas of expertise, came to speak to us: Hon. George McGhee, Walter Lippmann, Hon. William C. Bullitt, Gen. Curtis LeMay, Maj. A. P. Seversky, Margaret Mead, Mark Ethridge, Hon. Robert P. Patterson, Walter Reuther, Charles Thayer, Hon. Thomas K. Finletter, Adm. Forrest Sherman, Gen. Alfred Gruenther, Gen. Lyman Lemnitzer, Gen. Hoyt Vandenberg, Gen. Lucius Clay, and many others. Just being in attendance was a rare privilege. Gen. Orville Anderson, commandant of the Air War College, frequently took the platform and expounded predictably on his own concept for effective use of U.S. forces in war.

Each seminar met socially at least once, a custom that made us feel more a part of the student body. Agatha volunteered to work in the thrift shop and enjoyed her association with the others working there, wives of base people and students. I enjoyed playing golf with my seminar classmates and bowling once a week with the seminar team. We also exchanged dinners and cocktail parties with people in the class. In general, the treatment accorded us during our 10 months at Maxwell was similar in almost every respect to the treatment we received during our next 20 years of military assignments. People were friendly for the most part, but we also experienced small, petty actions by small, petty people. Before leaving Lockbourne, Agatha bought a new Singer sewing machine in Columbus. The price of the machine included sewing lessons for the making of one dress. She also purchased a dress form that was not right and had to be returned. When Agatha learned we were being transferred to Maxwell, she obtained a letter from the Columbus store to the Singer store in Montgomery requesting them to provide the lessons and another dress form to fit her figure. The Montgomery store complied cordially in every respect and even agreed to deliver the dress form to our quarters. When I opened the door and the delivery man saw me, however, he dropped the form on the porch, turned on his heel, and without a single word hurried to his car.

This kind of treatment of blacks by whites was the norm in Alabama in 1949. What a difference 40 years have made! I witnessed the difference when I attended the Gathering of Eagles at Maxwell in 1986. Many of the social events connected with this meeting were held in Montgomery, and the welcome given the Eagles was warm and completely consistent with the South's well-justified reputation for hospitality. Montgomery's leading citizens participated actively. On a visit to Huntsville in 1987 to be inducted into the Alabama Aviation Hall of Fame, I enjoyed the same kind of welcome.

Back in 1949, President Truman's executive order eliminating segregation in the armed forces created problems for Col. Leslie Mulzer, Maxwell's base commander, and the citizens of Alabama. The *Montgomery Advertiser* editorialized that the order was the act of a dunce and was "rendering the nation's military bases laboratories for social experiments." The Alabama House of Representatives requested that President Truman not enforce military integration in states with segregation laws. Without serious incident, Colonel Mulzer enforced Air Force directives at Maxwell's swimming pools and airmen's club. At Maxwell, as at other Air Force bases, legal, proper, and reasonable actions by commanders appeared to solve most problems in enforcing the new regulations. With its new concepts of equal opportunity and treatment, Maxwell Air Force Base set an example for the surrounding community and the whole state. Alabama chose to look upon that example with disdain, but in time it enthusiastically adopted these principles as its own.

Air Force integration progressed more slowly at some bases than at others, and in some respects Maxwell definitely lagged behind. This was not surprising, considering the powerful conservative forces in Alabama. In *The Air Force Integrates*, Alan Gropman describes visits made to seven Air Force bases in late 1949 and early 1950 by E. W. Kenworthy, executive secretary of the Fahy Committee, and Jack Marr. Kenworthy reported that about two-thirds of blacks on the bases he inspected lived in integrated conditions, with the remainder in service units. In all their travels, Kenworthy and Marr found only one all-black service unit—at Maxwell Air Force Base.

During our year at Maxwell, we drove to Tuskegee Institute to see old friends from pre–World War II days. We found little change from the Tuskegee Institute we had known. The changes were to come much later, after the violence that accompanied the civil rights demonstrations of the 1960s and subsequent actions by Congress mandating open public accommodations and voting rights for minorities. Since then, Tuskegee Institute has had better relations with the people of Alabama, and it is no longer shut off from the surrounding community.

Just before graduation from the Air War College, the class made a field trip to Norfolk Naval Air Station. We boarded a carrier, the *Philippine Sea*, from a submarine for a three-day indoctrination cruise aboard ships of a fast-carrier task force. The boarding was more exciting than I would have chosen it to be. Because of heavy seas, the Navy thought it was too dangerous to transfer us to the carrier by helicopter, and so they decided to use a breeches buoy—a sort of canvas seat used to haul people from one ship to another. Both the carrier and the submarine were under way with what I considered to be a lot of speed, perhaps 40 knots—surely enough to dunk me into the Atlantic and cause me to swallow more seawater than I needed or wanted!

I learned a great deal at the Air War College. Agatha uses the word "indoctrinated," and I have come to agree with her judgment. In retrospect, it does seem that the ideas and attitudes that the Air Force widely accepted and expressed about the Soviet Union were extreme and not justified on the basis of fact. The United States was riding high, with most citizens sharing a strong belief in our complete military superiority and an equally strong feeling that we were in the right and they were in the wrong. I recall the authoritarian manner in which I later parroted some of the concepts we had accepted at the Air War College. I preached this anticommunist doctrine for several years after I left the War College, and I remember how my father often applied his steady logic and sense of perspective to some of my dogmatic statements.

All of us at Maxwell were looking forward to the new assignments we would have after graduation. My orders were to report to the Pentagon as a staff planning officer within the Directorate of Operations, U.S. Air Force. I was not entirely happy when I learned of this assignment. Many classmates also received orders for the Pentagon, and most of them were disappointed because they wanted a command assignment. I was disappointed too, but mainly because Agatha and I would have to live in segregated Washington, with its housing problems and the other difficulties of day-to-day living that accompanied segregation. On the other hand, I realized that the assignment was a necessary step toward career advancement, and for that reason, it could not be all bad.

## A Western Holiday

As soon as Agatha and I learned that I had been assigned to the Pentagon, we started making plans to use our month's leave for a long trip across the western United States. Gen. Hoyt Vandenberg, Chief of Staff of the Air Force, spoke at the graduation ceremony on 16 June 1950, and we left early the next morning. Agatha is a great tourist; she has an insatiable curiosity about people and places. Our upbringing had emphasized the greatness of our country, and we were eager to see the vast areas west of the Mississippi, which we had not visited previously and knew almost nothing about.

Along the way, we reviewed our 10 months at Maxwell. We had not permitted Alabama's racial attitudes to bother us. These attitudes were not new to us, and I suppose we looked down our noses at what we deemed the stupidity of local people in the treatment they routinely accorded a large portion of the state's population. Perhaps our feeling toward some of the whites of Montgomery was similar to the feeling some city people might have toward so-called redneck country people when they encounter them for the first time. We felt no animosity toward anyone—certainly not toward our military associates—and we looked back with pleasure upon the various forms of learning we had experienced. I was grateful for the intellectual rigor of my classes and the chance to associate with my contemporaries. Several of my War College classmates had been at West Point when I was a cadet. At Maxwell they were as pleasant as any of the other students—apparently the shepherd had spoken, and the sheep had fallen into line. This situation was completely new to me; I had never had the chance to associate with my white peers before—not at the University of Chicago, not at West Point, and not during World War II in North Africa, Sicily, or Italy. Before Maxwell we had always been kept at arms' length and not permitted to join in the normal associations one would expect to have with one's military comrades.

The interstate highway system did not exist in June 1950, and we traveled at our own pace along roads that seemed to promise interesting sights. The interstate is safer, and one can make better time, but it does not offer the same view of the countryside. While we drank in all the wealth of beauty we saw, our thoughts during the first half of the trip dwelled almost exclusively on what we imagined as the wonderland of the West: California. It did not disappoint us, and the state's beauty was reflected in the spirit and warmth of its people.

We had some trouble finding a place to stay when we first arrived in Los Angeles. Unlike today, we traveled without a set itinerary or reservations, and the American Legion had taken over the city. After lots of looking, we found ourselves at a late hour in Glendale, where a kind Jewish lady recognized us as responsible citizens and rented us a comfortable room in her motel. We had a good time in Los Angeles. Some people we had known in other places lived there, including members of my fighter units in World War II. In general, we found the residents of Los Angeles to be warm and hospitable, and in some respects it was this visit that led Agatha to stay there while I did an unaccompanied tour in Korea in 1953–54.

We were in Los Angeles on 25 June when the North Koreans invaded South Korea. Despite my recent studies, I did not know much about Korea or Southeast Asia in general. I had served in the

European theater, and the European perspective was deeply embed-
ded in my attitudes and thinking. At the War College, my anti-Soviet
indoctrination had been emphasized to an extent that I immediately
recognized a threat to our world posture in the North Koreans' adventure. The United States was no longer the only nuclear power in
the world. The Soviet Union had exploded a nuclear device just a few
months earlier, and its friendly relationship with North Korea could
not be ignored.

I was proud of the alacrity of the U.S. military's response to the
North Korean attack. Far East Air Force (FEAF) Headquarters was
notified by Seoul shortly after the invasion started at 4:00 A.M., 25
June. By 6:00 A.M., Republic of Korea forces had engaged North
Korean forces along the border. FEAF Headquarters and all units and
bases had been alerted, and pertinent information had been passed to
Air Force Headquarters. By 27 June diplomatic red tape had been cut,
and the Navy and the Air Force had been ordered to aid the Republic
of Korea in repelling the invaders. By 28 June the B-29s of the 20th
Air Force had flown their first bombing mission against the enemy,
and by 29 June air attacks north of the 38th parallel had been authorized. These latter actions necessarily had to await the United Nations
Security Council action on 26 June, ordering a cease-fire in Korea
and calling on all United Nations members to support the Republic of
Korea and to withhold support from North Korea; and its action on
27 June, recommending that United Nations members "furnish such
assistance to the Republic of Korea as may be necessary to repel the
armed attack and restore international peace and security in the
area." As historians have often observed, these actions would have
been most difficult to achieve had the Soviet Union been present at
the critical Security Council meetings dealing with these matters.

The military response was fast under the encumbrances of the
existing international arrangements, but imagine how much better it
would have been if FEAF fighter units had been stationed in Korea
and if FEAF had been responsible for the air defense of the Korean
peninsula. In this much-improved scenario, the North Korean attack,
with the free daylight ride for its logistics movements along the roads
through the 38th parallel, might never have taken place. Instead,
with FEAF fighters stationed in Japan, the North Koreans were confident that their forces would be able to move easily into South Korea
and not be subject to air attacks. As matters stood, FEAF's sole mis-

sion with respect to Korea was to evacuate American nationals upon the request of the American ambassador. FEAF performed this mission, taking the necessary precautions to provide suitable air cover for the operation on 27 June.

The United States had tipped its hand in a 12 January 1950 speech by Secretary of State Dean Acheson, in which he outlined the defensive position of the United States in the Aleutians, Japan, the Ryukyus, and the Philippines. The inescapable conclusion was that the United States did not intend to defend Korea or Taiwan. Subsequent events proved the validity of this conclusion. The scenario followed after the invasion was in every respect the one described in Secretary Acheson's speech. The South Koreans defended themselves at first, and the United Nations joined later in the defense of the country.

I began to feel uncomfortable about being in Los Angeles on leave while there was a war being fought in the Pacific. I had been taught to ride to the sound of the guns, and I began to wonder who was carrying out my responsibilities while I was enjoying the pleasures of California. My discomfort grew as the days passed and newspapers told of the occupation of Seoul and other enemy successes. Agatha had always been a duty-first wife, and I had no difficulty convincing her that I should cut short my leave, curtail our planned drive north, and instead turn hard right and head in a more direct route toward Washington. In those days it took almost 10 days to drive across the country. I had been ordered to report to the Pentagon on 19 July, and I calculated that it would be easy to report a week early and pick up some of the heavy load that I expected was accumulating on my desk because of the war. Our rate of movement toward Washington was limited only by our ability to drive at a reasonable pace. We recharted our course, cutting out a planned stay in San Francisco.

Our decision to eliminate San Francisco grew out of the only really unpleasant incident we had experienced during the hundreds of miles we had covered since leaving Maxwell. We stopped at a place in northern California that advertised tourist accommodations with a large sign indicating vacancies. Agatha went into the office while I assembled our baggage. She asked to see one of the rooms, and the desk clerk was in the process of reaching for the key when I appeared in the door. Rather abruptly, but still rather smoothly, he announced that he had no vacancy. Obviously, he had taken Agatha for a Caucasian, and when in doubt a white bigot will not risk insulting another white person. Agatha gave the man a piece of her mind. We had not expected to find this kind of overt racism in supposedly liberal northern California. In a sense, we felt sorry for the poor man; perhaps what he had done made him feel more secure and important. Nevertheless, after Agatha had thoroughly berated him, we departed with a very sour taste in our mouths.

This kind of blatant discrimination was far from new in my life. It was usually much subtler, but it had always been present in one form or another. I had learned never, under any circumstances, to let my actions give any satisfaction to the enemy, and though we remember this incident almost 40 years after it happened, we did not permit it to ruin our trip. Had we done so, we would have led most unhappy lives indeed, because it was not an isolated incident.

I forget where we stayed that night. We were so mad we may have slept in the car. Psychologically, we were certainly ready to leave California and head east. After a brief tour of Montana and Wyoming, we drove back across the Midwest. The closer we got to Washington, the more we began to wonder what awaited us.

My parents greeted us warmly and welcomed us to Washington. Right away, however, we were faced with housing problems. There were plenty of houses and apartments in the area, but we and more than one knowledgeable real estate agent failed to turn up any that were both suitable and available to blacks. Mayfair Mansions, a new development in far northeast Washington, was the only apartment building we saw that we considered suitable. It had been built by Elder Michaux, a minister of local radio fame, to provide good housing for blacks. All the other housing available to us was old, smelly, and generally undesirable. In 1950 Washington's blacks were not socially mobile; those who had good housing stayed in it, and restrictive covenants prevented newcomers from moving into areas occupied by whites. It was easy for us to understand why Mayfair Mansions was full and had a long waiting list. This severe shortage of good housing for blacks in Washington continued far into the 1960s.

We finally got a one-bedroom apartment in Mayfair Mansions. After a few weeks, we were even able to obtain a three-bedroom apartment on Kenilworth Terrace, also in Mayfair Mansions. We liked this apartment and considered ourselves fortunate to live there. Today, the police and the Muslims actively fight drug racketeers for possession of the entire neighborhood.

## A Stint at the Pentagon

I reported early to the Pentagon, only to find that it had been a mistake to cut short my leave. For weeks I had nothing to do but fly the desk. I read all the papers that passed over that desk, and I probably learned something about Pentagon organization and routine. But I made no decisions worthy of my rank and experience. I was not alone; my desk was in a large, open room occupied by perhaps 20 officers and some secretaries—the Command Division of the Directorate of Operations. If the Command Division did anything, I would have been hard put to say what it was. I do not think I had a job description; my main activity was reading the rather small amount of correspondence that came to my desk, and I wrote a few minor messages and some internal correspondence within the Air Staff.

I was somewhat overwhelmed by the size of the Pentagon, though it was true that in five minutes one could walk anywhere in the building. I was more than somewhat overwhelmed by the complexity of Pentagon activity. I understood how the Pentagon operated from the large point of view, but trying to relate my particular role to that larger context confused me considerably during the early months of my assignment. I became acquainted with the people seated in my vicinity, and I tried to keep current with the details of events in Korea. The apparent lack of action by the Directorate of Operations in supporting the Korean War mystified me. Later, I learned that the important decisions were being made by General MacArthur in Tokyo, the Joint Chiefs, and senior visitors to the Far East, who reported their findings and recommendations directly to the Chief of Staff in messages that were not circulated at my level. Consequently, I had no way of knowing who was running the war and how it was being run. I read with deep concern of the daily disasters that our forces were experiencing. The war summaries told of the shrinking of the part of Korea controlled by the United Nations and the threat that we would be pushed off the Korean peninsula completely.

On the bright side, I read of the development of an effective joint operation by Gen. Earle Partridge, commander of the 5th Air Force, and Gen. Walton Walker, commander of the 8th Army. General Partridge was acknowledged as the first individual in the theater to recognize the importance of close air-support procedures and to take steps to implement them. I read of the close relationship between Gen. George Stratemeyer, the commander of FEAF, and General MacArthur. I watched from my desk as B-29 groups left the United States and, within days of their arrival in FEAF, participated in an interdiction campaign that destroyed the Korean bridges, rail traffic, and roads that had permitted the North Korean army to move so rapidly to the south. Later, when that army controlled all except a small corner of Korea's southern tip, I saw the surprising but highly effective use of B-29s in direct support of our frontline forces.

The coordinated Army–Air Force operation was right out of the book—Field Manual 31-35, *Joint Air Ground Operations*. Field Manual 31-35 had been jointly developed in North Africa during the critical days shortly after the invasion in 1942. It delineated a system perfected by the British in their campaign in the desert and later used so effectively by Gens. Elwood Quesada and Courtney Hodges in France and Gens. Otto Weyland and George Patton, Jr., in Germany. General Partridge and General Timberlake, his vice commander, had studied and exercised the provisions of FM 31-35 in a Far East Command exercise as recently as April 1950, so its principles were no mystery to them. Under General Timberlake's direction and with indispensable Army participation, the 5th Air Force quickly established the urgently required Joint Operations Center. The development of an effective operation was hindered by the complexity of coordinating the Navy and the Bomber Command, the fast-moving tactical situation, severe communications problems, and some interservice distrust. More than one problem had to be taken to Gen. Edward Almond, MacArthur's Chief of Staff, and some of the problems went even to General MacArthur for resolution. MacArthur, of course, got the truly knotty problems to solve, usually critical combat utilization problems involving his Army, Navy, and Air Force component commanders. The history of the Korean War shows the wisdom and soundness of his decisions.

My understanding of the Pentagon and the running of the war gradually improved. It turned out that I was correct about the inadequacies of the Command Division, which was eliminated and replaced by a new division, Operations and Commitments. Concurrently, the Directorate of Operations was completely reorganized and moved to the sub-subbasement of the Pentagon. As I look back upon these first days, weeks, and months in the Pentagon, it seems obvious to me that this reorganization was dictated by the Korean War and the imperative need for the Air Staff to adjust itself to the deeply wrenching effects the war was having on the Air Force as a whole. Support for the war was a new requirement that had to be accommodated along with all the other important Air Force responsibilities that did not disappear. The reorganization enabled the Directorate of Operations to keep abreast of the war and, more importantly, to organize itself so that it could actively support FEAF's mission and simultaneously monitor the actions of other Air Staff agencies in support of the war. Under the reorganization, the Directorate of Operations was headed by Maj. Gen. Roger Ramey, whose deputy was Brig. Gen. John Gerhart. Under General Ramey were the functional branches of the directorate: the Fighter Branch, the Bombardment Branch, the Reconnaissance Branch, and the Transport Branch.

I was made Chief of the Fighter Branch and given the Air Control and Warning Section, along with the mission of air defense operations. My most important job, however, was to supervise the fighter program of the U.S. Air Force worldwide. Our branch had to develop and maintain an awareness of all fighter unit activities in major commands by visiting the commands and talking to their representatives when they came to the Pentagon. The Fighter Branch had to consider all fighter activities on a day-to-day basis, maintaining an authoritative grasp of what was going on in FEAF and making sure that all messages were acted upon promptly and with careful consideration. It also had direct responsibility for maintaining information on the current capabilities of all fighter units (including Air National Guard units) to perform their assigned missions despite deficiencies in training, strength, or equipment. All these numerous responsibilities boiled down to the absolute necessity to do everything we possibly could to ensure the highest degree of combat capability in all fighter units, present and future.

As our position in Korea shrank in the dark days of July and August 1950, the Air Force was under pressure to neglect its general war mission, and it was tempting to put our ordinary tasks on the back burner. Fortunately, the Air Force in the Pentagon and in the Far East chose to carry out its responsibilities without endangering its worldwide responsibilities. One of the first actions I took in the Fighter Branch was to emphasize the key role fighters play in Air Force operations. I had a lot of seasoned help on my staff, all veteran fighter people with plenty of war experience. We got the idea of having little blue cards printed with the message, "What Have You Done for Blue Four Today?" The reverse side read, "Blue Four is the last member of the last tactical flight of a squadron formation, who does his level best to contribute, but is handicapped by turbulence, whiplash, neglect, and other forms of severe difficulty. Blue Four needs your help." We placed this card on the desks of Air Staff officers in key positions throughout the headquarters, including those of the Chief of Staff and his deputies, reminding them of the importance of Blue Four, the neglected tail-end charlie of fighter formations.

The daily routine at the Pentagon during the Korean War was extremely challenging. Unlike the early days of my assignment with the Command Division, after I took command of the Fighter Branch there were not enough hours in the day to do all the things that had to be done. There were no car pools in those days, and if there was work to be done, one stayed until it was done. Almost all the messages we handled were high priority, and a good many were "Operational Immediate." I routinely arrived at the office (I laughingly called it an office; it was a room only a little larger than my desk, my chair, and a chair for visitors or officers working in the branch) sometime between six and seven in the morning and left in the evening when the day's work was done. We always came in on Saturday mornings and sometimes on Sunday. When a vitally important action required our immediate consideration, we would go home late in the day and return at night.

We had an effective staff. I liked all my officers, respected their abilities, and was rewarded by their loyalty. I did not consider myself to be on the best of terms with General Ramey. He seemed to prefer dealing with some of my subordinate officers rather than dealing directly with me. There was so much work to be done, however, that I did not have a lot of time to be concerned with this relatively minor irritation. In those days, the mission dominated everything.

The Fighter Branch was involved in many actions that improved the posture of the Air Force, including in-flight refueling of fighter units to increase their range. Today, it is routine for fighter wings to fly the oceans on rotation to Europe and the Pacific. Even as early as the Korean War, fighter units began to fly long overflights of the Pacific. These flights were made possible by the strong efforts of such pioneers as David Schilling and Joseph Gurnow, who flew the first east-west flight in a jet fighter across the Atlantic from England to the United States in 1951. Even while the Korean War was going on, FEAF played a major role in fighter range extension with its tests of probe-drogue refueling. Prior to the development of the capability to refuel fighter units in flight, it was necessary to load aircraft on ships for the long voyage across the Pacific, with a resulting loss in capability, to say nothing of the expense. We improved upon this type of shipment by deck-loading fighters aboard Navy carriers, thereby avoiding the need to strip the aircraft down, but that improvement in no way approached the benefits of in-flight refueling. When SAC fighter units were rotated to FEAF during the second year of the Korean War, they flew all the way from their ZI base to Japan, using in-flight refueling for the California-Hawaii and Hawaii-Midway legs of the flight.

Air power was the decisive factor in the Korean War. It was air power that blunted the first North Korean attacks in the early days and later prevented the expulsion of the United Nations forces. FEAF established air supremacy early, by its defeat of the North Korean Air Force. Later, when the Chinese Communist Air Force entered the war from its politically protected Manchurian airfields, FEAF contained that MIG force in the northwest corner of Korea, permitting it to venture forth only to battle with FEAF F-86s and then scurry back to its sanctuary bases north of the Yalu. Normally, FEAF would have destroyed the enemy bases and regained air supremacy, but FEAF fighters were forbidden to cross a line 3 miles south of the Yalu. There was considerable discussion of the concept of hot pursuit, but hot pursuit across the Yalu was never authorized. The result was a disadvantage to FEAF and a great advantage to the Chinese, who had superb radar coverage on both sides of the Yalu, thereby permitting them to deploy their fighters advantageously and denying FEAF the ability to place our F-86s in the best striking position to combat the MIGs. Their MIGs greatly outnumbered our F-86s, but the end tally was 792 MIGs destroyed against 79 F-86s, of which 58 were lost to enemy air action, a victory ratio of more than ten to one. The reasons for this superiority were better training, tactics, and procedures, which effectively overcame some of the MIG's advantages over the F-86.

Within the Fighter Branch we were well aware of the controversy among FEAF pilot returnees about the A-1 gun sight installed in the F-86. At a Pentagon conference, 14 jet aces who had fought against MIGs recommended that the A-1 sight be removed from day fighters because of inadequate maintenance and replaced with the older, manual-ranging, gyro-computing sight. As a result of this conference, the Chief of Staff directed that FEAF and the Air Proving Ground Command evaluate the problem and recommend the proper course of action. The problem was solved by Col. John England, Chief of our Fighter Gunnery Section; it was decided to retain the radar-ranging features of the A-1 sight and redesign it to facilitate maintenance, thus reducing the number of technical personnel required. In my view, this important action set the proper course for the future. It was a step forward, instead of the backward step that returning to the manual sight would have represented.

The in-flight refueling project and the day-fighter gun sight problems are examples of significant actions I took over a period of time. In addition, I took many routine actions not as visible as these that contributed to the effectiveness of fighter aviation. One area that seemed to require endless internal review was the activation of Air National Guard aircraft control and warning units, their training, and their deployment at home and abroad. The Air Defense Command (ADC) was growing rapidly at this time, in response to the new Soviet nuclear capability. The Directorate of Operations set the policy that no contract flying schools be established in Air Defense Identification Zones and that no Air Force bases be reactivated in these zones for flying training without careful consideration of the ADC's problem of positively identifying hostile aircraft, because such actions might have exacerbated an already difficult situation.

The inspector general asked us to comment on a report entitled "Inadequate Training for Interceptor Pilots." The report criticized ADC interception of SAC bombers because both aircraft were operating with running lights on. Both ADC and SAC disapproved interception under blackout conditions until the proficiency of combat crews had improved to the degree that interception could be safely accomplished under blackout conditions. I supported their position. Training Command requested 54 F-94Cs and 33 F-89s to modernize Interceptor School aircraft. I agreed to modernization, but thought that Training Command was requesting too many late-model aircraft, and the number was reduced.

On another occasion, the Foreign Liaison Branch, Intelligence, asked that our office comment on the release of information to Switzerland on the use of the napalm firebomb. I objected to the release because there would be no assurance that this information would not reach enemy hands. I also originated correspondence questioning the condition of radar equipment to be placed along the North Atlantic route to support the movement of groups of fighter aircraft from the United States to the United Kingdom and Europe. Because the equipment had been poorly maintained, we recommended that an inspection system be devised and controlled by the individual commands concerned.

As part of a program to accelerate our visits to the major commands, I went on a 30-day visit to FEAF Headquarters and Korea-based fighter units. This trip to Tokyo and Korea was one of the most productive efforts of my first Pentagon tour. On more than one occasion, General Weyland expressed to me his personal appreciation for the Air Staff actions taken as a direct result of my trip report. These actions constituted a vitally important contribution to FEAF's combat capability. While there, I was briefed on FEAF's plans for the immediate future. I sent Col. William Paule to Headquarters, United States Air Force in Europe (USAFE), to discuss problems and procedures associated with the operational employment of the surface-to-surface Matador and other missiles. I reviewed a 4th Fighter Interceptor Wing combat evaluation report of the F-86E, which pointed out that the aircraft would need more thrust if it were to compete with the MIG. I also established a requirement for additional thrust for the J-47 and GE-27 engines.

The Vice Chief of Staff approved our recommendation for a 10-station augmentation of the Joint Chiefs of Staff air control and warning system in Alaska. I initiated action to deploy a fighter interceptor squadron to Iceland to complete the air defense capability in that area; took similar action in French Morocco, where the 316th Air Division was activated to coordinate air defense; and provided air defense divisions in Alaska and Greenland.

Also during my first tour at the Pentagon, I sought and received the Chief's approval to create the Thunderbirds, the official Air Force acrobatic team, which was to be stationed at the Training Command's

Luke Air Force Base. The purposes of the team were to demonstrate flying proficiency, create interest in the training and recruiting of aviation cadets, and on appropriate occasions, promote public interest in the Air Force. The decision to create the Thunderbirds was not taken lightly; it cost us dearly in equipment and manpower, but I thought that the benefits of such a program clearly justified the expense. I attended more than one of the Armed Forces Day air shows in which the Thunderbirds were the main attraction. The pilots were among the best the Air Force produced; their maneuvers required the utmost in skill and particularly in timing. Minor errors could result in loss of life to both pilots and people on the ground, to say nothing of the loss of valuable aircraft. My office held the major responsibility for the success of this state-of-the-art flying operation.

During this period, the Air Force was rapidly making the transition to jet fighters. In 1953 I attended a three-week jet indoctrination course at Craig Air Force Base in Selma, Alabama. After a week of ground school at Craig, I had two weeks of transition flights in the two-seated T-33, then solo, acrobatics, and a couple of formation flights. Formation flying, an important element of most fighter combat operations, was included in the course because of the difference in the way propeller-driven airplanes and jets react to throttle movements. A time lag between throttle movement and aircraft reaction in jets requires increased anticipation on the part of the pilot. The Fighter Branch had received numerous requests for additional T-33s, used primarily for instrument training and transition. I advised that until production reached current demand level, all tactical units would be equipped with one T-33 per squadron except for FEAF, which would be equipped with two T-33s for each jet fighter squadron.

This training was my first exposure to the jet airplane, and I enjoyed it very much. Because Pentagon staff officers in the Directorate of Operations were continually making decisions concerning jet aircraft, we arranged for all colonels to attend the instrument flying course at Moody Air Force Base. This course afforded senior officers the opportunity to become familiar with jet operations and instrument flying.

## Another Transition

My tour in the Pentagon was approaching an end. When I returned from Craig in April 1953, I learned that I was to be transferred to

FEAF. I immediately asked to attend the Combat Crew Training School at Nellis Air Force Base, Las Vegas, before leaving for the Far East, so that I would be fully qualified for combat operations whatever my assignment turned out to be. My orders assigned me to temporary duty at Nellis, followed by 30 days' leave before traveling to Travis Air Force Base, near San Francisco, and further assignment to FEAF Headquarters on permanent change of station.

Agatha had taken the Pentagon in stride, accepting the facts of life for a Pentagon wife: late meals, broken engagements, the appearance of neglect. Having spent a summer at the Art Institute in Chicago in 1934, she had always been interested in crafts and the fine arts. Wherever she happened to be, she looked for opportunities to add to her knowledge in these areas. In Washington she took silversmithing and ceramics at Catholic University, and she had one lesson per week in oils and portrait painting with an artist named Lazarus Gianpietro. She even gave me art lessons and had me painting the beautiful cumulus clouds that I saw in flight at altitude. When she bought a kiln and created some ceramics at home, I soon forgot the lurking fears I had about fire. In addition to these studies, she worked with the Red Cross at the Walter Reed Army Medical Center in physical therapy, mostly helping veterans regain the use of limbs, hands, and feet that had been frozen in Korea. She was also engaged in charity work with Jennie McGuire, the mother-in-law of an old friend, Elinor McGuire. Jennie, a member of the Washington School Board and a prominent citizen, organized women's groups to raise money for the city's poor. They raised substantial sums to purchase expensive medical equipment for Washington's hospitals. Agatha and I still saw a lot of each other on weekends. She would accompany me to the Pentagon on Saturday mornings and also on Sunday mornings if I had to go in then.

Agatha took classes in oil painting and investments at the YWCA in downtown Washington and was elected to serve as a student representative on the YWCA School Committee. At one meeting, the chairman announced an important change: the association was to integrate its school operation and permit "coloreds" to participate. The evening broke up with considerable buzzing about the change. Two days later, Agatha received a telephone call from her painting teacher. "Something terrible has happened at the Y," she said. "They are going to let coloreds attend classes." Refusing to teach "coloreds," she was going to hold her class at home in the future and invited

Agatha to attend. Agatha told the teacher she was shocked at her attitude, especially because she was teaching in a Christian organization, and informed her that she had been teaching a "colored" all along. "How do *you* know?" asked the lady. "Because you have been teaching *me*," replied Agatha. The teacher nearly had a heart attack. After a long pause, she said she would have to ask the other students if it was all right for Agatha to be in the class with them. Agatha replied that even if she offered her free painting lessons for the rest of her life, she would never take another lesson from her. Agatha laughs about this incident now, but it was not funny at the time.

I was not immune to continuing racial discrimination, either. During both of my tours in the Pentagon (1950–53 and 1961–65), my association with fellow officers was restricted to the office—it began with the workday and ended with the workday. Rigid segregation in the Washington metropolitan area made association of blacks and whites outside the Pentagon complicated, to say the least. We lived in different areas, and we could not go to restaurants, theaters, or other places of entertainment without the difficulties imposed by segregation. Arena Stage, located on New York Avenue near Ninth Street Northwest, was the only theater I know of that welcomed all patrons at the time; this policy was effective from its opening in 1950.

Fortunately, our lives in Washington were not all work (or education and voluntarism) and no play. South American dancing was quite popular in the early 1950s, and along with a group of others who were interested in rumba, tango, samba, and cha-cha, we hired a teacher and found a place to dance once a week. It was great. Agatha and I got so interested that we went to South America, she traveling commercially and visiting cities that I, as a nonpaying passenger on the Military Air Transport Service's weekly flight to Rio de Janeiro, did not get to see. In every respect, the trip was a grand success, so much so that we dreaded the return to the racist atmosphere of Washington. But soon we would be moving again—I on my way to the war in the Pacific, and Agatha to a solo existence on the West Coast.

The trip to South America had started with a near tragedy. I left the Pentagon in mid-afternoon and drove home at my normal speed-limit-breaking pace, causing an accident with two other cars in northeast Washington. My car had to be towed away, and the police took me with them to the station, where Agatha bailed me out for $20.

After we returned to Washington from South America, I found a notice from the Police Department asking me to show cause why I should not have my driver's license suspended for six months. At the District Building, I explained that there was no public transportation between my apartment in northeast Washington and the Pentagon, and that if I had my license suspended, Agatha would have her schedule disrupted by having to deliver me to and from work. Luckily, the people at the District Building let me keep my license, but they did not return the $20 deposit.

My tour at the Pentagon had proven immensely valuable to me professionally. The job had necessarily forced me to specialize in fighters, work that exposed me to across-the-board Air Force interests and philosophy. It was hard work, but it put within my reach a great deal of information and experience that was useful to me later in my career. I already looked back upon my time there with considerable satisfaction, and I was proud of the work done by the Fighter Branch. Three years after its creation, that office was recognized as the focal point for all information and activity pertaining to fighters in other than the specialized functions assigned to other Air Staff agencies. Our staff had been responsible for the direction and implementation of this division, including the aircraft control and warning program, building the fighter program to a high degree of capability despite production, manning, and base availability problems. We had used short-range programming techniques to make resources immediately available in support of FEAF's combat operation. In addition, we had pushed a worldwide program of exchange of information among major commands using Korean war data. In a short time we had developed operational air defense capabilities in the United States and far-flung areas of the world, where no air defenses had previously existed. Today, many decades later, I remain extremely proud of the outstanding results obtained by this small group of eager, highly skilled, dedicated, and hard-working officers, who made the Fighter Branch a powerful force in the Pentagon.

# ★ ★ ★ Respect

**9.**

*Even though the men of the 51st had always served under white commanders, I encountered no signs of skepticism or coldness at any time. Their attitude toward me was not only correct; they exuded enthusiasm, and I received the utmost in cooperation.*

The prospect of being separated from Agatha for a year in Korea was not a happy one. For 20 years she had been a constant source of comfort and support. Fortunately, I did not have to worry about her ability to exist on her own; otherwise I would have had a bad time of it. On the positive side, the new job would be an important step up in my career. For the first time I was to command an integrated tactical unit composed mostly of whites, but I anticipated no racial problems of any kind. Having served as chief of the all-white Fighter Branch in the Pentagon, I expected no surprises in the 51st Fighter Wing.

I also knew that in a foreign country racism would not be nearly the problem it was at home—a consideration that in itself would always make overseas assignments more attractive to me. Many of my friends and acquaintances understand why I always felt freer outside the United States. In this country I was treated as a black man first and a human being second. The attitudes expressed by many white Americans, in their actions if not in their words, were usually something quite different from the attitudes of one human being toward another possessing the same rights and entitled to the same respect. Whites in the United States generally respected other whites, regardless of their position in life. But at this time in my life blacks had never gained the same kind of respect.

I found the respect I had been denied at home in other countries. At age 16 I had visited France, Belgium, and Switzerland. For the first time in my life I had experienced a strange feeling of freedom: I was not a black American, simply an American traveler who happened to be black. I did not meet a single "ugly" Frenchman, Belgian, or Swiss.

A psychiatrist would be entitled to explore why I do not feel free in the United States by looking into my personality for an inferiority complex. But I do not have such a complex; rather, I have been conditioned by the treatment I have received from white Americans throughout my life. When I was a child, my father taught me that no one was better than anyone else. We were all equal. He taught me not to worry whether people liked me or not, but to earn their respect and respect them in return. He instilled in me the belief that people cannot be equal unless they respect one another. Failing to find that respect in the United States, he escaped the problem by spending as much time as he could out of the country, and in much the same way Agatha and I were to discover a degree of freedom overseas that we had never experienced here.

## Agatha Settles in LA

When I had returned from Italy in 1945, Agatha remarked that when I went overseas again and she could not go with me, she wanted a home of her own. During World War II she had moved from pillar to post, and even though she had been welcomed by her family, she had always wanted her own place. Now that I would be going to the Korean War, she firmly decided to live in Los Angeles. The decision was based on the few days we had spent there during our trip west in 1950, when both of us had fallen in love with the city. The climate, the warmth of the people, the atmosphere of activity, and the adult education programs were all factors in making Los Angeles particularly attractive. Specifically, Agatha wanted to pursue her interest in ceramics and to take other art courses. Today I am amazed that we made such major decisions in a rapid, casual manner. We just decided what we were going to do and did it. Now it seems that decisions of relatively little importance must be toiled over, delayed, worried about, and finally, after many misgivings, made.

I had to report to Nellis for jet combat crew training by 16 July 1953, and until then we were mostly on our own. We were excited to be leaving Washington and setting off on new adventures. After we concluded that it was too dangerous to tow our MG, I drove the Mercury and Agatha drove the MG. In the middle of the country, Agatha attracted the attention of a white Lothario who was also driving an MG. In those days MGs were not very common, and it was the custom of MG owners to blow their horns in greeting as they passed each other. Agatha's admirer followed us for many miles, cutting in and out, passing us and letting us pass him. As he pulled off the road at a motel, he blew his horn frantically and motioned for Agatha to join him. We both blew our horns back at him and shook with laughter as we stepped on the gas and continued our trip.

We did a lot of driving at night, being careful not to hit any of the many large jackrabbits, alive and dead, that were on the roads. We moved along in a carefree manner, unconcerned about getting Agatha comfortably settled. It seems that we refused to worry about future problems until we were in a position to do something about them—an ability that is sometimes lost as one grows older.

As it turned out, it was quite easy to get Agatha settled. In 1953 Los Angeles had a generous amount of relatively good housing previously occupied by Japanese Americans. They had lost this housing and all their personal property when they were forced on extremely short notice to move to the desert concentration camps our government created for them in the early days of the Pacific war. This policy resulted from the prevalent racist attitudes and wartime hysteria immediately after Pearl Harbor, when some people high in authority imagined that Japanese Americans might cooperate with the enemy if the country were invaded. Agatha made friends with one of the victims, an attractive, talented girl who had been forced to spend the war in one of the camps. There she taught other prisoners arts and crafts to spend the time profitably and give them a skill they might use someday. After the war, Angelenos welcomed the opportunity to purchase the abandoned homes, furniture, and other household items at drastically reduced prices. Because of this unfortunate situation, we quickly found a new modern apartment in an attractive neighborhood and furnished it as best we could until our household effects arrived from Washington. Agatha's landlady, Dorothea Bass, became our good friend almost immediately. (Years later she told us how reluctant she had been to rent to us because she suspected Agatha of being my mistress.)

In Las Vegas, by contrast, the apartment that Col. James Ulricson, the Nellis base commander, had found for me was not fit for human habitation. The reason was, once again, racial. Nellis had no jurisdiction over living conditions or quarters for blacks off-base; base commanders were not given this responsibility until much later. However, it came as a shock to see where the Air Force expected my wife and me to live just before I departed on a combat tour to Korea. The apartment was in a slum populated by unsavory characters, and I should never have been referred to it. It would have been far better for Colonel Ulricson simply to say that he could not help me and let it go at that.

Just as I began ground school preparation for the flying course in F-80 and F-86 combat crew training, the Korean War ended. My training continued, however, just as if nothing had changed, and I finished the entire course. It was certainly beneficial; I had not been active in fighters for several years, and at the age of 40 I definitely needed the training, especially in formation flying, acrobatics, gunnery, and rat racing—a maneuver in which the aircraft leading the formation executes acrobatic maneuvers followed in turn by the others, each maintaining its position in the formation.

I was determined to show up well in comparison with my 20-year-old classmates. Although I had more flying time than most of them, age made a difference, especially in the summer heat of the Nevada desert. The temperature was so high on the ramp—140 degrees—that one had to be careful not to touch the aircraft's metal surfaces with bare hands. I flew three missions a day, getting up at five in the morning. During the first couple of weeks I woke up tired, stayed tired throughout the day, and collapsed into bed shortly after dinner. Three years spent sitting at a desk at the Pentagon did not help.

I still loved to fly, however, and I was thrilled to be strapped into the compact, single-seated F-80. I always felt a first surge of exhilaration when I climbed into the cockpit, another when I started the engine, another when I pushed the throttle forward for takeoff, and yet another when I was airborne. It was one great feeling to ease into a gentle left turn and cut inside the airplane that had taken off ahead of me, putting me in close formation. I was in control, and the airplane was an extension of my body, just as my fingers were part of my hand. On the first flight of the day, the air was always smooth. The crystal-clear blue sky was broken only by the sharp edges of the mountains and the brown desert below.

After the F-80 half of the course, I felt better physically. It also got cooler in September, and I began to relax and enjoy the missions and my association with the other members of the class. I met some fine young men at Nellis, among them Alton Slay, who retired several years ago as commander, Air Force Systems Command. Many who had trained at Nellis had made all the difference in the air battles near the Yalu against the MIGs.

The F-86 course was practically a repetition of the F-80 course, but everything I had experienced before was multiplied by the superior characteristics of the F-86, known as "the Cadillac." This was the plane I would be flying in Korea. Although my air-ground work in dive-bombing and strafing was acceptable, I was not getting my share of hits in air-to-air gunnery. The gunnery sleeve was towed on a specified track. Flying off to the side in groups of four, we entered the gunnery pattern one at a time and fired. Although I never did get the results I was working for in air-to-air gunnery, I did better in 45-degree dive-bombing at 500 miles per hour.

Unless I had to fly on Saturday to catch up, I would drive to Los Angeles to see Agatha on Friday after I had flown my missions, stay until Sunday morning, and drive back to Nellis. I liked to gamble, but I was not allowed to enter the casinos on the strip. Las Vegas was as strictly segregated as any city in the Deep South, and its people did not have the charm possessed by many southerners. It was not until much later that blacks were allowed in the white gambling establishments.

Agatha and I wrote to each other daily and exchanged letters with our respective families; I learned from my father that President Eisenhower had appointed him to the Battle Monuments Commission. Although Agatha had been in Los Angeles only a few months, her wings were spreading rapidly and widely. She had already made many friends and was busy taking courses. Prompted by Essie Tucker, my sister's sister-in-law, she passed the real estate sales examination and became Essie's office manager in addition to working as a sales agent.

The time passed rapidly, and in October I moved to Los Angeles for one month's leave before leaving for the Far East. I would be in Korea for a year, and nobody assigned there was permitted to take any dependents with him. As 2 November approached, the day I was scheduled to report at Travis, Agatha and I reviewed the financial and living arrangements we had made for her to survive during my absence. My insurance was in order. I signed an unlimited power of attorney. Agatha had urged her parents and her nephew, Larry Melville, to come to Los Angeles to visit her, so I had every reason to believe that she would not be lonesome. We indulged ourselves in a little conjecture about life after Korea, guessing that the Air Force would give us at least two years in Japan, which would shield us from second-class citizenship in the United States until we were transferred back. This was indeed a happy thought. Government housing was generally good overseas, and we especially looked forward to expanding our understanding of other nations, peoples, and cultures.

Agatha stayed with me to the last moment, accompanying me to my point of departure. At Travis, an aerial port of embarkation near Sacramento, we got the VIP treatment: a five-room apartment on base that we rattled around in for the few days we were there. After a long boring flight to Tokyo, I checked in at the Dai Iti, one of many Japanese hotels that had been taken over by the military for temporary housing. I was impressed by the obvious industry of the Japanese, the rapidity of their personal movements, the speed at which they drove their taxis, the smells that dominated the atmosphere, their cleanliness, the neatness of everything I observed, the beauty of Mount Fuji in the distance. They said that the quality of one's day was measurably improved if the clouds lifted and one could see Mount Fuji early in the morning; it seemed true enough to me.

Over the weekend I traveled out to Johnson Air Base to see Ed Gleed, my former deputy at Lockbourne, who had a key assignment at Johnson. Ed took me to see George Evans, another officer who had served with us at Lockbourne. George was living nearby in disgraceful economy quarters, but they were the best he could find, and the only alternative was to leave his family at home and serve an unaccompanied tour. I realized I would face the same problem when I completed my tour in Korea. I agreed completely with George's solution because, after a time in economy quarters, it was possible, depending on one's rank, to obtain government quarters, which were almost universally good.

Early Tuesday morning I reported to FEAF Headquarters. General

Weyland was quite cordial; he went out of his way to remind me that my visit to FEAF a year and a half earlier had produced actions in the Pentagon that were highly supportive of FEAF's combat mission. He informed me that I would command the 51st Fighter Interceptor Wing at Suwon, Korea, and expressed the hope that I would enjoy the assignment. I thanked General Weyland for receiving me and returned to the Dai Iti to pack.

## Maintaining Combat Readiness in Korea

I assumed command of the 51st Wing on 12 November. Organized in much the same way as the 332d, it was composed of a wing head-quarters; a fighter interceptor group with three fighter interceptor squadrons (the 16th, 25th, and 39th); the 51st Air Base Group, with several air base squadrons; and a maintenance and supply operation, based at Suwon and Tsuiki, Japan. The assignment was a high compliment; I appreciated the honor at the time, and I am still grateful today.

In Suwon, I was met by Col. William Clark, who had commanded the wing since September. I was concerned about how he would receive me because I was taking a choice assignment from him and relegating him to a staff job in 5th Air Force Headquarters. But he welcomed me warmly—a tribute to the quality of his character and personality. A lesser officer might well have shown some resentment, in spite of the fact that I was in no way to blame for his change of assignment. Bill stayed with me for a few days settling his personal business. He assured me the wing was in good condition, an opinion verified by a recent inspection report. It was up to me to build upon an already strong foundation.

As of the 27 July armistice agreement, the wing's new mission was to maintain combat readiness. Active hostilities had ceased fewer than four months earlier, and the armistice was still shaky. I impressed this fact on all my people and kept it foremost in the con-sciousness of our day-to-day lives. We had to be able to fly combat missions on no notice and, at the same time, maintain the security of our airplanes, personnel, and materiel so that we could not be surprised by enemy action. Specifically, we were to fly patrol missions outside the three-mile limit along the east and west coasts of Korea, fly missions along the demarcation line between North and South Korea, escort photo reconnaissance aircraft along both coasts of North Korea, maintain our aircraft in a constant state of alert, fly special missions ordered by the 5th Air Force (radar calibration, joint training problems, and antiaircraft tracking missions), and conduct intensive training of combat pilots and maintenance personnel.

At one of my early staff meetings I asked for a detailed briefing on matters affecting morale. The post-armistice mission was cited as being a potential danger because in the coming winter months, a feeling might develop that our work had been done and we were being held in Korea unnecessarily. Fortunately, that feeling never materialized because of a general recognition of the chance for renewed hostilities. The morale briefing was encouraging because our recreation facilities were generally good. We did have one significant problem area: movies. The theater was a small, barnlike building with new but uncomfortable benches for seating, hot in summer (when films were shown on blacktop tennis courts) and cold in winter. Movies were free in Korea, but a rumor was circulating that the price of admission would be 25 cents after the first of the year—the same price charged at plush stateside theaters. The new charge never went into effect during my time.

I had another base under my command at Tsuiki, Japan, where the 51st Maintenance and Supply Group operated a rear echelon maintenance combined operation for all the Korean-based F-86 units. This important operation had two major morale problems: tour lengths of 18 months for unaccompanied personnel and 24 months for accompanied personnel, and bad assignments resulting from a constant shortage of skilled replacements. (In contrast, the standard length of a tour in Korea for all services was 13 months.) I sought unsuccessfully through command channels to alleviate these problems, talking to every senior Pentagon official who visited us, but to no avail. About all I could do was see to it that poorly qualified people received thorough on-the-job training.

I was satisfied with the briefings I received on troop morale, not only from the details given me during the staff meeting discussion, but also from my personal observations of men on the flying line and in their offices. I ate several meals in the airmen's mess and attended all manner of unit welcome and farewell parties, where I learned that the men felt good about the 51st in general and were eagerly awaiting the end of their 13-month tour. Nobody stayed in Korea for more than 11 months at that time, spending the other two months on leave or traveling, so there was a constant influx and outgo of people.

Even though my men had always served under white commanders, I encountered no signs of skepticism or coldness at any time. Their attitude toward me was not only correct; they exuded enthusiasm, and I received the utmost in cooperation. Although only a few blacks had been assigned to the 51st, it was clear to me that Air Force integration was working out beautifully. This was also true of my subsequent overseas assignments; integration was always particularly easy overseas, removed from the prevailing social restrictions of the United States.

My air base group commander, Col. Robert Bowles, whom I had known in the Pentagon, lived with me in a four-bedroom house. Our Korean houseboy, Yo Kim, kept the place clean and did the laundry, and the only complaint we had about our home was that the worst of the Korean winter overtaxed its heating capability. We did not have many overnight visitors because almost everybody found Japan a much more comfortable and enjoyable place to visit.

Operations accelerated markedly during December 1953. We flew more scrambles as a direct result of the increased vigilance of air defense personnel and an apparent change in the enemy's mode of operation. Our maintenance skills were at a low level; hence, the amount of flying time for training was less than desired. Our daily patrols of the east and west coasts seemed to cause an increase in enemy air activity at the times of our patrols, and there were reports that MIGs routinely followed our fighters. We saw a few of them, but made no contact. In addition to the coastal patrols, we flew fighter sweeps, escort missions of photo reconnaissance aircraft, combat air patrol, practice ground-control intercepts, camera gunnery, and weather reconnaissance. I flew with the 25th Fighter Squadron and the fighter group commander, Col. Harold Shook, an outstanding pilot and fine leader. All the air and ground personnel worked quite hard.

Considering the personnel turbulence that resulted from 11-month assignments, it is remarkable that our combat readiness was maintained as successfully as it was. Time was lost in the constant turnovers, the arrival of inexperienced people who had to be trained, the departure of people after a few months of work, rest and recuperation absences, and many unforeseen disturbances such as emergency leave and hospitalization. Yet the aircraft were maintained combat ready and the missions were successfully flown. I was impressed with the quality of the average officer and the average airman. They looked good, and they behaved well under any circumstances. Abuses of alcohol were infrequent.

## Relations with the Koreans

Korean personnel served as employees in our clubs and did other work that was mutually beneficial. They arrived early in the morning and departed the base en masse at night. This system encouraged good individual behavior and prevented practices such as shacking up. Sadly, the Koreans were treated as inferiors by most of our people, who referred to them as "gooks" and otherwise lived up to the reputation for ugliness and insensitivity that Americans earned in so many foreign countries.

Our commanders were without exception fine, strong, and respected men. My top staff was experienced and fully qualified, and my group and squadron commanders were mature individuals with substantial World War II background. Though FEAF had had no mission in Korea before the North Korean attack, its reaction had been immediate and effective. The top generals, the field officers, the junior officers, and the airmen did their jobs from the beginning of the war through the armistice. The leadership of the Air Force deserves great credit for producing an organization that performed so well under difficult conditions.

Two senior officers who had served with me during World War II were with me again in the 51st: Spanky Roberts and Bill Campbell. Spanky, the air base group commander at the time of my arrival, had been in my class in flying school at TAAF and served subsequently as my operations officer in the 99th, commander of the 99th after I left Italy to take command of the 332d Fighter Group, and my deputy commander in the 332d. He completed his tour in Korea shortly after I arrived and was replaced by Bob Bowles. Bill Campbell, one of the best officers I served with over the years, had flown the 99th's first mission over Pantelleria, commanded the 99th and the 332d, and had attended the combat crew training class following mine at Nellis.

When he arrived at the 51st, his initial assignment was air inspector. He did his usual superior job in this assignment and was rewarded with command of the 16th Fighter Squadron in the 51st. Personally popular, he was elected to the Board of Governors of the officers' club.

There was not much to do at Suwon other than one's duty. A few times I drove up to Seoul, where Koreans were better dressed than the destitute people of the villages. Korea had suffered severely from the war, and effects of hunger and destruction were plainly evident on the faces of its people. The 51st had adopted a Korean orphanage about a year before I arrived, and I occasionally visited the 450 children who lived there under the care of a resident Buddhist priest and a staff of Korean women. It was necessary to supervise the operation of the orphanage closely because of the honcho system, an aspect of the culture that had to be considered in all relationships with the Koreans. Yo was an example close to home. I was recognized by the Koreans as a honcho; hence, my houseboy was also a honcho. Unfortunately, Yo attempted to exercise his position as honcho on a couple of our air policemen. Reluctantly, I had to replace him with a boy and a girl who had been previously employed at the officers' club, but who could in no way match Yo's work.

I made informal inspections regularly, discussing current problems of mutual interest. In mid-December I made a formal inspection of the fighter group and its three squadrons and found everything in superior condition—quarters, headquarters, and flying areas. No orders had to be issued; quiet suggestions produced quick action. I also presented some Distinguished Flying Crosses and attended a pilots meeting and some classes for new pilots.

We attended Fighter Night at the club on 19 December. To my honest surprise, it turned out to be a birthday party for me (I had turned 41 the day before). There was a cake the size of an executive desk, a king-size steak dinner, and a hilarious show mounted by the 25th Squadron—spoofs of St. George and the Dragon and Little Red Riding Hood patterned after the television show "Dragnet." The Korean female employees did not understand English four-letter words, so there was no restrictions on language. It was quite a party.

The following day Lt. Gen. Samuel Anderson welcomed me to my first staff meeting of the 5th Air Force in Seoul. I liked the way the meeting was conducted. General Anderson had his say, and then his staff had theirs. One of the topics of discussion was the high number of recent aircraft and motor vehicle accidents. At Suwon an F-86 had been unable to get both gear down, landed with one wheel down and one up, swerved upon landing, and killed a man who had been taking pictures from the side of the runway.

The Christmas spirit was in evidence all over the base. Presents and Christmas cards were flooding the mail, and everyone seemed to feel kindly toward his fellow man. On Christmas Eve General Anderson visited us to join Adm. Arthur Radford, Chairman of the Joint Chiefs, and his party. The admiral told me that his brother-in-law, Col. Paul Davidson, had served as a regimental commander under my father when my father commanded the 4th Cavalry Brigade at Fort Riley in the early 1940s.

Many of us attended the holiday party at the orphanage and found that the visit contributed to our feeling of Christmas away from home. Santa Claus, a 51st Wing officer of suitable proportions, delivered presents to each child, including bicycles for the larger children and tricycles for the little ones. It was clear that the men of the 51st thoroughly enjoyed dispensing the gifts to our Korean wards, and I mailed all the stateside donors an official "Fighting 51st" Christmas card of thanks. We had to be vigilant to ensure that these contributions would stay with the orphans and not go to the honchos who would otherwise sell the bicycles and other items on the black market. We were at least partially successful, and our consciences were clear although we did not completely beat the system. There is no doubt in my mind, however, that the quality of life of some of the Korean children was improved as a result of our efforts.

I went unannounced to the orphanage from time to time to see whether the presents were still in the hands of the children. I had to threaten the priests and the other honchos with dire consequences if they sold the gifts for personal gain. At least I tried to threaten them. I could never depend on my interpreter to translate my admonitions strongly enough to impress the orphanage authorities. To do so would have been considered a transgression of the Korean caste system and proper interpersonal relationships.

In January 1954 we received news from the armistice talks. A disagreement about the repatriation of prisoners had escalated to the point that some people thought hostilities might be renewed. Not many of us really believed it could happen, but the result was an increased alert. Some alerts were more stringent than others. When Intelligence indicated, as in this case, we actually had pilots sitting in the cockpits—a rare situation called "strip alert." It wore out the pilots. At other times, crews and maintenance personnel were kept on the flying line, and at "base alert," our people were kept on base. The Chinese were concerned that instead of delivering Chinese prisoners to them we would send the prisoners to Taiwan, and that we would not deliver the North Korean prisoners who did not want to be repatriated. The armistice commission resolved the issue peaceably, and our alert was reduced.

I was awakened by a sharp knock on my door early on the morning of 2 February. Our chapel had been completely destroyed by fire, and all property and equipment had been lost. It had also been a near thing for our two chaplains; they escaped with some minor burns and smoke inhalation, but all their personal possessions had been lost. The cause of the fire was determined to be a defective stove. We developed a new respect for the dangers associated with our heating equipment, which had been tested beyond its limits in January. Temperatures had dropped to 4 degrees above zero, and the wind seemed to blow right through our quarters.

The end of January brought the end of the armistice talks crisis and our increased alerts. We resumed our former posture and operational routine. In February, essentially a month of boredom, we received a boost with the arrival of 40 skilled jet mechanics. Our maintenance skill levels had deteriorated to the point where the flying hours we could devote to training were fewer than we liked. We could now resume the much-needed training we had missed during the required January strip alerts, and the flying would alleviate the boredom. Almost at the same time, we received an additional 22 new pilots. This was great timing on the part of FEAF. Later in February I was pleased to receive a plaque from General Anderson for the best 5th Air Force flying safety record.

Agatha's daily letters told of the active social life she was leading in Los Angeles among a large group of friends. I admired the enthusiasm with which she attacked life; surely she must have experienced some down periods, but I find no evidence of them in the letters she wrote more than 35 years ago. Her mother and father completed a three-month visit and returned home to Connecticut; they had both fallen in love with California. Agatha herself was delighted in every way with the life she was leading. Through her real estate activities she became familiar with all parts of the city and worked with people of all races and nationalities. In the meantime, as the perennial schoolgirl she remains to this day, she attended classes in ceramics (at Los Angeles City College), painting, sewing, silversmithing, rapid-reading, modern dancing, Hawaiian and Spanish dancing, ballet, and, in spite of an old fear of putting her head under water, swimming. But no matter how busy she was, she wrote me at least one letter every day I was overseas, frequently augmenting them with packages of goodies. I also wrote to her every day, although my letters about life in Korea were not nearly as interesting as hers.

At the end of February temperatures moved upward in Suwon, and life grew more comfortable. All was well in our daily operations. I attended General Anderson's official farewell dinner in Seoul. The president of South Korea, Syngman Rhee, was present, as were Gen. Maxwell Taylor and our new FEAF commander, General Partridge. General Anderson's replacement was to be General Ramey, my boss in the Pentagon just the year before.

In early May we received a letter of commendation from Roger Lewis, the Assistant Secretary of the Air Force, who had visited us at Suwon and Tsuiki. In a personal letter to me he wrote, "I have nothing but the highest praise for you and your officers and airmen." Colonel Bowles, my commander at Tsuiki, also received a letter of commendation. And later that month, for the first time in the history of the wing, the 51st won the top position in the 5th Air Force rating system. I thought the rating system was fine when we came in first; at other times I did not think it truly measured the quality of our organization.

I learned that one of our squadrons was to be moved to Naha on Okinawa, and one each to Misawa and Chitose in Japan. I therefore led a group of 18 officers and men to Okinawa to examine the future squadron site. This trip was a morale builder. Our Air Force cousins treated us to all the hospitality we could absorb for three days, and we returned to Korea eagerly anticipating the changes that were in store for us.

One of these changes proved to involve me personally. On 6 June I was notified that I would be leaving the wing in July for reassignment to FEAF Headquarters. Presumably the redeployments accounted for this premature change of station. My immediate future was suddenly clouded in mystery: When exactly would I go? What would my new assignment be? How soon could I expect to get Agatha to Japan? When could I expect to get government quarters? What were the procedures for getting one's household effects to Japan? How could I get my car to Japan? Fortunately FEAF Headquarters soon sent me comprehensive answers to these questions. I was to be released by General Ramey as soon as I had indoctrinated my replacement, Col. Barney Russell, a classmate of mine at the War College.

The indoctrination process did not take long. I attended Fighter Night on 1 July, at which many embarrassingly complimentary speeches were made in my honor and I was given a large cake with "Sayonara Colonel Davis" written on it. I was moved by the kind words and the obvious sincerity of the speakers, but I was still glad to leave Korea. In 1954 it remained an impoverished, war-torn nation, albeit one with great human resources. Life there was hard, and I was looking forward to a more comfortable assignment and my reunion with Agatha.

About half the base came down to see me off the next morning. There was much impromptu fun; the pilots had over half the base transportation out, and drove down the runway in formation with their lights on. There were fireworks, a band, people in costume. I had never seen anything like it. For eight months I had enjoyed the experience of being in command without having to issue any orders. A mere suggestion would result in immediate action. The best part, of course, was that it all came out extremely well.

I wrote the following letter of farewell to all members of the 51st:

In leaving, I would like to express to you my sincere thanks and appreciation for your combined efforts which kept the Fighting 51st the finest unit of its kind in the Air Force. During the past several months we have completed the transition from war to half peace. Throughout this period, we have maintained a state of combat readiness, which has most certainly made itself felt in any enemy councils dealing with the possible renewal of hostilities in Korea. We have performed numerous missions in support of the UN mission. All of this has been accomplished under the adverse conditions of Korean weather, mud, dust, and isolation. The future will bring many changes, some of a nature that is not pleasing to those of us who have benefited for many months from the fine feeling of comradeship we have enjoyed. My hope is that each one of us will take with him, no matter where he may go, a part of the inspiration he has received from this great fighting organization. My association with the 51st has been the high point of more than 18 years of service. It has been a great privilege for me to serve with so many fine, capable people. Best of luck to every one of you and may we meet again.

Upon my arrival in Tokyo in July, I moved into the Sanno, a Japanese hotel that had been taken over by the American forces for the exclusive use of senior officers. It offered all the amenities, including a large dining room where excellent food was attractively served. It was good to live in the lap of luxury again. I immediately gave Agatha all the information I had about our move. Because I was to represent FEAF at the Air Force Fighter Symposium, to be held at Maxwell on 25 July, we could meet there and return to Tokyo together. Unfailingly industrious and resourceful, Agatha took care of all the details: inoculations, passport, selling her car. I think she wept a little when she realized she would have to relinquish her little robin's-egg-blue MG. Even today she reminisces about it.

## New Duties in Japan

I was going to be director of operations and training at FEAF Headquarters. It was the biggest directorate in the headquarters, composed of three divisions: Current Operations, which among many other things monitored the Indo-China War; Combat Operations, which ran exercises and directed missions; and Operations Evaluation. My boss was Maj. Gen. Jacob Smart, West Point class of 1932, a gentleman to whom I immediately took a liking. I was to replace Col. Richard ("Red") Smith, also West Point class of 1932, a War College classmate of mine, an artist, and a generous person.

As director, I would be responsible to the FEAF commander for developing and maintaining combat readiness at the highest possible level in all assigned units. Only four years earlier, FEAF had met an attack by the North Koreans. It could happen again, and everyone in a position of responsibility had to understand the gravity of our day-to-day situation. I defined combat readiness as the ability to react successfully to any reasonably imaginable threat. Our forces needed to maintain a realistic dispersal capability, and we had to have good enough intelligence to disperse our forces from their permanent bases in timely fashion. In June 1950 FEAF's reaction had been good; in the future it would have to be even better.

Once on the job I quickly established a routine. When I got to work in the morning, I read all the incoming messages and internal headquarters correspondence. Then I would make the rounds, conferring with the people who worked in the various divisions. At the same time I was developing my presentation for the Maxwell symposium and investigating the Tokyo housing situation, even though Agatha would make the final decision about where we would live.

Agatha flew from Los Angeles to Maxwell, where we met on 19 July. It was wonderful to be together again. While in Alabama we made a quick trip to Tuskegee Institute to say hello and goodbye to our old friends from years gone by. After the symposium we went to Los Angeles to say our farewells and engineer the move. I enjoyed seeing Agatha's friends, some of whom I had met before.

On our flight to Japan we experienced an 18-hour delay at Wake Island because of engine trouble, and we finally arrived in Tokyo after dark. Consequently, Agatha's initial impression was of a picture-book Japan: the lamps that lit the streets, people dressed in traditional Japanese garb, and a set of night sounds different from those of western cities. She was thrilled, and that positive first impression has stayed with her to the present time.

We checked into the Nikkatsu, a brand-new hotel that also made a favorable impression. At four the next morning, we were awakened by the noodle man's bugle. This also was a pleasant experience for Agatha, an enthusiatic traveler who relishes any opportunity to learn about the culture and lives of other people. We went sightseeing the next day and looked for private rentals, summarily rejecting everything we saw in Tokyo. Col. Ted Collagan and his wife, Rosemary, made every effort to make us feel at home and helped us look for a suitable place to live, but the rentals were almost all cracker boxes with no heat and no conveniences. The Japanese thought that wooden houses were too beautiful to cover with paint, and so too we came to believe. We were soon converted completely to Japanese concepts of beauty, and Agatha found Japan to be one of her favorite places in the world.

On our first night in Tokyo we went to a popular downtown restaurant distinguished by its location in a roof garden with a magnificent view for miles around. The food was beautiful to behold. We ordered sukiyaki; Agatha liked it, but when she returned to the hotel she became quite ill—so ill, in fact, that she has never eaten sukiyaki again. As a matter of fact, she does not care for any Japanese food, least of all the raw fish and some of the vegetables that are central to the Japanese diet. My experience of Japanese food was different from hers: I never liked it in the first place.

We ended up with a house that Capt. Howard Marsh and his wife, Mitzi, found for us in a suburb called Seijo Machi, which was cooler than Tokyo. Like most Japanese houses it had no central heating, a shortcoming we regretted when the weather got cold. We loved the area, however, and thought we would give it a chance. Many of my fellow officers stationed at FEAF Headquarters also lived in Seijo, and I joined a car pool with Howard Marsh and Maj. Andrew Kowalski. It was a pleasure to commute with these gentlemen, and in our conversations I learned about many matters that were not necessarily related to my job.

Agatha and I met our Japanese neighbors, many of whom came to our house to welcome us, and we were invited to become members of the Seijo International Club. A number of American Fulbright professors had chosen to live in Seijo, an educational center where many Japanese professionals lived. The community also had a train station providing excellent transportation to any destination in the Tokyo area. One could set one's watch by the arrival and departure of the trains.

Seijo was a charmingly beautiful and highly desirable location; the houses were large, attractively landscaped, and more private than those in the city. The occupant of each house was required to maintain a green-fence of trees, bushes, or plants. The yards were manicured to perfection. Each evening we enjoyed walking along the beautiful, peaceful lanes of the community, which illustrated so well the classical Japanese ideal of life in harmony with nature—an intimacy with the natural world and an awareness of it.

I felt completely free in Tokyo. It had been my experience that the "ugly American" is ugly to foreigners, but not necessarily to American blacks, when he was outside the United States. When he was overseas he tended to put blacks into the same category as other Americans; only when he returned to the United States did he again become ugly to blacks. At Nellis I had been directed to the other side of the tracks to live in an apartment that was not fit for any human being. Life in the Far East was obviously going to be extremely different. The warmth of the Collagans' greeting and assistance, Howie

Marsh's help in finding us a place to live, the cordiality of all the people we met—these were unlike any welcome Agatha and I had received in the military before.

## A Cultural Education

As a result of this unfamiliar feeling of freedom, we were delighted to be in Japan and determined to enjoy our time there to the fullest. It was a great advantage to live in Seijo Machi, where we learned more about Japan than we ever could have learned from books. We will always be grateful to Howie Marsh for guiding us there. The Marsh family became our friends and tour guides to Seijo and all of Tokyo, introducing us to their Japanese friends. We were to meet again in Germany.

Twenty-five years after leaving Japan we were still corresponding with our Seijo friends. We saw Paul and Nancy Ma, a Chinese couple, at regular intervals in Japan, Korea, Taiwan, and the United States. Paul was an international businessman in the import-export business. A group of Fulbright wives persuaded Nancy, an aristocratic lady who spoke some English, to offer Chinese cooking lessons, and Agatha was lucky to be included. Actually, they proved to be Nancy's guinea pigs—before long she was teaching in Tokyo. She later wrote several beautifully illustrated cookbooks in English, Japanese, and Chinese, and opened successful Chinese restaurants in Tokyo and Okinawa.

Arakawasan and Nittasan were two particularly close Japanese friends. Arakawasan, the widow of a man who had owned a lacquer business in Kyoto, lived within walking distance of our house. She was a small, slight lady who dressed in the traditional Japanese kimono, as did most of the Japanese women of the day. Although small in stature, she was very large indeed in her personality, intentions, philosophy, and determination. Agatha engaged her as her Japanese language teacher, but almost immediately she became much more, devoting herself to the task of teaching us about the Japanese people and their culture. It was easy for all three of us because she was well educated and spoke English fluently. She told us that because Agatha had shown much greater interest in the Japanese people than other Americans she had met, she would take great pleasure in showing her Japan and its people. She taught us how to look at the cherry trees and their blossoms, not the way most Americans looked at them, but carefully, as the Japanese did: to look at the branches on the right, then to see the clouds showing through the branches on the left; to see in the blossoms a life cycle similar to ours, from the bud (birth), to the full and admired blossom (youth), and then the withering of old age and death. We particularly enjoyed watching the expressions of serenity, happiness, worship, and sheer joy on Japanese faces during *sakura*, cherry blossom viewing.

Arakawasan took us to a tea ceremony at Waseda University and accompanied us to Kabuki and Noh, two forms of traditional Japanese drama, explaining the scenery, spectacle, and plot. She introduced Agatha to her friends in Seijo, some of whom lived in small houses, others in large ones, where they kept warm by sitting around a *kotatsu*, a recess in the floor in which charcoal embers burned. In every case Agatha was welcomed and shown through the home. All the Japanese were proud of their homes, which they kept scrupulously clean and neat. The emphasis was on simple elegance, a delightful Japanese concept known as *shibui*.

Agatha visited one home where an unusual cooling drink was served by the daughter-in-law of the lady of the house. The mother-in-law expected her daughter-in-law to work in the house as a servant, and she was not introduced to Agatha. After serving the guests, the daughter-in-law bowed and backed out of the room. Arakawasan explained that this arrangement was still the custom at that time; she was deeply interested in women's rights, and she must have objected to it. Later she took us to a meeting in Tokyo where a large group of women discussed the tactics they must employ to change this custom. All these women were fighting—in a reserved Japanese way—for their rights.

Agatha visited Arakawasan twice a week while we were in Tokyo. She also spent considerable time with Nittasan, a professional marriage broker. Nittasan had a husband and three sons who lived with her in Seijo; she also had a daughter who was in college in the United States. It was through Nittasan that we came to understand the age-old arrangements for marriage. She showed us her business books, filled with pictures of boys and girls of marriageable age, complete with full information on each one's family. Her mode of operation was simple. She interviewed family members, as well as the prospective bride and groom, until she could make an educated judgment on the prospects for a suitable match. Usually the mother of a prospective bride would take her daughter to some form of entertainment, a movie or a play. The father of the prospective groom would take his son to the same entertainment, where the boy and girl could see one another. If the interest was positive on both sides, Nittasan would negotiate between the families until further agreement was reached or until they agreed to break off negotiations. If the match was to proceed, Nittasan would arrange for the boy and girl to meet in a formal situation, which would probably lead to a closer relationship and ultimately to marriage.

Through Nittasan and Arakawasan we learned to appreciate many of the traditional Japanese attitudes toward life, religion, nature, and respect for people. We also came to understand the way the Japanese felt about family unity, the upbringing of children, and the importance of education. We particularly learned to respect Japanese talents in the arts and crafts. There was a Japanese saying that nothing manmade was perfect, but they tried to come as close to perfection as humanly possible. Our stay in Japan definitely enhanced our appreciation of some of the simple joys in life.

Agatha and I explored Tokyo together whenever my work permitted. Gene Steffes, an American who had a business in Okinawa, generously offered me the use of his right-hand-drive Consul pending the arrival of my own car. Driving carefully on the narrow, two-lane roads, which had open sewers on both sides, we experienced every smell the city and the wide agricultural fields could provide. We traveled into completely Japanese areas and wandered about without seeing foreigners of any nationality. We drove confidently in the city despite the tiny Japanese taxis that darted in and out from all directions. The police were invariably generous in assisting us, and when we had trouble communicating with them they would draw maps for us. We saw movies with English subtitles in Tokyo's huge, magnificently decorated theaters, live stage shows, and exquisitely staged productions in Japanese music halls. It took many weekends of exploration before we began to develop a balanced understanding of this awe-inspiring nation. When I was at work or away on a trip, Agatha explored alone. Tokyo was such a friendly place that when we left our house in Seijo, we did not even lock the door.

Matters remained relatively quiet on the diplomatic front until

Labor Day weekend, when they heated up, and I spent the holiday in Operations at our headquarters in the Meiji Building. The situation in the Formosa Strait was deteriorating. On the day Agatha and I arrived in Tokyo, Communist leader Chou En-lai had announced his country's intention to "liberate" Taiwan. A few days later President Eisenhower replied that the 7th Fleet would repel any invasion attempt. On Labor Day the Communists bombarded Quemoy and Little Quemoy, Chinese Nationalist islands immediately off the China coast. The Nationalists retaliated by bombarding the nearby Communist island of Amoy. No other significant military action took place at the time. The situation in the straits was viewed as being so serious, however, that on 12 September the National Security Council discussed proposals for military action against Communist China. The President rejected the proposals because of the danger of atomic war.

I visited Okinawa in late September. Bill Campbell commanded the squadron deployed there from the 51st in Korea. He was doing well. The situation had quieted down since the Labor Day flap, and the week-to-week service operation was fairly routine.

## An Unexpected Promotion

On 27 October 1954 I was notified that I had been nominated by President Eisenhower for promotion to brigadier general. This was not a routine promotion in any sense, nor one that I had been expecting. I tried to call Agatha and tell her, but she was out on one of her frequent adventures. Another officer in the headquarters, Art Pierce, had also been nominated, so Art and I had our pictures taken with our stars being pinned on by General Partridge. I do not remember my specific thoughts during the day, but I probably reminded myself that since I was now a general officer Agatha and I would not have to worry about the lack of heat in our house because we would move immediately into government quarters. I might also receive a raise, have use of a government car, and be reassigned to a command position—all possibilities that soon materialized.

As I approached the house that evening, I saw some odd Japanese signs attached to the wall around the house and its front and side. It turned out that they announced the arrival of Seijo's first general. Agatha had learned of my promotion from the signs when she returned from shopping in Tokyo. My neighbors had brought over food and drink, put the signs up, and waited to congratulate me on my promotion. I was moved by this outpouring of approval and friendship. The party went on for hours. We still have pictures of that memorable day in Seijo.

During the next few days I received hundreds of letters of congratulation from military people, as well as from American and foreign civilians. Some of the writers I knew; many were total strangers. I was grateful to them for taking the time to write, and I answered all the letters and messages. The following night Art Pierce and I had a well-attended and high-spirited joint promotion party at the Washington Heights Officers' Club.

Shortly after the promotion Agatha and I moved into an apartment in Pershing Heights, in the center of Tokyo. As much as we had loved Seijo Machi and its people, we were delighted to move into government quarters. Pershing Heights was impressive inside and out. Many tall old trees stood on the grounds, part of the elegant gardens around the buildings. Once the Japanese War College, the buildings had been converted into family quarters for senior officers—a few colonels, but mostly general officers. We had air-conditioning, wall-to-wall carpeting, and more than enough heat, even for cold-blooded Americans. In the morning on most days we could see Mt. Fuji from our dining area. We found ourselves thinking of the magic mountain as the Japanese did; contemplating it at breakfast, we could appreciate what the Japanese mean when they say the best things in life are free. Our conversations about and with Mt. Fuji became a daily ritual.

My work increased considerably, along with the demands for attending numerous social events involving people from FEAF Headquarters, the other services, and our superior headquarters, the Far East Command. I got less sleep, and we found ourselves on the go most of the time. I was asked to prepare the backup support for General Partridge's forthcoming visit to the Pentagon. This support had to come from all the staff sections of the headquarters, so it was necessary to arrange several meetings before writing, reviewing, and in some cases rewriting the staff papers the general would take with him to Washington.

Before leaving for Washington, General Partridge visited 13th Air Force Headquarters at Clark Air Base (formerly Fort Stotsenberg) and made an aerial survey of the Philippine Islands. I accompanied him and learned a great deal about the proper demeanor of a senior general toward junior officers. I was impressed by the size of the air base, its facilities, the large number of family quarters with new furniture and what I considered to be luxurious appointments, and the country club atmosphere. I also felt the weight of the recent history of the entire area: the initial air attacks on the Philippines by the Japanese in 1941, the Japanese landings, our surrender, Corregidor, MacArthur's departure by submarine, the Bataan Death March, the Leyte landings in 1944, and the Magsaysay presidency.

I also accompanied General Partridge on a surprise operational readiness inspection of a deployed location of the 18th Fighter Bomber Wing. Everyone who had been associated with FEAF in the early days of the Korean War was well aware of the necessity to be ready on no notice to implement war plans. General Partridge had been the commander of the 5th Air Force when South Korea was invaded, so he probably understood this necessity better than anyone currently in FEAF. I had always admired the general as a commander and learned things from being around him that I was sometimes not even aware of at first. During the inspection, I thought the wing did not show up well, and General Partridge did not come down on them as dramatically as I would have. But later, upon reflection, I came to realize that he had taken into consideration certain factors I had overlooked: personnel problems and evidence of dramatic improvement over recent performance. He probably shared my basic opinion, but having a broader perspective than I did, he chose to overlook some of the deficiencies.

While I was preparing for the general's trip I was designated officer-in-charge of a FEAF-wide command post exercise that would test FEAF's performance in the initial stages of a war. I worked on this exercise for a full month and a half before it began and discussed it intensively with key officers in local Army and Navy headquarters as well as our own headquarters. The war game, which I named Blue Racer, completely consumed my energies during January and half of February. It also effectively canceled the 14-day leave Agatha and I had planned and prevented me from going on an official trip to Washington.

Blue Racer involved everybody in our headquarters at least part-time. In addition to the regular correspondence, we had to handle Blue Racer correspondence—usually in the form of top-secret messages and disposition forms stamped "Blue Racer" to prevent them from being taken for a real-life situation. About 100 Army, Navy, and Air Force officers played the war game full-time for nearly two weeks—long enough to lend realism to the exercise. All the senior officers played the game, including General Partridge; the vice commander, Maj. Gen. Kenneth McNaughton; and my boss, General Smart. I suppose I made a nuisance of myself with my daily briefings and the exercise decisions in which I asked everyone to participate. The result, however, was that each officer got to know his part in the implementation of FEAF's war plan. The Army and Navy components cooperated beautifully, as did our top headquarters. Blue Racer favorably impressed Gen. John Hull, the Far East commander. His Chief of Staff, Lt. Gen. Carter Magruder, remarked to General Hull in my presence—and in the presence of senior Army commanders who had just completed a similar exercise in October—that it was "the best exercise ever conducted out here." After it was all over General Partridge sent me a letter of commendation, and I passed the accolade down to my Blue Racer staff.

With three other women, Agatha visited Hong Kong in February—the first of many trips she would make there during our tours in the Far East. She found it to be the most exciting place she had ever experienced. The sights of the city and the Kowloon peninsula were breathtaking: the teeming thousands of people, the narrow streets, crowded trolleys, tiny cars and taxis, multitudes of bicycles and rickshaws, the ferry between Kowloon and Hong Kong Island. Surely there was no more fascinating panorama of life to be seen anywhere.

Hong Kong also had a depressing side. Thousands of jobless, hungry refugees were living on the sidewalks in cardboard houses with a board for a bed, and in packing boxes on the hills surrounding Kowloon and Hong Kong. These boxes were set on levels dug into the side of the hill, and a single hill might be the home of 3,000 people. An effort by the Mary Knoll Sisters sought to relieve the misery and bring homes, jobs, food, and hope to the destitute.

On 2 December 1954 the Chinese Nationalists and the United States had signed a mutual defense treaty, quickly ratified by the Senate. On 24 January 1955 Congress passed the Formosa Resolution, which authorized the President to employ the armed forces of the United States "as he deems necessary to defend Formosa [Taiwan] and the Pescadores against armed attack, this authority to include the securing and protection of such related positions as he judges to be required or appropriate in assuring the defense of Formosa and the Pescadores." I visited the Pentagon in May to discuss FEAF's role in countering any threats to Taiwan. The 7th Fleet's role was clear, but FEAF had no capability on the ground in Taiwan, and its role was less apparent.

When I returned to Tokyo I reported to General Partridge and the senior staff on my talks in the Pentagon. Essentially the Pentagon approved of FEAF's proposal to deploy to Taiwan a headquarters capability with the mission of controlling the Chinese Air Force. In accordance with U.S. policy, it designated FEAF units in the interest of defending Taiwan and the Pescadores. At this point in the briefing General Partridge turned to me and asked, "Ben, how would you like to go to Taiwan?" To my surprise I heard myself saying I would be delighted. My meeting with General Partridge took place on a Wednesday. On Saturday Agatha and I departed Tokyo for Headquarters, 13th Air Force, at Clark Air Base in the Philippines. My orders designated me vice commander, 13th Air Force, with duty station on Taiwan; and commander, Air Task Force Provisional 13. Without question the job was going to be a challenge.

# ★ ★ ★ Citizens of the World

**10.** *My Air Force career was immeasurably accelerated by my assignment to Taiwan. From then on, largely as a result of the size and complexity of the problems ATF 13 was able to overcome there, my reputation as an effective commander and leader was firmly established.*

Generals Partridge and Smart left FEAF while I was still in Tokyo. Both Agatha and I felt they had set the tone for the good personal relationships that existed in the command, an accomplishment for which they deserved credit of the highest order. On 1 May 1955 I received the following letter from General Smart, my departing boss:

Prior to leaving FEAF, I want to thank you for the wonderful job you have done as Director of Operations and Training. Having you serve with me, and being able to rely upon you with complete confidence as I have done has been a great satisfaction to me. By the quantity and quality of the work you have done, you have freed me for other tasks, and for enjoying many an afternoon on the golf course, too. I sincerely hope that we can serve together again and I shall undertake to achieve this whenever I can offer you a job commensurate with your abilities. Ben, I believe you have a bright future in the Air Force. You are well known, well liked and highly respected by those who have served with you. Aggie is a great complement to you and a wonderful person in her own right. You two together can go far in making our Air Force a more valuable asset to the United States.

I appreciated General Smart's thoughtfulness. At this critical point I needed all the support I could get, considering the magnitude and difficulty of the assignment I was about to undertake. It was good to hear that my recent performance of duty had been regarded favorably.

From the discussions in the Pentagon only a few weeks earlier, I knew the thinking in Air Force Headquarters and the probable approach and attitude of Gen. Laurence Kuter, General Partridge's replacement as commander of FEAF. I compared the Taiwan situation in early June 1955 with the dark days of the Pusan Perimeter during the fall of 1950. In the latter case, the enemy had been on the verge of pushing us off the Korean peninsula into the sea. Only General Mac-Arthur's brilliant stroke at Inchon averted this disaster. The situation in 1955 also held the potential for disaster, but for reasons known only to the Communist Chinese we were permitted to develop our strength to the point that we could defend the island. When I assumed command the enemy had the initiative and the air capability to seriously threaten our ability to defend Taiwan. We needed to take several actions immediately that would enable us to provide a genuine contribution to the island's air defense. We were well aware of the enemy strength that confronted us across the Formosa Strait; our intelligence people credited the Communists with several thousand MIGs, a thousand IL-28 light jet bombers, some two hundred TU-4s (the equivalent of our B-29s), and five new airfields on the mainland with runways long enough to accommodate their jets. They also credited the enemy with the advantage of a centralized command structure.

I did not, however, create in my mind an enemy that completely dwarfed our capabilities. I knew of the announced role of the 7th Fleet, and I knew of the part that the FEAF fighter wings could play. From a visit I had made to Taiwan the previous February, I was familiar with the abilities of the Nationalist Chinese fighter wings, the skills of their pilots, and the determination of their military leadership and their government to fight and win. I also believed that the commitment that had been made by the President and Congress to the defense of Taiwan would ensure the use of other resources beyond the Pacific theater if they were needed. In 1955 the Korean War was less than two years behind us. The air superiority we had demonstrated in that war—a ten-to-one ratio of victory of F-86s over MIGs—could not have been forgotten by the Communists, and the Nationalist Chinese Air Force was equipped with some F-86s.

It was up to me to play the small part I had been assigned and to play it well; I was determined to do so. Agatha and I spent the night on Okinawa and proceeded to Clark Air Base the next morning, where I reported to my new boss, Gen. William ("Jerry") Lee. Before he took command of the 13th Air Force, Jerry had been known as the father of the Philippine Air Force; and rumor had it that he had taught Eisenhower to fly when they were both stationed in the Philippines in the late 1930s. He had commanded a bombardment group in Italy, and my fighters had escorted his B-24s on several missions in 1944–45. We did not know each other well, but we liked and respected each other. He and Mrs. Lee welcomed Agatha and me cordially and honored us with a reception.

After two nights in the Philippines we took off for my new duty station, Taipei, in northern Taiwan. There we were greeted by numerous Chinese officials and their wives, members of the American community, and my entire command—all two officers and seven airmen of Air Task Force Provisional 13 (ATF 13), who had arrived in Taiwan a few days before. After a warm greeting at the airport we were taken to the T'a Tung, a government guest house in Taipei, where we found an orchid plant sent to us from President and Madame Chiang Kai-shek. It was the Chinese custom on Taiwan to give orchid plants in bloom; when the bloom was gone the recipient was expected to return the plant to the donor, but we did not learn of this custom until much later. We stayed at the T'a Tung for three weeks, attending numerous luncheons, dinners, and cocktail receptions while I spent my days working and trying to find an adequate place to live.

## The Mission for ATF 13

From the moment I set foot on Taiwan, it was apparent that I had an enormous amount of work to do. From a command viewpoint the situation was far from the norm. Usually jobs in the military are assigned to an officer who does his job, making some minor changes along the way and, if possible, some improvements. When that officer completes his tour, he is succeeded by another who carries on in much the same manner. In Taiwan, however, we were starting from scratch. Agatha and I both realized that we were accepting a great challenge and a tremendous opportunity for a new brigadier general. If I succeeded we would reap the rewards of major achievement; if I failed I would shortly be replaced by someone who could produce the results desired by the Air Force—or in this case, because of the seriousness of the situation, by the United States. As it turned out, my Air Force career was immeasurably accelerated by my assignment to Taiwan. From then on, largely as a result of the size and complexity of the problems ATF 13 was able to overcome there, my reputation as an effective commander and leader was firmly established.

Overriding all other considerations was the immediate necessity for developing operational capability. The command structure that I was part of had interservice ramifications. The commander of the 7th Fleet, Vice Adm. Alfred Pride, would also be the commander of the U.S. Taiwan Defense Command in any war involving Taiwan. The Air Force position on roles and missions demanded that an Air Force officer command the air component of this command, and unless the Air Force could demonstrate capability, the battle for a satisfactory role would be lost before it began. My mission, in brief, was to create ATF 13 and develop in it a capability to control American units that would be deployed to Taiwan to defend against Chinese Communist attack. We would also control the Chinese Nationalist Air Force, which was already based on Taiwan and currently operating under the direction of the Joint Operations Center and the capable Commander in Chief of the Chinese Air Force, Gen. Wang Shu-ming, affectionately known as Tiger Wang. In event of war ATF 13 would become the air component of the Taiwan Defense Command, based on Taiwan. These command arrangements and plans were a direct reaction to Communist intentions to take over Taiwan, President Eisenhower's statement that the 7th Fleet would repel any invasion, the mutual defense treaty between the United States and Taiwan, and the President's congressional authorization to defend Taiwan and the Pescadores against armed attack.

The decision to move into Taiwan had come rapidly. No preparations had been made for the orderly development of ATF 13, no budget had been set aside, and no shipments of materiel had arrived. At first, Admiral Pride's headquarters was his flagship, and it was about a year before Taiwan Defense Command Headquarters was established on Taiwan. To make matters worse, no interservice agreements had been negotiated requiring the U.S. Army's Military Assistance Advisory Group (MAAG), the predominant American military organization on the island, to support me logistically.

My command slowly increased in strength. Officers and airmen reported in every day through the FEAF pipeline, some carrying everything they had brought with them to Taiwan. First and foremost, I had to make sure that when my unaccompanied airmen arrived, they would find a place to stay, a bed, a place to store their gear, and the assurance that they would receive their pay when it was due. I could have done nothing without the support of the Chinese, who furnished us with food, housing, and administrative space. We were given a building on Roosevelt Road in Taipei, which we used to feed and house our initial contingent of people.

It did not take me long to realize that my airmen could not exist indefinitely on a diet of Chinese food. This was one logistics problem that everyone could appreciate, and the FEAF surgeon supported us in this matter. Chinese food was fine, but not as an exclusive diet for homesick Americans. Before long my request for American Air Force mess personnel and equipment was approved.

In spite of inadequate administrative space, I also began to organize a headquarters that could operationally control Chinese Air Force fighter units and the American fighter units that would be deployed to Taiwan when needed. My command post was the Chinese Air Force Joint Operations Center. With the arrival of ATF 13, it became a combined joint operations center, from which any air war would be fought.

Almost all the people in my command had expected to be given some relatively cushy assignment in Japan, Okinawa, or the Philippines. Many of them had families with them, and some of the unaccompanied had probably chosen to go to Korea for a short 13-month overseas assignment. Instead, anyone coming to ATF 13 had been diverted from the assignment he thought he would get to a job on Taiwan with an organization that was just barely in the throes of being formed. I had a justifiable problem with those officers and airmen, especially the ones who had come with families—disappointment and upset when they found out they had been diverted to Taiwan, and more disappointment and upset when they had to shift for themselves, at least initially, to find quarters, with absolutely no assistance of any kind. I was in the same boat, so no one had to explain to me just how complicated that problem was.

When I approached the Chinese with our housing problems, they pointed me in the direction of the Military Assistance Advisory Group. Maj. Gen. William Chase, the chief of MAAG, was also the man who would command the Army component of the Taiwan Defense Command in case of war. He refused to accept any responsibility for our housing shortage, taking the short-sighted position that if ATF 13 people were permitted to live in MAAG housing, the arrival of his own men with families would be delayed. I could not imagine ever taking such a position myself. Army or Air Force, we were all Americans who had been sent to Taiwan to carry out an American mission. The real problem was the preeminent position of MAAG over ATF 13, both in their own minds and in the minds of the Chinese. I was unhappy with MAAG's attitude, but I realized I would have to get along with them. In those early days, they held all the cards.

MAAG's unreasonable delaying action cost our people a considerable amount of money and unnecessary discomfort. I was one of the victims of their selfish attitude; Agatha and I could not find a place to live for a while because there was so little to choose from, although everyone was congenial and there was no shortage of advice. We finally settled on an overpriced house that had been built by a Chinese banker expressly for rental to Americans. We moved in July and immediately ran into a sharp clash between East and West. Chinese servants in Taiwan had a monopoly on skilled help and could more or less set their own price. They also frequently took jobs for which they had no background or experience. If I fired them, they could live for two months on what I had paid them in two weeks. Agatha and I tried to beat this system, and we won some little battles but we undoubtedly lost the war. It was impossible to avoid losses in the Far East, as they used to say.

## Support from the Chinese

In an effort to solve my ATF 13 logistics problems I met with the Chinese, in the process establishing an excellent relationship and rapport with Gen. J. L. Huang, affectionately known as JL. The commander of the Combined Service Forces, JL was a powerful man physically and mentally. A winning personality with an infectious laugh, he possessed a wide array of talents, including the ability to stage inexpensive, culturally accurate, yet spectacular Chinese extravaganzas. His staging of the Moon Festival in celebration of the harvest was a feat of imagination and execution that made an exciting evening of entertainment.

As more of my people arrived, JL provided us with housing and administrative space, even though he was faced with the equally urgent requirement of providing school space for Chinese and Taiwanese children. Since the Chinese had fled from the mainland to Taiwan a few years earlier, they had been careful not to strain their relationship with the Taiwanese, descendants of the island's original inhabitants. The Chinese had to consider their relations with the Taiwanese in all their actions, and they were reluctant to disrupt plans for the schooling of either their children or the children of the Taiwanese to satisfy the military needs of Americans.

JL and I were to be friends for more than 20 years. My relationships with the Chinese in general, as with the Koreans and Filipinos, transcended any consideration of race, which was not always true of my relationships with American officers. JL did everything for ATF 13 that we asked of him; my only complaint was that he did not do it the day before I asked him. A Chinese virtue I had yet to develop was patience. This took a lot of effort on my part because I had been brought up in the "do it now" school. In time I learned that things often were best accomplished indirectly in Taiwan. It was not necessary to spell out in words of one syllable to JL or other Chinese officers the specifics of the help we needed; instead it was more effective to maintain a close personal relationship with these gentlemen, touching lightly on my immediate objectives. Miraculously, the word would filter down from them to their subordinates, and we would begin to receive support.

While I was struggling with the problem of how to take care of our people, we had to attain, with no delay, some degree of operational ability. It was very much a chicken-and-egg situation. Operational capability depended upon the performance of people, and their performance depended largely upon their belief that somebody cared about their welfare and that of their families. I tried to solve both problems at once. Fortunately, I had plenty of help from others who were as concerned about the welfare of our people as I was, or else we would not have survived.

When I arrived in Taiwan I called on Karl Rankin, the American ambassador; Yu T'a-wei, minister of defense; and General Wang. I had met General Wang on my first visit to Taiwan, in February, and I had been deeply impressed with his demeanor, his air of command, his keen sense of humor, and his mission-oriented attitude. Not only was he an inspirational military commander, he also had an artistic bent. An authority on Chinese opera, he composed, staged, and directed performances for his own opera company within the Chinese Air Force organization. He and I were immediately comfortable with each other, and I regarded him as a close friend from then on. I had the utmost respect for the job he had done over the years, and there was no suspicion of competition between us. Whenever my many problems threatened to wear me down, he was always willing to share some of the load with me. Because we shared high standards of performance, I could commiserate with him, for example, over an aircraft accident or poor performance on the part of a subordinate. A similar relationship existed between Agatha and Linda Wang, the general's wife, both of whom supported us in every joint effort we undertook. Their rapport and mutual understanding were especially helpful in our efforts to entertain distinguished visitors.

It surprised me then, and it continues to mystify me to this day, how key oficers in MAAG could fail to realize that the success of the American mission in Taiwan depended entirely on our cooperation with the Chinese. There is no accounting for likes and dislikes, and it is a fact that some Americans stationed on Taiwan liked the Chinese better than others. Agatha and I had no doubts; we admired and liked the Chinese people from the start, finding them to be invariably polite, considerate, and concerned about our welfare. We would have liked them regardless of the job I had to do on Taiwan, but our genuine good feelings were certainly a factor in the assistance we received and in my mission performance.

When I first called on General Wang I was given a thorough briefing by his chief of operations, Gen. Cliff Louie. Immediately after the briefing I scheduled visits to all Chinese Air Force installations on the island: Tainan, Chiayi, Taoyuan, Taichung, and Pingtung. These were purely educational visits for me, and I took advantage of them to meet and talk with as many Chinese Air Force people as I could. They inspired me to redouble my efforts to develop the kind of Chinese-American relationship that would enable us to prevail in the event of war. I was already familiar with the history of the Chinese Air Force on the mainland, and I was delighted to meet Chinese pilots and flight line personnel. They were impressive men. After a while I began to see in them characteristics of the fighter pilots I had known elsewhere. They walked with the same cockiness and used the same mannerisms that were familiar from my years of being around American pilots. The people who worked on the flight line gave me a similar impression: I had known them all before.

When I made my first visit to the Joint Operations Center, the day I arrived, we were already manning it side by side with the Chinese. They made us feel welcome and gave us no impression that they thought we were usurping their authority. I had two experienced officers, Col. Harold Scruggs and Col. Harry Downing, who exercised tact in developing an organization that would permit the Chinese operations people to carry out their responsibilities and permit us to operate with American fighter units in the same manner. It was not easy, and there were rough spots. Practically none of our people spoke Chinese, which sometimes made communication difficult, but many of the Chinese were able to converse with us in fluent English. Before long, we started to get to know one another as people. I was assigned a tall, handsome, charismatic Chinese Air Force officer as my aide—Maj. David Pan, recently returned from attaché duty in Tokyo. He anticipated my every need.

By September 1955, when we received the first deployment of a FEAF fighter squadron, we were ready to use it as planned. We were learning all the time and we made mistakes, but as we moved into October and November, we developed teams in the Joint Operations Center that were effective and smooth in their exercise of control. My director of operations, Colonel Scruggs, an experienced operator with impeccable credentials, was assisted by the chief of the Combat Operations Center, Colonel Downing. Several field-grade officers also grew rapidly into their jobs.

Late one night I received a call from the office of the minister of defense. Minister Yu wanted me to accompany him on a trip to Matsu the next morning, to return the next evening. Security necessitated the late invitation. General Wang; Maj. Gen. Harold Grant, deputy commander of the Taiwan Defense Command; and Gen. Edwin

Walker, deputy chief of MAAG in Taiwan, were also going. Our mission was to inspect the defenses of the four-island Matsu group. We met at 3:00 A.M. and boarded a PBY—an ancient U.S. Navy flying boat that always sounded as if it would be pounded to pieces by the water hitting the floats as it struggled for flying speed on takeoff. We landed at Matsu at first light so the PBY could depart under the cover of semidarkness. We were briefed by the Matsu command upon our arrival and took the opportunity to observe the state of discipline and the general appearance of the troops and their facilities.

Matsu was not a choice assignment. The island was barren, with only a few scrub trees. There were no creature comforts and no recreation—nothing to ease the monotony of a human being's existence. The troops had barely enough food to subsist on. The Communists frequently fired artillery from the mainland onto troop positions. We did not experience anything unusual, but we could see some evidence of enemy movement through binoculars. It was a long day. We walked many miles covering the areas we were encouraged to see and took off at last light for Taipei.

I was later to visit Quemoy, the other offshore island, with Minister Yu; General Wang; General Walker; and Rear Adm. George Anderson, the newly arrived commander of the Taiwan Strait Patrol. Quemoy was a garden spot compared to Matsu, but it filled all the criteria for a real hardship assignment. Matsu and Quemoy were not as specifically included in the U.S. defense commitment to the area, but the Nationalist Chinese were manning both garrisons with complete determination to stay. Losing either would have had a tremendously damaging psychological effect on the people of Taiwan because the offshore islands represented their last toeholds on the mainland.

We participated in our first major exercise in September. Two squadrons of the 18th Fighter Bomber Wing rotated to Taiwan from Okinawa, testing the control capability of the Joint Operations Center and accelerating our training. It was the first time we had been able to control this number of U.S. Air Force fighters. The results were not perfect, but looking back on the state of affairs that had existed two months earlier, I was much encouraged. The deployment also demonstrated our shortcomings in logistics. We developed firm plans for prestocking materiel on some of the minor airfields close to major Chinese Air Force bases and took action to get them implemented.

We felt the need to prepare for any contingencies because our intelligence people could not discern enemy intentions.

## Cross-Cultural Exchanges

A few weeks after our arrival in Taipei, Madame Chiang's personal secretary called and extended Madame Chiang's invitation to Agatha and me to spend a weekend at their guest cottage, next to the president's home on Grass Mountain. We accepted, and thus began an enduring association between us, Madame Chiang, and the president. The weekend was quiet and restful. About every hour a houseboy arrived with a tray of delicacies or drinks of some kind. The highlight of the weekend was dinner on Sunday with the President and Madame Chiang and Admiral and Mrs. Pride. Walking into the president's home was like visiting a museum. It was exquisitely decorated with paintings depicting scenes from the mainland. These and other art objects created an atmosphere we had never experienced before. Both President and Madame Chiang were charming in their welcome, and everyone was in good spirits. The president spoke only Chinese, and Madame translated all the English conversation for him throughout the dinner, although he revealed his understanding of English by laughing at appropriate moments when someone told a story. It was in every way a memorable weekend. We were gratified to receive this sincere expression of friendship and the implied promise of support.

The manner in which both Agatha and I were treated by President and Madame Chiang produced benefits that extended throughout the ranks of the Chinese hierarchy. A few days after we had dinner with them, Madame invited Agatha to tea—a meeting that turned out to have far-reaching consequences in accomplishing our mission. When Madame asked Agatha what she could do to make ATF 13 staff feel more at home during their stay, Agatha suggested that meeting Chinese people and learning about their life and culture would be a good start. No social and cultural activities were presently available to the ATF 13 family, and Agatha believed the lives of Americans and Chinese alike would be enhanced by such an association. Madame said she would look into the possibilities. Following her meeting with

Agatha, Madame called on JL's wife, Lucille, to plan an activity that might interest the American airmen and their families.

Lucille moved rapidly, meeting with Lillian Kiang, the wife of a businessman; Daisy Chen, the wife of a foreign service officer; and Agatha. They first organized a dance in downtown Taipei, and with the help of that man of many talents, General Huang, what started in a small way soon developed into an extensive program. By late August 1955, only weeks after we had arrived in Taipei, the Women's Service Committee to Allied Personnel was established. Consisting of the wives of Chinese government and military personnel and the wives of officers of ATF 13, it remained active throughout our stay in Taiwan and was instrumental in providing entertainment for all Air Force people on the island.

I cannot give enough credit to Agatha as the central figure who produced Chinese-American cooperation in its highest form while we were stationed on Taiwan. Daisy Chen was equally effective on the Chinese side. Agatha served on the committee as honorary patron and head of social services, contributing immeasurably to the morale of our people. I established a sponsorship plan under which new arrivals to ATF 13 were introduced to Taiwan and helped to find a place to live, and Agatha and the other members of the task force made a vital contribution to this enterprise.

In December 1956 Agatha addressed the assembled wives of FEAF commanders during our conference in Tokyo:

> Everyone has his own problems. They are all relative. We, who live on Taiwan, look at Japan, Okinawa, and the Philippines as "paradises" in the Far East. To us, they mean better housing, better base exchanges, better commissaries, better recreational facilities, and better contacts with the outside world.
>
> Life on Taiwan is never dull for we are always faced with problems, some that are easily solved and some that seem impossible. The Chinese have a characteristic patience that one gradually develops through constant contact with them. Things do not move along quickly, but somehow, someway, sometime, they get done. *Mei-yu kuan-hai*, which means "it is of no consequence, it does not matter," is a popular expression. However we, who are always in a hurry to get things done, become frustrated. By studying the people, their culture, their language, we would save ourselves a great deal of time and trouble.
>
> When Air Task Force 13 Provisional was first established in Taipei in June 1955, it was just a plan on paper. Today, 18 months later, it is a full-

fledged member of the Taiwan military family. It wasn't an easy job, and there were many setbacks. . . . Every man has had to take on additional duties to make ATF 13 a unit of which the whole Air Force may be proud. The wives have done and are doing all they can to be "goodwill ambassadors." All of us, officers, airmen, wives, children feel that we are one family working together to make life easier and more pleasant for each other.

She went on to describe the numerous charitable and community relations activities organized by the committee, among them its work with orphanages:

All of our activities were volunteer. Our noncommissioned officers and airmen did a marvelous job of community relations. Each of our squadrons adopted at least one orphanage. Last Christmas our two squadrons in Taipei sponsored parties for their "children." . . . Our third squadron was located at Linkou, about 18 miles from Taipei. Its orphanage was a very special one. Parents of the children had been evacuees of the Tachen Islands several years earlier. Some of the children had one parent living; others had none. Most had only sketchy knowledge of the fate met by their parents. The so-called Linkou Project was extremely popular among all of the men stationed at Linkou—Air Force and Army. Each man desiring to participate had to "adopt" an orphan. To do this he contributed $5 to the "fund." Some $1,500 was contributed. All of the money was used for a party and gifts. President and Madame Chiang Kai-shek were among the guests at the Christmas party held at the Chinese Women's Anti-Aggression League Hall. . . . Many of the men continued to support their "adopted" children by paying $5 a month, the cost of room and board at the orphanage. They frequently took their children out to parks, movies, the zoo, and Linkou for lunch. The men also assisted the children in their education. One can easily conclude that both the orphans and the American servicemen benefited greatly from this heartwarming relationship.

Just as she had studied Japanese civilization, Agatha became deeply interested in Chinese culture. She and two friends took a class in Chinese from Lillian I, wife of the former Chinese air attaché to Washington, Col. I Fu En. The class soon changed its focus to a study of Chinese traditions and developed an orientation pamphlet to be presented to new arrivals. An erudite Chinese scholar, Colonel Wu, familiarly known as Watermelon Wu, helped them by providing information about Chinese customs and family life. Colonel Wu frequently embarrassed Americans with his deep knowledge of American history, which was far superior to their own. Both Lillian and Colonel Wu dealt extensively with Chinese concepts, philosophy, and religion. It seemed to me that their strong belief in filial piety was one concept that would be worthy of emulation in any society.

Agatha took a fancy to the cheongsam, a dress with a split skirt and a Mandarin collar worn almost exclusively by Chinese women. These dresses were made of beautiful material. All she had to do was deliver a yard and a half of cloth to her tailor in the morning, and by the end of the day she would have a new dress. Initially she was the only American to adopt this mode of dress, and she heard murmurs of disapproval from the American community. Soon, however, many other women had followed suit. The Chinese considered the new practice a compliment to them, and it helped us in our campaign to foster good relations. By the time we left Taiwan, almost every woman in ATF 13 owned a cheongsam.

With Madame Chiang's help and at her suggestion, Agatha began lessons with Professor King, a teacher of Chinese painting who was fluent in English. In the Chinese method of teaching, the student sat and observed while the teacher painted a picture. Agatha took the finished painting home with her and returned to the next lesson with her copy, which the teacher then improved with his own strokes, thereby demonstrating approved technique and its results. After a few lessons she was able to create some paintings of Chinese scenes, which are displayed in our home today.

Agatha and I adopted many Chinese customs, particularly those associated with the protocol of dining at a round table. We thoroughly enjoyed the gaiety and enthusiasm that seemed always to be part of dinner in Taiwan. We never saw the same dish repeated, and I, formerly of the meat-and-potatoes school, never liked any food as much as I liked Chinese. There was another advantage—one seemed to be able to eat endlessly and never put on weight.

Not all our efforts were devoted to the Chinese, of course. Much work was done by our people stationed and settled in Taipei to make the arrival of newcomers as easy and smooth as it could possibly be. Concurrent travel was authorized for all officers, warrant officers, noncommissioned officers (NCOs), and airmen first-class who had completed more than seven years' service. We developed a sponsorship plan, assigning a sponsor to each newcomer to send him orientation information, welcome him, and escort him during the days immediately after his arrival. Our command furnished transportation, and sponsors always met both single and accompanied personnel. We always provided two wives from the officers' or NCO wives' clubs to greet and assist families assigned to our command. The Chinese Foreign Affairs Service Department Band met all ships at the port of Keelung, about 18 miles from Taipei. Pretty young Chinese girls presented each woman with a large bouquet of flowers as she stepped off the gangplank, and a similar warm welcome was given those arriving by aircraft. I attended orientation meetings of newcomers and sought to help them understand what we were trying to achieve, reassure them, and alleviate any unhappiness they might feel because they had been diverted from their original assignments.

Although my life on Taiwan was busy, I always found time to play golf on the championship course at Tamsui, on the ocean a few miles' drive from Taipei. Agatha and I went on a boar-hunting trip one weekend to Hualien, on Taiwan's rugged east coast. Richard Chuday, my American aide; his wife, Nancy; General Chen, the vice commander of the Chinese Air Force; Gen. Loh Ying Teh; Major Pan; and Colonel Larson, Air Force Section, MAAG, made up our formidable hunting party. We did no damage to the denizens of the Taiwan wild, but we were in good company and enjoyed associating with the other hunters. Shortly after our return to Taipei I was honored by the graduating class of the American School of Taipei by being chosen as the graduation speaker.

## ATF 13 Achieves Combat Readiness

ATF 13 continued to progress operationally during the winter and spring of 1956. Our people learned the details of their jobs, and our frequent exercises became easier to accomplish. Prestocking of materiel improved, and the visiting squadrons became familiar with the probable area of operation in case of armed conflict. In March Minister Yu; Adm. Liang Hsu-chao, Chief of the Chinese Navy; and I visited Matsu. I observed a change for the better in the living conditions of the troops, and the equipment available to the garrison had greatly improved. About this time I was accurately quoted in the local press as stating, "The Reds won't tackle Taiwan because we are too strong here. We are training and working alongside the Nationalists and familiarizing them with our equipment. Together with MAAG we attempt to create more initiative. The longer we work together, the more trained personnel we get. The difference between Taiwan and other places where we have military advisers is that on Taiwan we have today the framework for combat operations—immediately available in the area where war can occur at any time. And we are committed to defending Taiwan." ATF 13 had progressed from zero capability in summer 1955 to a genuine operational capability in spring 1956 at minimum cost militarily. An accurate summation might be that the United States was now in a reasonable posture to carry out its treaty commitments to Taiwan.

In March 1956 Karl Rankin made the obviously proper decision to include ATF 13 personnel in the MAAG housing list, an action we had fought for since the early days of our presence on Taiwan. Houses at Tien Mu, a suburb of Taipei, and the MAAG compound had been built by the Chinese Bank of Taiwan and leased to MAAG. Lt. Col. John Phillips, deputy commander of my air base group, carried this battle to ultimate victory despite MAAG's dog-in-the-manger attitude. The forces of justice won out, and our people began to occupy Bank of Taiwan housing on the same basis as MAAG personnel. Agatha and I moved into a reasonably sized Bank of Taiwan house in Tien Mu; life was not perfect there, but it was better.

My other major personnel problem was solved a few weeks later. On 4 April 1956, 10 months after my arrival on Taiwan, General Wang presented me with a key to the new ATF 13 Headquarters compound. At the ceremony American and Chinese flags were slowly raised to the tops of two flagpoles as the Chinese Air Force Band played martial music. I spoke on this proud occasion, pointing out that the compound represented an outstanding example of Sino-American cooperation: it had been built with American money, under the direction of American engineers, and by Chinese contractors. The Chinese were pleased that the dual-purpose design would enable the buildings to be converted to classrooms in peacetime. The successful completion of this project resulted in a substantial heightening of morale in ATF 13. At the same time I was grateful for the strong support we had received from General Wang and JL, and the unseen support we had received from the Chinese chain of command up to and including President and Madame Chiang Kai-shek.

Between 4 and 6 May 1956 General Kuter conducted Operation Roundup, assembling commanders of the air forces of Australia, Cambodia, France, Korea, Pakistan, the Philippines, England, Tai-

wan, Thailand, the United States, and Vietnam in the Philippines for
three days of meetings on the importance of close international relationships between the various air forces. This conference was so beneficial that the participants unanimously urged similar conferences in
the future throughout the Far East. As General Kuter had prophesied,
although there were vast differences among these air leaders, they
came to recognize that their aims were not as much at variance as
some had thought, and their divergent viewpoints did not interfere
with their ability to gain significantly from the discussions. The conference also provided a few days of relaxation, enabling the conferees
to get to know one another under informal conditions and leading to
invitations to visit their respective countries.

I personally developed cordial relationships with leaders in the air
forces of Japan, Korea, Taiwan, the Philippines, and Thailand. General Kuter's concept of cooperation with host countries in the Far East,
which differed from our previous practice of behaving as domineering
representatives of a victorious power, pushing aside everything that
got in our way, was to pay great dividends in our future efforts to
achieve national objectives in the Pacific.

Agatha left Taiwan on 1 July to visit our families in the States. She
had not been home in almost two years. Although I missed her sorely,
I was glad for her to get a change. It could not be denied that Taiwan
was a hardship station, and the trip was a shot in the arm for her and
her relatives. Much was being written in stateside newspapers about
the dangers we were facing daily in Taiwan, and it was definitely
reassuring to her family to be told the unvarnished truth. Agatha had
a wonderful time, and she deserved it. Throughout our service, I
never heard a single complaint from her about the hardships or worries she experienced countless times in many different places.

August was a bad month for both of us, starting with a dinner
party at Frank Smolken's home in Taipei. Frank, a concessionaire for
the post exchange in Taipei, was noted for his warm hospitality, and
everyone always enjoyed his parties. He had recently reupholstered
and refinished his furniture, and the lacquer used in the refinishing
caused Agatha and me considerable trouble: she awoke the next
morning with a mild itching on her left arm, which increased the
following day as the blisters filled with fluid and spread. I took her to
the MAAG dispensary, where the nurse suggested applying oatmeal
poultices. When that did not do the job, Major Pan made a correct

curbstone diagnosis of Chinese lacquer poisoning. Many people on the mainland were allergic to lacquer, and he was familiar with the disease and its cure. He cooked some herbs that were known as a cure for lacquer poisoning, but they did not help. By this time Agatha had developed large blisters filled with fluid everywhere except on her face and asked to be taken to a hospital in Okinawa. The people at the dispensary admitted defeat and were glad to accede to her request.

Fortunately she arrived at Okinawa before the onslaught of Typhoon Emma and was placed in an Army hospital. Her condition was confirmed as lacquer poisoning, and her treatment began just as Emma hit the island with the worst winds (180 knots) and the most destruction in memory. She and the rest of the patients were moved from the Army hospital to the second floor of the supposedly typhoon-proof Marine hospital, along with 28 pregnant American military wives, all scheduled to deliver within three months. Emma roared in that night, and over a period of hours 26 babies were delivered, some prematurely. Sanitary conditions deteriorated to the point that the health of all patients was seriously threatened. They survived with some difficulty, Emma blew herself out, and after 10 miserable days, Agatha returned to Taipei. She was very lucky. Though sick, she ate C-rations for several days. The doctor who released her commented that when she arrived she looked as if she had walked through a furnace, but she recovered without a single scar anywhere.

I had gone to Okinawa to see Agatha before the storm hit, and when I returned to Taipei I developed a medical problem of my own. I had been given penicillin for a sore throat and bronchitis and developed severe swelling of my entire body, especially the throat, neck, and head. Lying on the bed, I wondered whether I would be able to continue to breathe. I was alone in my quarters at the time, but fortunately I was able to crawl to a telephone and summon an ambulance. The swelling continued for several days. After a time, it was determined that I was allergic to penicillin. It was well recognized that medical care of Americans on Taiwan was less than adequate; the Navy clinic had only one overworked American doctor. I was sent to the hospital at Clark for treatment, but even there it took a long time for the swelling to subside, and for a while the prognosis was questionable.

## Distinguished Visitors and a Tearful Departure

The United States went to great lengths to demonstrate to the world, and especially to the Communist Chinese, its interest in Taiwan. We hosted a steady stream of distinguished visitors from the start, and it never really let up. We provided briefings, receptions, and dinners. Two aircraft loads of congressmen arrived in October 1956, including Senators Everett Dirksen and Earle Clements and seven members of the Military Affairs Committee, headed by Congressman Melvin Price. This group was entertained by President Chiang Kai-shek. The traditional Double Ten celebration (on the tenth day of the tenth month, commemorating the Chinese revolution of 1911) demonstrated the military might of the Chinese Nationalists. The parade was perfectly executed, and the military equipment that passed in review was impressive.

Shortly after Double Ten we celebrated Armed Forces Day. For this particular celebration, at the suggestion of the American embassy, wives of diplomats, military personnel, and civilians volunteered to prepare ditty bags filled with personal items and bags of powdered milk to be distributed to Chinese soldiers in the hospitals. Groups of people from the various American agencies visited the hospitals and presented these items to the soldiers. Unfortunately, although the soldiers were pleased with the ditty bags, they did not like powdered milk and threw it away. Otherwise, the day was an outstanding success. Madame Chiang attended and greeted everyone who participated.

During the first weekend in November I was the guest of the Chinese Navy to observe one of their exercises. President Chiang Kai-shek was also aboard. The fact that the ship was a new freighter that the Chinese had captured from the Russians two years earlier made the visit especially interesting. I was much impressed with the ship. Of the crew of 60 Russian seamen, about 40 had sought asylum in the United States. During dinner that evening with the president, there was some discussion of the effect President Eisenhower's reelection would have on the situation in the Formosa Strait. I thought that the mere fact that the election was over created a new opportunity for action. Not being a political expert, however, I listened and kept my counsel. The consensus of those participating in the discussion was that we had to watch the world situation carefully because whatever happened, the status quo would probably not be maintained.

Tiger Wang and I exchanged birthday parties in each other's honor on 18 November and 18 December, respectively—both lively occasions. On Christmas Eve Agatha and I, three other American couples, and four Chinese couples demonstrated the old Western custom of caroling to the Chinese community. We sang at the president's chapel on Grass Mountain and many other places, including the military housing area, two Chinese Air Force clubs, and the hospital. The Chinese voices were trained and cultured; we Americans provided the volume and the enthusiasm. We received numerous Christmas presents from the Chinese (among them four live turkeys, which we shared with orphanages), and Agatha stayed up until 4:00 A.M. wrapping presents for Chinese officials and friends.

Among the other holiday festivities, we attended a small dinner party given by the president's son, Gen. Chiang Ching-kuo, and Madame Chiang Ching-kuo. General Chiang was to succeed his father as president and skillfully guide the destiny of Taiwan internationally during his regime. He was a most charismatic personality, a charming host, and a successful player of the traditional Chinese "finger game," with a reputation for never having lost a match. Apparently, success at the finger game is determined by one's ability to read the intentions of one's opponent, a talent that must have made General Chiang a formidable negotiator. After dinner, he entertained us with his repertoire of magic tricks. Both General and Madame Chiang Ching-kuo made us feel very much at home.

In January 1957 I received news that I would be leaving Taiwan in early April. My replacement was to be Brig. Gen. Fred Dean, who would arrive before I left. General Dean had an outstanding reputation, although I did not know him well. There was no doubt in my mind that he would be a fine replacement and understand the critical nature of person-to-person relationships with the people of the Chinese Air Force. Furthermore I was confident that he would avoid the mistakes some Americans assigned to MAAG had made in dealing with the Chinese.

Agatha and I regretted leaving Taiwan. We loved the island, the people, and the life we had lived there, and we felt deeply the strong bonds of friendship that existed between us and the Chinese. I had been ordered to report to U.S. Air Force Headquarters, which could mean another assignment to the Pentagon, and we were in no way eager to return to the United States, especially not to segregation in Washington. We had thoroughly enjoyed living as free citizens of the world in Tokyo and Taipei, and we would have much preferred to spend some time on leave in the States and depart immediately on another overseas assignment. But at this time we had no way of knowing what the Air Force had planned for us next.

In March I relaxed and enjoyed the outpouring of goodwill I received from the people I had worked with during the previous 22 months. We were honored with many dinners, luncheons, and gifts: a tea given by President Chiang Kai-shek the day before my departure; the award to me of the Cloud and Banner, the highest decoration awarded by the Chinese government, for my "outstanding contribution toward the strengthening of Chinese air power"; a dinner banquet given jointly by Minister Yu and Gen. Peng Meng-chi; and a farewell reception in our honor by Vice Adm. Stuart Ingersoll, the commander of the Taiwan Defense Command, and his wife, Jo, at the Grand Hotel.

We had a tearful departure from Sungshan Airport. Several hundred people came out to see us off, including many members of the diplomatic corps, and both Agatha and I felt the emotion of the moment. The past 21 months had been the most challenging and satisfying experience of my military career, barring only my combat tours with the 99th and the 332d. In Italy and Taiwan alike, I had learned and matured as a commander. Although I had spent more time in the Mediterranean, Taiwan had been equally demanding.

We had made many true friends among the Chinese. Working together, we had accomplished our individual and collective goals. All the people I had been privileged to command, both officers and airmen, had performed to the limit of their ability. No less deserving of praise were their wives, who had contributed immeasurably to the success of our operation. All had undergone hardships and selflessly given of themselves in the interest of our organization and our country. Our Chinese friends had also supported us faithfully, and we could not have done our job without them. I will never forget Gen. Tiger Wang and the Chinese Air Force. I remember all these associates fondly even now, more than 30 years later. It was a pleasure and an inspiration to know them and work with them.

# ★ ★ ★ Little America

## 11.

*We led a much quieter life in Germany than we had led in Japan or Taiwan. A Little America, Ramstein was largely isolated from the native population. It was surprising how many Americans traveled all over Europe to see places but made no effort to know the people in whose country they lived.*

I requested travel to my new station through the embassy route: Bangkok, Calcutta, New Delhi, Karachi, Dhahran, Khartoum, Tripoli, Nouasseur (today Casablanca International Airport), and the Azores. In Tripoli I had the pleasure of visiting one of my flight leaders from World War II, Maj. Clarence Jamison, an old friend who had been one of the mainstays of the 99th in the air battles over Sicily. En route to the States from the Azores, we lost an engine and were forced to turn back just short of the point of no return. Agatha says I helped push the airplane along and that I seemed to be unduly interested in how the other engines sounded on the way back to the Azores. After a quick turnaround, we took off again and finally made it to McGuire Air Force Base, near Fort Dix, New Jersey.

I had been out of the States for two years, and Agatha had been gone almost as long. I took leave, and we visited both our families. I was still sweating out my new assignment. Although my orders read "Hq. USAF," there was still some chance I would not have to serve another tour in the Pentagon. Things broke my way, and in mid-May

237

1957 I received orders assigning me to Ramstein Air Base, Germany, as Chief of Staff, 12th Air Force.

Both Agatha and I were delighted. Before leaving Washington, I ordered and paid for a Renault Dauphine, a small French car, under the condition that it would be delivered to me at our port of debarkation. We sailed to Europe with first-class accommodations aboard the *America* in early June. When we arrived, five representatives of the Renault Company met us at Le Havre and delivered our car, presenting Agatha with a large bouquet of long-stemmed roses. Some months later I read an ad for the same car in the *Stars and Stripes* quoting a price for military people of $100 less than I had paid. I wrote to the Renault Company in Paris and promptly received a check for that amount.

## Settling in at Ramstein

After driving through France and Spain we arrived at Ramstein Air Base and were taken to our palatial quarters—more than enough room for us to rattle around in, and a far cry from the austere conditions we had recently left behind in Taiwan. Maj. Gen. John Gerhart, commander, 12th Air Force, and his wife, Helen, welcomed us warmly and entertained us at dinner the night of our arrival. My predecessor as Chief of Staff, Brig. Gen. William Bell, had been a classmate at the War College. He and his wife, Barbara, were our first neighbors, and both of them made us feel very much at home. Barbara and Agatha were given a joint farewell and welcome party by the wives' club, after which the Bells departed for reassignment in the States.

Our quarters occupied half of a large, three-story building reserved for the deputy commander and Chief of Staff of the 12th Air Force. During World War II competition for limited resources had obliged American forces to endure primitive living conditions, but now the deutsche mark reparation funds made our German air base facilities far superior to those we had experienced in the Far East. Paid by the West German government as part of its responsibilities to NATO and authorized to be spent only in West Germany, the funds made the difference between our West German bases and bases elsewhere in the USAFE command area.

Maj. Gen. Gabriel P. Disosway, who had been a first classman at West Point when I was a plebe, arrived three days after me and took command of the 12th Air Force. Mrs. Disosway would not arrive for several weeks. I concluded at once that General Disosway and I would have a good relationship. He was an unflappable individual, relaxed yet alert, and a highly intelligent and capable leader. One of his major talents was the ability to see immediately and clearly the solutions to complicated problems. As Chief of Staff, I attended most of the initial briefings presented to him by staff officers or wing commanders on aircraft accidents. By their very nature briefings should be clear and concise, and General Disosway invariably cleared away any excess verbiage that obscured the facts of what actually had occurred. He was never unpleasant and kept his sense of humor, but he always established the facts. I liked him, his mode of operation, and the way he exercised his command. We took a German class together, played golf on Ramstein's championship course, and became bridge partners.

The 12th Air Force was the most powerful tactical element in USAFE, commanded by Gen. Frank F. Everest, with headquarters in Wiesbaden, Germany. Its 40,000 people were widely based in Germany, Morocco, France, and Libya. It was composed of 11 wings, including one guided missile wing. In the event of war, the 12th Air Force would fight under the operational control of the 4th Allied Tactical Air Force (ATAF), a NATO command with headquarters in Trier, Germany, commanded by Major General Timberlake, who had helped me locate my group at Lockbourne 12 years earlier. Along with other members of the 4th ATAF and units of the Royal Canadian Air Force and the French Air Force, the 12th Air Force was responsible for the defense of a broad expanse of territory in France and Germany.

A tactical air force with a majority of fighter aircraft and fighter bombers, the 12th also had all-weather interceptors, light bombers, tactical reconnaissance aircraft, and guided missiles. All these were modern jet airplanes, including the F-84F Thunderflash, the new RB-66, and the F-100 Supersabre. Many 12th Air Force squadrons were completely equipped with F-100s; others were undergoing transition training. Our fighters were capable of delivering either atomic or conventional weapons. The guided missile wing was equipped with the TM-61 Martin Matador, a surface-to-surface tactical missile that was launched from a specially designed trailer by the combined force of a jet engine and a powerful rocket. It was a pilotless aircraft with the advantage of requiring no runway for takeoff. Electronically guided, it would fly at almost the speed of sound to its target, carrying an atomic warhead or conventional high explosives.

The 12th was committed to the NATO policy of resisting aggression and retaliating against an attack from the East. Under these conditions it was prepared to absorb an initial blow, but would be required to disperse and deploy at a moment's notice. Throughout my time in Germany—a period of continued East-West tensions in the wake of Soviet-crushed resistance movements in Poland and Hungary—we watched political developments through our command's intelligence and advisories from higher headquarters. Our surveillance of the prospective enemy and our evaluation of the threat were detailed and constant, and we moved frequently from one stage of alert to another, depending upon the situation. The pilots and aircraft crews of the 12th Air Force routinely maintained alert 24 hours a day, seven days a week, guaranteeing that there would be no Pearl Harbor in Europe. They were prepared to retaliate immediately upon release by the Supreme Allied Commander in Europe, Gen. Lauris Norstad.

The operational wings of the 12th had been deployed in France and Germany in accordance with the role each was expected to play in carrying out its mission. The 10th and 66th Tactical Reconnaissance wings—our eyes and ears—were equipped with RF-84F, RB-66, and RB-57 aircraft carrying the most up-to-date photographic equipment. The photographic processing centers at their bases, Spangdahlem and Sembach, were capable of processing and transmitting reconnaissance information to higher headquarters in a matter of minutes. Bitburg Air Base, also in Germany, was the headquarters for the 36th Day Fighter Wing. Its squadrons were deployed at bases throughout West Germany and were equipped with the F-100. One of its squadrons was permanently deployed to Camp New Amsterdam under the operational control of the Royal Netherlands Air Force. The 86th Fighter Interceptor Wing was located at Landstuhl Air Base, close to Ramstein. Its squadrons were also deployed throughout the 12th Air Force area. Their equipment was the F-86D interceptor, equipped with 24 Mighty Mouse rockets. They maintained alert around the clock and actively investigated all unidentified planes. Landstuhl was also the home of the 501st Tactical Control

Wing, which operated a network of radar and communications sites all through the forward area of the 12th's zone of operation. Radar scopes of the 501st Tactical Control Wing continuously watched over the skies of central Europe. Because of radar characteristics, most of the sites had to be located on barely accessible mountain peaks. The 701st Tactical Missile Wing had its headquarters at Hahn Air Base, Germany. Its crews periodically took their missiles to North Africa for launching exercises over the desert range near Wheelus Air Base, near Tripoli. We had four fighter-bomber wings located on new bases in France—Chaumont, Etain, Toul-Rosières, and Laon. Three operational squadrons equipped with the B-57 Canberra bomber were also located at Laon.

In order to be effective in my job, I had to visit all these bases and learn about their operations. My July 1957 visit to Wheelus Air Base was especially valuable. There I flew a training mission in a TF-100, the two-seated version of the F-100, with Capt. Bruno Giordano, chief of tactical standardization and suitability at the USAFE Weapons Center. We flew over the ranges used by USAFE units during their regularly scheduled visits to Wheelus for gunnery training. During the flight Captain Giordano gave me an excellent demonstration of his skills as a combat fighter pilot.

At the end of July I hosted a reception for 72 Air Force Academy cadets who visited Ramstein as part of a summer tour of military installations in Europe. I spent most of the day with them and was much impressed with their reactions to our briefing on combined operations and the mission of the 12th Air Force and 4th ATAF. After lunch we took them to Landstuhl, where they visited various operational sections.

## Reorganization

In the late fall of 1957 a cutback in the Department of Defense brought many changes to USAFE. Much confusion resulted, and it was difficult to keep up with what was going on. I did learn that effective 9 December, I was to become Deputy Chief of Staff, Operations, for USAFE. Although I was still a temporary brigadier general, this was a major general's assignment with responsibility for England, North Africa, and all of Western Europe except Spain. Operations, intelligence, and communications would be located at Ramstein, and all the supporting functions would be located in Wiesbaden; a major part of the justification for this reorganization was Ramstein's more survivable facilities in case of nuclear attack. Under this plan, I would remain at Ramstein to create a new operations unit as part of the consolidation of our USAFE and 12th Air Force functions, whereupon the headquarters of the 12th would be closed. The plan would place all former 12th Air Force tactical units in Europe directly under USAFE Headquarters, while nontactical bases formerly assigned to the 12th would be reassigned to the USAFE support wing at Wiesbaden Air Base.

This reorganization proved to have substantial operational advantages. It placed USAFE Headquarters at Ramstein, the heart of the existing facilities for wartime operational command, and created a USAFE support headquarters in Wiesbaden. The change did, however, create a major morale problem among the people who had to move. Practically all the operations staff from Wiesbaden, who would join me at Ramstein, were unhappy about leaving the attractive features of Wiesbaden for rural Ramstein.

Agatha understood my need for help, and she made a strong and effective contribution by calling on the wife of each of my new USAFE operations staff officers. She was particularly interested in getting to know the German people on more than just a casual basis. She was active in the German-American Club in Kaiserslautern, and soon made several lasting friendships with its German members. One was the Baroness von Gienanth, wife of a former German diplomat. They had married while both were interned in the United States during World War II. We exchanged visits with the Gienanths while we were stationed in Germany and maintained a correspondence with them for several years after. Ernst Krupp, a talented young artist from whom Agatha took oil painting lessons, was another close friend. Herr Krupp was also an entrepreneur with a keen eye for business; recognizing a potential market for Christmas trees in the area's large American population, he planted 10,000 trees.

We would have found this part of the world busy and exciting had we not lived in the Far East. Official dinners, cocktail parties, coffees, luncheons, teas, and other forms of entertainment were regular activities, but we were leading a much quieter life in Germany than we had led in Japan or Taiwan. A Little America, Ramstein was largely isolated from the native population. It was surprising how so many Americans traveled all over Europe to see places but made no effort to know the people in whose country they lived. Of the 2,000 Air Force wives eligible for membership in the German-American Club, only 17 currently belonged. The Germans did not have the initial warmth of the Chinese nor the graciousness of the Japanese, but after several meetings one could easily develop a friendship. Breaking through the social strata in Germany was not as difficult as in the Far East, nor as easy as in the States.

Agatha has always thrived on her relationships with all kinds of people, but she particularly enjoyed her German neighbors. I did, too. We ate, drank, and made merry with them over the holidays, getting to know, understand, and like them better in the process. We liked their emphasis on family life and the respectful attitude they had for one another. We were impressed by the way they trained their children—strict and orderly, but at the same time gentle. We found their love of art, music, knowledge, nature, and cultural traditions to be inspiring. And we thought their ability to laugh and enjoy themselves was truly exhilarating. Agatha and I felt we were getting a close look at the German people, and we liked what we saw.

My new job as Deputy Chief of Staff, Operations, was much better than the one I had given up. I was closer to the troops, and I was concerned with practical operational problems in Europe, the Middle East, and North Africa. It kept me extremely busy, and I frequently worked past six in the evening. I enjoyed every minute of it, even though it was a frantic assignment that dealt with a hundred different subjects every day, all of which were of extreme importance and required my close consideration. When I traveled I would invariably find my desk piled with papers upon returning. In early January 1958 I flew twice to Paris for meetings involving all the 15 nations of NATO. These were high-level meetings, with three four-star generals and an assortment of lower ranks in attendance. Following Paris I went to England for three days to visit 3d Air Force installations. The facilities in England could not compare with those we were blessed with in Germany, and deficient housing for our troops stationed in England constituted a serious morale problem; there were few creature comforts. In early February I traveled to Italy, Africa, and Turkey, returning home only long enough to replenish my clothing. In Naples I visited our NATO command, Air South, and at Wheelus I flew a gunnery mission and visited one of our USAFE fighter units in training there. In Turkey I visited Ankara, the capital, and our important air base at Adana. I left feeling that I did not care if I ever saw that worn-out-looking country again, but when I visited other places in Turkey later, I changed my mind.

One of the most interesting events Agatha and I attended while we were at Ramstein was a bar mitzvah, to which we were invited by Edna and Aaron Cohen. Aaron was an American civilian who worked for the Air Force. Both Agatha and I were truly impressed with the obligations a person assumes when he becomes a Jewish adult. The responsibilities enumerated in the ceremony to one's self, one's parents, and one's fellow human beings are awesome. It was a beautiful occasion, and all present shared in the love and understanding that it expressed.

The major event at Ramstein during 1958 was the arrival of the 4th ATAF from Trier. With it came a multitude of American, French, Canadian, and German families, who brought new life, activities, and ideas. The people of the 4th ATAF transformed the base; they got along well with each other and knew how to enjoy life. We of Little America found the international atmosphere refreshing.

My job tightened up twice during that year. The Lebanon crisis kept me working the longest hours I had ever logged in my life. The complicated situation was characteristic of the Middle East: it started with the assassination of King Faisal of Iraq and progressed with an appeal from President Camille Chamoun of Lebanon for U.S. help. President Eisenhower ordered marines from the 6th Fleet to land in Lebanon and moved 10,000 American troops from Germany into the area. USAFE's 322d Air Division responded in timely fashion, moving the troops first to our base at Adana and then into Lebanon. I maintained an around-the-clock surveillance so that I could assure General Everest that our command was carrying out its part of this critical operation. Emergencies of all kinds were possible, and I had to stay awake to deal with them and answer any calls for information from higher headquarters in Europe or the United States. I lost a lot of sleep, but everything turned out well, mainly because our military professionals carried out their assigned missions in an exemplary manner. I visited the area after matters quieted down and had the privilege of lunching with Adm. James Holloway, Commander in Chief, Special Command, Middle East, on his flagship in Beirut harbor.

The situation in Berlin also flared up around this time when we received a report that an enemy fighter had intruded into our airspace. General Disosway and I happened to be in Berlin together at the moment. We were not able to verify the incident, but we had to respect the possibilities, so we returned posthaste to Ramstein. Luckily, the emergency passed without incident.

## Excursions throughout Europe

Official business took me to the Pentagon at the end of March. While I was gone, Agatha drove some 600 miles through Germany with Freda Caldwell, a friend of long standing. Freda's husband, Lang, was an Army pilot stationed in Wiesbaden. When I returned from Washington we exchanged news of our separate doings, and after a week together at home we were ready to go again. This time I had four days of conferences in Paris. They ended on a Thursday, so I made arrangements for us to spend a weekend in Brussels. We particularly enjoyed the drive to France through the Saar and Luxembourg. The weather was perfectly beautiful, and we looked forward to Paris in the spring. How lucky we were to be stationed in Germany!

In Paris I attended an exercise directed by the British field marshal Bernard Law Montgomery, first viscount of Alamein, dealing with NATO's strategy against the current Soviet threat. In October 1942 Field Marshal Montgomery had turned the Germans back at Alamein in North Africa, the first major Allied victory after numerous setbacks. He was a rival of Eisenhower's during the war, and he carried so much history with him that it was a privilege to sit at his feet and hear what he had to say. He was a wonderful old man.

In Brussels we went to the World's Fair. The United States and the Soviet Union were still fighting the cold war in the late 1950s, and the European press was playing up the superior quality of the Russian pavilion compared to the American exhibition. We visited the American exhibition first, and then with a quick look over our shoulders in deference to my many security clearances, we walked into the Soviet pavilion. I did not think I was a likely target for kidnapping, but I did possess a considerable amount of classified information, and the thought did cross my mind. Agatha had always maintained that Americans tended to underestimate the Russians, and while we were inspecting a model of an extremely large Soviet airplane I made the mistake of saying the model could not be an accurate representation of an existing airplane. Someone else looking at the plane heard my remark and offered that he had seen the real thing on the ground in Moscow and that this was indeed an accurate model. I could not wait to get back to Ramstein and talk to our intelligence people. The Brussels World's Fair was held several months before the Soviets launched the first manmade satellite, Sputnik, which gave many Americans, including me, a healthy new respect for Russian technological capabilities.

The people at USAFE Headquarters routinely worked so hard that they did not have the opportunity to get to know the people in the commands with whom they were dealing. Many misunderstandings had arisen because not enough attention was paid to the development of sound person-to-person relationships. To correct this imbalance, General Disosway combined business with pleasure by convening a 12th Air Force commanders conference at a lovely resort on Lake Geneva at Evian-les-Bains. He also invited the wives to attend, making it possible to give them information that would be valuable to future duty performance throughout the command. All of us had a good time at Evian, and I was able to discern immediate positive results when we got back to Ramstein.

For years I had been hankering to see the bases in Italy from which I had flown during World War II. Agatha was completely agreeable to driving from Ramstein to Italy and back on a sightseeing trip. We surprised my parents in Rome, where my father was inspecting the American cemeteries at Anzio and Florence in his capacity as a member of the Battle Monuments Commission, and all of us enjoyed the impromptu reunion. We spent three days together in Rome and made them promise to visit us in Ramstein.

Except for the major airport at Naples—Capodichino—I could not find the airfields I had known in 1944–45. I had operated two squadrons for three months from Capodichino, and everything there was familiar, but at Montecorvino, Ramitelli, and Cattolica, all I could see were fields of waving grain. I could not visualize the places where the pierced steel plank had been spread to create a runway. I did see Lake Lesina, which was near Ramitelli to the south, but everything else was completely unfamiliar.

Our real vacation of the year was a Mediterranean cruise, for which we had applied soon after arriving at Ramstein. The Military Sea Transport Service furnished the ship, and we embarked at Livorno for Naples, Athens, Istanbul, Izmir, and then back to Naples and Livorno. Naples remains our favorite Italian city. Athens was a sad disappointment, partly because we were recovering from food poisoning from the ship mess. What was once the center of the ancient world seemed dormant. The ruins of the Acropolis helped us imagine the glory of what had been the first great civilization of the western world, and we did enjoy walking around the Parthenon, but the modern city of Athens, with its half-built houses and dirt side streets, seemed sadly declined.

Istanbul was a different story. At the pier we were welcomed by the "Star-Spangled Banner" and the Turkish national anthem. The ultimate multicultural city, Istanbul was old and new, East and West, Moslem and Christian, European and Asian. Minarets, domed mosques, spires, and skyscrapers lay before us. It was without question one of the most fabulous cities we had ever visited. There was too much to do, too much to see, too much to buy, and very little time. After we sailed back to Naples, we took the romantic Amalfi Drive by moonlight to Salerno, one of my stopping-off places during World War II. We immersed ourselves in the beauty of the Bay of Naples, silently comparing it to the harbors in Hong Kong, Rio de Janeiro, and San Francisco. From there, I flew back to Ramstein, while Agatha took the train. The cruise had been a tremendous success, more than we could have imagined.

My work slowed down a bit after the cruise. December was especially busy for Agatha, with parties almost nightly in addition to her activities with the German-American Club, her German-American cooking class, painting, and the base thrift shop. She was a member of the committee that created the shop, a valuable addition to the military community. It had opened with next to nothing, but soon was contributing regularly to the American Youth Activities program and dividing the rest of the profits among worthy projects.

All the parties we went to were attended by an international crowd; Canadians, French, and Germans from the 4th ATAF added immensely to the gaiety. It continued to be our good fortune to observe and participate in the joining of hands and hearts of peoples of other nations. Christmas Eve we had dinner with Gen. and Mrs. Paul Stehlin, a French couple. General Stehlin, the senior French officer in the 4th ATAF, was later to become Chief of Staff, French Air Force. Christmas night we had dinner with Cardinal Francis Joseph Spellman, and the day after Christmas we had a typical German dinner with Baron and Baroness von Gienanth. Agatha and I had two cocktail parties during this period. Peace and joy were abundant at all of these occasions.

Agatha started 1959 with a meeting of the board of the German-American Club, which she always enjoyed. She and I had three international days in succession: a formal dinner dance by Gen. and Mrs. Amadée La Dousse; a tea the next afternoon by Air Commodore H. M. ("Cars") Carscallen of the Royal Canadian Air Force and the 4th ATAF, and his wife, Nancy, our new neighbors; and on the third day, cocktails with Anne Marie and Paul Stehlin. We were certainly being royally entertained by the top echelon of the 4th ATAF. The new arrivals obviously felt that we liked and respected them, and they wished to show their appreciation for our welcome.

Early in January Agatha went to Berlin with Sonya Eastburn, a native Berliner and wife of Col. Charles Eastburn, commander of the Army post at Bad Kreuznak. Agatha and Sonya had met several years earlier at the Army hospital in Okinawa where Agatha had been treated for lacquer poisoning. Recently they had encountered each other at a party at Vogelweh, the largest Army base in the area. Sonya's mother and father still lived in Berlin, and Sonya planned to take her little boy, Billie, to see his grandparents. She offered to show Agatha the Berlin she had known as a child. Agatha jumped at the opportunity, and they traveled together on the American military train. Agatha had visited Berlin years before the war with her sister, Edith, and she had been impressed with its cleanliness, beauty, neatness, and character. For several days Sonya gave Agatha a personal tour of the spots she had known as a child and a teenager, and Agatha was grateful to see Berlin through the eyes of a German. Sonya was upset about her parents' living conditions. Before the war they had lived in a large apartment, but the wartime bombing of the city had destroyed much of its housing, and the government converted most large apartments to provide space for thousands of homeless citizens. Sonya's parents saw their quarters reduced to a small portion of what they had been, and they had to use a community bathroom. Berlin was no longer in ruins by this time, however; it looked neat and clean, and there was merchandise in the stores.

The operation of the USAFE Headquarters had settled down to a comfortable routine. I supervised six staff offices, each with enormous responsibility: plans, programs, operations and systems evaluation, operations services, manpower and organization, and the USAFE command post. Each of these directorates was headed by a colonel, and subordinate to them were field-grade officers. They were all experienced, capable, conscientious, and hard-working people, and I felt no qualms about our ability to meet any contingency; several of them had served at base level in USAFE and knew how to obtain any answers they did not have at their fingertips. I insisted that our officers travel to our bases, learn of problems in their incipient stages, and solve them before they got too big for us to handle. I believed that our posture must be read by the enemy as one of strong and effective alert, so that they would not be tempted to take adventurous actions. Our people always performed in a highly satisfactory manner, and I was consistently proud of their performance.

Agatha and I made numerous friends on the base, including Ary Murray, wife of Lt. Colonel Frank Murray, a legal officer. As chairman of the tour committee of the Ramstein Officers Wives' Club, Ary had arranged a tour to Rothenburg ob der Tauber, a quaint town that was famous for its history and architecture, and Agatha was scheduled to be Ary's roommate on the weekend outing. I had been feeling unwell for days and went to the hospital several times about my condition, but each time the doctors could find nothing wrong. I did not want to interfere with Agatha's trip, particularly because of the commitment she had made to Ary, but I felt so sick that I decided to turn myself into the Landstuhl hospital. Agatha wanted to cancel her trip, but I insisted that she go and she reluctantly agreed.

Rothenburg is one of the oldest and best-preserved cities in Germany. Local laws prevent inhabitants from modernizing the exteriors of their houses. Agatha painted a beautiful scene from the town that we still enjoy. She was particularly impressed by the Eisenhut Hotel, which had remained in the hands of one family for over 300 years. She had been amazed that some of the American women on the trip never left the hotel and played bridge the whole time, apparently interested only in getting away from home.

Agatha thought I was sick from overwork during the Lebanon crisis, but after 72 hours in the hospital the doctors diagnosed my condition as infectious hepatitis. Shortly before, I had been in Spain and Africa, and that may have been the source of the hepatitis. The upshot was that I had to spend six weeks in the hospital on a salt-free, low-fat diet supplemented by vitamin pills. There was no medication; I had to avoid rich food for several months and drink no alcohol for a year. Visitors had to wear gowns and sterilize their hands upon leaving. I was very sick only for the first 10 days; the rest of the time I stayed in bed reading—I became an authority on Hitler and Germany from 1918 through 1945. Initially I had no interest in anything and was deeply depressed—one of the symptoms of the disease, I was later told. Someone brought me a hydrangea plant and told me to water it several times a day; watching it grow more beautiful with the passing of each day cheered me considerably. Agatha gave up most of her activities so she could spend every day in the hospital with me. Her encouragement and attention accelerated my recuperation.

Eventually I was permitted to go home, with the understanding that I would spend another two weeks in bed and take 10 days' leave after that. I was grateful to the doctors, nurses, corpsmen, and thoughtful friends who had showered me with visits, cards, plants, flowers, and words of encouragement. I wanted to make it up to them, but I did not know how. I felt much better, however, when Agatha answered the telephone one day and called upstairs to tell me I had been nominated for a second star.

The doctors pronounced me recovered in June, and we headed for a week in Denmark. We were met by Dorie and Col. (later Lt. Gen.) Maurice Casey. Mo was the air attaché at the American Embassy, and both he and Dorie were superb representatives of the United States. They went out of their way to anticipate our needs and make our visit a happy one. We enjoyed Copenhagen, but for the first time in my life I was bothered by a feeling of weakness. It took at least a year for it to disappear.

General Everest's departure from the command had long been forecast without any tangible confirmation. We did suspect that he was indeed leaving when we were invited to a large dinner for him at the von Steuben Hotel in Wiesbaden. Not long after came the announcement that Gen. Frederic Smith would be our new commander and General Everest would move to Tactical Air Command at Langley Air Force Base.

## Relocation to Wiesbaden

I made a quick trip to the Pentagon to secure Air Force approval of another reorganization plan for USAFE, reversing the big change that had occured more than a year earlier. Now the 17th Air Force would be created as a subordinate unit of USAFE, and Headquarters, USAFE, would be redeveloped as a major command with a full-fledged staff at Lindsay Air Base, a large compound of office buildings in Wiesbaden without a runway. I and my office would move to Wiesbaden, as would USAFE's intelligence and communication staff.

The trip was a success, and my problem now was to sell the reorganization to the European command and Supreme Headquarters Allied Powers Europe (SHAPE). I made an initial approach in Paris, and shortly thereafter I got a call from General Smith telling me of some reservations and concerns that General Norstad had expressed. Because the 4th ATAF was properly located in the center of any wartime operations, and because the Commander in Chief of USAFE wore a second hat as the commander of the 4th ATAF, all considerations seemed to fit logically into place with the new plan. Apparently General Norstad wanted to reassure himself that the United States would retain control of nuclear weapons and their use in the early stages of a war. General Smith and I went to SHAPE together, and after a short visit with the staff and a meeting between General Smith and General Norstad we were able to return to USAFE with our reorganization plan cleared for implementation. General Smith assured me that General Norstad's reservations had been satisfactorily resolved.

The move to Wiesbaden pleased many people, including me, because they would no longer have to travel from Ramstein to attend meetings several times each week. Agatha was also pleased, for it would give us a chance to see city life in Germany. It was a little hard to leave our palatial home in Ramstein for smaller quarters in Wiesbaden. But there was much to see, do, and appreciate, all of which led to a better understanding of the German people. Kaiserslautern had been interesting and provincial; Wiesbaden was interesting and rich—the home of many millionaires and other people of means. We had the feeling that it was a city of old people who had come to enjoy the shadow years of long and successful lives, and the local entertainment seemed to be geared to these connoisseurs. We felt lucky to be permitted to experience the joys of art, music, and nature. The Far East had awakened these feelings in us; in Wiesbaden they would be nurtured. We missed our friends at Ramstein, but the people of Wiesbaden were equally kind, and our circle of friends continued to grow.

We received numerous invitations for the Christmas holiday celebrations, all of which we had to decline because of a message from Air Force Headquarters. President Eisenhower had designated me his special ambassador to attend the ceremonies incident to the independence of Cameroon, which would be held at Yaoundé and Douala from 31 December to 3 January 1960; and the inaugural ceremonies incident to the reelection of His Excellency William V. S. Tubman as president of the Republic of Liberia, which would be held at Monrovia from 3 to 7 January. A subsequent message stated that Agatha had tentatively been authorized to accompany the delegation, which would be headed by our ambassador to the United Nations, Henry Cabot Lodge, Jr. On 16 December we left for the States.

For the first time in six years we were thus able to spend Christmas with Agatha's family. Agatha glowed with the happiness of being back in the fold. We visited our sisters in New York (as well as the Metropolitan Museum of Art and the new Guggenheim Museum) and the senior Davises in Washington. Unhappily for us, Ambassador Lodge decided that his wife would be the only woman in the delegation, but Agatha never complained. After I left for Cameroon, she spent some time with her parents and her sisters (and visited the Museum of Modern Art and the Whitney Museum). I met her in Frankfurt on 10 January, and I could tell that this visit home had been exactly the lift she had needed. She was radiant.

I had never before been to Cameroon, the most recent African nation to achieve independence. It was a primitive place, but I believed it was far better off independent and in trouble than safe and sound under French colonialism. Many knowledgeable diplomats doubted that the right man was president, but they were not concerned because elections would be held in a few months. There was internal strife, however; about 35 people were killed while I was there as a result of attempts by the opposition party to seize power.

In Liberia I saw great improvements since I had attended President Tubman's inauguration in 1948 as a member of my father's delegation. I enjoyed seeing my many Liberian friends, and President Tubman was especially gracious in his complimentary references to my father. There was only one difficulty: attending reviews, luncheons, dinners, balls, garden parties, and sports events in formal clothes in broiling temperatures. Agatha had asked me to bring her back some primitive carved figures, but I could not bring myself to do it. The only ones I could find cost $60; they had been imported from Nigeria, where I knew they sold for $8. So Agatha had to settle for pineapples, grapefruit, and oranges.

She and I were gradually becoming acclimated to our new lives in Wiesbaden. With her usual verve, Agatha joined the local German-American club and readjusted her personal activities. Herr Krupp had lost many of his painting students with the great exodus from Ramstein, so he commuted to Wiesbaden once a month and Agatha continued in his class. She also supported my work; the day after she returned from the States, she had invited a group of women to join her in developing a six-month plan of social activities for our operations people. A year and a half before, people had been unhappy about moving to Ramstein from Wiesbaden. This time nobody was disgruntled; everyone was happy to be in Wiesbaden, and an activities plan to bring colleagues and their families closer together was enthusiastically welcomed.

We met lots of new people in the support elements of the headquarters who had lived in Wiesbaden while we operators had lived at Ramstein. They all seemed friendly and enthusiastic. I had plenty of work that kept me occupied all day long, before and after formal office hours. Previously I had been concerned mainly with operations; now I was concerned with everything that took place at USAFE, and I developed closer relationships with all the command's units and staff agencies.

In March Agatha and I flew to Istanbul, where I addressed the Turkish War College. While I visited the War College Agatha explored the city with Nancy Poinier, who had lived there more than two years. We met members of the local American colony and were proud to see that they were working to eradicate the image of the ugly American. Many of them spoke to the Turks in their language, and some of the Turkish officers, who were responsible for the success of their War College, were quite fluent in English. My speech went as well as it could, considering I could not speak to my audience in their own language. I did not have an interpreter, although one was available to assist in the question-and-answer period. Fortunately the audience already knew something about my subject—the organization of USAFE, its mission, and its part in NATO in peace and war—and my talk was supplemented by charts that in themselves answered many possible questions. It was clear to me from the question-and-answer period that I had been understood, so the time had not been wasted.

Before returning to Wiesbaden Agatha and I visited Ankara, where we saw the impressive Ataturk Memorial. Kemal Ataturk, the founder of modern Turkey, is credited with liberating Turkish women from their absolute domination by Turkish men. The nation was greatly modernized and effectively brought into the 20th century under his leadership.

On the way home I also addressed the German War College in Hamburg. Even though I could not speak German well enough to make my presentation in that language, most of my audience understood English, and my visual aids again helped considerably. After the formal presentation, I responded to many thoughtful questions through an interpreter.

When we got back to Wiesbaden I received word of my promotion to permanent brigadier general. This promotion was important to me because it indicated overall approval of my work, and it meant I was on my way to the rank of permanent major general. Permanent major generals could serve 35 years before mandatory retirement; lower ranks had to retire after 30 years.

## Agatha Ventures behind the Iron Curtain

Agatha's next adventure was a bus trip to Moscow via Prague, Warsaw, and Minsk. Some of her companions started out with fixed ideas about the Russians—ideas tinged by the anti-Soviet prejudices absorbed from our schoolbooks, our newspapers, and the pronouncements of our political leaders. Some of them found it difficult to admit an interest in how the communist world lived, for fear that their interest would cause eyebrows to be raised. It seemed impossible to talk to some of them on the subject, because they would immediately look with suspicion at the inquisitive one.

Agatha was fascinated to look out of her 17th-floor Moscow hotel room window—up at the sky and down on the broad avenues filled with bustling adults headed for the subway and children marching and singing in the streets to celebrate the end of the school year. The Russians were friendly, eager to help, and anxious to talk, which surprised the Americans. In Gorki Park she and several companions tried to stand in the long lines leading to the display of parts of Gary Powers's U-2 aircraft, which had been shot down by Soviet antiaircraft guns. As was their custom, the Russians ushered the Americans to the head of the line, where they saw some of Powers's clothing, the gold coins he had taken to evade capture, and the poisoned needle with which he was supposed to commit suicide. From Moscow Agatha took her first ride in a commercial jet, flying to Leningrad in the very aircraft whose existence I had doubted at the Brussels World's Fair. She was impressed by this city of canals and beautiful buildings, but most of all she was delighted with the treasures of the National Museum of Art.

Agatha made the journey east because she had been curious, and she came home even more curious, with many unanswered questions in her mind. She regretted that more Americans did not visit the Soviet Union; she believed that we should not turn our heads and look the other way, refusing to acknowledge our common humanity. Many service wives had regarded the trip as something courageous, but she hoped that in the future more American wives would venture beyond the Iron Curtain to satisfy their curiosity and perhaps to lose some of their preconceptions. When she returned home in early July, she arranged a party for those who had made the trip so they could discuss it in the presence of their spouses, whose security clearances had prevented them from going.

The rest of the summer was business as usual: visits to USAFE bases, and briefings and entertainment for the endless flow of official visitors. In early September I went to London on an official visit to 3d Air Force Headquarters. Agatha traveled by train, but on the way she got on the wrong car and found herself en route to Amsterdam. Believe it or not, some thoughtful, cooperative railway officials made the necessary phone calls to enable her to make her connections. A train at Utrecht was delayed five minutes for her, and the ship at the Hook of Holland was delayed 10 minutes. When she told me this story I could hardly believe it. It was just one more example of how generously we were treated in Europe compared with what we ordinarily experienced in the United States.

Agatha spent a week in Berlin with me at the end of October. This was our second trip to Berlin together, and we were happy to see that progress was being made in the concentrated effort to restore the city. Modern buildings had been constructed on many of the previously empty, bombed-out plots, and the new subway addition was nearly completed. We stayed at Wannsee, a suburb, on a beautiful estate that had been owned by the man who had invented the zipper. Pete Brinitzer, a high-ranking civilian employee, showed us around the city. He was a fascinating young man who knew everything about everything. We saw a refugee center and the document center where all the records of the Nazi party members and SA and SS troops were kept. We saw documents signed by Hitler, Göring, and Himmler. Also on display were the hideous lampshades made of human skin, products of the concentration camps. It was hard to comprehend that the German government had held such enormous power less than 20 years before. Pete made all the difference in our visit to Berlin; his knowledge of the city and the Germans was unsurpassed, and he was able to develop our understanding of many things we would have missed without his help.

Agatha made a final European trip of 1960 in late November. She had planned to go to Vienna and Budapest with Ary Murray and her son, Paul. Ary, a native Hungarian, had not seen her mother in 15 years. Paul had been one year old when he last saw his grandmother, so it would have been a most happy Thanksgiving for them. Unfortunately, at the last minute Ary was denied a visa, so Agatha went alone on the trip, which turned into a series of alarming incidents. Ary had asked Agatha to deliver a package containing some medicine, coffee, and a sweater to her mother. The air attaché called on Agatha at the hotel to see if he could be of any assistance, but when the subject of delivering the package came up, he thought it would be too dangerous. He drove past the house but did not stop, because Ary's mother could have been put in jeopardy for associating with Americans. While he drove around Budapest he constantly turned his head, apparently checking to see whether he was being followed. Agatha said he was as nice as he could be, but she was quite uncomfortable about the whole situation. Each time she returned to her room she was concerned about whether it had been entered and whether she would be questioned about the coffee in the package. Eventually she gave the coffee to the attaché and took the package back to Ary. She had found Budapest depressing, and her adventure a little frightening.

We spent Christmas with our families in the States and returned to Rhein Main on 2 January 1961. I left with General Smith for the U.S. Air Force commanders conference in Puerto Rico a week later. While we were there, General Smith informed me that I would be leaving USAFE the following summer, probably to command the Western Air

Force of the Military Airlift Command, with headquarters at Travis Air Force Base. This was music to my ears, but I refused to believe it until I had seen my orders. Certainly I would have preferred another assignment overseas, but the likely alternative—Washington and the Pentagon—was extremely distasteful to me.

One of the most enlightening evenings we spent in Wiesbaden was in the home of Col. and Mrs. Charles Price. Colonel Price had done missionary work in Germany in the early 1930s while he was a student at Brigham Young College, and had developed a keen interest in the people, their culture, and their political and social life. Upon his return to Germany in the 1950s, he revisited places and people and delved with a sincere and unbiased attitude into what had really happened during the war, seeking out people who had known and believed in Hitler. Eventually Colonel Price incorporated his findings into a talk packed with data and illustrated with pictures taken by Hitler's personal photographer. We saw Hitler through the eyes of those who loved and admired him; they had lived in a world of pageantry, of mass hysteria, and of fervent belief that the führer was their savior. We left Colonel Price's home hoping that he would give many other Americans the privilege of hearing about his years of investigation.

In April I received orders sending me to Washington and the Pentagon. The wondrous, exciting years of living abroad in an atmosphere of complete acceptance and freedom were coming to an end. After this initial shock came two softening blows. I had been assigned quarters at Bolling Air Force Base, and I was granted permission to return home the "long way around" the world.

Later that month I escorted Italian generals and missile teams to Cape Canaveral. There we met Wernher von Braun, the brilliant German engineer, who assisted the Italian teams in their missile firing exercise. I was grateful to him for the close personal attention he gave us, which helped the Italians produce excellent results.

May was short. Agatha and I had much to do before our sad farewell to the life we had loved. At the end of the month we drove to Brussels, where I represented the Air Force and spoke at the Memorial Day services at the Henri Chapelle and Ardennes American cemeteries. It was a proud, sad day for all of us. The ceremonies were conducted in French, and all the Americans who participated spoke fluent French. It was the only time in our seven years overseas that we had attended an official program where it was not necessary to have an interpreter.

Our last two weeks in Wiesbaden were filled with auf Wiedersehen parties and with completing the details of our move back home. On 17 June we took off for Tripoli, Libya, on the first leg of our trip to the United States and the start of our second trip around the world. Germany, like Japan and Taiwan, had become another happy memory.

# ★ ★ ★   Manpower

## 12.

*One must have almost superhuman endurance to obtain any satisfaction from working at the Pentagon, because one hardly ever sees concrete evidence of change. I could certainly count some successes during my tour in Manpower, but most of them seemed to take place on paper, and therefore they were not among my proudest accomplishments.*

After 10 days in New Delhi, we flew to Taipei. Word of our visit had gotten around, and we were given a royal welcome at the new terminal building at Sungshan Airport. It has been said that it is not wise to return to a place where one has spent many happy days. But even though the time and the place had changed, the people of Taiwan were still our dear and loyal friends.

The austerity program seemed to be losing its grip on life in Taipei. Visible progress had been made since our emotional departure four years before: new buildings, houses, roads, bridges, schools, businesses, and redevelopment areas. The man on the street looked better dressed. We were thrilled to see the results of this rejuvenation.

The social life of the city had not changed, and something had been planned for our every waking moment. Interpreters were no longer necessary. Friends who had been speaking little or no English when we lived among them were now fluent. Chinese women were playing golf and wearing sports clothes on the golf course, although the cheongsam remained. We were royally entertained by Madame Chiang and others. The Chinese Air Force guest house we stayed in was filled with flowers, the phone rang continually, and friends dropped by to see us. The visit was much too short, but when we left we were not as sad as we had been four years earlier. In 1957 we had no hope of ever returning, but now we were confident we would be back again. In many cases Americans develop a good relationship with their foreign hosts while they are overseas, but the relationship does not last after they leave. Not so the Davises. We have returned to Taiwan several times over the years, and we have always been made to feel that we were returning to our second home.

## Back in Washington

After visiting Honolulu, we landed at Travis Air Force Base on 13 July 1961 and took off for Washington the next day. Our new quarters at Bolling Air Force Base were a far cry from what we had left behind in Germany. Originally we had expected to live in one of the large sets of quarters reserved on Bolling for general officers, but I was ranked out of the more desirable set of quarters by Ted Timberlake, who had been promoted to lieutenant general. Instead we were assigned a duplex, the other half of which was occupied by the base commander, Col. Wilson Wood. Washington was still a strictly segregated city and would remain so throughout my second tour, but at least this time we had relatively decent housing. Old friends from Tokyo, Taipei, Ramstein, and Wiesbaden called and came to see us. We talked about the carefree days we had spent overseas, friends we had left behind, and the many worthwhile lessons we had learned from our brothers and sisters in foreign lands.

All in all, we enjoyed Washington during the early 1960s except for the leaden backdrop of segregation that hung ominously over this beautiful city. President John F. Kennedy held a White House reception celebrating the Emancipation Proclamation on Lincoln's birthday, 12 February 1963, to which my parents, Agatha, and I were invited. We attended the reception because in those days a White House invitation was a command performance. Even so, we were reluctant to go because the conditions under which black people continued to exist in the United States were no cause for celebration. Given the blatant fact of those conditions in Washington and elsewhere, we felt that it was completely inappropriate and false to glorify the Emancipation Proclamation.

During this second Pentagon tour President Kennedy was assassinated, and Rev. Dr. Martin Luther King, Jr., gave his famous "I have a dream" address at the Lincoln Memorial. Dr. King's speech seems to have grown in influence and to obtain more attention than when it was given. Even then, however, Agatha and I were deeply moved by his words, and they still inspire us today. Martin Luther King's life and philosophy continue to influence the struggle for human rights in nations all over the world.

We followed the events of the civil rights movement closely and with deepening interest. The hatred and senseless violence that characterized many of those events struck close to home when Samuel Younge, Jr., the son of a close friend of ours, was murdered in Tuskegee for daring to use the white men's room in a gasoline station. In the murderer's eyes, the act was justified because the boy was breaking the law.

President Lyndon B. Johnson's civil rights program, with its emphasis on voting rights, aimed at improving the lot of all downtrodden people in the United States. We strongly supported it, although active military duty was still so far removed from the political process in the 1960s that the idea of our campaigning for such legislation was beyond comprehension. Not until much later did it become appropriate for military people even to vote, and I can remember the shock experienced by older personnel when the policy was officially endorsed. We left the United States again in 1965, before the height of the violence by white reactionaries, and returned in the summer of 1968, when some of the major actions by black activists had already taken place. When news of happenings in the States did reach us abroad during those years, often on Armed Forces Radio, it was sketchy and out of date. For this reason only the major events came to our attention, and we felt detached from many developments.

Years later, when we were in Washington for a White House dinner, we drove through areas of the city that had been torn by racial violence in the late 1960s and were astounded by the extent of the unrepaired damage. Dr. King had preached nonviolence, and had he lived his tactics might have prevailed. With his murder, however, rioting broke out in many American cities, in an eruption of the accumulated history of racial hatred and oppression in this country. It was difficult for Agatha and me, so used to the relative racial calm of our lives overseas, to understand this tragic violence that seemed to dominate both blacks and whites in the United States. We deeply appreciated President Johnson's contribution to the positive changes that were taking place at home; during that time of turmoil, the country was fortunate to have a leader with his vision and courage. Since his administration, the nation has suffered from the absence of a leader like Lyndon Johnson, truly a man of the people.

I approached my second assignment to the Pentagon with mixed feelings. Eight years earlier the prospect had seemed much more mysterious and overwhelming than it did now. On the other hand, my background and experience had prepared me better for my job in the Directorate of Operations than they did for my impressive-sounding new position: Director of Manpower and Organization of the U.S. Air Force. I knew that I would be concerned with the distribution and management of the manpower allocated to the Air Force by the Department of Defense, but I was completely unaware of the myriad problems and details associated with the job.

When I reported for duty I called on my new supervisor, Lieutenant General Strother, the Deputy Chief of Staff for Operations, the former commander of the 15th Fighter Command, and my boss when I had commanded the 332d Fighter Group in Italy. I had always liked and admired him, and I was comfortable working for him. According to Alan Gropman in *The Air Force Integrates,* General Strother had opposed the racial integration of the armed services, saying as late as 1974, "I think they rushed into it too fast; they've almost ruined the services." If he in fact held this view, it would not have surprised me. In the early days of military integration, an extremely high percentage of Air Force senior staff held similar opinions. General Strother and I were quite busy, however, and discussed only matters relating to our work.

After calling on General Strother I returned to my office on an upper floor of the Pentagon, quite an improvement over the space I had occupied in the sub-subbasement for three years. I listened to a briefing by my executive officer, Lt. Col. Orville Fisher, an energetic person who had served many years in the manpower business and knew everything there was to know about it. He was just the kind of executive officer I needed, because my knowledge was limited at that time and remained limited on the intricate details of some manpower documents. My deputy, Col. Edward Rector, a former Flying Tiger and a valuable talent, was also knowledgeable on manpower and well versed in the ways of the Pentagon.

The last gentleman I met that first morning was Victor Cavagrotti, a data analysis expert. Vic was Chief of our Data Analysis Branch, a group of officers and civilians who had the mission of providing me with a continual evaluation of the Air Force manpower system. I placed great reliance on Vic to help me maintain impeccable mechanics throughout the manpower system. This effort was important because our credibility with the Department of Defense determined to a great degree their acceptance of the positions we presented to them. Vic was highly skilled in his work and served our office well. He stayed with me for most of my tour and left the Air Force only to accept a high position with the Civil Service Commission.

Through several briefings I learned that the overall mission of the Directorate of Manpower and Organization was to determine how many people it took to get the Air Force job done, what skills these people should have, and which of the three categories of manpower we should use—military, civil service, or contract services. I then would pass these manpower requirements to the Deputy Chief of Staff of Personnel, who recruited, trained, and assigned people in the proper skills and grades to meet our needs. Perhaps inevitably, I never had enough spaces or grades to meet our total manpower requirements. To develop the requirements, I formulated plans, programs, and policies that related to them, thus covering the total Air Force requirements for military and civilian personnel and contract services. Our basic policy was to allocate all available manpower to the commands; withdraw manpower spaces in accordance with unit, mission, or workload changes; and require the commands to place manpower requirements for which resources were not available in a deferred status until authorizations became available through program changes.

## Improvements in Manpower Management

Before long I realized that this job was simple in concept but extremely complicated in practice. The part played by the Office of the

Secretary of Defense, Robert S. McNamara, added to the complexities. That office had full program control, and sometimes it was difficult to ascertain their intentions. I attempted unsuccessfully for three years to increase the ratio of the top six airman grades from about 59 to 66 percent of the total force. Toward the end of my tour I found that my approach had been wrong: I had never convinced the Defense Department that the Air Force had a valid method of computing the basic requirement.

I was more successful in refining the method of computing Air Force requirements for rated officers. The General Accounting Office had been highly critical of the former system, and as a result my office set guidelines for how much time a pilot or navigator would spend in aircrew or related duties and how much he would devote to education, command, and staff development. I set only a small requirement for officers on active flying status beyond the age of 45, or 22 years of rated service. The General Accounting Office expressed satisfaction with our new system and stated that this method of computing rated officer requirements was acceptable. About this time our ongoing study of pilot requirements indicated a shortage and the need for an increased pilot training rate. The Defense Department approved an increase of 1,500 and later of 2,000, indicating their credence in our rated officer computing system. I maintained a close and cordial relationship with the people in the department, including Gus Lee, the deputy in charge of manpower. Invariably courteous and considerate, he was a gentlemanly public servant.

I also had to relearn the workings of the Air Staff. Great changes had occurred since my service there eight years before, and I found it necessary to develop new relationships with key people in the various offices. They could either help us improve our staff actions, thereby ensuring their success, or let us bloody our heads against stone walls. Fortunately I found everyone helpful and cooperative. The routine of Pentagon work was totally different from what I had been accustomed to. I now found it completely unnecessary to arrive at work before 8:30, and to my surprise and some consternation it was usually quite proper for me to go home about 5:00. Bolling operated a boat to transport general officers to the Pentagon and back to Bolling after work, but I found the rigid schedule inconvenient and started driving my car. After going to the office on a few Saturday mornings to read papers I had not understood during the week and to chat informally with the duty officer on manpower matters, I found no reason to continue. What I really needed was increased knowledge on the large subjects—the budgetary process, the operation of the Air Staff and the Office of the Secretary of Defense—to guide me in making the correct management decisions. I went through an entire budget cycle, a year or more, before I was able to separate the wheat from the chaff and exert my influence where it would render some genuine value to the Air Force.

Soon I made my first appearance before the Armed Services Committee, which breaks down the appropriations bills for the military services. Appearing before this committee meant appearing before congressmen who had served for many years and knew much more about the subject than someone who had recently arrived for duty in the Pentagon. I had to defend the portion of the Air Force budget that applied to my area of interest. But after this first experience I felt no real concern about making a good showing at congressional hearings, primarily because I had developed considerable understanding of how much money we needed to carry out our various projects, and the people who helped me prepare my testimony were experts in anticipating what committee members would ask. My assistants also worked closely with the pertinent committee staffs, preparing me so thoroughly that I was never surprised. During my tour I appeared several times before the House Appropriations Committee; the Manpower Utilization Committee of the House Post Office and Civil Service Committee; and the Senate Appropriation Committee's Subcommittee on the Department of Defense. Lt. Col. Jeanne Holm, who became the first female general officer in the Air Force, was one of our manpower experts, and she gave me superb assistance.

My efforts in one direction were particularly productive. Using the basis of vastly increased duties and responsibilities, I developed new grade standards for each operational flying unit of the Air Force and directed the commands to apply these standards to their units. For the first time, lieutenant colonel grades were authorized in all flying units, and the number of major grades increased. These important actions ensured full utilization of the rated inventory and provided for much better career progression in the operational career field. I obtained 4,000 additional lieutenant colonel grades under Public Law 87-194 and transferred major grades from nonoperational areas to meet the requirements for crew and crew supervisory positions.

In another important manpower action, my staff conducted a study on the use of senior NCOs as supervisors. To develop a factual basis for the study, I sent a policy letter to the major commands asking them to review work areas in which senior NCOs were working beneath layers of officer supervision. Because this situation was detrimental to the morale and career motivation of officers and NCOs alike, I asked commands to put NCOs in more responsible positions. At the same time I worked with the functional staff agencies to remove policy and directive restrictions that prohibited senior NCOs from performing certain officer-level duties and functions. As a result senior NCOs began functioning as personnel records custodians, daily transaction authenticators, equipment and control accountable officers, theater officers, and certifiers of tuition assistance applications. All these jobs had formerly been performed by officers.

I also reviewed the size and number of intermediate organizational echelons, hoping to find ways to expedite the decision-making process. It was clear to me that the Air Force needed to adjust some of its organizational concepts to meet the demands of modern operations. Our forces and the weapons they employed demanded instantaneous responses and quick decisions from commanders and their staffs. This required a tight, clearly defined command structure unencumbered by support or housekeeping functions, and a combat commander relieved of all but his primary wartime mission. When I commanded the fighter wing at Lockbourne, I was responsible not only for the management of the tactical aspects of operational readiness, but I also had to manage an extremely large and diversified industrial community. My span of control included supervision of nineteen functions. In our new standardized organization, my span of control would have been reduced to the direct supervision of only five functions, and my traditional wing staff would have been almost eliminated.

This new organization became standard for the entire Air Force. Responsibility for the entire day-to-day operation of any particular wing was delegated to the commander's three "alter egos"—two deputies and a support group commander—who would oversee operations and training, materiel, and housekeeping or support activities, respectively. As a result the commander would be able to concentrate on his combat mission. Once the organization of the wing was revised, the decision-making process could be further streamlined by taking the same approach to intermediate headquarters between the wing and its major command. In this case I eliminated staffs that did not contribute materially to the resolution of functional problems at the intermediate command level. In effect, I cut out the middleman.

A perfect example was to be found in the Air Defense Command, where I eliminated the functional staffs from its 21 sector headquarters. From that time on, functional matters were handled at the division headquarters, and each sector commander was free to devote his energies to his primary mission of air defense. My review eliminated an air division in the Air Defense Command and three regional headquarters in the Air Force Communications Service. I eliminated inspection functions at all echelons below the major command headquarters and consolidated these important functions at the major command headquarters. I also consolidated the Air Force Postal System in Europe under a single administrative head and created a single, worldwide mission headquarters to manage Air Force special investigations activities.

After I had been back at the Pentagon for a year and developed some ideas about how our operation could be improved, I took a survey trip to the Alaskan Air Command in late November 1962. This was not a popular time of the year to visit Alaska; I chose to make the trip then to avoid accusations of boondoggling. A Distant Early Warning (DEW) system had been built during the late 1950s to provide early warning of possible Soviet transpolar attacks. Our SAC aircraft maintained a 15-minute alert during periods of emergency, a margin that could mean saving our combat aircraft from being destroyed on the ground. I had been told of an interesting experiment being conducted in DEW stations involving intensive cross-training efforts of airmen in numerous skills, with the objective of reducing the number of people assigned to these isolated sites. This initiative had succeeded primarily because the men had no place to go and nothing to do beyond their duty. At these remote stations a cook could also be a radar operator, a driver, and a maintenance technician. It worked well on the DEW line, but its use elsewhere was questionable. The advantages of the program were that a minimum number of people were sent to the DEW line, and those on duty were glad to be kept busy with different kinds of work.

My office also supervised contract services. We developed a policy that the Air Force must perform combat and direct support functions with our own personnel to ensure combat capability. To implement the policy, I published an Air Force regulation directing an in-service capability to perform combat and direct-support functions—not only cockpit positions, but also all Air Force work that, if not accomplished, would result in an immediate impairment of combat capability. The regulation prescribed what kinds of work might and what might not be contracted and under what circumstances. Because of obvious differences between overhauling aircraft engines and feeding troops, for example, I tailored contract services procedures to functional areas. The Department of Defense determined how much military manpower, civilian manpower, and money was available, with little or no flexibility.

This particular effort was never-ending, and sometimes it seemed as if I could not win. I continually received opposing congressional inquiries: Why was the Air Force using in-service resources instead of contract services? and Why was the Air Force contracting for a service instead of using its in-service capabilities? My office did a reasonably good job of maintaining in-service capability, but because of a lack of skills we found it necessary to grant more electronic contracts than I would have liked. We did, however, convert the Aleutian segment of the DEW line and operation and maintenance of Air Defense Command power plants, refrigeration equipment, and training programs from contractor to military manning. We also developed a number of well-controlled and highly successful contracting programs, such as contractual feeding, and continually reviewed activities in indirect combat support to realize our goals of effectiveness and economy. In Turkey and Saudi Arabia, for example, we used contract services for vehicle maintenance, supply, civil engineering, and feeding; in-service feeding cost 3 cents more per meal than contract feeding. On one occasion, Air Force Logistics Command requested contract services for mess hall operations at Wright-Patterson Air Force Base, but when I determined that the contract service would cost $32,000 more, the command withdrew its request. The debate over the use of contract services and assigned manpower continues to this day.

The Department of Defense gave me the difficult job of identifying functions and manpower to be transferred from the Air Force in the process of activating the Defense Supply Agency, an attempt to centralize the purchase and distribution of items commonly used by all the military services. The timing of the transfer assumed great importance because it could not be allowed to weaken the existing Air Force logistical system, which supported our weapon systems. In addition, new workloads were being imposed on the Air Force by the activation, thus creating a new requirement for manpower resources. The Department of Defense also directed the Air Force to provide logistic support to the new agency in the performance of its mission and functions. Although the Air Force intended to provide this support, it had to be careful not to endanger or compromise its own missions in both operational and logistical support. All these conditions had to be specifically covered in written interservice support agreements between the Air Force and the Defense Supply Agency. These arrangements progressed slowly but well.

## Standardizing Work Centers

When I arrived in Manpower and Organization in 1961, I found the fledgling Manpower Validation Program (MVP). It had not yet grown to the point where many people outside of my staff had even heard of it, but it had started to formulate ideas on the standardization of work centers in command organizations. The ideas suggested that central control of manpower utilization could be achieved only with the establishment of a common policy in a number of areas: positions and grades; organization; the mix of military, civilian, and contract personnel; workload; tasks; procedures; equipment; physical layout; and facilities. In the beginning, we merely attempted to confirm the distribution of manpower resources and more accurately determine the manpower required to perform the Air Force's many functions. Each command developed and applied its own standards, while we retained quality-control review.

We started with only a few manpower validation teams, but soon, encouraged by the acceptance of the commands, I took three actions that became the basis for the expanded Management Engineering Program (MEP). First, I asked Air Force personnel to guarantee complete manning in those functions where MVP standards were being applied. The concept was simple and direct: work-center manpower standards stated precisely the numbers of people, by skill, required to perform a given volume of work, and this total complement of personnel had to be provided or the unit would be unable to perform its assigned mission. Second, I sent a personal message to all commands based in the continental United States, stressing that MVP standards would provide the greatest possible effectiveness because they had been developed by experts who had closely examined the function to be performed at the local level. Third, I asked the Air Training Command to institute formal training for people entering MVP and later to include in its training courses the broader aspects of management engineering. Air Training Command set up a ten-week course for officers and an eight-week course for airmen. Both were "career progression" courses, and they covered manpower validation methods and standards.

MEP gradually gained momentum, and we began to achieve our goal of common manning standards. When I left the Pentagon in 1965 we had 1,438 people assigned to management engineering, and there were 147 teams throughout the Air Force worldwide. In one of my last actions with the program, I organized a worldwide management engineering conference at Orlando Air Force Base in January 1965. It was well attended, with guest speakers from the Bureau of the Budget, the Department of Defense, and industry, and participation from the Federal Aviation Agency and the Royal Canadian Air Force, which had also adopted MEP. The story of MEP was well summed up in a letter from General LeMay, who referred to it as a program that provided an effective and continuing capability unequaled by other manpower surveys: "The Management Engineering Program is giving us solid manpower requirements which, because of the scientific methods involved, are recognized by higher authority. Each command has, in MEP, a professional tool to achieve more effective use of manpower."

Agatha and I enjoyed getting to know the Manpower people. Agatha organized women's groups and activities. The directorate sponsored one black-tie dinner dance each December at the Bolling Air Force Base Officers' Club; we still receive an invitation every year. During this time Agatha also took sewing, oil painting, silversmithing, ceramics, weaving, and woodworking lessons. I studied lapidary at the Fort McNair Hobby Shop, and Agatha used my stones with her silver settings to make cuff links, rings, pins, necklaces, and earrings.

I found working with my hands extremely rewarding and relaxing; it was the one place where I could see definite results. One must have almost superhuman endurance to obtain any satisfaction from working at the Pentagon, because one hardly ever sees concrete evidence of change. I could look back with solid satisfaction to my first Pentagon tour from 1950 to 1953. The fact that the United States had been fighting in the Korean War undoubtedly contributed to that feeling of accomplishment; some of the actions I had taken had translated measurably into an increase in combat capability in FEAF. I could certainly also count some successes during my tour in Manpower, but most of them seemed to take place on paper, and therefore they were not among my proudest accomplishments.

One benefit of living in the nation's capital was the opportunity to see many visiting dignitaries whom we had previously met in our work and travels. Agatha and I were on the so-called protocol list and we received a constant stream of invitations to diplomatic affairs. General and Mrs. Wang came to Washington frequently, and we always enjoyed their company; General Wang now represented Taiwan at the United Nations. We knew air attachés from Canada, Italy, Israel, India, Yugoslavia, Germany, Greece, Taiwan, Belgium, and Korea, and we frequently attended functions at the embassies of the Soviet Union, France, Belgium, Yugoslavia, Canada, Taiwan, Korea, Liberia, Ethiopia, Italy, and Turkey. During periods of tension between the United States and the Soviet Union we were sometimes told not to attend a particular function at the Soviet embassy, even though we had already accepted the invitation. We regretted not attending, because parties at the Soviet embassy were always lively. We also spent much time with former American embassy associates whom we had known in Taiwan, Korea, and Germany, and we attended official dinners given by the Chief of Staff and the Vice Chief of Staff of the Air Force for foreign visitors.

Agatha was invited to join a Department of State welcoming group, the Hospitality Information Services, sponsored by Mrs. Arthur Goldberg, wife of the Secretary of Labor, to help the families of foreign diplomats become familiar with Washington and its environs. She learned a great deal about the city through this activity, escorting foreign visitors to places of interest. She was also a member of the board of Barney Neighborhood House, which operated a community center on 16th Street in northwest Washington, and of the board of the Military Wives Association.

In December 1963 we spent 10 days in Rio de Janeiro, where Col. Claude Brown, the assistant air attaché, and his wife, Dottie, catered to our every interest and showed us everything there was to see. Both the Browns were fluent in Portuguese and obviously on excellent terms with the local inhabitants. Aware of my interest in lapidary, they took us to the home of an expatriate German who had developed a business in the manufacture of mosaic tabletops. The mosaics had been made from stone he had excavated himself; he kept a large supply in piles around his home and generously gave me as many as I wanted to use in my lapidary work. Brownie and Dottie took us on several tours of the areas surrounding Rio, and through their kindness we were able to see parts of the country we had not seen before and gain new understanding of Brazil and its people.

## Early Involvement in Vietnam

Late in February 1965 I visited the Far East with Col. John Kern (later a major general and a Director of Manpower and Organization) and Major Morgan, both of whom worked in my directorate, to review manpower requirements in the Pacific region, including Vietnam. We went first to 13th Air Force Headquarters at Clark Air Base in the Philippines, then to Vietnam, Thailand, back to Vietnam, Hong Kong, Taiwan, Okinawa, Japan, and home to Washington. At each location I saw people I had served with in the past.

Clark was as relaxed as Saigon was tense. At this time our involvement in the Vietnam War was beginning to expand, and I had to deal with the important subject of juggling Air Force manpower to cover additional and unforeseen requirements. Maj. Gen. Joseph Moore, a senior Air Force commander in Vietnam, discussed future manpower requirements and timing with me. The Air Force had to do its part in the war under the assumption, in accordance with national policy, that we would fight it within our existing resources—that is, without calling up reserves and National Guard units. It is possible (though hardly profitable) today to severely question the wisdom of that policy.

In 1965 we were being told that the United States was at war with North Vietnam to stop the loss of other nations to communism, which could adversely influence our interests in the Pacific—the domino theory. This simplistic view of the situation was held by many people in high places and accounted in large degree for the disaster we experienced there. By now we have learned that it is not possible to simplify situations in the Far East, or at least that such simplifications do not often represent reality. The French had learned in their war with the Vietnamese that conventional European military tactics were thwarted by enemy actions they did not know how to deal with—"melting away" into the jungle, night operations, tunneling, booby traps, and other highly effective techniques. The United States fell into exactly the same situation.

Much to the relief of our military and civilian personnel in Vietnam, their families had been sent back to the States to remove them from danger. We were about to begin an important bombing operation called Rolling Thunder, in which a lot of hope had been placed. My major interests were professional, and I left the geopolitical aspects of the war to the denizens of the White House and the Joint Chiefs of Staff. Everyone we met was optimistic and in high spirits, from General Westmoreland on down through the Army and Air Force chains of command. I attended General Westmoreland's daily staff meeting and got the distinct impression that his people knew exactly what they wanted to do, but were finding that doing it was exceedingly difficult.

I visited Bien Hoa and Can Tho, where I saw Dick Rowland and renewed acquaintance with Air Vice Marshal Nuyhen Cao Ky, head of the Vietnamese Air Force. I had met Marshal Ky in the mid-1950s in the Philippines when General Kuter had entertained the heads of several national air forces in the Southeast Atlantic Treaty Organization. Marshal Ky and General Rowland obviously had a good relationship. We flew to Bangkok, where Bert Cumby, an American embassy officer and a good friend, held a reception in my honor. Esther Cumby, Bert's wife, had been a high-school classmate of Agatha's in New Haven. I visited the active air bases at Korat, Udorn, and Takhli. Vietnam had been full of war, but Thailand was beautiful and warm, and the people seemed happy even though they were poor. We returned to Saigon and attended another briefing, which told us of the loss of six aircraft on 3 March and the recovery of five of the pilots. After a heartwarming visit to Taipei, where I saw many old friends, we pushed on to Okinawa, Japan, and back to Washington.

It had been an educational trip, and I enjoyed seeing the people who had welcomed us so enthusiastically. When I got home, my job changed. I became Assistant Deputy Chief of Staff, a kind of holding position for a senior general officer who might soon be promoted into a new job outside the Pentagon. I say "might" because this kind of thing was never certain. A few weeks later, I was notified that I had been nominated by President Johnson for promotion to lieutenant general. I also learned that I was to go to Korea as Chief of Staff, United States Forces in Korea; and Chief of Staff, United Nations Command.

# ★ ★ ★ Affairs of State

*When Agatha and I arrived in Korea in May 1965, we were starting out even in our ignorance of its people. We soon learned to appreciate their indomitable spirit. As strongly as any of the nationalities we had met anywhere, the Koreans were fierce in their determination to succeed in all their efforts—military, educational, economic, and governmental.*

**13.**

It took us a week to get to Seoul. Along the way I was briefed at Headquarters, Pacific Air Force, in Hawaii; and Headquarters, 5th Air Force, in Japan. Just before Agatha and I left Tokyo we were greeted by my new aide, Maj. Duff Huettner, who had come over from Korea to give us some idea of what we could expect to do immediately after our arrival in Seoul. A week after leaving the States, we were met at Seoul's Kimpo Airport by Gen. Hamilton Howze, Commander in Chief, United Nations Command, and commander, U.S. 8th Army, who seemed to have brought a host of other people with him. I received honors from the Chief of Staff of the Republic of Korea Air Force, Lt. Gen. Park Won Suk.

We left with Mrs. Howze and Gen. and Mrs. Edward Burba in a helicopter piloted by General Howze. I got to know Ed Burba well and came to admire him as a capable Army officer during the remaining months of his tour. We were taken to our quarters, which we liked immediately, and were graciously entertained that evening by General and Mrs. Howze.

I reported to Headquarters, United Nations Command, at Yongsan the next morning to receive honors at Knight Field. Agatha took a seat in the spectator stands next to one of the women she had met the night before. Immediately she was told she should not sit there because wives sat according to rank. Agatha's rejoinder was, "I don't have any rank." At this point laughter eased the situation, and Agatha eventually sat where she was supposed to. This incident made her one of "the girls." We learned later that, according to command protocol, wives were expected to wear a hat and gloves to the numerous honor guard ceremonies welcoming official guests. Agatha attended the ceremonies she was expected to attend, but sans hat and gloves. We wonder today whether the honor guard protocol has survived the wives' revolution in the military services.

My honor guard ceremony was faultlessly executed. I thanked the honor guard commander, stopped to greet the spectators, and proceeded up the stairs with General Howze to my office. After showing me through headquarters and introducing me to the people I would be working with, General Howze escorted me to the briefing room, where I heard the command briefing for the first time. I was to give this briefing countless times to people possessing security clearances, and the unclassified version to other visitors.

From the time we arrived in Korea we felt very much at home. Night after night we were treated to official dinners and receptions by the liaison officers of the United Nations members represented in Korea. General Howze accompanied me when I called on American and Korean officials and members of the diplomatic community, and Mrs. Howze accompanied Agatha on similar visits. We were particularly pleased to have dinner with old friends, Adm. and Mrs. Liang Hsu-chao. Admiral Liang, chief of naval operations when we lived in Taiwan, was now the ambassador from Taiwan. He told us that ours was not an official dinner, but an opportunity for friends to spend an evening together, and we were touched by his sentiment. On the occasion of my call on Kim Ok, mayor of Seoul, I was graciously welcomed and with much ceremony presented the key to the city. In similar fashion, when I called on the governor of Kyunggi, I was presented a key inscribed, "In token of the friendship of the people of Kyunggi Province."

My association with Admiral Liang in Taiwan had been close and personal. In Korea I was to develop several similar relationships, first with the United Nations liaison officers who represented their nations as members of the Armistice Commission, and also with the diplomats stationed at their embassies in Seoul. Life in Korea was intensely social, and Agatha and I considered ourselves fortunate to be able to develop lasting friendships with members of the diplomatic corps. These personal relationships often extended far beyond official business.

A nation's accomplishments are utterly dependent upon its human resources, and we were aware of Korea's recent history and advancement. We had lived four years in Germany, one year in Japan, and two years in Taiwan since my previous tour in Korea. I had also developed some familiarity with the peoples of the Philippines, Thailand, and Vietnam. Consciously and unconsciously we had made comparisons, perhaps unfairly in some cases, but we found that our initial judgments about the Far East often turned out to be wrong. In 1953–54 I never came to know any Koreans other than the priests at the orphanage. I had liked my houseboy, Yo, but our relationship did not go deeper than the thinnest possible surface, and I barely recognized any of the other Korean employees around the base. I credit myself with an open mind that tends to push aside superficialities, but in the case of the Koreans I missed out completely. When Agatha and I arrived in Korea in May 1965, we were starting out even in our ignorance of its people. We soon learned to appreciate their indomitable spirit. As strongly as any of the nationalities we had met anywhere, the Koreans were fierce in their determination to succeed in all their efforts—military, educational, economic, and governmental. The results of this determination are crystal clear today.

## A Joint Command

Any future war in Korea would be fought by the United Nations Command, composed of the forces of the nations committed to furnishing troops and headed by the commanding general of the U.S. 8th Army. The United States maintained a force of about 40,000 assigned to the 8th Army, many deployed along the demilitarized zone. The zone had been established by the armistice, which had been in effect since the end of active hostilities in July 1953, and was carefully administered by the armistice commission. The commanding general of the 8th Army, an American four-star general, simulta-

neously commanded all the American forces on the Korean peninsula. All our military services contributed to the Military Assistance
Advisory Group, which maintained constant association with its opposite numbers in the Korean armed forces.

As Chief of Staff of the United Nations Command, I held the second highest military position in the United Nations military hier-
archy. Three weeks after my arrival, General Howze was replaced by
Gen. Dwight Beach as my boss, followed by Gen. Charles ("Tick")
Bonesteel a year later. In the military organization to be adopted in
time of war, all the Korean military forces would be under General
Beach's command, which also included the U.S. 8th Army, the
Korean Military Advisory Group, and military assistance groups for
the Korean Navy, Air Force, and Marine Corps. At Osan, Korea, the
U.S. Air Force maintained a Korean advisory group, an Air Force
headquarters, and units that would also be under the United Nations
commander in time of war.

On 26 May, after being in Korea for two weeks, I participated in a
field exercise involving all the U.S., Korean, and United Nations
forces in Korea. During the exercise I traveled over all of South Korea,
visiting Army, Navy, Air Force, and Marine headquarters. At night I
listened to briefings and made necessary decisions. It was highly
educational to be simultaneously part of a joint command (the U.S.
Forces in Korea) and the combined United Nations Command. My
primary duty was to operate Headquarters, United Nations Command in Korea, at Taegu. Remembering Pearl Harbor and the crossing
of the 38th parallel by the North Koreans in 1950, I was fully conscious of the importance of what we were doing.

The tour for unaccompanied U.S. officers and men in Korea was
13 months. It was desirable to train personnel in two intensive field
exercises during their tours to teach them their jobs under simulated
emergency conditions. All my visits to subordinate units included
briefings that delineated the military situation as it applied to that
unit. Without exception, these briefings were professional, reflecting
the excellence of both unit and staff training. The Army maintained a
high standard of living in the field; I lived in a house with my aide,
and excellent food was served at a table with a white tablecloth.
When I left home wearing my steel helmet and .45-caliber pistol,
with my trousers tucked in my boots, Agatha told me I was too old to
be playing cowboys and Indians. But I enjoyed being back in the field

and associating with a fine group of military professionals. It was also good to get away from the incessant round of cocktail parties and dinners that were the routine in Seoul.

## Agatha's Liberal Education

After we were settled Agatha began to pursue her liberal education on the Korean people. She had a car and driver at her disposal, and my Korean aide, Major Oh, accompanied her on her frequent trips in search of knowledge. Major Oh, a highly educated officer, seemed to enjoy acting in the capacity of guide and interpreter.

Agatha believed that to know about people, one must live with and among them and know their language. She did the next best thing she could do under the circumstances, taking in the beautiful sights and the ugly squalor, the wide avenues and the back alleys, the modern homes and the shacks. She visited our live-in housegirl, Peggy Kim, in a Korean hospital when she had a gall bladder operation. The privately owned and operated hospital staff provided professional services, but Peggy's family was required to furnish food and personal care. Her mother stayed in the same room with her for three weeks, took care of her, and fed her a diet of rice soup. Agatha described the hospital as depressing, dirty, and with an overpowering stench. Peggy recovered and, after a time, returned to work.

Agatha visited shops and hand-drawn carts, heavily laden with merchandise. She asked Major Oh questions and carried on lively discussions with him about everything they saw. She attended a few union meetings of Korean workers. Major Oh also took her to visit a women's jail. She found it neat and orderly, with each cubicle occupied by one woman quietly sitting on the floor, and no evidence of crowding. In a larger room she observed women prisoners taking a class in hairdressing. When schoolchildren passed by—boys in blue suits and caps and girls in middy blouses and blue skirts—the conversation turned to the importance of education to the Korean family. Korea was a highly literate nation; students competed strenuously to attend the best middle schools, high schools, and colleges. The honor of the family was at stake when a child took an entrance examination, and educational achievements determined what kind of a job he or she would get later on. Classes were large; Agatha visited one school where there were four first grades with perhaps 50 students in each room. Discipline governed the system, and the atmosphere for learning was ideal.

Agatha also maintained her associations with the women of the American community and counted several of them as friends. Together, they toured the South and East Gate markets, packed with merchandise manufactured in Korea and black-market items from U.S. exchanges and commissaries; glass factories that used Korean children for labor, some of them no older than nine or ten; brass factories where beautiful objects were made out of artillery shells that had been expended by the United Nations Forces in range practice; student demonstrations against the Korean government, where the tear gas made their eyes water; silk factories in Inchon; and wig factories, where the wigs, popular items in New York, were made of human hair. Agatha developed active relationships with the wives of Korean officials, too, joining a painting class with a group of Korean Air Force wives, a flower-arranging class at the home of the Minister of Defense and his wife, and a Korean chapter of the Red Cross. She worked regularly at the American USO in Seoul, which provided overnight accommodations and homemade cakes for American soldiers visiting the city on pass or leave from frontline divisions.

Both she and I remained busy from dawn until late at night. Besides nightly cocktail parties, receptions, and dinners, we were obliged to attend national days at each of the embassies (in return, we expected to see representatives of other countries at the American embassy for our celebration of the Fourth of July). About this time I stopped drinking all forms of alcohol and found that almost immediately I felt better, slept better, and met the next morning more easily. I was not to drink alcohol again until long after I returned to the States.

At the end of August Agatha and I traveled to Taipei for a couple of days, and then to Hong Kong. We found outstanding economic progress in Taiwan and a prosperous Hong Kong, with few of the bargains we had become accustomed to a decade earlier. Our stay in Hong Kong had to be cut short because of a visit to Korea by Adm. U. S. Grant Sharp, Commander in Chief, Pacific. This was the first of many times that I would meet Admiral Sharp; I found him to be one of the most pleasant and congenial people I had ever met, and I always enjoyed his company. Perhaps part of my reason for liking him so much was his low-key approach to problems and the fact that he liked to develop solutions on the golf course.

On 11 October the United Nations Command held the second of its two major annual exercises to get the men who had arrived during the summer into the field. I believed there was no satisfactory substitute for these two exercises, which gave us confidence that we could react reasonably well in a crisis. About the same time we conducted a ceremony honoring the Tiger Division, an infantry unit Korea was sending to Vietnam. This action was of vital interest to the U.S. effort because it showed Korean support for the war we were fighting in Vietnam and encouraged wider participation by other nations. The deployment of this division also had genuine value for the Koreans: they could rightfully bask in the warm gratitude of the United States, and the 20,000 men in the Tiger Division stood to gain considerable training, experience, and personal and family economic benefits. The Tiger Division acquitted itself with distinction in combat in Vietnam. In a letter to my sister about this time, I wrote, "We think Korea is acting the way a true friend should act, and we don't think we have very many true friends, when we need them. So, we think on a quid pro quo basis, that Korea deserves a ground swell of gratitude from the U.S. and more military and economic assistance."

On 24 October I traveled to Pusan to conduct a ceremony celebrating the anniversary of the establishment of the United Nations. The UN was represented by individual liaison officers from Israel, New Zealand, Turkey, Italy, Sweden, Australia, the Philippines, the Republic of Vietnam, Thailand, Canada, Great Britain, Ethiopia, and the United States. They were invariably a fine group of officers—cooperative, cheerful, and intent upon representing their countries in a creditable manner. When I left Korea in 1967 the United States was capably represented by Maj. Gen. Marvin Demler, the senior member of the United Nations Command Military Armistice Commission. The commission frequently conducted meetings with the North Koreans at Panmunjom. I was never permitted to visit Panmunjom because of my security clearances, but Agatha made the trip twice.

I worked closely with the U.S. embassy in Korea. Winthrop Brown, our ambassador during most of my tour, was replaced just before I left by William Porter. I was proud to be part of Ambassador Brown's operation, and I felt privileged to attend his weekly staff meetings at the embassy. George Newman, the deputy chief of mission, and I supplemented these meetings with weekly luncheons, alternating between his quarters and mine. I particularly liked George and his wife, Mattie, and considered them effective representatives of the United States. Joel Bernstein, Chief of the U.S. Operations Mission, thoroughly understood what was happening in Korea and correctly forecast more than 10 years in advance that Korea would take off economically. I did not believe him at the time, but I am glad he was correct in his assessment.

In every respect Korea was much improved over my tour in 1953–54—still very poor, but making enormous progress. The Koreans still found it necessary to devote most of their resources to defense, even though 12 years had passed since the conclusion of actual combat in the Korean War. Even in the mid-1960s, they were showing signs of entrepreneurial genius. Korean groups sent to the States to study American unions returned with a sophisticated understanding of the best features of these operations and put them into practice. Applying these techniques to labor-management relations, they won concessions for the Korean employees of U.S. and private agencies. When artisans from Taiwan came to Korea to teach woodworking, they found their students capable and easy to teach. Korean-manufactured guitars were well made and popular in the United States. Few Americans, however, recognized these talents that were there to be seen if only they had looked more carefully. Korea's eventual prosperity resulted at least in part from the advice and economic support of the United States. Our embassy arranged for many visits of American industrialists to Korea during my tour. They came and actively invested within the limits of Korean law. In any event, the United States is now fortunate to have a strong, capable ally in the North Pacific.

## A Round of Guests and Visits

November 1965 brought many distinguished visitors to Korea. One prominent group of senators and congressmen was headed by Senator Russell of Georgia. They were closely followed by the Chairman of the Joint Chiefs of Staff, Gen. Earle Wheeler; Secretary McNamara; and Hanson Baldwin of the *New York Times*. We were able to meet all their requirements, and we were pleased to host them. It was through such visitors that we were able to keep in touch with events in the States.

Agatha and I visited Japan for physicals in mid-November and received clean bills of health. Although Korea was not an island, it was possible to get restless there, and this was our first trip away since August. We visited friends, and I attended the Pacific Air Force Commanders Conference. Being stationed in Korea had isolated both Agatha and me from the Air Force, and the opportunity to associate with other Air Force people brought us up to date psychologically and factually. I was glad to learn that I would also be invited to the annual Air Force Commanders Conference, to be held at Ramey Air Force Base, Puerto Rico, in February.

Christmas came and went happily. I played golf with the temperature in the 20s, the ground frozen, and the wind a brisk 30 knots. General Beach, an avid golfer, also took the exercise in spite of the elements. From time to time Gen. Charlie Chang, Chief of the Korean Air Force, would call me up and suggest a game at Seoul Country Club. I never turned down Charlie's invitations. He still visits the United States frequently, and we play the Andrews Air Force Base course. The Korean Air Force was in particularly good hands while Charlie was Chief, though all his predecessors or successors have been top drawer.

Immediately after Christmas I visited the American troops holding the line north of Seoul. I went first to Headquarters, I Corps, at Ui Jong Bu, where I was briefed on troop dispositions, emergency war plans, and current problems beyond I Corps's ability to resolve. From I Corps, I went to Headquarters, 7th and 2d Infantry divisions. Lt. Gen. John Heintges, commander, I Corps, and Maj. Gen. John Chiles, commander, 2d Division, had been in my class at West Point. As usual, I found it inspiring to be in the field among people who were at the cutting edge of the job we were all trying to do. I spent the night with forward elements of the 2d Division and was favorably impressed with the demonstrated spirit of the units and people I met. Every soldier I saw was a fine representative of the U.S. Army. Obviously a high state of discipline was being maintained.

I left Agatha in Seoul for a week in February while I attended the Air Force Commanders Conference in Puerto Rico. Arrangements had been made for the conferees to meet in Washington and travel together to Ramey. I joined Robert Friedman, Fred Dean, Maurice Preston, Raymond Reeves, Eugene LeBailly, and Winston Wilson— people in positions similar to mine from the far-flung corners of the globe. After arriving at Ramey I learned that Generals Smart and Strother would be retiring. I also learned that Thomas Morris of the Department of Defense had wanted me to be assigned as Director of Manpower in the department, but Gen. John P. McConnell, the Chief of Staff, had disapproved because I had just started my tour in Korea. I enjoyed the change of climate and associating with the people at the conference, but these constituted my only real benefits because I was fully familiar with the subject matter of the presentations.

After I returned from Puerto Rico, Agatha and I were invited to an informal dinner by the former prime minister of Korea, Paik Tu Chin. Although Minister Paik was in retirement, he retained his deep interest in affairs of state. We were graciously received in the Paiks' attractive home, and gifts of Korean silk were presented to the women. With pride the Paiks mentioned the exploits of the Tiger Division in Vietnam, commanded by Gen. Chae Myung Shin. We also discussed the American dilemma with respect to Vietnam and the lack of unity among the American people in their attitude toward the war.

All of us, including the host and hostess, enjoyed the evening. Dinners like this did not always go so smoothly; although Korean men were often fluent in English, only a few of the women spoke English, and most Americans were unable to converse at all in Korean. But there was no language problem that night, and the conversation did not lag. Whenever understanding was less than complete, we and the Paiks had both learned to bridge the language barrier with a smile.

We had now been in Korea a year. Our house had been completely redecorated, and it was almost ideal from April through November. During the winter the heat was not quite powerful enough to keep it comfortable for me, but I emulated the Koreans by wearing more clothing. So much was going on that we never had a chance to get bored. We were contributing positively to an important mission, and in the process getting to know many interesting, friendly colleagues who eagerly shared their philosophies of life and added to our appreciation and understanding of Eastern civilizations.

In late May 1966 I spoke at Tachikawa Air Base in the Tokyo area to a group of newly appointed American Eagle Scouts. They were an impressive group, young men who could already look back upon practical accomplishments of an important nature. Their enthusiasm was inspiring. I was honored a few months ago when an Air Force officer in his late thirties reminded me of that evening in Tachikawa, when he had become an Eagle Scout. Agatha and I returned the next night to Yongsan, where Admiral Sharp and the ambassador to Vietnam, Henry Cabot Lodge, Jr., were soon to arrive.

In early July all Americans in Korea were honored by the visit of Secretary of State and Mrs. Dean Rusk. We attended dinners given by Ambassador Brown and Minister of Foreign Affairs Lee at the Chosen Hotel. Secretary Rusk spoke of the role of the United States in the world and particularly in Korea. Secretary Rusk also signed a Status of Forces Agreement (SOFA) with Korea. Existing in nations where the United States maintains substantial military forces, SOFA is a government-to-government agreement covering virtually any subject the signatories want to include. In the case of Korea we were in the driver's seat, with something to lose and perhaps little more than goodwill to gain in Korean-American relations. The subject of sovereignty was a touchy point. Before the signing, American forces were under the sole administration of Americans; after the signing, they ceded some of that sovereignty. Under SOFA detailed arrangements had to be made, for example, to cover the importation of goods into Korea by Americans, who until that time had not paid Korean taxes. It was a particularly sensitive subject for the American military, because for the first time Americans could be tried in Korean courts for violations of Korean law. Many made dire prophecies of maltreatment—throwing "clean American soldiers" into "filthy Korean jails" and so on. The agreement provided for the establishment of a United States–Korea Joint Committee, the first meeting of which was to be held on 9 February 1967—the day SOFA entered into force. The agreement was close to me personally because, as the senior U.S. representative on the committee, I was charged with its administration. The development of the agreement was thrown into my lap by the U.S. embassy because of my position with the United Nations Command and its critical role in the implementation process. SOFA had to be carefully handled on both sides, and it was my job to persuade the committee that it was to the benefit of both nations to give a little in order to gain a lot.

General Beach completed his tour in late summer and was replaced by General Bonesteel. Agatha and I had greatly appreciated our friendship with Flo and Dwight Beach, and we admired the manner in which General Beach had discharged the responsibilities of his important command. I remain proud of the warm letter I received from him just before he left Korea, in which he cited my "sound advice and recommendations, which have made my task easier and more enjoyable." We welcomed General Bonesteel and his wife, Al, with an informal party planned by Agatha on the theme of "This Is Your Life," a popular television show.

I kept General Bonestee[1] informed of the activities of the Joint Committee and obtained his prior approval for any position I took on SOFA. Fortunately he was a sensitive, understanding, and intelligent leader and understood the larger diplomatic issues. The Koreans also realized that the Americans could pick up their marbles and get out of the game at any point, so it was to their advantage to be reasonable. The SOFA talks went smoothly, and I was pleased with the contributions made by both sides. The American embassy was happy, and so was the prime minister.

## Paving the Way for LBJ

In the late fall of 1966 the shadow of a larger-than-life figure, Lyndon Baines Johnson, fell across the Korean peninsula. He arrived by way of Vietnam and Kuala Lumpur to express his gratitude for the deployment of the Tiger Division —exactly the kind of support for his Vietnam policy that he had needed. The preparation for President Johnson's visit occupied much of my time for more than a month, and things were often hectic. On one such day, shortly before the President arrived, I went to my office early to receive briefings on weather and intelligence and then proceeded to a meeting with Ambassador Brown to discuss whether we had enough helicopters in Korea to meet all requirements. We reviewed whether it would be desirable for the President to spend time with the American community during his stay, which places he would visit, the preparations being made at those places, and the rehearsals we planned in preparation for the tour. I returned to my office to discuss other facets of the problem, had lunch, went to the airport by helicopter to meet Maj. Gen. Buck Anthis, a visitor and friend, and then returned to my office, where I saw more people involved with the planning. Late in the day I left for the embassy and yet another meeting.

Days such as this one had begun weeks earlier. Coordination with the Koreans had been constant and thorough. Our waking and sleeping hours were dominated by small details, such as stationing schoolchildren along the President's route and deciding what messages they would carry on their posters; and large items, such as security. Rehearsals were held frequently, some of them dummy rehearsals designed to thwart any hostile intelligence operatives. William Stinson, the White House coordinator for the visit, and Robert Livingood of the Secret Service, who was in charge of security, kept their eyes and ears open and demonstrated a keen interest in everything that went on.

On 13 October Bill Moyers, head of the President's advance party, arrived to review our plans and, to our relief, approve the work we had done. Now we could make final arrangements for the President's arrival on 31 October. This last stage of preparation, involving communications, baggage, transportation, press, and supervision, would make or break the operation. Take the simple matter of baggage, for example. Shortly after the President's aircraft had landed at Kimpo, some 400 weary travelers with the presidential party had to be reunited rapidly and efficiently with their luggage. This was just one of thousands of details I and my task force had to attend to before the end of the month.

A few days before President Johnson was scheduled to arrive I learned of my mother's death. I was ultimately responsible for the military participation in the visit, however, and I could not leave the job to someone else. Consequently, I was unable to return to the States. President Johnson arrived promptly at his scheduled time of 3:00 P.M. He and Mrs. Johnson were received by President and Mrs. Park and introduced to senior Korean dignitaries. Because time was limited, only a few Americans were privileged to meet the President at this time. Agatha and I were among them, and I was astounded to hear him express his condolences about the death of my mother. President Johnson demonstrated his absolute command of all situations confronting him throughout his stay. He was greeted by a crowd of 2 million cheering Koreans, and the 10-mile route to City Hall Plaza was lined with children carrying posters printed in English with the words, "President Johnson, We Love You." Factory workers joined the teeming crowds, and cadets from the Korean military, naval, and air force academies stood at a respectful "present arms." As the motorcade moved through an area of rice paddies, President Johnson got out and picked up a piece of earth—the gesture of an American farmer to Korean farmers. He continued to leave his car with Mrs. Johnson from time to time to greet individuals along the motorcade.

At City Hall Plaza a massive crowd of between 250,000 and 300,000 welcomed the guests. Secretary Rusk was reported to have stated afterwards that he had been with President Kennedy in Berlin and Naples, and that President Johnson's welcome in Seoul was the equal of those two occasions. Presidents Park and Johnson spoke to the crowd, which greeted them with cheers. At this point President Johnson executed another coup; observing that Mrs. Johnson's hair was in disarray from the wind, he combed it out with his own comb.

Following the speeches and the welcome at the plaza, President and Mrs. Johnson proceeded to their villa at Walker Hill, a hotel in the Korean resort area. They were given a short rest period before calling on President Park in his office, where gifts were exchanged. After a state banquet at the capitol, the presidential party moved to Citizens' Hall, a large auditorium seating several thousand people, for an energetic, joyful presentation of Korean music and dancing. Thus ended the first day—so far, so good.

The next day went rapidly, with visits to Korean and American troops in the field. Deeply interested in seeing how our laborious plans and rehearsals would be implemented, I was fortunate to be part of the presidential party. The Koreans delivered an impressive demonstration of karate, breaking stones and blocks of wood with their hands and sometimes with their heads, but more important, leaving everyone present with an impression of tough combat readiness—exactly the impression we had intended to create. At lunch with the American frontline troops, the President reminded them why they were in Korea and offered an eloquent explanation of why our nation was fighting a war in Vietnam. I found his speech to be compelling and completely reasonable. He certainly won the hearts of his audience, and a few grizzled veterans even shed tears.

After lunch we flew by helicopter to a rural area south of Seoul. We landed on a hilltop, from which the president had a good view of the countryside and the crowd of perhaps 40,000 schoolchildren and farmers who had gathered to greet him. After he received a briefing on rice paddy rearrangement, rural electrification, agriculture, reforestation, and irrigation, he discussed his own experience with rural electrification in the Texas of his youth. The President thanked the village elders for receiving him and presented them with a television set. His hosts dedicated the hill as Johnson Hill in memory of his visit.

The party then returned to Walker Hill for President Johnson's reception for President Park. There was one alarming episode during the reception when the lights went out, leaving a thousand people in darkness and everyone, particularly the Secret Service, extremely perturbed. The President and his party were rushed to a small room off the main floor until the lights were restored. In another unplanned event, a pair of lady's underpants were found on the floor near the receiving line. A quick-thinking member of the staff stood on them until they could be surreptitiously removed.

On the last day of the visit, Mrs. Johnson made a ceremonial contribution of a tree to be planted in a central place along one of Seoul's boulevards. An extremely approachable, unaffected person, Lady Bird made a lasting impression on those who were privileged to meet her. The President laid a wreath at the Tomb of the Unknown Soldier in Seoul's national cemetery. The entire party then moved to the National Assembly, where the President again spoke, lauding the Korean efforts that had produced striking developmental progress despite the ravages of war. He emphasized the cooperation between Korea and the United States and cited the excellent results attained by hard work on the part of both nations. Helicopters took the presidential party to the airport, where the President made a moving speech to the large American-Korean group assembled to bid him farewell. With a small American flag in one hand and a small Korean flag in the other, he conducted a Korean girls' band in "The Yellow Rose of Texas." The departure was a truly emotional experience.

Americans and Koreans alike were pleased with President Johnson's visit. Everyone in the U.S. embassy and General Bonesteel's command considered it a brilliant success. All who participated in the planning and execution received official recognition for their contributions from the White House over the President's signature, and the wording used indicated beyond a doubt that the letters had been personally inspired by the President. I received two personal letters from him, and one each from Ambassador Brown and General Bonesteel; all four went far beyond the routine letters of commendation normally written in military channels. Other letters arrived, including one from the Deputy Under Secretary of State, William J. Crockett, expressing thanks from President and Mrs. Johnson. I was delighted to pass on these commendations to every person who had worked with me on the project.

## Another Tour of Duty Ends

On Christmas Day 1966 Agatha and I, Sgt. Maj. C. E. Forman of the United Nations Command, and my driver, S. Sgt. Robert Olenski, visited the 2d Infantry Division to be oriented on selected activities of the 1st Battalion, 38th Infantry Regiment, and to have dinner with the troops. We arrived at the demilitarized zone orientation battalion conference room and toured the Tactical Operations Center. After dinner we toured the facilities of Company B, 1st Battalion, and returned to Yongsan. It was a refreshing experience to talk with the people who were doing such an important job for the command— and we found the troops were being exceedingly well fed.

On 9 February 1967 the Republic of Korea and the United States held the first meeting of the Joint Committee on SOFA. The meeting opened with a statement by His Excellency Chung Il Kwon: "In view of the traditional bonds of friendship that have tied our two peoples, it is my firm belief that the Korean Government and the U.S. military authorities will go about implementing the specific provisions of the pact with sincerity and fairness." Ambassador Brown replied, "Now that the Agreement is in force, we must make every effort to insure that it is carried out effectively, to our mutual advantage. The Joint Committee, which meets officially for the first time today, is entrusted with the day-to-day task of carrying out the Agreement. If the Committee does its job well, it will act quickly on little problems and thus keep them from becoming big problems."

One "little problem" that might have developed into a "big problem" was the exercise of criminal jurisdiction by Korea over American service personnel. Fortunately the Korean government, in its own words, used "utmost restraint" in this regard. At the last of the 13

committee meetings I attended, on 13 July 1967, my Korean counter-
part, Yoon Ha Jong, a member of the Ministry of Foreign Affairs,
stated: "The ROK [Republic of Korea] government has always kept in
mind the significance of ROK-U.S. joint interests in implementing
fairly and smoothly various provisions of SOFA, including those related to criminal jurisdiction." I replied that "the U.S. authorities
would continue their efforts to reduce the number of incidents and to
punish promptly and adequately U.S. personnel covered by the SOFA
who are found to have violated Korean laws."

SOFA was a distinct triumph for both the United States and the
Republic of Korea. It had been in effect for almost six months with
little controversy among Koreans or Americans when I departed the
country. I was awarded the U.S. Distinguished Service Medal for my
part in developing the administrative procedures for SOFA. Needless
to say, I had received generous help from the U.S. members of the
Joint Committee, and the Korean members and Yoon Ha Jong deserved the highest possible marks for their understanding and spirit of
cooperation.

Early in May 1967 I received orders to leave Korea on 31 July and
report to Clark Air Base in the Philippines as commander of the 13th
Air Force. I regarded this change of assignment as a step up and an
expression of approval for my work in Korea. Almost simultaneously
I received notification of an award for professional achievement from
the University of Chicago, where I had been a student in 1931–32. I
thanked the University of Chicago Alumni Association for the award
and expressed my regrets for not being able to attend the awards
ceremony. Just prior to my departure from Korea, on 28 July, Chung
Il Kwon awarded me the Order of National Security Second Class in
recognition of my "contributions to the modernization of the ROK
Armed Forces." I was also presented the key to the city of Seoul by
His Honor Kim Hyun Ok, the mayor.

Vice President Hubert H. Humphrey returned to Korea as President
Johnson's personal representative for the inauguration of President
Park as the sixth president of the Republic of Korea. Vice President and
Mrs. Humphrey and the other members of the delegation were met by
the foreign minister, Kyu Hah Choi, upon their arrival on 30 June and
honored with a state reception at Walker Hill. The inauguration
ceremony took place at Capitol Plaza the next day in the presence of
thousands. Vice President Humphrey sent me a letter expressing his

pleasure upon "seeing the enthusiastic and smooth way in which all the elements of the country team operated to make the visit a success. This cooperation is certainly an indication of the dedication and high morale of our men and women in Korea." I was delighted to pass on the substance of the Vice President's remarks to our hardworking military team.

Agatha and I were not eager to leave Korea. Our associations with our friends and colleagues had been unfailingly pleasant, and we had appreciated the chance to serve in yet another important mission. We recognized, however, that our more than two years in Seoul constituted a full tour. As we prepared to leave, we reflected upon our arrival in Seoul in mid-May 1965. Almost all the many people we had called on officially had been strangers to us, as we were to them, and the calls had been obligatory and "correct." By contrast, the calls we now made in the days before our departure were warm, friendly goodbyes—one friend to another. We were grateful for having had the opportunity to serve in Korea, and my time there was one of the high points of my service in the Air Force.

★ ★ ★    **Courtesy**

## 14.

*Many Filipinos distrusted and hated Americans, and many Americans held much the same attitude toward Clark's thousands of Filipino employees. Both groups stood to benefit by developing more positive feelings toward one another. None of us could be satisfied with the current situation which, despite high-blown oratory on both sides, had existed for many decades.*

The American military presence in the Philippines had been a point of contention among Filipinos since the U.S. Army first occupied the islands in 1898 after the Spanish-American War. Before I left Korea I was visited by a group of Filipino media people and warned about the extremely poor relationships that existed between local Filipinos and the Americans at Clark Air Base. The resulting newspaper articles referred to me as the "brown brother" of the Filipino people and expressed the belief that I, a victim of racism in the United States, might fully understand the racial situation at Clark Air Base. In their view, that situation was potentially explosive, and they thought that I might be able to help. I did not understand the details, but the validity of their perspective was confirmed to me later both by Filipinos in the diplomatic service and by Americans.

My father had told stories about his assignment in 1917 to the black 9th Cavalry Regiment at Camp Stotsenburg (Clark's former identity as an Army base). Ever the student of his profession as a cavalryman, he had researched the engagements of German and French cavalry units in World War I and lectured his fellow officers on the probable future role of United States cavalry, recommending changes in weapons that he believed would enhance cavalry effectiveness in offensive operations. During the war he was promoted to lieutenant colonel, opening the possibility of his assignment as a squadron commander and presenting the Army with the problem of what to do with a black officer of his rank. In 1920 his regimental commander recommended his reassignment to Camp Stotsenburg solely to avoid having a black officer in the same regiment with white officers. My father deeply resented being assigned to the Philippines and thus being prevented from participating in the war in Europe. He knew that he was being discriminated against, and in times of despair said he would rather be a civilian. He realized, however, that few other opportunities existed for him elsewhere.

My father served as provost marshal for part of his stay at Camp Stotsenburg and observed black market trade in U.S. materiel, particularly weapons. Filipinos were continually trying to bribe military personnel out of one kind of merchandise or another, and at times the temptations became so great that Americans had to succumb or ask to be relieved of their duty. I never found out whether my father encountered this problem personally, but as provost marshal he had certainly been in a vulnerable position. As I was to discover during my time in the Philippines, some of the same kinds of problems continued to undermine our mission there four decades later.

In 1935, the year the independent Commonwealth of the Philippines was established, General MacArthur visited the islands as a military adviser. After the events of World War II, including the dramatic recapture of the Philippines from the Japanese in 1944, the armed services became dependent on our important military bases at Clark and Subic Bay, which we leased for millions in annual payments. The new Republic of the Philippines signed an agreement with the United States in 1947 granting us the use of military bases for 99 years. Even after the sovereignty of the Philippines over American bases was recognized in 1956, however, internal opposition to our presence continued, resulting in the shortening of the 1947 lease and the closing of some of the bases.

I had not been at Clark Air Base since 1965, when I traveled to the Far East from the Pentagon, and Agatha had not been there since we were stationed in Taipei 10 years earlier. We were greeted upon our arrival on 31 July 1967 by Col. Jesus Singson, the Philippine liaison officer at Clark, and Mrs. Singson; Maj. Gen. Michael Ingelido, who was to be my vice commander, and Mrs. Ingelido; Mrs. William Westmoreland, the wife of General Westmoreland, my West Point classmate and commander of U.S. forces in Vietnam; and a host of other people. Kitsey Westmoreland resided at Clark, as did the wives of several other Army officers who were serving tours of duty in Vietnam. General Ingelido introduced the people who had been kind enough to come to the flying line to greet us, and we had an opportunity to exchange a few words with them before we left in a motorcade to our huge, elegant plantation quarters. There a small reception had been arranged. The next evening we attended another reception in our honor at the Clark Air Base Officers' Club, given by General and Mrs. Ingelido. We were extremely pleased with the warmth of the welcome we received.

## Mission of the 13th Air Force

As commander of the 13th Air Force, I had a vital and complex mission. In the words of the mission statement, I was to "conduct, control, and coordinate offensive and defensive air operations in accordance with tasks assigned by the Commander-in-Chief, Pacific Air Forces" and "maintain assigned and attached forces at a level of readiness to ensure successful execution of general war, contingency operations, and cold war plans." This meant I would answer to the commander of the 7th Air Force, with headquarters in Saigon, who was responsible for the overall conduct of the air war in Vietnam. I would be in charge of logistics for most of the fighters and bombers involved in that war, but the operational aspects of the war were not within my purview. The part played by the 13th Air Force in the building and support of the bases in Thailand was essential to the operation of the Air Force units there, and it was our job to support the bases operationally controlled by the 7th Air Force. In order to do the job properly, I had to be aware of what was going on in the war, but by the design of our higher headquarters I would have no hand in the decisions about its actual conduct. My mission also included representing the Air Force in the Southeast Asia Treaty Organization (SEATO) and interdepartmental and interservice activities within the 13th Air Force area of responsibility.

Clark Air Base was the principal base in the 13th Air Force, housing the 405th Fighter Wing, the 5th Tactical Control Group, the 6200th Materiel Wing, and the Jungle Survival School. Equally important for the war being fought in Vietnam was the Air Force hospital, a large modern facility with aerial evacuation capability and medical care comparable to that of the best stateside hospitals. The 13th Air Force operated a joint air defense control center at Clark in conjunction with the Philippine Air Force and furnished F-102 interceptors for the air defense mission. Some 400 miles to the south, near Cebu City, were the 463d Tactical Airlift Wing and the 606th Military Airlift Support Squadron. To the north, on Taiwan, was the 327th Air Division, with headquarters at Taipei Air Station. This unit commanded Air Force personnel assigned to Ching Chuan Kang, Chiayi, and Tainan. In Thailand, serving on the Royal Thai bases of Udorn, Ubon, Nakhon Phanom, Takhli, Don Muang, Korat, and Utapao, major Air Force units were fighting the Vietnam War under the control of the commander of the 7th Air Force. The 13th Air Force supported all these units, and to carry out this mission Clark had become a major procurement, supply, and aircraft maintenance center for Air Force units throughout the southwest Pacific.

On 2 and 3 August I called on key American and Philippine officials recommended by the American embassy in Manila and my staff. First, in the absence of Ambassador William Blair, I called on Minister James M. Wilson, deputy chief of mission. I then proceeded to Camp Aguinaldo, where I was accorded military honors during a call on the Philippine Secretary of National Defense, Ernesto S. Mata, and our air attaché, Col. William Lawley. The next day I visited Gen. Victor Osias, Chief of Staff, Armed Forces of the Philippines; and Brig. Gen. Jose B. Ramos, commanding general, Philippine Air Force. When Ambassador Blair returned to Manila, he took me to call on President Ferdinand Marcos. At the same time Mrs. Blair took Agatha to call on Mrs. Marcos, who graciously gave her a tour of Malacañang Palace.

Agatha and I were favorably impressed by President and Mrs. Marcos. From our perspective in 1967 and 1968, they seemed to be acting in what we felt were in the best interests of their country and ours. I knew that the Marcoses presided over a nation shot through with corruption, involving the highest elements of Filipino society, and I was well aware that the Philippines was a nation composed of a wealthy minority upper class and a large majority underclass that existed in misery beyond comprehension. But we Americans in the military were mission-oriented and did what we were supposed to do within the bounds of our official instructions. This was also true of the American embassy. One could say quite truthfully that the United States and the Philippines are still partners today in the dishonesty and corruption that tightens the yoke around the necks of the Filipino people.

Apparently the Filipino press was keeping close watch on my activities. One article concluded that I had a pro-Filipino attitude because I had called on top defense and armed forces authorities within three days after assuming command. It also pointed out that "previous USAF chiefs never even bothered to make courtesy calls on Filipino officials." Mine was not exactly a pro-Filipino attitude, but I did consider myself to be pro-humanity. The 13th Air Force mission involved working in concert with Filipino officials, and in making the calls I was simply following what I considered to be appropriate protocol. I was deeply interested in meeting people who could contribute to the goodwill of Filipinos toward Americans. After all, the 13th Air Force had 33,000 Filipino employees at Clark and Mactan, whose attitude toward their American supervisors could have great effect upon their performance.

My next calls were in Bangkok, where I met with Prime Minister Thanom Kittikachorn and made a courtesy call on the Royal Thai Air Force Commander in Chief, Air Marshall Boon Choo Chandsuhekasa. Over three days I visited Don Muang, Korat, Ubon, Udorn, Utapao, Takhli, and Nakhon Phanom. I was impressed with the quality of these Royal Thai Air Force bases and the evident spirit of the Air Force people who were busy fighting a tough war. The North Vietnamese were getting plenty of technical, materiel, and direct combat support from their allies and becoming more capable every day. The briefings I received were encouraging, however, in that our units were also being well supported from the States and the 13th Air Force.

I spent some extra time at Takhli, visiting Col. Rachan Vannarot, commander of the 4th Fighter Wing of the Royal Thai Air Force; and Col. John Giraudo, commander of the 355th Tactical Fighter Wing. Later, at Udorn, I had the honor of presenting the Legion of Merit to Gen. William Lindley, deputy commander, 7th/13th Air Force, based in Thailand under the existing command arrangements. Before returning to Clark I visited Col. Harold Aderholt and his 56th Commando Wing at Nakhon Phanom Royal Thai Air Force Base. Harry was most enthusiastic in his exercise of command and was obviously an inspiring leader. Considerable work remained to be done at NKP, as the base was called, and it took a man like Harry Aderholt to produce the desired results. He was getting the job done as rapidly as could be expected, considering the mud he had to contend with.

Shortly after I arrived in the Philippines President Marcos reorganized his armed forces, thus triggering a series of turnover ceremonies and courtesy calls. I returned to Camp Aguinaldo to call on Gen. Segundo P. Velasco, the new Chief of Staff of the Philippine armed forces; and Brig. Gen. Emmanuel S. Casabar, the new Philippine Air Force Chief, at his headquarters at Nichols Air Base. Agatha called on Mrs. Casabar, offering her congratulations. Just a few days later, Mrs. Segundo Velasco, wife of the Philippine Chief of Staff, hosted a tea party at the officers' club in Camp Aguinaldo honoring Agatha and Mrs. Herman Kossler, wife of Admiral Kossler, commander of U.S. naval forces in the Philippines.

On 26 August Agatha and I held a large reception at the Clark Air Base Officers' Club for American and Filipino guests from Manila and the area surrounding Clark. The party was conceived as part of an effort to develop better relationships with the people of our host country. Agatha set the tone with a warm letter of invitation. The dress for men was *barong tagalog*, the traditional Filipino shirt, and some of the American women wore Filipino dresses. The party was very well managed by our protocol people—obviously they had done parties before. My efficient protocol officer, Capt. Barbara Patton, did her usual outstanding job. Air Force couples acted as hosts and hostesses for their Filipino guests, even furnishing quarters for those who wanted to spend the night before returning to Manila. We were highly pleased with the splendid attendance at this dinner, considering that for some it required a two-hour drive from Manila and that many had never received an invitation to a social affair at Clark Air Base.

My next visit was to Mactan Air Base, near Cebu City, where there had been some harassment of Americans by Filipinos. Mactan employed about 3,100 Filipino civilians, and I was convinced that it had some of the same relationship problems that existed at Clark. At

Mactan I met the commander of the base, Col. Henry G. ("Spike") Hamby; Col. L. J. Mantoux, commander of the 463d Tactical Airlift Wing; and Lt. Col. Archie Grant, the 606th Military Support Squadron commander. Colonel Mantoux's briefing described his unit's far-ranging support missions to Vietnamese bases, and Colonel Grant discussed the day-to-day details of his support operation at Mactan. I spoke to the officers and NCOs at the base chapel and paid courtesy calls on the military and civilian leaders of Lapulapu City, Mandaue, and Cebu City. Mayor Eulogio E. Borres presented to me the key to Cebu City. Agatha went sightseeing and shopping with Mrs. Frazier Meade, the wife of the American consul. That evening we were honored with a formal reception. Mactan was a pretty good distance from the rest of civilization, but we enjoyed the visit and the kind, pleasant people.

August had been an exceedingly busy month that kept us moving day and night. When I was at Clark, my day started with briefings to learn what was going on in the world, with a pointed emphasis on Vietnam, intelligence, and operations. The day was invariably interrupted by the arrival of visitors to whom I had to give attention. Late in the month I flew to Saigon to call on General Momyer, under whom I had served during World War II, to assure him of my faithful support and to learn as much as I could about his operations and the contribution the 13th might be able to make. At my first staff meeting after returning to Clark I was happy to report that the 13th had a reputation for getting the job done.

Immediately after I returned I presented the coveted Air Force Outstanding Unit Award to the 5th Tactical Control Group, Col. S. D. Berman, commander—the third such award the group had won since it arrived at Clark in 1959. According to the citation, 5th Tactical personnel had executed 17 major deployments and six operations in support of combat exercises. The group was credited with improving tactical air-control system concepts, procedures, and techniques throughout the Air Force. After the ceremony I flew to Fort Bonifacio, Rizal, where I called on Brig. Gen. Romeo C. Espino, commanding general of the Philippine Army, and Agatha called on Mrs. Espino.

These continuing courtesy calls were critical to improving Filipino-American relationships. They gave the participants an opportunity to meet face-to-face and judge one another's sincerity. It was my hope that I passed the test on every occasion, because it was vitally important to all I hoped to achieve. Agatha and I made a nonmilitary call together on the queen of the Negritos, a group of small black people who lived at Clark Air Base under the protection and patronage of the U.S. military. Negritos had acted as scouts for Filipinos and Americans in the Spanish-American War and against the Japanese during World War II. As compensation they lived at Clark Air Base in their own compound with the support of both the Americans and the Filipinos. When we called on the queen, she received us with all the dignity of a royal personage.

Agatha and I were particularly looking forward to a visit to Taiwan and seeing the changes that had occurred since our departure in 1957. I knew of the construction of a new base at Ching Chuan Kang, better known to Americans as CCK. During my time in Taiwan I had always bombarded visitors from Washington with our belief in the military need for such a base, but few of them were farsighted enough to believe it would ever be built, and I was delighted that it had finally become a reality.

I had covered many a mile in fewer than 40 days in the command, and in my last introduction to a major 13th Air Force base I visited the 327th Air Division on Taiwan. I took the opportunity to be re-united with many old friends for whom I had the utmost respect and affection. At the airport, I was met by Gen. William Pitts, the commander of the 327th Air Division; Gen. Lai Ming-tang, the commander of the Chinese Air Force, and his wife, Dei Fong; General Lai's deputy commander, Gen. Loh Ying-teh; Vice Adm. John Chew, the commander of the Taiwan Defense Command; Gen. Levi Chase, an old friend and a great fighter pilot, who would succeed General Pitts; and Gen. and Mrs. Richard Ciccolella. General Ciccolella was now the Chief of MAAG in Taiwan; he and I had served together in Korea.

As usual, Taiwan did not disappoint me in any respect. A new prosperity had taken hold, and I was pleasantly surprised with the tremendous development that had taken place over the years. While in Taipei I met with my old friend, the minister of national defense, the Honorable Chiang Ching-kuo, later to be President Chiang Ching-kuo; Gen. Kao Kuei-kuo, Chief of the Chinese General Staff; and the American ambassador, Walter P. McConaughy. I called on Admiral Chew at the Taiwan Defense Command Headquarters, and I was briefed on 327th Air Division activities by General Pitts. I also

called on my old friend Gen. Lai Ming-tang at Headquarters, Chinese
Air Force. I then made a heart-warming visit to the ATF 13 compound, which General Wang and I had jointly dedicated more than
10 years earlier in the spirit of Sino-American unity. The next day I
visited CCK, Tainan, Chiayi, Taoyuan, and the Joint Operations Center, demonstrating to me beyond all doubt the vast improvements in
capability that we and the Chinese had made on Taiwan. Agatha
enjoyed the visit to Taiwan as much as I did; she was able to renew
friendships with many Chinese women to whom she had been close
during our tour. One of her closest friends on Taiwan was Lillian I,
who had put so much effort at her side in the creation of the information booklet that became a bible for Americans assigned to Taiwan.

## Improving Filipino-American Relations

A day or so after our return to Clark, Agatha conducted a highly
significant meeting in our quarters of wives of officers and enlisted
men to rejuvenate the Clark Women's Welfare Association. She explained that those present had been selected to represent the thousands of military wives in the Clark area, and that their ideas and
personal support were sorely needed in the development and inten-
sification of the base's volunteer and community efforts.

The association had two functions: education and medical welfare.
In the process of planning social and welfare work on and off base,
the members were always busy attending coffees, luncheons, executive board meetings, teas, and more coffees. Their work benefited the
Nepomuceno Elementary School in Angeles City, the Manibang Elementary School in Porac, the Santos Ventura School in Mabalacat,
and many others near Clark Air Base. The Marisol Clinic in Angeles,
Welfareville in Manila, and two seminaries in San Fernando also
benefited. It was Women's Welfare that made it possible for 100
worthy Filipino students to continue their secondary education. Each
student received 100 pesos, which paid most of a year's tuition.
Women's Welfare contributed much more than money; their volunteers spent thousands of hours taking children in the Clark Air Base
area to doctors for the repair of harelips and cleft palates. Women's
Welfare paid for surgery and treatment, and some Filipino doctors
and hospitals contributed their services. The association regularly

contributed money to the Philippine Tuberculosis Society and made special contributions to ease the effects of natural disasters. On base they routinely baked cookies and cakes for hospital patients, bachelors, and unaccompanied airmen. I was proud of this group and grateful for their efforts to improve Filipino-American relations.

Our social life also moved into high gear. We were invited to a cocktail party at the home of Col. and Mrs. Felix Pestana. Felix had been the Filipino liaison officer to the United Nations Command in Seoul during my tour there. On 10 September we attended a dinner given by President and Mrs. Marcos in Senator Michael Mansfield's honor. A week later Agatha and I received a message from President Johnson's social secretary, inviting us to a black-tie dinner at the White House in honor of the president of the Republic of Niger and his wife. At the dinner we were further honored: I sat at the President's table, and Agatha sat at Mrs. Johnson's table. In President Johnson's handwriting, my place card read, "With highest regards and respect, Lyndon B. Johnson." I had come a long way from West Point.

Back at Clark, I stuggled with the problem of Filipino-American relations, which was as serious as the journalists I had met in Korea had portrayed it to be. The day after my arrival at Clark, the president of the Filipino civilian labor association at the base was murdered, and his body was thrown over the fence onto the base. To my knowledge, the murder was never solved. Not long after, thousands of demonstrators converged on the main gate to protest the base's firing of more than 350 houseboys and mess attendants. These people, who had lost their jobs because of a change in financial procedures, were paid from base funds and were not personal employees of military personnel. Col. Philip Rawlins, the base commander, solved this problem posthaste, but in these early days small crises and incidents were reported almost daily.

I was determined to make a personal effort to demonstrate to Filipinos that our military policies were based on a people-to-people attitude that held them in high esteem as human beings, and that we intended to treat them fairly and honestly as valued employees of the U.S. Air Force. Many Filipinos distrusted and hated Americans, and many Americans held much the same attitude toward Clark's thousands of Filipino employees. Both groups stood to benefit by developing more positive feelings toward one another, and the 13th Air

Force's mission performance would thereby be certain to improve. I knew from experience that U.S. military personnel were always more effective when they had respectful relationships with their hosts. None of us—Filipino or American—could be satisfied with the current situation which, despite high-blown oratory on both sides, had existed for many decades.

I invited a large contingent of Filipino media people to a press dinner at Clark Air Base on 25 October. In my opening remarks I pointed out that Ambassador Blair was the American government's spokesman on matters concerning foreign or domestic policy, and I could address only military matters concerning the 13th Air Force. The 13th was assigned by the U.S. Air Force to support the mutual defense agreements between our nation and sovereign nations in its area of responsibility. All our efforts were aimed toward one goal—to help stop the spread of communism in Southeast Asia. Our primary operational mission in the Philippines was air defense, a mission we shared with the Philippine Air Force. The Joint Air Defense Control Center at Clark was manned by personnel of both air forces who worked side by side, and our staffs cooperated closely to ensure the success of the mutual air defense program.

Then I moved to the matter of the employer-employee relationship between Clark and its Filipino employees. The U.S. Air Force, I stressed, provided equal opportunity and treatment for all employees. It was our desire to eliminate any unfair dominance by management and substitute wholesome cooperation. In place of mistrust we sought the full confidence of our employees. Air Force officers and supervisors wanted to eliminate all defensive attitudes and instead be open-minded in all matters that could lead to improved relations. Our people had to be sincere in their dealings with their employees and never permit phoniness of any kind; they had to help our employees instead of merely criticizing them; and they had to replace apathy with enthusiasm. Maximum productivity by the Filipino-American team could be reached only through mutual honesty and respect.

I mentioned the many opportunities for developing relationships between Americans and Filipinos extending far beyond Clark Air Base—person-to-person ties that could transcend cultural differences. Professional relationships between Filipino and American doctors and lawyers could be further developed; already, Filipinos and

Americans worked side by side in the Clark hospital and the Central
Luzon Filipino-American Lawyers League. Commercial relationships
with merchants in Filipino communities, the landlords of the housing
we rented off base, and the employees of hotels and entertainment
establishments we visited provided other such opportunities. I closed
my talk with the assurance that we would make every effort to encourage Americans to participate in an exchange of ideas with members of the local community. We could develop an atmosphere of
mutual understanding only so long as the Americans and the Filipinos made an effort to know one another.

At this point I opened the evening to questions, some of which
follow:

*Question:* What are the benefits to the Filipinos [of working at Clark]
beyond payroll?
*Answer:* Schools at Clark where children of the Philippines associate with
Americans and Americans associate with Filipinos.

*Question:* We are invited here tonight for a very informal dinner and
cocktails. May we come to your base at any other time to look things over
and look for stories?
*Answer:* Yes, very definitely—and you are welcome.

*Question:* What part does Clark play in Vietnam operations?
*Answer:* We provide logistic support to the Vietnam operations. We do not
participate in actual combat.

*Question:* But you consult the Philippine government on any action which
is not within the purview of the treaty? I mean in cases where the base is
used for purposes not specified in existing treaties?
*Answer:* That is correct, sir. As a matter of fact, all uses of all military bases
in the Philippines are in accordance with military base agreements, and
they do not provide for offensive military operations from the Philippines
by U.S. forces.

*Question:* There is the current impression here in Angeles City in Pampanga that some insiders in Clark, probably Americans, are in cahoots
with pilferers in military materials, including armalites [the AR16, a popular automatic and semiautomatic rifle, highly prized among terrorist
elements], because how can anybody steal armalites inside Clark without
the connivance of probably some insiders in Clark Air Base? What do you
say to that impression, sir?
*Answer:* Well, I would say that there are undoubtedly people on Clark Air
Base who are engaged in pilferage, without question. And I would say at
the same time that there is an accelerated movement on Clark Air Base by
Colonel Rawlins and by his people to reduce substantially the amount of

pilferage that goes on. It takes many forms and again if you consider that there are here on Clark Air Base, on any one day, more than 60,000 people, I think you can understand that the opportunities for pilferage and black-market operations are very great. But it's not in the interests of the U.S., nor is it in the interest of the Philippines for pilferage and black-market activities to continue. And for that reason we are doing all we can to stamp them out.

*Question:* General Davis, there has been some criticism about unequal pay between Filipinos and Americans.
*Answer:* Yes, I've heard about this, and of course we all know there is unequal pay. I have looked into this quite extensively already, and there are a couple of things I will say about it. First, there's unequal pay in the U.S. military service between employees in Oklahoma and employees in Maine. We pay employees who are not general schedule employees in the Department of Defense according to prevailing wage rates in the U.S. We do exactly the same thing in Germany, France, and in the Philippines. We also consult with the Philippines government on the rates that are paid our Filipino employees and these rates are paid on the basis of agreement between our government and your government. There is no equal pay and I think the reason is that there is an interest on the part of the Philippines, as there is in our country and our practice, to avoid undue disturbance of the local economy.

Col. Robert B. Good, my director of information, furnished me a file of newspaper reaction to our press dinner and news conference. I was not displeased with what I read. The reply to the press on the pay question attracted most of the attention, and the attitude of the Philippine media on the question of unequal pay was entirely predictable.

I believed then, as I do now, that the relationship between Filipinos and Americans could be improved by the application of leadership on both sides. It would not be easy; many Americans displayed an arrogant attitude, and the Filipinos' resentment was grounded in historical events that would not soon be forgotten. There was also the question of race—an inescapable ingredient in a matrix of cultural and economic problems that were no single person's fault. I did not confuse myself with thoughts of glowing success, but I was positive that I could contribute to the development of a new attitude. I sent copies of my speech and press conference to concerned personnel in the U.S. military and leaders in the various Filipino communities, hoping to convince supervisors at Clark and Mactan that improving Filipino-American relations would pay dividends in higher effectiveness and productivity.

## Meetings and Greetings

November was another month for meeting and greeting, and I had little time to do much else. In many cases I was renewing old relationships, and the visitors also gave me much current information on military matters that had not reached me through normal channels. Toward the end of the month I had an important speaking engagement at the Rotary Club in Makati and used it to put in a plug for Filipino-American unity and friendship. Members of the club were influential people who could effectively support our efforts. On the last day of November Agatha and I joined the governor of Tarlac, Mrs. Lazaro Domingo, in the celebration of National Heroes Day. Filipinos and Americans marched together in tribute to the gallant men and women of the Bataan Death March, and unknown soldiers were memorialized in an interment ceremony at a new monument.

Early in December our staff surgeon, Col. Arthur Tarrow, and I visited Camp O'Donnell, at the deployment site of the 656th Tactical Hospital of the 1st Medical Service Wing. We found the unit in a tent complex. It had everything necessary for the operation of a modern field hospital: surgical, dental, and general medical services, along with a power plant, food services, and living facilities. Each of the tactical hospital units at Clark held three five-day deployment exercises a year to give them experience in erecting and operating a mobile field hospital. Each unit was designed for quick deployment; its equipment was stored on pallets that could be fitted with a complete staff into four C-130 aircraft, and it could be mobilized and on its way within six hours of the initial call. These units were prepared for whatever demands might be made on them, whether to serve in a disaster area or a war zone.

Back at Clark we welcomed Maj. Gen. Ken Dempster, who replaced Mike Ingelido as my vice commander. Ken and Helyn and their two lovely daughters were a most welcome addition to the base, and we celebrated their arrival with a large reception attended by people from our embassy, the Filipino Defense Group, and senior Filipino and American military officers and their wives.

I spent the second week of December visiting all the 13th's bases in Thailand, receiving briefings and presenting decorations that had deservedly been won in combat operations. Just before Christmas I spent three days at CCK with General Chase; the 327th was doing a consistently fine job. Agatha kept busy with the activities of the Women's Welfare Association while I was away. After Christmas we attended a dinner at the invitation of Mayor and Mrs. Rafael del Rosario of Angeles; a barrio party given by the Governor of Pampanga, Francisco G. Nepomuceno, and Mrs. Nepomuceno at the Camp Olivas Officers' Club, also in Angeles; and a formal dinner by General and Mrs. Velasco at the Officers' Club at Camp Aguinaldo.

In January 1968 I encountered a problem at Mactan. A private Filipino airline had reportedly been denied the use of emergency lighting facilities at Mactan when the airport's power unit broke down. Spike Hamby assured me there had been no intention of denying the use of these facilities to civilian airlines. I did not believe, however, that this answer was sufficient to satisfy anyone, so I ordered an inquiry to look into the possibility that certain individual servicemen may have been responsible for the alleged incident. Because it involved Filipino-American relations, the problem was sensitive and could not be swept under the rug. It was certainly against U.S. policy to refuse assistance to other aircraft using the Mactan alternate international airport, especially in times of emergency.

Another problem involved the selling of high-powered guns to Filipino underworld people. I confirmed that some U.S. Air Force personnel may have been criminally involved and directed that an effort be made to pinpoint the guilty individuals. At a press conference at the local U.S. Information Service office, I characterized these problems and others as bubbles on the surface; a fundamentally sound relationship existed between Filipinos and Americans, and conflicts could be resolved by heart-to-heart discussions in a spirit of understanding and fair play. I also expressed my view that surface troubles were frequently aggravated by a lack of goodwill by Americans, Filipinos, or both. Although the problem of equal pay for Filipinos for equal work was not voiced at the press conference, it was discussed in some of the press reports. Although I believed the U.S. position on this subject was logical, I did not expect that I or any other American could convince Filipinos that our practice was good for their economy.

I visited the 463d Tactical Airlift Wing commander, Col. Thomas Twomey, at Mactan and was briefed on their missions to Vietnam— Tuy Hoa, Tay Ninh, and An Khe. Their mission, furnishing materiel, was vitally important to the war effort, and they were frequently under fire during landings. Back at Clark I was delighted to welcome Cols. Hal Shook, John Giraudo, and Roland McCoskrie, who had much to say about current operations in the Vietnam War. This kind of discussion was the best way of finding out what was really going on—far better than a stand-up briefing. Then I left for Thailand, where I spent the rest of the week discussing our support mission performance with our fighter-wing consumers at Korat, Takhli, Ubon, and Udorn.

General and Mrs. Chase visited the base from Taiwan at the end of January, accompanied by three senior Pentagon civilians. They were closely followed by Gens. Earl Hedlund, Francis Gideon, Marvin McNickle, and Joseph Deluca. This group was primarily interested in our major mission, logistics, so we were especially glad to see them. Col. Robert Gates took them on a tour of the 6200th Materiel Wing and entered into extensive discussions with them. Some improvements in the 6200th base-level supply system had recently been accomplished with the installation of a Univac 1050-II computer, a 15-unit, remote-control, teletype system. The visitors were especially interested in this system because Clark's supply account was the largest in the Pacific Air Force, with over 90 percent of its effort in support of Southeast Asia. The new system provided a more efficient means of processing issue requests and getting goods to the customer.

In March I spoke to the Rotary Club in Baguio, again expressing my interest in improving Filipino-American relations. It was my hope that we Americans would conduct ourselves in a manner befitting guests in a host country. I mentioned our discussions with incoming servicemen on Filipino attitudes toward foreigners and explained the combined effort Filipinos and Americans made in the air defense of the Philippines—for example, the exercises in which intruders were intercepted by Air Force F-102s and Filipino F-5s. I also described the joint manning of the Air Defense Control Center and told of presenting the U.S. Air Force Commendation Medal to Maj. Caesar A. Soriano, Philippine Air Force, for his outstanding achievements there.

Major Soriano's award was one of many I presented while in the Philippines. At Clark I presented the red, white, and blue Outstanding Award Streamer to the Pacific Air Force's Jungle Survival School for its exceptional airmanship, leadership, and devotion to duty from 1 July 1966 to 31 March 1967, when the unit trained 6,318 combat crewmen in jungle survival, recovery, and rescue procedures, thereby making a huge contribution to successful operations in Southeast Asia. I also presented the Air Force Cross to Sgt. Russell M. Hunt in a ceremony on the Clark parade ground before assembled troops. Sergeant Hunt was the fifth person to receive this, our nation's second highest award for valor; he was one of only two living recipients. A mechanic on an HU-1F helicopter, Sergeant Hunt had distinguished himself by extraordinary heroism on a combat mission in Vietnam on 31 March 1967. The citation read:

> On that date Sergeant Hunt's aircraft was shot down while participating in the evacuation of a beleaguered party of American and Allied ground forces. Despite painful injuries and continuous hostile fire, Sgt. Hunt rendered aid to increasing numbers of wounded personnel. When hostile actions forced the movement of the ground party, Sgt. Hunt assisted in carrying his mortally wounded aircraft commander in an exhausting trek to a designated landing zone. He again exposed himself to the hostile field of fire to give manual landing directions to recovery helicopters, refusing evacuation, until all seriously wounded personnel had been airlifted from the scene.

In response to a request from the Philippine government for the loan of air traffic control radar, the 13th Air Force provided not only a complete set of radar equipment, but also technical personnel to operate and maintain the unit at Manila International Airport, the focal point for all domestic and international air traffic operations for the Philippines. In early March Imelda Marcos, assisted by Agatha and Mrs. Nilo de Guia, wife of the Philippines Civil Aviation Authority director, cut the ribbon marking the completion of the installation.

The succession of important visitors continued, including General Westmoreland, who made one of his infrequent trips to Clark in March 1968. Westy gave us his impression of the previous month's Tet offensive as an American victory, an assessment that seems to have been borne out by the events of later years. He also said that it was absolutely necessary for him to take the important role of television reporting into account in the conduct of the war. Secretary of the Air Force and Mrs. Harold Brown spent a night at Clark before going to Bangkok. We entertained them at dinner and were delighted by their enthusiastic appreciation of the Philippines. Comedian Bob Hope and the stars of his USO show sandwiched in a stop at Clark between a two-week tour of Vietnam and a trip to Guam. The entire group of entertainers moved through two wards of war casualties at the hospital, posing for pictures with patients and interspersing lots of ad-lib wisecracking. They were obviously tired from their extensive and concentrated tour, but they gave more than their all in entertaining the hospital patients.

## Bad News from the States

Two pieces of news from the States during this period distressed me and Agatha very much. We learned of President Johnson's 31 March address to the American people announcing his decision not to seek reelection. Agatha's feeling and mine was that the United States had immeasurably increased its stature as a nation during his administration by improving the lot of all its citizens. Not only were blacks better off because of the president's leadership and policies, but the laws mandating legal segregation and denying voting rights and equal use of public accommodations to blacks had been declared unconstitutional. Gradually these laws were removed from the conscience of the entire population. It was President Johnson who had provided the courage and determination to bring about these practical and basic changes in the lives of both white and black Americans. We doubted that his successor would be inclined to pursue his policies with the same vigor.

Then, while playing golf on Clark's golf course—putting on the 15th green, as I remember it—I was delivered a message announcing the assassination of Rev. Dr. Martin Luther King, Jr. This news disturbed us deeply, and we interpreted his murder as a precursor of actions that could eliminate hard-won gains in civil rights. We had lived abroad for more than three years, and thus had no feel for the changes that had recently taken place. We were aware of King's march on Selma, Alabama, and the demonstrations and rioting that had accompanied the efforts of the civil rights movement, but we could not predict the course of events that were to follow. We deemed it highly unlikely that the United States would elect another president with the power, inclination, and guts to continue the move toward genuine citizenship for all Americans. We also had no inkling that we would be returning to the States within a few months.

Two unifying events highlighted Filipino-American relations during the spring of 1968: the 14th annual national convention of the

Defenders of Bataan and Corregidor; and the turning over by our ambassador, G. Mennen Williams, of the Pacific War Memorial, which the United States had erected on Corregidor. President Marcos and Ambassador Williams signed the formal commemorating documents in a colorful ceremony under the blazing sun of Corregidor.

Late in May Agatha and I flew to Davaó and the Del Monte pineapple plantation in Mindanao. In Davao, as in Manila, we found startling examples of great wealth and abject poverty side by side. It was an enlightening experience to meet the owners of large estates and observe their opulent lifestyle. A similar situation existed near Clark Air Base, but the contrasts were less startling there. We also visited the Philippine Packing Corporation and its general manager, George Richardson. It was especially interesting that the Filipinos and the Americans were completely integrated from top to bottom in their work, workers and executives alike. The grounds of the plantation were gorgeous—bougainvillea, orchids of every kind, and handsome tropical trees and bushes everywhere. We were taken through the fields, the cannery, the schools, and the homes. The Richardsons held a dinner for us in their home the first night, and on the second we were invited aboard a new German ship that lay in the harbor, awaiting a load of canned pineapple for shipment to Europe.

Upon our return to Clark Air Base, we learned of my reassignment as Deputy Commander in Chief of the U.S. Strike Command at Mac-Dill Air Force Base, near Tampa, Florida. Agatha and I were unhappy to leave Clark, especially after being there less than a year, but I had been in the military service long enough to let disappointments roll off my back. We adjusted in exactly the same manner as we had always adjusted. There were some good features associated with being transferred to the States: both of us wanted to see our families again, we had many friends on the East Coast whom we had not seen for years, and it would be interesting to assess the recent changes in U.S. society. These thoughts, however, were the products of my perennial optimism. At heart we did not look forward to living again in the South. Overseas we had experienced freedom, equality, and friendship—qualities of life that had been missing for us in the United States.

Agatha and I had long planned an official trip in early June to Indonesia and Australia. In the process of making our obligatory calls in Djakarta and Bali, we were fortunate to see some of the country and learn a bit about the Indonesian people. We then flew to Darwin, Australia, which until then had been nothing more than a name on the map for me. It had been the location of a key Allied base during World War II, and I thought it must be a city of some size. We had been told that we would drive through downtown Darwin on our way to the motel. After driving a while and noting the rural nature of the countryside, I asked when we were going to arrive in Darwin. We had already driven through it.

That evening we ate at a restaurant where a young woman was being feted on the occasion of her 21st birthday—a very important day in the life of an Australian. After we had been seated, our presence in the dining room was announced, along with the names of the officials who had met us, the guest of honor, and the people celebrating her birthday. Several people from the birthday party and other tables in the restaurant came to our table to welcome us effusively. Later in the evening, the guest of honor brought her birthday cake to our table and asked me to cut the first piece. She then shared the cake with us and people at the other tables in the restaurant. One gentleman, a member of our welcoming party at the airport, stated most hospitably his intention to arrange a visit through the outback for us upon our return trip. At the time I thought the promise was made in the enthusiasm of the evening, and I did not expect the trip to materialize. Leaving Darwin we flew to Sydney, where we learned to our horror of the assassination of Robert Kennedy.

We loved Sydney in every way—the harbor, the zoo, the opera house, but most of all the people's warmth and enthusiasm. The drive around the city was fascinating, as were all our experiences there. After Sydney we visited Canberra and Melbourne before flying back to Darwin en route to Clark. The strangers we had met there had not forgotten us; we were met by four cars well-stocked with food and drink, and we spent our last day in Australia in the bush watching kangaroos, emus, lizards, echidnas, koala bears, turkeys, ducks, geese, and other forms of wildlife in their natural habitat. On our last night in Darwin we accepted an invitation to a party on a naval ship lying in the harbor. It was another evening of gaiety with Australians, who indeed seemed happiest when they were welcoming foreigners.

We had one month more to spend in the Philippines. Early in July we made one final trip to Hong Kong, Bangkok, and Taipei to make farewell calls and some last-minute purchases. Returning to the Philippines, I called on Ambassador Williams; President Marcos; Secretary of National Defense Mata; Gen. Manuel Yan, Chief of Staff, Armed Forces of the Philippines; and General Guevara, the commanding general of the Philippine Air Force. Agatha followed a similarly rigorous schedule. We met at the Oasis Hotel in Balibago, where Governor Nepomuceno gave me a plaque naming me an "adopted son of Pampanga."

Just before we departed Clark the vice mayor of Angeles City presented me with a municipal board resolution adopting me as an honorary citizen. This action was especially satisfying because it represented authentic testimony that the relationship between Angeles and Clark Air Base had changed for the better. In the same vein Colonel Tarrow was presented with the Presidential Merit Medal by President Marcos for "enhancing an effective working relationship between the Philippine medical profession and the United States medical group." About the same time President Marcos conferred upon me the Legion of Honor "for promoting mutual respect and understanding between personnel of the Philippines and the United States Armed Forces and demonstrating deep concern for the professional development of the Armed Forces of the Philippines, particularly the Philippine Air Force."

During our last days at Clark numerous affairs were held in our honor, culminating in a farewell reception given by General and Mrs. Dempster. On 18 July we flew in a Military Airlift Command C-141 to New Delhi and took off the next morning for three days in Madrid. There we rested, walking about the city, visiting the Prado, and window shopping. We made no purchases, but we recovered from the jet lag and the stiffness in our muscles from sitting long hours in an airplane. We left Madrid for McGuire Air Force Base at noon on 23 July and landed there a few hours later after a long but pleasant trip. In one week I would be reporting to MacDill Air Force Base for yet another adventure.

# ★ ★ ★  Strike Command

**15.**  *Each morning as usual, General Conway and I would attend the morning briefing; on some days we would have other discussions, or a visitor might have to be briefed, but frequently I would go to MacDill's golf course. I found myself with a perpetually guilty feeling that I did not seem to be able to shake.*

About a week before I left the 13th Air Force I received a cordial message from Adm. Paul Blackburn, Chief of Staff, U.S. Strike Command. He summarized the schedule projected for the day after my arrival, 1 August 1968, from the honors ceremony to dinner that evening at the quarters of Gen. Theodore Conway, the commander in chief.

As I was soon to learn, the Strike Command was the quintessence of precision. Each event for my arrival had been elaborately planned in advance, including a 10-minute meeting on the flight line with local news media representatives. Admiral Blackburn enclosed a précis of media attitudes toward the military establishment and military personalities, along with the suggestion that I thank the reporters for coming to MacDill and speak as follows: thoughts about my new assignment; the significance of joint-service cooperation toward achieving common missions and objectives; comments on my experience as commander of the 13th Air Force; recognition that Tampa was a community in which the military and civilian sectors had an outstanding record of working together; and my hope that, after settling into my new assignment and getting to know more about it, I could meet with reporters again. In a return message I assured Admiral Blackburn that I was grateful for these arrangements and I looked forward to meeting him.

The schedule was followed exactly as planned. Although I had allocated Air Force manpower to the Strike Command when it was created and studied its intended functions in detail, in one day of briefing I learned much more about it than I had known before my arrival. Strike was only a few years old. Organized in the early 1960s as a unified command operating directly under the U.S. Joint Chiefs of Staff, it had operational command over all assigned combat-ready ground and air forces of the U.S. Continental Army Command and the Air Force Tactical Air Command based in the continental United States. It was responsible for combining assigned Army units and Air Force tactical air units into mobile, flexible, rapidly reacting joint forces under single direction. By the nature of its organization, it could deploy "fire-brigade" joint task forces of any size, anywhere, for any measured response required to support national policy. Its prepackaged joint forces were designed to bring hostilities of any scope or type to a successful conclusion. This mobile joint task force concept held great promise for national security. Through the immediate deployment of these versatile, air-mobile, joint-action forces, conflict already under way would be dealt with promptly, thus minimizing the risk of escalating hostilities.

The Strike Command had been assigned three major missions: to provide a general reserve of combat-ready forces to reinforce other unified commands; to plan and conduct contingency operations as directed by the Joint Chiefs of Staff; and to plan for and conduct peacetime military activities in the command area known as Middle East/Southern Asia and Africa South of the Sahara (MEAFSA). The officers and enlisted men of the Strike Command came from the Army, Navy, Air Force, and Marine Corps. Within the headquarters, the deputy of each directorate and his chief were from different services. For example, the director of operations was an Army major general; the deputy was an Air Force brigadier general. A senior foreign service officer from the U.S. Department of State was assigned to the headquarters as a political adviser to the commander in chief and held the title of ambassador. A scientific adviser also served on the Strike Command staff. He was assigned to the Joint Operations

Analysis and Test Group, a special branch of the headquarters with responsibility for operations analysis, testing, and assessing joint tactical warfare concepts and procedures for the employment of assigned Army and Air Force forces. Also located with the Strike Command at MacDill Air Force Base was a 700-man unit of Army and Air Force communications specialists and all their equipment, which was entirely air-mobile. This unit, the Command Communication Support Element, could provide rapid, long-range communications for two Strike Command joint task force headquarters deployed simultaneously overseas from their operating locales.

## Strike Command's Record

Strike Command's record in joint training was outstandingly good. It had provided continual training of land/air and sea personnel in exercises of all kinds to more than a half million personnel in Army and Air Force units. Its major exercises in the United States had involved up to 100,000 soldiers and airmen and 1,000 aircraft. It had conducted 10 minor exercises per year in the United States, each involving 150 to 1,500 ground and air personnel. It had also conducted major overseas exercises, augmenting other unified commanders. In Big Lift, 1963, Strike Command had airlifted 15,000 troops to Europe in 63 hours and 20 minutes, together with a composite air strike force of tactical fighters, reconnaissance aircraft, and assault transports. In Delawar, 1964, Strike had deployed 6,800 troops and 133 aircraft for joint maneuvers with Iranian forces. In Deep Furrow, 1965, it had deployed 4,000 troops and 140 aircraft for participation in a NATO exercise in Turkey; similar exercises took place in 1967 and 1968. In Bold Shot/Brim Fire, 1968, it had deployed 7,500 troops and 64 aircraft to Vieques Island, Puerto Rico, to conduct a joint assault-training exercise. And in Focus Retina, 1968, it had deployed 7,500 troops and 64 aircraft from Pope Air Force Base, North Carolina, to participate in a joint maneuver with troops of the Republic of Korea.

Strike Command had also been effective in times of crisis. In 1964 it had provided a Joint Task Force Command element and the airlift forces for the joint Belgian-American rescue operations at Stanleyville and Paulis, the Congo, liberating 2,000 hostages from Congolese rebels and airlifting them to safety. In 1965 it had augmented the commander in chief, Atlantic, with the 82d Airborne Division, a tactical fighter squadron; reconnaissance aircraft; and assault airlift during the Dominican Republic crisis. In 1967 it had provided non-combatant, logistic airlift support to the Democratic Republic of the Congo. And at the time of my arrival the command had already augmented the commander in chief, Pacific, with the overseas movement of more than 500,000 Army and Air Force personnel for Southeast Asia operations.

The Strike Command had also been deeply involved in humanitarian operations. In 1965 it had evacuated U.S. nationals from West Pakistan during Pakistani-Indian hostilities and sent a medical team with 20,000 pounds of medical supplies to Somalia to treat more than 7,000 Somalians suffering from malnutrition and disease. In 1966 it had airlifted 500 tons of sorghum wheat grain to famine-stricken areas in Chad, and airlifted over 30 tons of food and medicine and evacuated civilians of many nationalities to safety during a mercenary-led rebellion in the Congo. In 1967 it had airlifted food, medicine, and clothing to the citizens of Guerrero, Mexico, who were isolated by widespread flooding, and in 1968 it had airlifted 177,000 pounds of food to flooded areas in Ethiopia.

Admiral Blackburn's briefings during my first two days in the command acquainted me with the mission of the command and the part I would play in it. Agatha and I were warmly welcomed by everyone we met. The local press carried a full report of our activities, presenting every piece of information available about our past lives and experiences. Invariably the articles were written in a highly complimentary vein, but they tended to stress our race—because we were not white, the articles spoke of us as if we were exotic, somehow essentially different from other human beings. They accurately described our lives in the military and reported on our personal attitudes, activities, and hobbies. Some of the articles went back to World War II, and almost all of them told of my recent tour as commander of the 13th Air Force. We had been out of the United States for more than three years, living under circumstances in which our race had not assumed the importance it seemed to have in the minds of the people around MacDill. Undoubtedly our race had been well known at our overseas stations, but it certainly was not emphasized. We were relieved, however, that we were not made to feel uncomfortable at

MacDill, either officially or socially. In fact we both felt that we would enjoy being stationed there and saw no obstacles to a pleasant tour.

This feeling was encouraged by a series of welcoming coffees in Agatha's honor by the MacDill Officers' Wives' Club, the Noncommissioned Officers' Wives' Club, and the Strike Command women. Everyone seemed motivated by a spirit of goodwill, further exemplified by a large dinner party given in our honor by Maj. Gen. and Mrs. William Thurman at their quarters. The Thurmans invited their friends from the Tampa area to meet us, thus assuring us of the welcome of the civilian community.

My new boss, General Conway, had been a first classman and a cadet battalion commander when I was a plebe at West Point. Agatha and I both remembered him from our first days in Korea in 1965, where he had been deputy commander, 8th Army. There was no doubt in my mind that we would enjoy serving with the Conways. General Conway was in my estimation a fine leader of military people and a considerate human being with personal attributes that drew people to him. El Conway, his wife, was also a friendly and considerate person, apparently well liked by everyone. She and Agatha became immediate friends, and it was obvious that all four of us would be able to work together in harmony.

The Strike Command Headquarters wives met regularly, sometimes at MacDill and other times off base. Mrs. Conway was always present, and her personality sustained the closely knit feeling that existed among the women. Just as important, her efforts favorably influenced the morale of Strike Headquarters. The other women at the base felt free to discuss any and all subjects with her, and they also knew they would find sympathy and understanding with Agatha, usually leading to the resolution of their problems.

Shortly after our arrival, for example, some of the black wives stationed at Macdill asked Agatha to help get cosmetics and hair preparations for black people made readily available to them through the base exchange. Up until then they had to travel to black neighborhoods off base to purchase these items at considerable expense and inconvenience. Agatha discussed the problem with El Conway, and shortly thereafter the desired items appeared on exchange shelves.

General Conway celebrated Strike's seventh birthday a few weeks after my arrival. The energy he had applied to the command accounted for the progress that was there for all to see. Among other accomplishments, he had created a special study group to determine new joint operational concepts for the strategic mobility of U.S. military forces from 1970 to 1975. The study, headed by Gen. Howard Kreidler, Deputy Chief of Operations, was analyzing all aspects of Strike capability to deploy and employ joint forces in contingency operations or to reinforce other unified commands worldwide. It considered organizational changes, existing and new equipment, and weapons systems that would be available in the first half of the coming decade. General Conway had also instituted language training in French and Arabic for Strike Command members who held concurrent Joint Task Force assignments in the MEAFSA area. Progress continued on a new Strike headquarters building, with occupancy scheduled for the spring of 1969. Exercises, "no notice" and planned, tested the rapid-deployment and communications capabilities of assigned forces. Bold Shot/Brimfire, just conducted at Fort Campbell, Kentucky, had involved 1,600 Army, Navy, Air Force, and Marine personnel. Seven other exercises had been conducted during 1968, each highly successful.

## An Orientation Trip Abroad

Shortly after my arrival at MacDill I called on General Momyer, commander, Tactical Air Command, at Langley Air Force Base, where I received a briefing on the air forces committed to Strike. I made a similar call on Gen. James Woolnough, Continental Army commander, at Fort Monroe, where I was briefed on the committed army forces. By this time I was comfortable in my job and more than ready to go on an orientation trip through the MEAFSA area: Liberia, the Ivory Coast, the Congo, Uganda, Ethiopia, and Iran. Key members of the Strike Command staff accompanied me, and all the major staff elements of the headquarters were represented. The trip offered a fine opportunity for me to get to know these people better and to learn more about the operation of the command.

Completely by chance, on our arrival at Roberts Field in Liberia I had the pleasure of seeing President Tubman, who happened to be there when I landed. He graciously recalled my last visit to Liberia in 1961, when I had been a member of Ambassador Lodge's delegation to the inauguration of President Ahidjo of Cameroon. After I called

on Ambassador Ben Brown and met with Liberian government officials, we visited the Barclay Training Center. There we were briefed
on the state of training of the Liberian armed forces and given an
estimate of their capabilities.

We departed the next day for the Ivory Coast, where we were
briefed by the embassy and the military. I found the Ivory Coast
impressive; its reputation as an African Paris seemed to be merited.
After a two-day visit, we went to the Congo, where I was granted an
audience with President Joseph Mobutu and briefed by the American
ambassador. Our next stop was in Uganda, where we were met by the
commanding general of the Ugandan armed forces, Idi Amin. General Amin had not, at this point, achieved full governmental power. I
found him, at least on this occasion, to be congenial, friendly, and
likable. He staged several striking demonstrations of his troops' military prowess and educated us about Ugandan culture. Our stay in
Uganda was in every way interesting and pleasant. Years later it was
difficult for me to reconcile the Idi Amin revealed as a murderer and a
scoundrel with the man who had received us so courteously.

From Uganda we went to Addis Ababa. The warm welcome we
received there was surely related to the large amounts of food we had
airlifted to Ethiopia to help ease the effects of the disastrous floods
earlier in the year. We were briefed by the Ethiopian military on the
current war they were fighting with Somalia. Following our discussions, we were taken to Jigjigga, on the front line of the war. I was
shocked by the conditions there. The Ethiopian soldiers were dirty
and unkempt. Their food was handled in a manner that can only be
described as filthy. Although they lived in a building that was solidly
built, there were no provisions for effective heating. The Ethiopians
considered these conditions normal; I considered them harsh beyond
belief. The fighting was sporadic, and neither side seemed to be doing
much damage to the other. We were also taken to Asmara, in Eritrea.
By contrast to Jigjigga, it was an attractive place, peaceful and pleasant, with much evidence of the Italian occupation three decades
before.

In Teheran we were met at the airport by a large MAAG delegation
headed by the Chief, Maj. Gen. H. A. Twitchell. We were briefed in
some detail on MAAG's activities and the Iranian armed forces. The
emphasis the United States was then assigning to Iran was evident in
everything we saw and experienced: the large number of personnel

assigned to the advisory group, the relatively high rank and caliber of its U.S. members, and the active participation of Iranians in exercises involving large numbers of men and modern armaments. By the time we finished our schedule in Iran, all of us were more than ready to return to MacDill.

I was glad to get home. Agatha, as usual, had gotten along fine during my absence, attending sewing and catering classes in Tampa and working as a volunteer in the base thrift shop. I had been so busy that I had not been able to miss playing golf, but when it stopped raining in the fall I was able to start playing frequently. To my way of thinking Tampa and Washington each had six months of poor weather: MacDill from April to October and Washington from October to April. By early October we were approaching the good six months of Florida weather, and my relationships with the people I saw from day to day were equally pleasant. I had come to understand the nature of my job, which consisted largely of regular traveling about the country participating in command exercises, spreading the message of Strike Command at service schools, and speaking in the interest of the military.

General Conway designated me the Joint Task Force commander of Brass Strike III, a maneuver to be conducted 2–4 October at Fort Bragg, North Carolina, with 81 aircraft and 3,000 paratroopers. General Conway was the overall commander of the exercise, which included close air-support demonstrations of TAC F-4s and Continental Army Command "Huey Cobra" and UH1D helicopters, an airborne ground-landing assault by Army troops and helicopters, and static displays of weapons and equipment. The F-4 Phantoms and the Huey Cobras displayed the ample firepower they could produce with conventional weapons. The F-4s used rockets, aerial cannon fire, 500- and 750-pound bombs, and napalm in reducing prepared "enemy positions" and other "targets" to rubble. The Army's gunships used M-5 grenade launchers, nose-mounted machine guns, and 2.75-inch rockets during their attacks on "aggressor" positions. At Pope Air Force Base, TAC's C-130s gave loading and unloading demonstrations. Paratroopers of the 82d Airborne Division showed their effectiveness during a quick-reaction loading demonstration aboard the C-130 and during the personnel paradrop that followed. The Airborne troops were resupplied in the demonstration area using the Low Altitude Parachute Extraction System. Brass Strike III was a smooth operation with no safety violations, demonstrating the effectiveness of the training that had produced it. I was extremely pleased with the quality of the cooperation between the Army and the Air Force.

Agatha and I were deeply grieved by a telephone call in mid-October telling us that her father had died suddenly. In his nineties, he had been sick and under the care of a doctor, but was believed to be recuperating. Considerable responsibility rested with Agatha as the strength of the Scott family, so she left for New Haven to help ease her mother's problems. Agatha had always carried on a detailed and lively correspondence with her father, and the loss was especially great to her. Mr. Scott had reared five children through the depression, put a son through dental school at the University of Pittsburgh, and educated four beautiful daughters who went on to lead full, successful, and happy lives. I had had the privilege of knowing him for almost 40 years; throughout that time, he had been a constant supporter on whom all of us could depend. We still miss him today, more than 20 years later.

During the winter I visited Bronze Plate, an eight-day training exercise conducted at Army and Air Force installations in Georgia and Florida. More than half our 700-man Communications Support Element was involved in a test of field communications to train the participants in airlift deployment. Military Airlift Command C-141s flew 400 men and 200 vehicles from MacDill to Georgia bases, and others drove to Cross City Air Force Station, Florida. During the exercise a C-130 packed with communications equipment provided simultaneous airborne voice-and-teletype contact between short-range stations and to points up to 5,000 miles away.

I also commanded the Joint Task Force in an assault exercise on Vieques Island, just southeast of Puerto Rico. Some 2,700 troops of the 82d Airborne Division from Fort Bragg participated. General Conway and I observed the final phase of this action from a helicopter above the island. In other activities I attended a three-day Air Force commanders conference at Ramey Air Force Base in Puerto Rico, made trips to several Air Force installations, presented the Strike Command briefing to the Army War College at Carlisle Barracks, Pennsylvania, and visited the Air Force Academy in Colorado.

In late February 1969 we bade farewell to Admiral Blackburn, who was transferred to the Pentagon, and welcomed Adm. John

Lynch, his replacement. Soon after, I visited Gen. Howell Estes, commander in chief of the Military Airlift Command and a West Point classmate of mine, at his headquarters at Scott Air Force Base, Illinois; I was particularly interested in seeing first-hand the preparations that the Military Airlift Command had to make prior to a major deployment from the United States to Korea. I traveled with full Strike Command staff representation to Korea via Alaska and Japan, to Thailand via Hong Kong, thence to Uganda, the Congo, Surinam, and finally back to MacDill. The staff was headed by Ambassador Bell, the political adviser to Strike's commander in chief, and included senior representatives from each Strike agency. This eight-day trip enabled us to observe the deployment, the arrival of troops in the objective area, and their functioning under the exercise plan. In Korea we visited the commander in chief, United Nations Command, which was being augmented, and the 314th Air Division in Osan, which controlled all air operations under the United Nations Command. I also made two separate trips to Europe: one to Headquarters, 17th Air Force at Ramstein, followed by a four-day visit to Nuremberg for a major NATO exercise; and the other to the annual Supreme Headquarters Allied Powers Exercise at Gen. Lyman Lemnitzer's headquarters in Brussels. General Westmoreland, then Chief of Staff of the Army, was in attendance, along with General Estes.

At MacDill, Strike Command had a constant stream of visitors, the most prominent of whom was King Hussein of Jordan, a quiet and personable monarch who had survived far beyond the expectations of our intelligence people. His brother, Crown Prince Hassan, accompanied him. We were also visited by Air Chief Marshal Arjan Singh, commander of the Indian Air Force, and his wife, Teji, and senior officers from France and Iran. On Armed Forces Day we celebrated the opening of our new headquarters building, which provided the entire staff with improved facilities.

### Agatha Makes the MEAFSA Tour

It was customary in the Strike Command for the deputy commander in chief to make one trip to MEAFSA during his tour with authorization to take his wife along as a passenger and observer. The valid fiction was that the wife would confer with dependent wives of the military people who were stationed at the various MEAFSA bases and make recommendations that, if reasonable and capable of being implemented, would improve the lot of families living under hardship conditions. Agatha had looked forward to this trip, which would take her to some places she had not seen before, and I was particularly eager for her to go. She made all the difference, as far as I was concerned; her observations were always keen and to the point. The trip would last 17 days, enough to test the endurance of even the seasoned traveler.

Accompanied by many capable and congenial people from my command, we first flew to Monrovia, Liberia. This was my fourth visit to the country, but it was all new to Agatha. She liked the Liberians she had met at their embassy in Washington, and she was delighted with the warmth and delightful sense of humor of those she encountered in Monrovia. On our first day Maj. Gen. George P. Seneff and I visited Ambassador Ben Brown and met with the Liberian Secretary of Defense and Gen. George Washington, Chief of Staff of the Liberian armed forces. Agatha visited Liberian homes and went shopping. In the evening, Ambassador Brown gave a large reception in our honor. More than 400 people attended, including the entire diplomatic corps, all the key members of the government, and many prominent people from civilian Monrovia.

Our next stop was the charming city of Abidjan, capital of the Ivory Coast, where we stayed at the ambassador's residence. I was glad to visit the country a second time, because Ambassador and Mrs. Morgan were among the most effective and well-liked representatives of our nation overseas. I also hoped to meet President Felix Houphouet-Boigny, world-renowned for his political and economic acumen. In addition, it was an opportunity for Agatha to see the "Paris of Africa." We were met by Ambassador Morgan, who accompanied me on my initial courtesy calls.

The next day General Seneff, Col. Hugh E. Quigley, and I were given a helicopter tour of Abidjan and a drive through the port and industrial areas, while Agatha visited all the places of cultural interest with Peggy Morgan, Ambassador Morgan's wife. Responding to questions from the local press, Agatha revealed her interest in the rights and education of women:

> What I have noted and what impressed me most is that the city of Abidjan is undergoing a considerable urban development. . . . I visited the Univer-

sity, where I admired the greenery, the beautiful structures, and the ease of moving from one building to another without getting wet during the rainy season. But I did not meet many young girls at the university. Is it due to the fact that they stayed at home to prepare for their exams? The population is very hospitable and a stranger in Ivory Coast does not feel himself to be in a foreign land. The sincere hospitality must be the reason for this. Therefore, I leave Abidjan with happy memories, hoping to return here again.

Peggy Morgan, a lovely, charismatic, generous lady, was warmly greeted by all the Ivorians she met. She had worked at the hospital as a regular volunteer, and she was obviously well liked by the staff and the patients. Prior to a buffet dinner given by the Morgans in our honor that evening, the ambassador and I were received by President Houphouet-Boigny, who fully lived up to his reputation. His knowledge of world affairs and the strength and wisdom of his personal beliefs were borne out by his comments. After returning to MacDill, I was particularly gratified to receive a letter from the defense attaché of the Ivory Coast stating that our call on President Houphouet-Boigny had given Ambassador Morgan a rare opportunity to sound out the president on important African matters.

Our three-hour flight to Kinshasa went rapidly, with animated conversation about Monrovia and Abidjan and the people we had met. We had covered the first third of our trip, and everything had gone extremely well. In Kinshasa, capital of Zaire (formerly the Congo), a reception was given in our honor. We departed Kinshasa for Lubumbashi—formerly Elizabethville. There, General N'Zoigba, a battalion commander, and his wife had arranged a dinner in our honor. The evening was somewhat difficult because of language problems, but the general and I were able to converse in French, and we developed a warm friendship during the course of the evening.

Upon our arrival in Nairobi, Agatha and I were greatly surprised and pleased to see the familiar faces of John Lim, the Korean ambassador to Kenya, and his wife, Kay. The Lims had been good friends in Seoul just three years earlier, where John had been the secretary to the Prime Minister. Learning of our impending arrival from Wendell Coote, the U.S. chargé d'affaires, they had come out to meet us. Mr. Coote later conducted an embassy briefing. The most thorough in-country briefing we had yet received, it summarized the political situation in Kenya, gave details of the government operation, and discussed key personalities such as President Jomo Kenyatta and Vice President Daniel arap Moi. Current problems, domestic and foreign, were discussed, and we were briefed on the border war with Somalia. We were also appraised of the newly formed East African Community, which aimed to create a common economic market among Kenya, Tanzania, and Uganda. The economic summary was optimistic, based on Kenya's political stability, sound economic policies, and the determined efforts of its people. The greatest barriers to orderly economic development were shortages of skilled workers and citizen entrepreneurs. The current per capita income was $112 per year. A significant contribution was being made by the 263 Peace Corps workers presently serving in Kenya, most of whom worked in agriculture or taught in government-supported secondary schools. The briefing ended with a discussion of information efforts by our government and operations by the large number of U.S. firms in Kenya.

The next day we called on the Minister of Defense, Dr. Njoroge Mungai, and officers of the Kenya Army and Air Force. In the afternoon we were taken on a tour of the Nairobi Game Park in a Land Rover driven by our guide, Frank Minot, representing the African Wildlife Leadership Foundation. Mr. Minot took us to within a few feet of a large pride of lions and cubs playing with each other in the sunshine. At first we felt somewhat timid, but the lions did not pay any attention to us and we soon felt quite comfortable. We did not get out of the Land Rover, however. Mr. Minot then drove us to a watering hole, where we assumed a strategic position and watched rhinos, ostriches, zebras, giraffes, and gazelles warily approach to drink. The park was teeming with wildlife, yet it seemed peaceful, beautiful, and completely unintimidating.

Agatha and I departed Nairobi for Amman, Jordan, early on the morning of 20 June 1969—our 33rd wedding anniversary. We do not normally make a big occasion out of our anniversary, but I did feel that a trip to Jordan was a fitting celebration. The ambassador to Jordan, Harry Symmes, and his wife, Joan, were at the top of our list of State Department representatives—and we don't go overboard in our praise of government servants. We stayed at their residence. Our briefing at the embassy covered many of the complexities of the current political situation in the Middle East, and then we attended a military retreat in my honor at Headquarters, Royal Guards Brigade, performed by the Arab Army Massed Bands. This retreat was the most impressive ceremony I have ever witnessed. From the top of the highest hill overlooking Amman we had unlimited visibility, and the view was magnificent. The men in the bands were resplendent in their colorful uniforms, their instruments reflected the sun brilliantly, and their military bearing was impeccable.

While we were in Amman Agatha and I called on Crown Prince Hassan, whom we had met on the occasion of King Hussein's visit to MacDill. The crown prince had been especially cordial, and he insisted that we call on him when we visited Jordan. We were delighted to be introduced to Her Royal Highness Princess Sarvath, whom Prince Hassan had met in London while he was studying at Oxford and Princess Sarvath's father was stationed there as Pakistan's ambassador. Our call was informal and relaxed, livened by the presence of Princess Sarvath's mother, a former delegate to the United Nations and then Pakistan's ambassador to Morocco.

The Symmes treated Agatha and me as members of the family, and it seemed as if we had known them and their two children, Rebecca and Peter, for a lifetime. The family was scheduled to go home on leave soon after our departure for Teheran. Unfortunately, an engine on our C-135 acted up and we were unable to leave as scheduled. At first we were to be delayed a day, but we had to wait three days before an engine part was flown to Amman from Spain. We begged the Symmes to permit us to move to a hotel, but they would not hear of it. The only concession they made to the situation was to ask us if they could take some items out of the house to store them while they were on leave in the United States. I wanted to hide for embarrassment, but they would not let me. The Symmes were gracious throughout, and we finally departed.

Although we had kept Teheran informed about our airplane troubles, we must have caused them problems with our inability to stay on schedule. General Twitchell met us in good humor and carried on as though nothing untoward had happened. He presented us with an itinerary booklet with detailed information about U.S. military missions, the Iranian armed forces, principal Americans in Iran, principal Iranian government and military figures, the city of Teheran, and the religions and religious customs of Iran. I studied it with great interest.

While I carried out my official calls in Teheran, Agatha enjoyed the sights. She visited the vault of the Central Bank, where the crown jewels were on display, and was much impressed by the beauty of Golestan Palace's garden, shade trees, and tiled pools. Her last visit was to the bazaar—the world's largest. Maj. Randolph Jameson, my highly esteemed aide, accompanied her and barely avoided a major tragedy when he climbed a ladder to look for metal trays on the second floor of a store. As he was reaching for a tray in the dark, a noiseless electric fan cut the right side of his face a fraction of an inch from his eye, frightening him with the possibility that he could lose his eyesight and with it his flying career. Fortunately, though deep and bleeding profusely, the cut did no permanent damage. Randy was taken to the Mission hospital, where it was determined that the injury was not serious. Needless to say, Agatha lost all interest in shopping that day, but eventually she did go back and buy the tray.

We departed Iran early the next day for Spain, determined to take advantage of the remaining 48 hours of our tour. We were billeted at Torrejon, a SAC base near Madrid operated by the Air Force. After visiting the Prado and shopping in Madrid, we came to the realization that our trip was over. It had measurably improved our professional and cultural understanding of the countries of the MEAFSA region; we had been much enlightened by the interesting people we had met, and we were especially grateful for their many kindnesses.

## Retirement Approaches

Back at MacDill I called on General Conway and reported to him on our tour. He would be retiring within a month, and I greatly regretted his departure. He had been good for the command, and it had prospered under his stewardship. It had improved its posture and its state of training in exercise after exercise. Provided it was given the required forces, it was prepared to carry out its mission. Its day-to-day operations, however, left much to be desired, through no fault of anyone in the command. It was a simple fact that the forces of the Army and Air Force over which Strike exercised operational command were no longer available for further exercise because they were fighting a war in Vietnam. And it appeared that one such war was more than enough for the nation to handle. General Conway informed me that for this reason, activity at Strike Command was being reduced even below the level of activity that had existed during previous months.

Each morning, as usual, General Conway and I would attend the morning briefing, a formal affair that brought us up to date on our area of interest and intelligence matters indicating possible direct involvement by Strike. On some days we would have other discussions, or a visitor might have to be briefed, but frequently I would go to MacDill's golf course. I found myself with a perpetually guilty feeling I did not seem to be able to shake. It just did not make sense to sit in a large office with nothing to do.

In early July I sought an appointment with Gen. John P. McConnell, the Air Force Chief of Staff. In as pleasant and diplomatic a manner as I could muster, I described Strike's inactivity and requested an assignment that would give me work demanding more of me than I was currently expending. As a permanent major general with more than 33 years of active commissioned service, I knew that I would be statutorily retired in less than two years, unless I voluntarily retired earlier. General McConnell offered me nothing, so I chose the voluntary retirement route, giving the Air Force ample time to replace me by the date I chose to retire, 1 February 1970. I felt considerably better after my meeting with the Chief. Immediately after my return to MacDill I informed General Conway of my planned retirement, but the information remained classified for six months. The decks had now been cleared for me to move on with the rest of my life.

General Conway's replacement as commander in chief was Gen. John Throckmorton, commanding general, 3d Army. General Throckmorton had been a year ahead of me at West Point, so I recognized him from cadet days. General Conway retired on 31 July; he and El continued to live in the area, so we saw them from time to time. General Throckmorton received honors on 4 August, followed by the usual round of parties, receptions, and dinners. A quiet and friendly man, General Throckmorton liked to play golf as much as I did, so we found much in common on the greens. Agatha and Mrs. Throckmorton, however, did not hit it off well, primarily because Mrs. Throckmorton preferred to deal with her through one of General Throckmorton's aides, a practice Agatha would not tolerate.

In October I received a cordial letter from Bill Shuler, one of my West Point classmates and president of the Washington chapter of the class organization, telling me that the chapter had voted unanimously to nominate me for the Benjamin F. Castle Award. The nomination had been written by Philip S. Gage, class secretary and a fellow cadet in M Company. I wrote Phil to thank him for his generous characterization of me, which was the basis for my nomination. I had no mixed feelings about accepting the award—to refuse it would have been ungracious. Through the years several of my classmates had expressed regret about the way I had been treated at West Point, and I held no grudges. A large silver tray was presented to me on Founder's Day at Bolling Air Force Base in March 1972. The inscription on the tray read: "Benjamin F. Castle Award To: Lt. Gen. Benjamin Oliver Davis, Jr., U.S. Air Force, West Point 1936, For Outstanding Service and Dedication to his Country and Alma Mater."

On Veterans Day, 11 November 1969, I spoke at the dedication of a new school in Compton, California—Lt. General Benjamin O. Davis, Jr., Junior High School. I stressed the need for the United States to maintain a strong defense posture. I recalled the quality of the American youth I had met in Southeast Asia, their ideals, the sacrifices they were making in the Vietnam War, and the contribution they were making to world peace. I also pointed out the fact that American youth in the United States, viewing the imperfections in our society at home, were imbued with the same kind of idealism in their efforts to right wrongs and improve the lot of their people.

Following the dedication I attended a reunion of veterans with whom I had served during World War II—fighter and bomber pilots, navigators, and technicians I had known more than 20 years earlier in Africa, Sicily, Italy, and the United States. What was then known as the Tuskegee Air Force AMVETS Post 99 held its reunion banquet at the International Hotel in Los Angeles. Today a national organization named the Tuskegee Airmen, Inc., continues to serve, primarily in youth education.

Naturally I began to think about what I would do after I retired, discussing it with Agatha from time to time through the summer and fall of 1969. Having made the transition, I would now advise any person contemplating retirement from any career he or she has been working at for a long time to consider the possibilities as carefully as possible. Barring unexpected catastrophe, I would have many years to live after retiring at the age of 57. My first major decision was to work constructively. Any job I took would have to be challenging and meaningful. I had no desire to accumulate vast wealth, but I would not work at a job in which the employer had calculated my Air Force retirement pay and assumed that he would not have to pay me as much as he would someone else. Many such employers hired retired military people because they did not want to pay for the years of experience and expertise the retiree had developed in the service. I did receive a definite offer from the Assistant Secretary of Defense, Manpower, for a job dealing with racial matters in the Department of Defense. I turned it down because it did not carry enough authority for me to be effective, and I did not like the idea of being chosen for a job on the basis of my race.

As soon as the news of my impending retirement became known in the Tampa area, I was offered a job as a professor at the University of South Florida. I did not give this opportunity much consideration because I did not want to teach and felt that had I taken the job, I would be doing my prospective students an injustice. I was also offered an unspecified job at Pepperdine College in Los Angeles. This offer was more attractive because Agatha and I thought we would enjoy living in Los Angeles, so we accepted Pepperdine's invitation to travel there, see the college, meet the people, and actively consider their offer.

We were met at the airport by Maj. and Mrs. Ronald Rasmussen. Ron had been General Beach's aide during my tour in Korea. Upon hearing of my impending retirement, he had suggested to the people at Pepperdine that I might be an asset to the college. We liked the people at Pepperdine and its ambitious plans for the future, including a move to a new campus at Malibu. We were impressed with Dr. Norvel Young, Pepperdine's president, and Norvel's wife, Helen, who entertained us in their home and introduced us to faculty members and their spouses. We visited the site of the new campus at Malibu and were taken to a Church of Christ service at which the singer Pat Boone spoke. We had dinner with one of Pepperdine's major benefactors, I suppose so she could look us over. We enjoyed the evening, although we were wary of the strong religious influence of the Church of Christ. If Pepperdine had offered me a well-defined job at a reasonable salary, I might have taken it. As it was, Dr. Donald Bibbero, our escort, never told me what the job was or the salary they had in mind. When he saw us off at the airport, I asked the nature of the job. The answer was, "What do you want to do?" Then, when I repeatedly asked the salary, he sheepishly told me $15,000 a year. Both Agatha and I were amused by the offer and rejected it immediately.

A few other job offers came to me from other parts of the country, but by December 1969 I had decided to enter George Washington University, obtain a master's degree in business administration, and join the business world. In 1969 many people considered the MBA to be a key that opened all sorts of doors. I spent many hours preparing for the Educational Testing Service's graduate management admission test, learning just how much I had forgotten over the years and that I could not work as rapidly as I had once been able to do. Fifteen thousand young people with much more recent schooling than mine took the test, so I was pleased to be notified that I had passed at a sufficiently high grade to be admitted to the George Washington School of Government and Business Administration. Once we had rented an apartment in Arlington, Virginia, I would be all set to matriculate on 1 February 1970.

## Cleveland Beckons

After my impending retirement had been made public, I received hundreds of letters, telegrams, and telephone calls complimenting me on my service in the Air Force and expressing regret about my retirement. I thanked all the writers for their kindness. My approaching retirement also came to the attention of Mayor Carl Stokes of Cleveland, the first black mayor of a major city in the United States, who visited me at MacDill to discuss the possibility of my joining his administration as director of public safety. He told me that he would give me a "free hand" in cleaning up the "mess" I would inherit in the position. The visit was kept secret from the press: Mayor Stokes wanted to be sure that no information be leaked about my possible appointment. I took the mayor in to meet General Throckmorton, but I did not inform anyone of the reason for his visit. After we talked he had dinner in my quarters and then returned to Cleveland. Agatha accompanied us to the airport. On the way she told Mayor Stokes that she hoped the job would not be political, and he assured her it would not be. He also invited her to come to Cleveland for a visit.

We liked Mayor Stokes. A handsome man with much charisma, he could exude charm when he wanted to. We recognized that the job he was offering was an opportunity to serve in an administration that was important to the nation. The job met my criteria—it was challenging, constructive, meaningful, and the pay was adequate. It was also a job that involved working with men—policemen and firemen—and there was no doubt in my mind that I could lead them effectively. I had been doing that most of my life.

Mayor Stokes sent the current safety director, Joseph McManamon, to MacDill to brief me on his responsibilities and the general situation in Cleveland. Of course I knew the city from my early days; in winter it could be a dismal, gloomy place. Its people were its redeeming feature. A wonderful group of Americans, Cleveland's people were a very special type of Ohioan. Even the Clevelanders who move to the Washington area are still Clevelanders at heart: public-spirited, generous, and unpretentious.

Before I committed myself to taking the position, I wanted Agatha to be certain that she could live in Cleveland. She saw the city at its worst, in midwinter, and she did not have the proper clothing for the 9-below-zero weather that greeted her. However, Beth Lambright, sister of a prominent Cleveland doctor, Dr. Middleton ("Middy") Lambright—both friends of Mayor Stokes—took good care of her. Agatha was whisked to the presidential suite of a downtown hotel and given the ultra-VIP treatment during her two-day stay. Mayor Stokes had a cocktail party in her honor at his home; Mrs. Stokes was a friendly and enthusiastic hostess. Agatha was sold by the genuineness of her welcome.

Soon afterward we informed Mayor Stokes that I accepted his offer. He would handle the publicity for the appointment, and we would say nothing. A few days after Agatha returned from Cleveland I flew to Lawton, Oklahoma, where a new high-rise apartment complex for senior citizens in the Lawton–Fort Sill area was to be dedicated in honor of my father. He was in ill health and could not attend the dedication, so I represented our family and thanked Jackson Webb, the director of the Lawton Housing Authority, for the honor bestowed upon us. During my absence, a group of Cleveland reporters visited MacDill and confronted Agatha with the rumor that I had accepted the job of Cleveland's safety director. Agatha received them cordially even after their 11:00 P.M. telephone call but, in accordance with our agreement with Mayor Stokes, gave them no information.

At Strike Command Headquarters, I walked around to say my farewells. In my own office, I thanked everyone for all they had done in my interest during the year and a half I had served in Strike. The life of a general officer is made easier when he is fortunate enough to have the expert assistance of efficient, capable, and tactful aides whose personalities and good judgment permit them to perform in a manner that reflects favorably upon the officer they represent. Navy Lt. Dick Chuday in Taiwan, Maj. Tony Postero in Korea and the Philippines, Maj. Randy Jameson in the Philippines and Macdill, Maj. Richard Jackson at Macdill, and S. Sgt. J. D. Moore in Korea, the Philippines, and MacDill all had these qualities, and all were highly effective. Their wives also contributed greatly. My aides—all volunteers—were outstandingly good representatives of the Air Force in appearance, demeanor, and effectiveness. In recognition of their excellent service, I awarded them Commendation Medals. I also decorated my administrative assistant, M. Sgt. Robert Eskridge, for his outstanding duty performance.

The MacDill Officers' Wives' Club honored Agatha with a farewell luncheon a few days after her return from Cleveland, and Ambassador and Mrs. Bell held a dinner in our honor. Agatha then got down to the serious work of packing and generally getting us ready to leave. She had a successful yard sale and disposed of many items that would not fit into the apartment we would be renting in Cleveland. A week of dinners and lunches was capped by a retirement ceremony on 22 January 1970. General Throckmorton pinned a second cluster on my Distinguished Service Medal and made some generous comments. On 26 January I put my uniforms away, never to be worn again, and we drove away from MacDill.

Agatha and I had now reached a vitally important milestone in our lives. I was grateful to the Air Force for giving me an opportunity that did not exist for me anywhere else in the United States. It had given me a flying career, something I had always wanted. It had educated me at West Point, and it had handed me a Regular Army commission as a second lieutenant upon graduation. Initially the military had treated me badly, but eventually it had rewarded me with important assignments in Africa, Europe, the Middle East, and Asia. I lived almost 14 years overseas in these assignments, developing an appreciation of and respect for people at all levels of life—people who were different in appearance and culture from Americans, but who had the same aspirations. I learned to recognize arrogance and its killing effects on human relations. I also learned the meaning of the phrase "the equality of man."

Through good experiences and bad, I had lived $37\frac{1}{2}$ years under military control. I had found little redeeming at West Point or Fort Benning. The three years at Tuskegee Institute were socially pleasant but professionally wasted. I appreciated the few months we spent with my mother and father at Fort Riley only because they were there. I had good years at Maxwell and the Pentagon, despite the discrimination that interfered with my life in the Washington area. I had in fact lived under complete segregation from June 1936 until August 1949, but flying airplanes had certainly helped ease the pain. The remaining 17 years were almost completely enjoyable, however, and I could look back upon substantial contributions to the Air Force and improvements in human relations that I could not have foreseen in my early years. I could never have had another career to compare with what I had experienced in the Air Force. I had seen much of the world and its people, and my understanding had been broadened enormously.

I was now stepping into the uncharted sea of the civilian world, where I had no experience and where I might encounter difficulties I could not foresee. Agatha wanted me to be challenged, so that I would not suffer the mental and physical deterioration that often seemed to go along with retired life. Now, as an editorial in the *Tampa Tribune* put it, we were on our way to "a new combat zone." "Cleveland has had a rising crime rate and severe racial troubles," the editorial stated. "Firemen and policemen have been shot by snipers. Many policemen complain that Mayor Stokes has not supported them in handling violence." It concluded by saying that law enforcement required highly capable leadership. It was my hope to provide that leadership.

# ★ ★ ★ Politics

## 16.

*It was difficult for me to resign as safety director. In hindsight, I probably should have prepared myself by learning more about Cleveland and its political milieu before taking the job. On the other hand, I might well have dug up all sorts of facts and still taken the position, believing that I was capable of surmounting the difficulties.*

Over a period of hours on 23 July 1968, seven people had been killed and 15 injured in a shooting incident in the Hough area of Cleveland's predominantly black east side. Three of the dead and 11 of the injured had been policemen. For five days after the shooting, looting and arson had resulted in property damage to 60 separate business establishments, damaged or destroyed, valued in excess of $1 million.

Cleveland Police Department surveillance vehicles had earlier been dispatched to the area to conduct moving surveillance on the home of Fred ("Ahmed") Evans. The department had received a report that Evans and his group, the Black Nationalists of New Libya, had assembled an arsenal of weapons and were planning to assassinate four prominent black Clevelanders and a policeman. The incident apparently started when a sniper fired at a police tow truck that was picking up a ticketed and abandoned Cadillac, wounding the driver of the truck.

On the night of the shooting, Evans was arrested and charged. The Grand Jury of Cuyahoga County returned seven first-degree murder indictments against him, and at the trial almost a year later a jury found him guilty on all counts. He was reported in newspaper articles to have stated that he received money to support his group from Cleveland: NOW! funds administered by the Hough Area Development Corporation, and that his group had used the money to buy guns and ammunition. Cleveland: NOW! was a community development program devised by Mayor Stokes to raise money for the benefit of the city.

The Hough shootings further polarized public sentiment in a city already torn by racial strife. The election of Mayor Stokes had been viewed by many of Cleveland's citizens as the beginning of a dream come true. This group of people—integrationists—thought that Cleveland's future lay in a society composed of a mixture of blacks and whites in all areas of American life. Many people in other parts of the country considered the election of a black mayor in a city with a population of more than 60 percent whites to be a promise of better things to come. Another group of blacks—separatists—believed strongly that the salvation of black Americans lay in control of their own environment and destiny. This group envisioned separate schools in separate black areas, administered by black police and black fire departments and served by black-owned businesses.

Mayor Stokes, supported by both integrationists and separatists, was torn between his attempts to satisfy the objectives of both groups. He had successfully controlled the city throughout his first administration in spite of the polarization resulting from the Hough shootings, and he was able to control the agenda of the separatists sufficiently to prevent actions by them that might have destroyed his bid for reelection in 1969. The problems of black-white relations generally and the specific problem of the function of the police in the race-torn, crime-ridden city remained, however.

It was the latter problem that apparently led Mayor Stokes to offer me the job of safety director. I accepted because I wanted to support his historically important administration. I considered him a true servant of all the people of Cleveland, and I was determined to help him succeed. Having attended junior and senior high school in Cleveland and one year of college at Western Reserve, I had come to like the city and its people. I realized that substandard city-center living conditions were at the heart of many of Cleveland's problems, and such fundamental matters had to be addressed before other improvements could be achieved. Cleveland's problems were similar to those of all large cities: the vicious cycles of racism, poverty, addiction to narcotics, and crime that continue to afflict our young people. I knew that Cleveland's difficulties could not be corrected in five minutes or five years by waving a wand, but I looked forward to doing what I could to alleviate them. It seemed to me that if anyone could accelerate change, Carl Stokes could.

## A Promising Beginning

When Agatha and I arrived in Cleveland on 31 January 1970 we were greeted by Middy and Beth Lambright. Middy brought us up to date on the seemingly continuous crisis in Cleveland officialdom. The current scandal involved the new police chief, William Ellenburg, the former police chief of Grosse Pointe, Michigan, who had been appointed by the mayor only a few days earlier. On 28 January a City Hall reporter had learned of an investigation of Chief Ellenburg by the *Detroit Free Press*, which alleged that some years earlier he had accepted payoffs from a member of the Mafia to protect an abortion racket. News of this investigation was spreading, although it had not yet hit the newspapers.

Early the next day, Sunday, I walked to City Hall to visit my new office. I met there with Richard Peters, the mayor's friend, former aide, and confidant, and a man regarded as a political professional. Our meeting was cordial, and it improved my understanding of some of the city's personalities. I could not interpret the full import of all the political nuances he casually insinuated, but it was a beginning. In the afternoon I taped a television talk show hosted by Dorothy Fuldheim, whom I liked immediately and quickly learned to trust.

That night Agatha and I were invited to dinner at Mayor Stokes's home. It was a pleasant affair, mostly attended by the mayor's official family, all of whom were strangers to us. We liked Mrs. Stokes, a charming hostess. The evening was disturbed somewhat by city business. Most of the men, including me, repaired to a back room (not smoke-filled) to discuss the Ellenburg crisis. Chief Ellenburg was present at this meeting, which must have been embarrassing to him. Under an eight-column banner headline that day, the *Plain Dealer* had broken the news of his alleged involvement in the abortion racket. I was given a lesson in politics when the mayor went on a three-channel television hookup that night and defended his actions in failing to investigate Chief Ellenburg properly, stating that the *Cleveland Press* and television stations had not, unlike the *Plain Dealer*, assumed Chief Ellenburg's guilt. The mayor obviously believed that attack is the best defense.

On Monday Agatha and I attended a large welcome luncheon sponsored by the city and given in our honor at the Hilton Hotel. Mayor Stokes introduced me. The reception from all the people present was warm, and everyone seemed to be extremely pleased that I had accepted the position. I met many Clevelanders from my high school days, 1925–29, and was intrigued that I recognized many of those who came up to reminisce. That evening I attended my first city council meeting, where I was also well received by the council and the large group of citizens in attendance. These meetings, held on Monday evening at 7:00, were habitually watched on television by a large audience and faithfully reported in the newspapers.

Chief Ellenburg held a press conference on 3 February, but he was not effective in defending himself. For this reason, and possibly for reasons Mayor Stokes discovered on a quick trip to Michigan, Chief Ellenburg submitted his resignation the next day. The mayor immediately appointed Inspector Lewis Coffey, a veteran with 31 years in the department, as police chief. Chief Coffey served as chief during my stay in Cleveland. I found him to be a man of impeccable character, and I never had anything but high marks for his performance.

Within a few days of our arrival Agatha and I had dinner with Beth and Middie Lambright at their home. Beth invited Lynn Coleman, a former classmate of mine from Central High School, who had lived nearby on East 85th Street when we were teenagers. Lynn, now a sergeant in the Police Department, said the department was shot through with racism. I was not surprised; it seemed that racism and the suspicion of racism abounded everywhere, among whites and blacks alike. I determined to try my best to reduce it wherever I could. I also learned from Lynn that though black police officers belonged to the white police officers' union, they also had an organization of their own.

For the first several months, although a spirit of cooperation and close support existed between Mayor Stokes and me, we had little opportunity to talk specifically about the problems I faced as safety director. We saw each other at city council sessions, social affairs, and neighborhood meetings, but the mayor was busy with many matters that did not concern me, and I had the administration of the Department of Public Safety to keep me occupied.

My first responsibility was ensuring the safety of the citizens of Cleveland through the Police Department, the Fire Department, the Office of Traffic Management, and the Dog Pound. For me to be effective, I had to get to know the people of these departments, so I set up a schedule that would permit me to visit all the police precincts and fire stations at an early date. I told the department chiefs that future visits would be unannounced. I also obtained a briefing on traffic management plans and budget. Needless to say, my schedule met with constant delays because emergencies were always arising, such as a fire of major proportions or incidents of street violence. I worked constantly, however, trying to get to all sites in the city. I concluded that each department, if properly led, could respond in a manner that would produce the results all of us wanted.

In my first official duty, I visited the Police Department and was favorably impressed with the appearance and demeanor of the officers I met. I was issued a special invitation to visit the Mounted Unit, a particularly valuable asset in those days of frequent demonstrations. I paid a similar call on my fire chief, William Barry, and later the same day I visited Traffic Management and the Dog Pound. When it came time to appoint an Assistant Director of Public Safety, I got in touch with the Air Force, interviewed some likely candidates, and selected Lt. Col. William Hendrickson, who was in the process of retiring. Bill did a good job for me.

Unless I decided to walk, my movements about the city were efficiently handled by Detective Harlin Worthington, an active member of the Police Department, who was assigned to protect me and drive my official car. A fine man, Harlin took his job seriously. He was concerned about my safety during the demonstrations I attended, some of which were violent, and took precautions to counter any possible assassination attempt on the frequent occasions when I returned home late at night. He kept his eyes open, and he was thinking and anticipating all the time.

I was soon introduced to another facet of my job. A demonstration was in progress at Cleveland State University, just a few blocks from the center of the city. I was told it was peaceful, but I attended anyway, hoping to find out what I could about dissatisfaction among student groups. I do not remember the cause of the demonstration, but I was pleased to be able to meet with the student demonstrators and discuss their apparently mild grievances. I was to spend many an hour and day at schools and colleges in efforts to keep things quiet. I observed some violence, but none was ever directed at me.

My major concern was, of course, the Police Department, which had been engaged in an ongoing struggle with City Hall since the election of Mayor Stokes. Racial antagonism was the root of the problem. Many white policemen, who made up the majority of the force, thought they had no support from City Hall, claiming that the mayor and his staff, many of whom were black, had usurped the police force's authority and were obstructing the exercise of legitimate police powers. In some respects, these men were right. Given this nearly impossible situation, it was my job to convince the police that they could depend on me to protect their interests in City Hall. To my surprise, I was able to accomplish this feat in short order. Chief Coffey and his people gave me their trust, and among themselves they began to believe that City Hall would support their legitimate interests. On one hand, I was careful not to interfere with police prerogatives; on the other, I expected the police to realize that City Hall was dealing with sensitive political issues.

## Taking the Pulse of the Community

I accompanied Mayor Stokes on the first of a series of town meetings between members of his staff and the public, designed to enable people from City Hall to learn about neighborhood problems and improve the climate, attitudes, and personal relationships in the city—as well as to strengthen the mayor's position and standing. City Hall actively solicited invitations from various citizens' groups for us to come and address issues that concerned them. I attended several of these meetings in different parts of the city and profited immensely from them. After the mayor opened the meeting with a statement and introduced us, we would respond to questions from the floor. At each meeting I stressed my strong belief that we could only have an effect on crime through total community involvement—getting to the root causes of the problem with genuine improvement in human relations. It was my conviction that responsible citizens had to get involved and oppose the relatively small number of people, whites and blacks, who undermined the positive elements of our society. A virulent hatred of police existed in some areas of Cleveland, just as some police actively hated certain groups, particularly black nationalists. I would describe our intensive training program, which required each policeman to know the essence of the Bill of Rights and to carry its principles in his heart as well as his head. It was the policeman's duty to protect the innocent, apprehend the guilty, and preserve the peace, maintaining the delicate balance between the rights of the individual and the rights of society as a whole. Many of these community meetings were attended by dissatisfied, angry, and hostile people who had come to express their grievances. I welcomed all comments, whether friendly or unfriendly. Following the meetings, I briefed my office people on the concerns expressed by the participants and asked them to take appropriate action to correct any deficiencies that had been uncovered.

I was constantly interviewed on television and had no difficulty handling the questions, the answers to which seemed obvious to me. Once I appeared on Merv Griffin's show in Philadelphia, and I was interviewed almost weekly by Norma Quarles or Dorothy Fuldheim. These appearances helped me immensely in my performance of duty. Soon I was recognized by many people I met on the street, and they frequently offered me valuable ideas I could use in my work. Likewise, I received a steady stream of letters, practically all complimentary, some offering me valid suggestions for improved law enforcement. I answered each of them—keeping the people in my office very busy! My office door was open to everyone, and many individuals and groups came to see me.

The job entailed a vast variety of activities and functions. I had lunches with Birkett Williams, a former safety director, and with the former mayor of Cleveland, Anthony Celebrezze. As part of my public relations campaign, I played in a golf tournament at the Canterbury Country Club with David Frost. The next day I attended the Advertising Council's luncheon for the Cleveland Indians and sat next to an old hero of mine, Rapid Robert Feller, one of the greatest pitchers of all time.

At the Indians game on the opening day of the season I was interrupted by a call from Mayor Stokes, leading to the first of many trips to Collingwood High School. The situation at Collingwood represented a threat to the tenuous peace that had been established there between black and white students, who had feuded before the Easter holidays. Members of Black Unity, a separatist group, were making a concentrated effort to recruit additional members at Collingwood, and the school administration was resisting their tactics because of the resulting disruption. Mayor Stokes had earlier requested the National Guard, and they were currently on alert at their armory in Shaker Heights. I dealt with the situation by staying calm, refusing to argue, listening to both sides, backing up the authority of the school administration, and attempting to prevent confrontation and violence. After several days the school resumed its normal operation, and the National Guard alert was relaxed.

In Glenville, a suburb, I attended a community meeting and visited West Technical High School. Such meetings were always helpful because I would pick up information on community-police relationships. The specter of the Hough shootings remained in our consciousness, and it was important to discourage actions that might inflame elements of the community. The Glenville Area Neighborhood Council sponsored a reception honoring Agatha and Dolores Coffey, wife of Cleveland's new police chief. About 2,000 people attended the reception, and its theme told the whole story: "All Segments of Cleveland's City Government Working Together for the Betterment of Our Community." The affair brought together—for the first time—the diverse elements of city government that were almost constantly in conflict with each other: City Hall, the Police Department, the Fraternal Order of Police, the Cleveland Firefighters Union, and the Cleveland Council. (Tish Brown, wife of Councilman Virgil Brown, was a prominent force behind this important effort.) This represented a dramatic attempt to defuse some of the virulent hatred that existed.

Agatha appeared on television shows, too. Soon after our arrival she remarked in one such appearance that she would like to become involved in volunteer work, stating specifically that she preferred actual working assignments to honorary positions on committees or boards. The television audience took her at her word: she received numerous invitations to participate in community affairs and became extremely busy. Her activities included, but were not limited to, the Red Cross, the United Police Wives, the Firemen's Wives, the Council on Human Relations, the Campfire Girls, the Hospital Auxiliary, the Safety Council, and the Hammill Day Care Nursery. She was involved in all sorts of meetings, teas, and visits. She participated in the kickoff for the tuberculosis fund-raising drive and visited several of the public schools in the company of Mrs. Paul Briggs, wife of the school superintendent. We went together to visit the Hough Community Opportunity Board, and Agatha became a member of the board of the Juvenile Detention Home for delinquent boys. She did consent to be a trustee of the Tuberculosis and Respiratory Disease Association, but only on the condition that she could also be a working volunteer. We had an interesting time every night, telling each other about our experiences during the day.

Both of us felt happy with our new lives. We believed we were being productive, and we were enjoying what we were doing. Frequently, we strolled around the city to enjoy the spring weather. Once we walked to a large but peaceful demonstration in the public square attended by hundreds of people and a large number of ethnic demonstrators from the city's many diverse neighborhoods. As usual, the Police Department was well represented, with officers at strategic points on foot. Members of the department's impressive Mounted Unit were also present. Astride their beautiful horses, these police were effective counters to the extremist demonstrators who frequently showed up at large rallies. They were skilled in handling crowds, well trained, and exceptionally well disciplined. At a demonstration at Western Reserve College in sympathy for the student victims at Kent State, it was the mounted police who maintained control and prevented the violence that threatened to take over at several critical points during the afternoon.

Sometimes Agatha and I went to the West Side Market, where we struck up an acquaintance with the vendors. I played golf at more than one of the city's beautiful and well-maintained public golf courses. Cleveland also maintained an excellent, inexpensive public transportation system. But Agatha and I agreed that the best thing about Cleveland was the friendliness and candor of the people themselves. Like me, she soon became an enthusiastic Cleveland booster.

The city's reputation for racism, however, was not unjustified. Within weeks of our arrival, an African graduate student at Western Reserve was severely beaten in a laundromat in Murray Hill, an Italian area. The hoodlums who beat the man announced that Murray Hill was off limits to blacks. I issued a directive to Chief Coffey to increase police attention to Murray Hill so that citizens of both races would be protected. I announced that all areas in Cleveland must be safe to all citizens, that no area was off limits to any law-abiding person, and that my enforcement directive to the Cleveland police would be strictly observed and enforced. After speaking to a councilman representing the area, I received an invitation to the Italo-American Brotherhood dinner at Murray Hill, where I was courteously entertained in Old World tradition. On the surface it was a pleasant evening, but I have my doubts that even today, 20 years later, blacks are welcome in Murray Hill.

In late spring I inducted a large number of new men into the force and officiated at a promotion ceremony for deserving older policemen. The new men, who had just completed their training, were most impressive in their appearance and demeanor, and their families were as proud as they were. I made a few remarks on this important occasion, directed at both the police and the public. For the police to do their duty, I said, it was imperative for them to have the support of both their families and the public. The police and the public had mutual responsibilities. Although I did not mention it on this occasion, crime in Cleveland had in fact been reduced. The number of complaints about police actions or inactions had dramatically dropped, the police were now generally perceived as doing a good job, and police morale was high. Most important, a climate of goodwill was beginning to develop between the city's blacks and whites, even in the most troubled neighborhoods. The basic problems remained, but on this day, at this time, there was a feeling of hope, which I shared.

In June 1970 I was appointed by President Nixon to the Campus Unrest Commission, designed to prevent tragedies like the ones that had occurred at Ohio's Kent State and Mississippi's Jackson State in early May, when students had been shot and killed by national guardsmen. The White House requested permission from Mayor Stokes to make the appointment. He regarded it as a compliment to the city and, upon learning that my absences would not be frequent or protracted, agreed. I was happy with the assignment because of the nature of the problem and the people I would be working with. The tasks outlined by the President for the commission were challenging and vitally important for the nation.

## Conflict and Resignation

Matters were going well in June. I believed I was making genuine progress toward uniting the city in a way that had never before been accomplished. I had created substantial goodwill among disparate groups of people, and I had been able to develop respect where only hatred had existed before. There were, however, glimmerings of trouble ahead. Articles in the *Cleveland Press* described personality differences between the mayor and me. The Cleveland *Call and Post*, a black newspaper sympathetic to Mayor Stokes, stated that I had allowed "heavily armed police task forces" in black areas and claimed that I did not do the same for white areas. I had no reaction to this typical antipolice statement, which was justified in some respects by earlier police actions. I discussed with the mayor more than one inflammatory and antipolice speech that had been made by black revolutionaries supported by his administration. Especially considering the misuse of city funds that had led to the Hough killings, I thought that the actions of such extremists should have caused them to be cut off from city support. In my opinion their statements were jeopardizing public safety, which led me to recommend effective counteraction. The mayor, however, was committed to remaining the man in the middle.

Mail sent to my office continued to comment favorably on the job we were doing to bring ethnic and racial groups together. It also seemed, however, that certain unfriendly, separatist elements were unhappy we were doing so well. Even in late June, it was still my strong belief that with the mayor's complete support we could be successful. Unfortunately, over the next few weeks, that support did not develop. It became apparent that I could not survive in my position without the support of other elements of the city administration, much less when those elements attempted to thwart my mission. The police were sworn to arrest violators of the law, and I was not going to ask them to look the other way.

Mayor Stokes, an astute politician, was fully aware of the deterioration of my support within his administration. During my last month in office, I spoke with him on several occasions about the city's support of self-declared racists and enemies of law enforcement. I did not identify those enemies for the press because I thought that a public confrontation between me and the mayor would not be profitable to anyone, least of all the city of Cleveland. In addition, I had come to understand the political balancing act that was part of the mayor's job, and I respected him for his efforts under adverse conditions. For my own part, I tried to act intelligently in my performance of duty, making a serious and strong effort to help the mayor in any

way I could within the bounds of proper discharge of my responsibilities. However, even though he had promised me a "free hand" in
the job when he visited me at MacDill, it became impossible for me to
act effectively under the constraints imposed upon me. Consequently,
on 27 July, I submitted the following letter to the mayor: "I find it
necessary and desirable to resign as Director of Public Safety. The
reasons are simple: I am not receiving from you and your administration the support my programs require, and the enemies of law enforcement continue to receive support and comfort from you and
your administration. I request your acceptance of my resignation at
your earliest convenience."

My resignation provided a field day for the news media. Some
writers were of the opinion that I should have given the euphemistic
"for personal reasons" as the basis for my resignation. Many other
key people who had left office during the three years Mayor Stokes
had been in office chose this route, but I could not do so. Large
numbers of citizens had enthusiastically welcomed me to Cleveland
and given me their full support, and I believed they deserved an
honest explanation for my abrupt departure. If I had remained in
office under the existing conditions of severe conflict between me and
City Hall on the nature of my duties, I would have had to surrender
all the principles under which I had operated. I would have been
forced into preferential treatment of extremists who were breaking
the law, thus violating the Police Department's essential mission: enforcing the law equally for all citizens. The issue came down to this
simple point, and it was perfectly clear that I could not and would not
ignore it.

Although the mayor had assured Agatha and me when we first
talked that the job of safety director was not political, it had inevitably
dragged me into the political arena. In the struggle between blacks
and whites, separatists and integrationists, police and law violators, I
had taken the side of both the blacks and the whites, the integrationists, and the police in the proper performance of their duty. Mayor
Stokes was demonstrably on *all* sides simultaneously, including that
of various law violators and those who supported them. Among those
whom I considered enemies of law enforcement were Harllel Jones,
the Rev. Baxter Hill, the Rev. Arthur LeMon, the Cleveland Council of
Churches, the *Call and Post*, the Friendly Inn Settlement House, and
the United Committee to Combat Fascism. Mayor Stokes considered

these people and groups to be pillars of the community; to me they were the opposition, and furthermore they were being actively supported by people in City Hall. When Mayor Stokes presented this list to the media, I elected to remain silent, neither confirming nor denying its accuracy.

Some of the mayor's political supporters harassed me one morning by having a group of 20 to 30 women appear in front of my apartment building and block my departure for the airport until I had listened to a message they had composed in support of Mayor Stokes. They almost made me late for my flight to a Campus Unrest Commission meeting in Washington. This was political hardball, and I did not like such tactics. Over the past months I had seen many unfriendly demonstrations in the interest of one cause or another, but it was a new experience to have one organized against me. On the other hand, I received hundreds of letters from all over the nation and some from foreign countries. Almost all thanked me for the efforts I had made in the interest of the city and indicated support for the position I had taken. I recognized that some of this "favorable" mail was really anti-Stokes mail, but I also believed that the mayor had taken many political steps that were not in the best interests of the city.

It was difficult for me to resign as safety director. I had failed, and I knew there was no other interpretation that could be put on my resignation. I was particularly concerned about the effect it would have on Agatha. Happily settled in Cleveland, with already many friends and pleasant relationships, we had intended to put down roots. This unexpected breakup of our new home must have caused her considerable anxiety, but she never complained. She agreed with the action I had taken, feeling that I had no alternative under the circumstances, and adjusted to the changes that came our way with a stiff upper lip. With help from a great lady like Agatha, I simply could not lose.

In hindsight, I probably should have prepared myself by learning more about Cleveland and its political milieu before taking the job. On the other hand, I might well have dug up all sorts of facts and still taken the position, believing that I was capable of surmounting the difficulties. Regardless, I now had to pick up the pieces, find other employment, and get on with my life. In a sense, it all turned out for the best. Once it became apparent that I could not continue, it was to everybody's advantage for me to cut my losses and move on.

**New Horizons**

Soon after arriving in Cleveland I had received a letter from Dr.
Norvel Young congratulating me on my job and, in the same paragraph, making me an open-ended offer of a job at Pepperdine College
whenever I saw fit to take it. I thought again of Pepperdine after my
resignation but rejected the idea. I also considered jobs with General
Dynamics, Emery Air Freight, the Bank of America, and Xerox. I
listened to the local Republicans and the local Democrats, who had
some ideas about my running for mayor of Cleveland, but I had no
interest in leaping from the frying pan into the fire.

In the meantime the work of the Campus Unrest Commission had
begun with several meetings in Washington to orient its members,
discuss procedure, and develop courses of action. In establishing the
commission on 13 June, the President asked it to identify the principal causes of campus violence; assess the reasons for breakdown in
the processes for the orderly expression of dissent; suggest specific
procedures through which legitimate grievances could be resolved;
and find ways to protect and enhance the right of academic freedom,
the right to pursue an education free from improper interference, and
the right of peaceful dissent and protest. The former Governor of
Pennsylvania, William Scranton, was our distinguished chairman.
The other members were Martha Derthick, a former Clevelander,
then associate professor of political science at Boston College; Bayless
A. Manning, dean of Stanford University Law School; James Ahern,
police chief of New Haven, Connecticut; Erwin Canham, editor in
chief of the *Christian Science Monitor;* Dr. James Cheek, president of
Howard University; Revius Ortique, a New Orleans lawyer; and
James Rhodes, a junior fellow at Harvard and lecturer in education at
the University of Massachusetts. The commission worked intensively
for three months and met the President's deadline for submitting its
report, which was released to newspapers for their use on 27 September 1970.

The commission conducted public hearings in Washington; Los
Angeles; Jackson, Mississippi; and Kent, Ohio. It met often in executive session and had its staff conduct intensive investigations in Jackson, Kent, and Lawrence, Kansas. The commission staff visited numerous other colleges and universities and reviewed the contributions of several consultants. Our report recommended that govern-

ment officials at all levels make efforts to bring hostile factions within their jurisdiction together; that law enforcement officers be better trained and equipped so they could deal with campus disorders firmly, justly, and humanely; that universities, supported by students, faculty, and trustees, improve their capability for responding effectively to disorder; and that students accept the responsibility for presenting their ideas in a reasonable and persuasive manner. In its conclusion the commission observed that the government must continue progress toward its national goals of ending the war in Vietnam and achieving racial and social justice; that failure even to appear not to be pursuing these goals could provoke further campus protest; that the federal government must champion everyone's right to dissent nonviolently and promote the evenhanded enforcement of the law everywhere; that governments at all levels should encourage work, service, and internship opportunities, so that those who do not want to attend college would not feel forced to do so; that massive financial aid for black colleges and universities, increased aid for higher education generally, and expanded programs of student financial aid should be provided; and finally, that the President, by example and instruction, should offer the compassionate, reconciling, moral leadership that was required to bring the country together again. The members of the commission unanimously concurred in these recommendations, but they were not well received in the White House, probably because President Nixon felt that too much responsibility for action was being placed upon his presidency.

In early September John Volpe, former Governor of Massachusetts and at that time Secretary of Transportation, came to Cleveland to speak. He sought a meeting with me, but I was out of the city on business with the Campus Unrest Commission. Upon returning I called the Department of Transportation and requested an appointment with Secretary Volpe at an early date. He offered me the job of Director of Civil Aviation Security, a newly created position with the mission of combating the rash of hijackings of commercial aircraft to Cuba, which had increased rapidly in recent weeks. I accepted with no delay. A glutton for punishment, I had welcomed challenges all my life, and this would not be the least of them.

Secretary Volpe took me to the White House, where we met President Nixon in the Oval Office. Attorney General John Mitchell and J. Edgar Hoover, Director of the FBI, were also present. President Nixon

forthrightly offered his proposed solution for the war against hijacking: to neutralize the hijacker and permit the plane to proceed safely
to its destination. My appointment was announced on 21 September.
I found temporary quarters at Fort Myer while Agatha stayed in
Cleveland, preparing for our permanent move to Washington. Without further delay I went to work, organizing my office, recruiting
knowledgeable people, and developing concepts of operation.

# ★ ★ ★ Piracy

## 17.

*The very basis of civil aviation security had to be the capability at each airport complex to protect aircraft, passengers, terminal buildings, cargoes, hangars, fueling systems, and air navigation facilities from any form of unlawful act. I came to believe that the current situation demanded leadership and assistance by the federal government.*

Television comedians were making jokes about aircraft hijackings in 1969 and early 1970. Fortunately, the public began to realize that the subject of hijacking was not to be taken lightly. Most of the jokes stopped in September 1970, when Arab terrorists seized and destroyed four airliners: a Pan American 747 in Cairo and planes belonging to TWA, BOAC, and Swissair in Jordan. A $50 million capital loss in aircraft was sustained, but this was overshadowed by the 600 lives put in peril. Those aboard the 747 had an extremely close brush with death. The terrorists aboard that aircraft mistimed their explosives, and the plane blew up 90 seconds after landing at Cairo. Had it not been for the evacuation instructions given to the passengers by the Pan American crew on the flight from Beirut, most of them would have died. For many days television audiences around the world witnessed the helplessness of the hundreds of passengers held hostage on the Jordanian desert. Their safe return was made possible only after long and delicate diplomatic moves by the White House and the State Department in concert with statesmen from other nations.

Piracy is an old crime, and the U.S. policy on it has remained constant since 1815. When he was Secretary of State, James Monroe faced the Barbary pirates with a simple and unequivocal statement: "It's the object of the United States to put an end to these odious practices." President Nixon was equally direct in his announcement: "The menace of air piracy must be met—immediately and effectively." During the 1960s there had been almost 100 hijackings in the United States, the great majority taking place after 1967, during the Nixon administration. Most had amounted to demands for air transportation to Cuba. Although expensive and unsettling to the traveling public and embarrassing to the airlines and the nation, these hijackings were not nearly as serious as those that took place in the Middle East in September 1970. Now the threat was to lives and costly property; hijacking had become an act of terrorism and sabotage.

For the five years I was with the Department of Transportation, I was the federal government's spokesman on all matters pertaining to civil aviation security. The job was worldwide in scope. I dealt personally with the representatives of many nations in Europe, the Middle East, Asia, and Australia. My staff and I searched for ways to put an end to all kinds of hijackings. Improved security on the ground and in the air might reduce incidents of hijacking in its simplest form—the demand for transportation—but it would not solve the larger problem, which included terrorism and sabotage. Within a relatively short time, with effective assistance from the federal government and commercial airlines, we were to solve the domestic hijacking problem. Terrorism and sabotage, however, remained extremely serious threats. In the United States we had not yet experienced the kind of terrorism that occurred in the Middle East in September 1970, but we must be ever vigilant in our defense against the threat of it. This threat is now recognized as related to the drug problem, which should require security in its highest possible form throughout the transportation system.

As soon as I moved into my new office in the Federal Aviation Administration (FAA) building on 20 September 1970, I conferred with several officials who had been working on the hijacking problem. My office was part of the Office of the Secretary of Transportation, and I reported directly to the Secretary. The Administrator of the FAA, Jack Shaffer, headed a large nationwide organization that until the recent creation of the Department of Transportation had been a separate operating agency. He and his administration now reported to the Secretary. Under this new arrangement, which continues to cause some problems today, the FAA (along with the Federal Highway Administration, the National Highway Traffic Safety Administration, and the Coast Guard) lost considerable prestige. My mission constituted a usurpation of FAA's authority over civil aviation security, but I had to use the services of a large FAA office that had been charged with carrying out essentially the same mission.

It is truly a wonder that Jack Shaffer and I did not come to blows about our respective authorities, but we did not. At first the civil aviation people at FAA dragged their feet and seemed to delight in placing roadblocks in my path, but it did not take long for them to realize that I did not stand on ceremony, I had no political ambition, and I was mainly interested in solving our common problems. From then on I began to receive full cooperation from FAA people, without whose energetic and capable assistance nothing good could possibly have happened. All of us managed to swallow pride of position and work together to improve our nation's security posture.

## Learning from Abroad

Secretary Volpe and I visited some of the busiest European airports, which were doing all they could do to address the hijacking problem. Leaving the States on 26 September, I carefully inspected the security at Dulles International Airport before boarding a TWA jet for Rome. I did not observe any glaring defects at Dulles, where the FAA "airport plan" was in operation. Under this procedure passengers were screened on the basis of physical and behavioral criteria such as age, sex, type of ticket bought, and use of credit. These criteria made up a passenger "profile," and their use had been approved by the American Civil Liberties Union.

Before the passengers boarded the aircraft, TWA gave each a small plastic bag in which to put watches, rings, change, and other metal possessions. Magnetometers were then used to detect the presence of any additional metal objects, such as a gun or knife, on the person of the passenger. When the passengers reached the aircraft, their hand luggage was opened and inspected. Any individual considered a security threat would have been searched by an airline security official, but we did not have anyone searched on this occasion. During these early days some travelers objected to the inconvenience of screening, but the public generally came to recognize the need and accept the requirement.

When we made our intermediate stop in Orly, the Paris airport, we disembarked and went into the terminal while the aircraft was being serviced. A French security officer with a big tommy gun held each passenger back when we reboarded until a French TWA employee told him to let the passenger proceed for boarding. Hand luggage had already been carefully searched at check-in. Each man, including me, was patted down and had to remove his hat for inspection. I could not understand why they did not search the women—after all, Leila Khaled, a Palestine Liberation Organization terrorist, had been arrested in a hijacking attempt on a British aircraft less than a month earlier.

Rome was warm and beautiful. Secretary and Mrs. Volpe flew to Europe with President Nixon aboard Air Force One, and I met them at the Excelsior Hotel. At the President's news conference, Secretary of Defense Melvin Laird and Secretary of State William Rogers stood closer to the President than Secretary Volpe. Members of the White House staff commented that for political purposes, it would have been preferable for Secretary Volpe, an Italian American, to have been seen on American television by the 20 million Italian Americans in the United States. This was my first of many times to meet Mrs. Volpe, a lively, gracious, and friendly personality.

I inspected Fiumicino—Rome International Airport—the next morning with Secretary Volpe and discussed security with airport officials. Fiumicino seemed to have some rather large holes in its security system, among them allowing various kinds of workers to visit parts of the airport where they did not need to be. We then traveled to Zurich, Frankfurt, Paris, Amsterdam, and London, observing first-hand the procedures used and following up our discussions at the working and ministerial levels. From London we flew to Boston, where I left the Secretary and flew to Washington.

John Volpe had been the guiding force in the antihijacking program throughout his tenure at the Department of Transportation, which had started in January 1969. Faced with an unusually high number of hijackings that month, he ordered the FAA to form a task force of aviation, security, legal, and medical experts to find a way to stop hijackings. This was not easy—it took 18 months for them to come up with a procedure that worked. Properly applied, that procedure turned out to be infallible in preventing the transportation-to-Cuba type of hijacking. Eastern Airlines tested the FAA's passenger screening system in its operations. Its success was astounding; from being the most likely airline to be hijacked, Eastern rapidly became the least likely. One hijacker admitted choosing another carrier because he knew Eastern was screening passengers.

It was impossible to know for certain whether hijackings had actually been prevented through the use of the FAA system. Over a two-year period, about 300 arrests were made for attempting to board an aircraft with a gun, and 19 for possessing other weapons, including hand grenades. Most people believed, however, that some of those arrested would have attempted a hijacking had they been permitted to board as passengers. Unfortunately, even in the face of Eastern's success, other airlines were reluctant to adopt the FAA system.

After the loss of the four aircraft in the Middle East, Secretary Volpe recommended that President Nixon order a force of federal sky marshals to fly on U.S. air carriers as an armed deterrent against hijacking attempts. The President accepted the recommendation, and the Secretary presented to the International Civil Aviation Organization (ICAO) a request for concerted international action. He was successful in persuading the ICAO to recommend to its member nations a convention calling for the return or punishment of persons hijacking aircraft.

After I was appointed Director of Civil Aviation Security, the airlines became, on the whole, more involved with screening. I would have preferred all flights to be screened, and I was not satisfied with the long-odds gamble by some airlines that one of their planes would not get picked off. We soon had several hundred sky marshals flying on domestic and international flights of U.S. carriers. It was impossible to say with certainty that they deterred any hijackings, but I thought that many potential hijackers would be dissuaded by the possibility of being killed or captured. We did not yet have a blueprint for solving the entire hijacking problem, but we were taking many actions that would form a foundation for further measures.

Secretary Volpe was the ideal boss, and I found it a pleasure to work for him. He was supportive, he knew what was possible and what was not possible, and he was always ready to listen and help solve problems. I associated with many cabinet members during my career, but none operated at a higher standard. His leadership was such that every one of his subordinates appreciated his concern for their welfare and responded accordingly.

On 6 October 1970 I flew to Fort Dix, where our first class of sky marshals was in training. Their average age was 29; half were college graduates, three-fourths were military veterans, and several were former policemen or airlines security men. There were also a few former customs inspectors, several detectives and engineers, and one research analyst. More than 8,600 men had applied for 2,100 positions. The chance to travel, especially on international flights, was an attraction, but the fact that all would be trained as security officers in the U.S. Customs Service seemed to be the major reason for the positive response. Their training included classwork and practical courses in the martial arts and marksmanship.

I welcomed the members of the class to the program, stressing its importance to the safety of passengers on commercial aircraft and warning them to be ever vigilant. Many innocent lives were under their protection. I described the part they would play in the overall air security picture and the efforts being made by the Department of Transportation to have all nations agree to return hijackers immediately to their point of origin or to try them as hijackers in the country where they landed, thus removing the safe-haven privilege. We were aided in this effort by member countries of the ICAO.

I delivered several other speeches where I thought it would be useful to outline the department's intentions—in New York to the northeastern chapter of the Society of American Travel Writers, and in Washington to the Aviation and Aerospace Writers Club. With the recent Middle East terrorist actions, it seemed appropriate to reassure the traveling public as much as possible. American air travelers on the whole never appeared to become overly alarmed about their safety on our commercial aircraft.

While I was busy learning my new job, Agatha took care of everything that needed to be done in my absence. She found an apartment with a perfect view of Washington in Arlington, Virginia, where we live to this day. Finding a desirable apartment was no small task in October 1970. The Department of Defense had at least taken the lead in listing only apartments open to military applicants without regard to race, color, or creed. Agatha was apprised of this fact by my former protocol officer in the Philippines, Captain Barbara Patton, who was now stationed at the Pentagon. Barbara suggested that Agatha look at an apartment at Normandy House, a building on the Department of Defense list. When Agatha visited the apartment she rejected it immediately because of its restricted view. The Normandy House manager then took her to London House, where she saw a three-bedroom apartment that from every standpoint—especially the view—was ideal. Fortunately London House was under the same management as Normandy House and committed to equal opportunity housing. After some deliberation we moved into London House on 27 October, and we were delighted with it. From our windows we had a wide panorama of the Potomac and the city beyond. We could see Georgetown, aircraft touching down at National Airport, the Jefferson Memorial, the Lincoln Memorial, the Washington Monument, the Capitol, the Kennedy Center, Roosevelt Island, and all points in between. Twenty years later we still feel lucky to have found London House. The view from the ninth floor is always spectacular: morning, noon, and night, fall, winter, spring, and summer. The Defense Department's policy of approving only real estate listings by equal opportunity housing owners has had a beneficial effect on the lives of its members stationed in the Washington area. But Arlington still seeks solutions to landlord discrimination even today.

## A Strategy for Security Evolves

It became clear to me early on that Americans could learn much from Israeli security operations, even though many details of their system were not directly transferable to ours. Consequently, in early November I combined a trip to Tel Aviv with one that Agatha had planned to take to Israel with Ruth Miller—a Cleveland friend—and 10 other women. The purpose of my trip was to learn in detail the basic reasons for Israel's success in warding off the hijackings that had been inflicted upon other nations. Israel boasted a record of truly effective operation. Its small airline, El Al, was regarded as a prime target by terrorists, and the country's enemies were everywhere, not only in the Middle East. According to intelligence they surrounded Kennedy Airport, where we boarded El Al for our trip, and other airports used as transient stops. El Al did have the advantage over other passenger airlines of operating only a small number of aircraft on a relatively limited schedule of daily flights. Even more important, it was determined to survive without loss of life and valuable aircraft. Many prominent Israelis flew El Al and were vulnerable to being kidnapped by Middle Eastern terrorists. El Al had used sky marshals successfully, but it also understood and emphasized ground security at airports and airline terminals. At the Kennedy terminal, each passenger, his hold baggage, and his carry-on baggage had to undergo detailed screening.

I spent three days in Tel Aviv conferring with Israeli security officials and making inspections and observations at the airport. They forthrightly informed me on helpful details. Everywhere I went I found an overwhelming determination and spirit; visiting Israel was an inspiring and thrilling experience to me from every standpoint. Agatha and I went our separate ways—I to work, and she to the detailed schedule that Ruthie Miller had devised for her group. Several in the group, including Agatha, had friends or relatives who were Israeli citizens.

Gradually I began to arrive at some conclusions. The absolute importance of effective airport security was foremost. Along with it came the shocking realization that we had no airport security in the United States except at the two airports owned and operated by the federal government—National and Dulles. I heard many frightening stories about the absence of airport security: two teenagers found asleep aboard a parked jet airliner at Logan Airport in Boston; an unguided tour by an insurance investigator of a parked 747 on the ramp at Los Angeles; unforced entry of three parked 727s by drunks ostensibly looking for liquor at Rochester. A 16-year-old boy hijacked a National Airlines 727 from Mobile, Alabama, simply walking aboard without a ticket and pulling out a loaded pistol; and a 14-year-old slipped aboard a Delta DC-9 at Birmingham, threatened a stewardess with a loaded automatic, and demanded a flight to Cuba.

The very basis of civil aviation security had to be the capability at each airport complex to protect aircraft, passengers, terminal buildings, cargoes, hangars, fueling systems, and air navigation facilities from any form of unlawful act. Since the beginning of aviation in the United States, the federal government had not involved itself in airport security matters, leaving these problems to airport operators, airlines, and local authorities. I came to believe that the current situation demanded leadership and assistance by the federal government to ensure the safety of U.S. national and international air commerce. I also realized it was imperative to establish regulations accelerating the implementation of airport security measures. The security problem could only be solved through a team effort by airport operators, airlines, local law enforcement, the federal government, and the traveling public.

It was up to me to stimulate this kind of teamwork. I asked the head of the Air Transport Association, Stuart Tipton, to schedule me to speak to a group of presidents of the major air transport companies during a visit they were making to Washington. Airline presidents had to begin placing more emphasis on security than they had in the past, provide incentives for proper performance, and punish failures. I did not ask much of these busy men, and I was careful not to tell them how to run their big, complicated, and important businesses. My sole request was that they have their security officers report to them on a regular basis on their effectiveness. I named these officers, whom I had met all over the country, and stated my respect for them as professionals. If the airline presidents carried out my suggestion, their employees would soon catch on to the president's personal interest, and some rather miraculous and startling things would begin to happen. In the 1970s it was an inescapable fact that security was as important an element of safety as the airworthiness of the airplane, the qualifications of the pilot, air traffic control, and navigational aids. I forecast that airline operations, marketing, and flight safety people would begin to recognize the airline security officer as an indispensable member of the airline team.

I also visited Boston, Seattle, and Houston, where I met with the Air Transportation Security subcommittees of the Air Transport Association to educate myself on progress being made at the working level. The meetings, not always encouraging in the early days of the program, were attended by representatives of airlines, airport management, customs, the FBI, and the FAA—all intensely interested in developing a safer operation by keeping dangerous people and things off airplanes and away from operational areas. In each case I closed my short talk with a statement of my strong belief that the responsibility for security belonged equally to the airlines, airport management, and the federal government.

Each airport was different, but three basic concepts could be applied to all of them: vehicular access controls, people access controls, and vehicle and people identification systems. At many U.S. airports, people and vehicles had open access to runways, taxiways, and ramps. It was clear that we could not permit airports to continue to be public parks. When people could freely wander around multimillion-dollar investments in aircraft and facilities, there was little chance to stop those intent upon doing damage. It was important that the public have free and easy access to the airport's public facilities only and that identification be required for every vehicle and person permitted beyond the public areas—for example, food service personnel, baggage handlers, and the vehicles they used. Carte blanche passes for all areas of the airport would not be issued; a mail handler had no reason to be where aircraft were serviced, and a line mechanic had no reason to be in the cargo-handling area. I had visited foreign airports and found that some of them used a photo-identification badge keyed to six zones of access. The airport manager's badge authorized access to all six zones, but a food handler's badge authorized access to only one.

Mrs. Max Schenk, Hadassah national president, spoke at a semi-annual meeting of the Washington area Hadassah chapter shortly after I returned from Israel. I had been invited to speak at the same meeting, but I was completely upstaged by Mrs. Schenk. Two months earlier she had been aboard the El Al plane en route to London from Amsterdam that Leila Khaled and an unnamed Palestinian male had attempted to hijack; Khaled had sat in the seat next to Mrs. Schenk. In dramatic fashion Mrs. Schenk described both hijackers, the Israeli sky marshal, and the successful defense of the aircraft, during which the male hijacker was shot and killed and Leila Khaled was captured and tightly bound, hand and foot. I spoke briefly about my visit to Israel and my desire to study Israel's antihijacking system, applying its principles where possible to our situation. After Mrs. Schenk's eloquent presentation, there was not much left to say.

My father died on Thanksgiving Day 1970 at Great Lakes Naval Station Hospital at age 93. He had overcome many obstacles during a long and rewarding career in the U.S. Army, and had enjoyed about 20 years of retired life in Washington with his wife of almost 50 years, our Mother Sadie. Upon her death in 1966 he had moved to Chicago to live with Elnora and her husband, Jimmy. Elnora and my father had dearly loved each other all their lives, and the care she gave him was complete. She and Jimmy kept Agatha and me informed about his condition, and we visited them whenever we could. My father's military funeral was held at Arlington Cemetery on 30 November. During the funeral I thought about my long and happy relationship with this remarkable man. I had always given him my full respect, and I do not recall any serious disagreements or harsh words of any kind between us. Elnora, Jimmy, and Agatha were at my side. Many long-time Washingtonians filled the Fort Myer chapel, among them many relatives and close personal friends of mine, including Gen. Ira Eaker and my boss, John Volpe. To my surprise, I found myself overcome with grief, and I am experiencing the same feelings as I write these words two decades later.

I continued my travels, accepting invitations to discuss the government's antihijacking program. Agatha and I had dinner with Congressman Charles Vanik and his wife, Betty, one of the women in Ruthie Miller's group. With our recent trip to Israel in common, the conversation was in no danger of lagging. I spoke at a meeting of the Air Force Association in the Tampa Bay area and renewed acquaintance with former comrades at Strike Command who were still stationed at MacDill. I also attended a party in Arlington given by Matt Byrne, who had been the executive director of the Campus Unrest Commission. Ramsay Clark, the former Attorney General, was in attendance. Matt was interested to hear from me that President Nixon had remarked that our Campus Unrest Commission report had been a good one, but that Governor Scranton had gone a bit overboard at the White House press conference in stressing the part that had to be played by the presidency. Unfortunately, the report's recommendations were not conscientiously implemented.

## More International Inspections

I traveled to London's Heathrow Airport in a 747, my first ride in that airplane. It made me feel like I was in a house moving down the runway for takeoff—big inside and extremely stable. We cleared the ground long before I realized that we had reached takeoff speed, and we still hardly seemed to be moving. At Heathrow I spent two hours walking from one end of the airport to the other; it seemed quite secure. After a two-hour flight on Alitalia Airlines, I arrived in Rome and found Fiumicino little changed from what I had seen five months earlier. Recent bad experiences had made both Heathrow and Rome especially conscious of the importance of security, but Heathrow seemed the tighter of the two airports.

Over the weekend I went on tour in an embassy car to Pompeii, Naples, and Salerno. This trip conjured up many memories of World War II. I spent Monday in meetings at Fiumicino with the security people. They talked a good game, but I did not feel that I learned much. On Tuesday morning I left for Hong Kong by way of Bombay and Bangkok. When we landed in Athens I visited the El Al terminal, which was up to their high standards. But it was in Hong Kong that I saw state-of-the-art airport security for the first time. Kai-Tek, the Hong Kong airport, had put into effect a system exemplifying how the access of vehicles and people to critical airport areas should be controlled. It had enforced a complete personnel identification system, and the security operations were beautiful to behold. I was convinced that I had never seen a more secure airport, and that I would never see a better one.

My next stop was Seoul, which I could not believe until I had closed my eyes and opened them several times. I should have had a clue from my ride on Korean Airlines from Hong Kong to Seoul. Everything on the plane had been of the highest quality, and I was pleased to see the Koreans operating a modern commercial jet so efficiently. Security at the airport was being given plenty of attention. On my first trip to Korea, years earlier, the landscape had been predominantly A-frames and rice paddies. Now I was deeply impressed with the new government building for cabinet ministries, and the new Chosun Hotel was as fine in its appointments as any I had ever seen. I had dinner with a West Point classmate, the United Nations commander, Michael Michaelis.

In Japan I was briefed and given a demonstration of the security at Tokyo's airport, Haneda. As usual, the Japanese seemed to have everything under control. I then left on the long trip to Australia, visiting only Melbourne, where I gave more information than I received. I could truthfully say, however, that everywhere I went I found an understanding of the threat and realization of the need to improve security and screen passengers. The hijackings of the previous September had made a strong impact.

Agatha received a cordial letter from Mrs. Volpe, telling her of an

executive retreat planned for Department of Transportation executives in mid-April at the Coast Guard Academy in New London,
Connecticut, and expressing the hope that she would be able to
attend. Agatha was delighted to accept. The idea of the retreat was to
allow all agency heads to get together away from the normal activities
of their offices and conduct sessions without interruptions. Secretary
Volpe was in attendance throughout, and his warm personality relaxed everyone. Mrs. Volpe contributed greatly by her informal,
friendly interactions, and by the end of the retreat all of us felt much
more at home with each other. From a professional standpoint it was
helpful to get to know people in the department and their families
informally.

President Nixon had recently appointed me to a three-year term as
a member of the Board of Visitors of the Air Force Academy. Agatha
and I left on our spring visit to the Air Force Academy just a few days
after returning from the Coast Guard Academy. Our leader was Col.
Wayne A. Norby, Chief of the Air Force Academy Activities Group,
Headquarters, U.S. Air Force. In his quiet way, Colonel Norby made
everything go extremely well. As a member of the board for three
years and chairman during the last year of my appointment, I can
attest to his outstanding performance during some critical and controversial times among some high-ranking and, in some cases, opin-
ionated people; the subject of admitting women to the Academy
engendered especially high emotions. I was glad to see the Superintendent of the Academy, my West Point classmate, Lt. Gen. Albert P.
("Bub") Clark. Bub and I had worked together in the Pentagon when
he had been Director of Military Personnel and I had been Director of
Manpower and Organization.

While the board was being brought up to date on activities and
programs at the Academy, each of our wives received a cordial letter
from Gen. John Bennett, commander of nearby Fort Carson, inviting
them to an aerial helicopter tour of Fort Carson and Colorado
Springs, a briefing at his quarters on his operation, and a luncheon
with the wives of some of his senior commanders. Agatha enjoyed
the day immensely, particularly the long-range view of Colorado
through crystal-clear air and bright sunshine. At his briefing, General
Bennett spoke of the high quality of his dining halls and the ethnic
food nights given for his soldiers, at which Italian, German, Chinese,
and other ethnic foods were served. At this point, he turned to

Agatha and singled her out with the statement, "And Mrs. Davis, we also serve soul food." Always quick on the trigger, Agatha remarked that neither she nor I had ever tasted soul food. Later several of the other wives at the briefing voiced their criticism of the statement, recognizing it to be silly and racist.

During May I had an important audience at a meeting in Miami of the International Association of Airline Security. I had met many of these people during my travels, and I was frank in my criticisms of shortcomings that should have been eliminated by this time. In Daytona Beach I also addressed the annual convention of the American Association of Airport Executives, a group with considerable power. They ran our nation's airports and could make the difference between a secure operation and one that made the entire system vulnerable. At the Naval War College in Newport, Rhode Island, I reviewed the hijacking problem and was helped with a lively discussion from the floor that produced some valuable recommendations on crowd control. I submitted some of these recommendations to the security subcommittees, but the consensus was that they were too restrictive and would alienate passengers.

In the late spring of 1971 Secretary Volpe asked me if I would be interested in a new assignment in the Department of Transportation. Adm. Willard Smith, then Assistant Secretary of Transportation for Safety and Consumer Affairs, would be retiring, and the Secretary asked me whether I would be willing to replace him. He considerately pointed out that I could hold my current job indefinitely, but if I became Assistant Secretary, a political position, I would be subject to the uncertainty of being replaced with a change of administration. I accepted Secretary Volpe's offer. I was nominated for the position by the President in mid-June and routinely confirmed by the Senate. In the news release announcing the nomination, Secretary Volpe stated:

> As Director of the Department of Transportation's Office of Civil Aviation Security, General Davis has done an outstanding job working with the airlines, airport operators, and other government agencies on the security problems facing our air commerce industry. In his new job he will coordinate the Department's safety and consumer activities and direct the hazardous materials, pipeline safety, and transportation security programs. I am confident his leadership will be a vital element for the success of our efforts.

# ★ ★ ★ Transportation

**18.** *Transportation is a public service, and therefore its benefits had to be assessed in terms of broader societal goals. If a proposed facility had environmental effects that were too severe, then it was open to question whether the community would really be served by it.*

Civil aviation security was just one of many important issues I now dealt with as Assistant Secretary of Transportation for Safety and Consumer Affairs. When Secretary Volpe announced my nomination in 1971, he stated that I would be in charge of a new attack on cargo thefts, estimated to total $1.5 billion a year. He cited the case of a jailed thief who had told Senate investigators that, with little trouble, he stole $100 million worth of goods from various airports over a four-year period. Senator Alan Bible's Select Committee on Small Business estimated that in the previous year railroads had lost $250 million in freight thefts; maritime shipping, $210 million; airlines, $110 million; and truck theft and hijacking, $9 million. The Secretary stated that the department would mount a concerted, interagency drive to eliminate crime in transportation. He also announced that he had sponsored the establishment of the Interagency Committee on Transportation Security to work with a wide range of agencies and had designated me as his representative on the committee.

The solution of the cargo theft problem could lead to enormous benefits for the entire domestic transportation system. To provide specific information on cargo theft, the Interstate Commerce Commission, the Civil Aeronautics Board, and the Federal Maritime Commission were already setting up uniform loss reporting systems. The Department of Transportation would focus on preventive techniques such as personnel identification, packaging, locks, guards, alarms, and communication systems. I was completely in agreement with this arrangement.

The offices under my supervision were headed by genuine professionals. I found to my great delight that they knew their business and that I could depend on them. One of my first visits was with Philip Bolger, who ran the Office of Safety Program Coordination, a "master control" room where analysis and evaluation brought together all the safety efforts in the Department of Transportation. A former Navy test pilot, Phil had worked many years in safety and was an expert. Through me, Phil's office acted as the Secretary's primary safety adviser. It conducted in-depth safety reviews, analyses, and studies resulting, for example, in tighter FAA regulations, notably in the areas of general aviation and air charter operations.

Across the hall was Ann Uccello's Office of Consumer Affairs. Ann, a seasoned politician, had been mayor of Hartford, Connecticut. A major function of her office was to improve communication between the government and users of transportation goods and services. The department had taken a variety of approaches, including the publication of news of special interest to the transportation consumer, but the Office of Consumer Affairs provided the all-important personal touch. In hearings conducted all across the nation, travelers were given an opportunity to be heard on safety, comfort, convenience, and other related concerns. People with special problems—the elderly, the disadvantaged, the handicapped—had been given particular consideration. All these views went into the evaluation process along with blue-ribbon advice from our Citizen's Advisory Committee on Transportation Quality. Through this process much of the public's advice found its way into department programs. I thought this was one of the most valuable systems I had seen for carrying government to the people, to the benefit of both.

Next I visited Joseph Caldwell, the Director of Pipeline Safety. I knew exactly nothing about gas and liquid pipelines, and I frankly stated my need for help to Joe and his staff. My education consisted of briefings and a series of field visits. Joe's office was directly responsible for safety regulation of the nation's sixth largest industry, encompassing some 1 million miles of pipelines and serving 41 million customers.

My orientation continued with a visit to William Burns, Director of the Office of Hazardous Materials. His job was to protect the public and the environment from hazardous materials in transit: explosives, flammable and combustible liquids, radioactive materials, flammable solids, etiologic agents, poison gases, corrosives, and compressed gases. Prior to the creation of the Department of Transportation, hazardous materials had been regulated by modal authorities—land transport by the Interstate Commerce Commission, water shipment by the Coast Guard, and air shipment by the FAA. After the Department of Transportation came into being, Secretary Volpe set up the Hazardous Materials Regulation Board, chaired by Bill Burns, to establish firm cooperation among these agencies. Problems specific to one mode were thus brought to the attention of all the other modes. This arrangement was important because 80 percent of all hazardous material shipments were transferred from one mode to another in transit.

Industry was developing and shipping ever-increasing numbers of hazardous substances, and government had to learn to cope with new technologies. Chemical production in the United States had increased dramatically, and highways, railways, waterways, and air had become channels of shipment for such commodities as toxic gas and radioactive material. Spectacular leaks and explosions had occurred, most of them involving ground conveyances such as trains and trucks. These mishaps had led Congress to pass the Hazardous Materials Transportation Control Act of 1970. Under this act my office was required to establish a centralized, all-mode, accident-reporting system feeding into a uniform data bank. The system was designed to collect and evaluate information and to determine where corrective measures should be taken.

## Focus on Cargo Security

I renamed my old Office of Civil Aviation Security "the Office of Transportation Security" to reflect its all-mode mission of cargo security. Richard Lally, one of the most capable civil service officers I

had met, was now Chief of the office. Dick had had a highly successful career in FAA air transportation security, so this new job was
tailored to his capabilities. He and a team of airport ground security
specialists hired by the FAA set to work to solve the theft problem.

In the beginning we had little idea who was stealing what cargo,
by what method, or to what degree. Many people looked to organized crime as the culprits in cargo theft and pilferage, but we soon
found that the facts did not bear out that assumption. So Dick took
another approach, based on the premise that the key to reducing
theft-related cargo loss was prevention. An important initial discov-
ery was that only 13 commodities accounted for 90 percent of all
theft-related losses of the thousands of commodities handled by any
general commodity carrier. It thus became immediately apparent that
cargo thieves were a selective breed. The top 10 commodities stolen
were clothing, electric appliances, auto parts and accessories, hard-
ware, alcoholic beverages, food products, tobacco products, rubber
and plastic items, technological instruments, and jewelry. All these
items had at least one thing in common—they were readily salable. A
single hijacking of a truckload of alcoholic beverages, fur coats, or
frozen beef, which could put a small carrier out of business, earned
the hijacker 10 times as much as the $4,500 realized in the average
bank robbery, and at considerably less risk.

Estimates indicated that the take from hijacking and theft of trucks
was many times the $8 million the FBI said was taken from banks
each year. But these appallingly large figures represented a mere 10
percent of the total theft losses in the transportation industry. Burgla-
ry of a transportation facility's premises accounted for another 5 percent, but this kind of theft entailed a certain amount of risk, some
skill in planning, and organization for disposal. No such talent was
required for the other 85 percent of the cargo stolen in 1972. The
prime requisite for the thief seemed to be opportunity and, unfortunately, opportunity was everywhere. Dick and his people discovered
the surprising and unglamorous fact that 85 percent of stolen cargo
simply moved out the front door, aided and abetted by helpful employees. It moved through the front gates of transportation facilities
during normal operating hours in the possession of persons and on
vehicles authorized to be on the premises. The average cargo thief
turned out to be the platform man on the shipper's dock, a clerk, a
terminal manager, or even a corporate official. It was the man or

woman on the inside, ostensibly responsible for protecting the company against pilferage, who was creating this steady drain on the transportation economy.

With this information the Office of Transportation Security arrived at its first major conclusion: transportation management had to take the initiative to prevent cargo theft by eliminating opportunity. Our office determined that management supervision could reduce theft losses dramatically through a continuously operating program of checking and counterchecking, thereby taking the initiative away from the cargo thief. I was much pleased with the first year's accomplishments in cargo security and eager to receive the next progress report.

Agatha and I were happy with our life in Washington, which was substantially different from both our experiences in the military and our short time in Cleveland. During this period I began taking on many other important activities that were not related to my immediate job. In 1973 I held active membership on 35 boards, many in the Washington area but some as far away as California. For six years I served on the board of the Retired Officers Association; I particularly enjoyed my membership in this fine, large organization, which provides important services to retired military people. I also served with the Association of Graduates of the United States Military Academy, the National Safety Council, the National Defense Transportation Association, the Institute of Aerospace Safety and Management, the National Education Institute, the Air Force Historical Foundation, the Air Force Academy Foundation, the Domestic Council Committee on Aging, the Domestic Council Committee on Drug Abuse, the Cabinet Committee to Combat Terrorism, and many others.

I was extremely busy for my five years with the Department of Transportation. I enjoyed the challenges of the day, attending meetings, reading the voluminous office correspondence, listening to briefings. I liked all the people I worked with. I had three bosses during this time; when John Volpe was appointed Ambassador to Italy, he was replaced by Claude Brinegar, an executive of the Union Oil Company of California, followed by William T. Coleman, a brilliant lawyer with a national reputation, who after Harvard Law School had served as clerk in the office of Associate Justice Felix Frankfurter. Secretary Coleman had been in one of my commands at Godman Field at the end of World War II.

After Agatha and I had been living at London House for 16 months, we discovered that, for no apparent reason, we were paying more rent than any other tenant. In addition, I had reported by letter that several items in the apartment needed fixing but received no reply. Unhappy with this treatment, in early March we talked with Robert Kogod, the president of the management company, and in a few days all the deficiencies were corrected. Mr. Kogod acknowledged that we had been paying more than the tenants of other three-bedroom apartments, reduced our rent, and refunded our overpayments. Since that time there has always been a sign posted in a prominent position in the manager's office: "Equal Opportunity Housing."

Discussions among London House tenants revealed widespread dissatisfaction, not only about inexplicable differences in rent among people with comparable apartments, but also with inadequate building maintenance: leaking gas stoves, dripping air conditioners, and broken plumbing. A major security problem had also arisen from the lack of doors on the building's garage. Eleven cars were broken into one night. One tenant lost all four wheels from his new Cadillac, and the following night the replacement wheels were stolen. After discussing these problems with the tenants, Agatha took the initiative to organize the London House Tenants' Association. She wrote a letter to each tenant, citing the numerous maintenance and security problems and the fact that a tenants' organization would be more effective than individual tenant action. Response was positive, and she became president of the London House Tenants' Association. The association met regularly over a period of many years, measurably improving building operations. Garage doors were installed, and prompt and effective attention was given to security problems. No meetings of the London House Tenants' Association have been held in recent years because tenant-landlord relations are now satisfactory.

## Parties, Speeches, and Official Business

Now that I was Assistant Secretary, it was much easier for Agatha and me to get to and from official affairs. A car would pick me up at my apartment and wait for me at my destination until I was ready to go home. We frequently attended parties at the embassies of the nations where I had served or with whom I was currently working, as well as to affairs given by Washington-based offices of companies doing business with the government. Many of the people attending these official parties were deeply interested in the wide range of transportation matters that were primary to my job. Safety in all modes of transportation was a popular subject, and of course our antihijacking activities interested many different groups, particularly the commercial aviation people. Agatha and I regularly saw friends from far-flung locales who had reason to come to Washington: Tiger Wang, now the Republic of China's Ambassador to the United Nations; Charlie Chang, retired head of the Republic of Korea Air Force; Helen Dibble, our close friend from Tuskegee; Ambassador and Mrs. Winthrop Brown, who had been our friends in Korea; and many others who got in touch with us while they were in town. We also renewed many friendships we had made duing the seven earlier years we had lived in the Washington area. Our social life was very active indeed. Agatha supported me all the way, as usual. Still the kind of person who maintained a lively interest in everything around her, she took courses in dressmaking, tailoring, and silkscreening.

I worked hard, traveling often to speak at the many international meetings I had to attend in Europe, as well as the Far East. My speech writers conferred with me before and after they gave me drafts to consider. On some occasions, often close to elections, they had instructions from on high to include certain items—for example, some boilerplate references to Vice President Agnew that I simply ignored. I used the items if they were true and not distasteful, and I had no difficulty at all in giving Secretary Volpe the fullest possible credit for all his official actions. I was annoyed, however, when the Nixon administration would stress the race of black appointees without mentioning their abilities.

President Nixon had been reelected by a more than comfortable margin, and at Secretary Volpe's Christmas party in December 1972 the atmosphere was not nearly as gloomy as it would have been had the victory gone to the Democrats. A sword of Damocles, however, hung over the presidential appointees who had faithfully followed White House orders and submitted their resignations, effective 20 January 1973. (All presidents follow this practice to give themselves flexibility in making appointments in their new administration.) Doubts over the status of these appointees caused the conversation to lag irretrievably after "Merry Christmas"—all present realized the necessity to avoid what might be a painful subject. I was one of the few who had already received a call from the White House telling me that I would be retained. The department did sustain one major loss: Secretary Volpe would leave us to become Ambassador to Italy.

The Office of Environmental Affairs, headed by Martin Convisser, joined the Office of Transportation Security in February 1973. Marty and his people had been extremely productive. Their office had filed more environmental impact statements with the Council of Environmental Quality than any other government agency. The objective of the Office of Environmental Affairs was to promote environmental responsibility as an integral part of fast, safe, and efficient transportation. Marty defined "efficiency" as the total value of a transportation service as measured against the combined monetary and environmental impact cost. Transportation is a public service, and therefore its benefits had to be assessed in terms of broader societal goals. If a proposed facility had effects that were too severe, then it was open to question whether the community would really be served by it. Severe impacts, which could negate the value of a transportation outlet, included displacement of a significant number of families, destruction of valuable natural areas and wildlife habitat, and a threat to public health through substandard air quality, water quality, or noise. I considered Marty's operation to be sound, and working with him and his people was always a pleasant experience, even when not everyone in the department agreed with all the positions we took.

The idea of evaluating a transportation project's broader implications was also mandated by the Airport and Airway Development Act of 1970, which required that the opinions of the affected community be solicited through public hearings and that those hearings address the economic, social, and environmental results of a proposed airport project. The project had to be consistent with the plans of the community, and airport operations had to be compatible with land use in the vicinity. FAA was required to consult with the Department of the Interior and the Environmental Protection Agency on environmental impacts of major airport developments. Similarly, the Federal Highway Administration and the Urban Mass Transportation Administration were affected. The 1966 law creating the Department of Transportation mandated special efforts to preserve the natural beauty of the American countryside, public park and recreation lands, wildlife and waterfowl refuges, and historic sites. It stated that transportation should not use publicly owned land from a park, recreation area, wildlife refuge, or historic site unless there were no feasible or prudent alternative, and unless planning minimized harm to the affected public land.

About this time representatives of the Cleveland Club of Washington notified me that I was to be awarded the Harold Hitz Burton Award. After receiving the award I found that I had been listed as one of a relatively small group of distinguished Clevelanders on the club letterhead. Agatha and I retain great affection for Cleveland, and we still hear frequently by telephone and letter from our friends there.

World and national events did not permit me to neglect our antihijacking, antiterrorism mission, which had continued to effect improvements in 1970 and 1971. The rate of successful hijackings had decreased from a peak of 82 percent in 1969 to 67 percent in 1970 and 44 percent in 1971. We had gone from no policy and no defense to a viable government program that was drastically reducing the hijacking rate.

The decisive year proved to be 1972. In March, following three acts of bomb sabotage against domestic airlines, President Nixon ordered the regulatory program into effect. We were now determined to stop the hijacker on the ground, intercepting him before boarding. This objective called for tougher regulations, more magnetometers, more guards, and tighter ground security. In May 1972 the government allocated $3.5 million for electronic detectors, and the FAA took most of the sky marshals off the planes and reassigned them to the boarding gates. The fine young men in the sky marshal service had performed a valuable service when we were beginning the fight against hijackers and we had no other defense. There had been a calculated risk in putting men with weapons aboard airplanes and ordering them to shoot under certain circumstances, but the sky marshals were well trained and indoctrinated, and they demonstrated that they merited the trust that had been placed in them. After the new procedures were in place, the sky marshals were no longer needed to ride shotgun. The new system produced a sharp rise in arrests at airports and a wholesale confiscation of weapons.

Meanwhile, there were ominous developments abroad. The Black September faction of the Palestine Liberation Front turned to mass murder. In May three Japanese fanatics hired by the Arab terrorists shot up the crowded terminal building at Tel Aviv's Lod Airport, killing 27 innocent people and wounding 80. In September the terrorists staged their massacre at the Olympic Games in Munich, leaving 17 dead as a shocked world watched on television. Federal officials were deeply concerned that Black September would transfer this kind of mayhem to the United States because of our firm friendship with Israel.

Instead of international terrorism, however, domestic crime suddenly descended on civil aviation. Desperate criminals fleeing the law saw the airlines as a means of escape. In late October 1972 four men wanted for murder and bank robbery shot their way on board an Eastern plane in Houston, killing an airline employee and wounding another. The hijacked plane went to Cuba. Just 12 days later three wanted men, one an escaped convict, took over a Southern Airways jet out of Birmingham. Brandishing pistols and hand grenades, the three sent the plane on a 29-hour, five-stop flight around the eastern United States. The hijackers eluded an FBI trap, shot and wounded the copilot, seized ransom money amounting to an estimated $2 million, and finally directed the plane to Cuba.

These hijackings were perpetrated by criminals of the worst kind, fugitives from the law with little to lose, willing to shoot people down with no compunction. We knew we had to move quickly before the inevitable repeat performance, with even more tragic results. We analyzed the existing security system, determined what improvements could be implemented to achieve complete passenger screening, and sent our recommendations to the White House. President Nixon approved the plan, and shortly after the Birmingham incident new security procedures were announced. From this time forward we had blanket screening and inspection of passengers and luggage—the same system used today in every major U.S. airport. All these measures had been under discussion for some time and were part of our contingency plans; thus, we were ready to implement them immediately. For many months thereafter not a single attempt was made to break through the security shield and seize an airplane. We could not expect this success rate to hold forever, but we would continue to refine the system, introduce improved electronic devices, and recommend further changes.

Shortly before the new security regulations were published, Dick Lally and I traveled to Brussels to attend an international conference on terrorism. Our delegation was headed by Ambassador Armin Meyer, the chairman of our Cabinet Committee to Combat Terrorism. We found that the international community had progressed considerably in its thinking on this vital subject. I also accepted an invitation from the government of Israel to revisit their country and discuss mutual air-security, ground-security, and antihijacking problems. They made the proposition particularly attractive by inviting Agatha as well.

We were met in Tel Aviv by Col. and Mrs. Yehuda Guy, who escorted us everywhere for the entire week of our visit. Yehuda was Deputy Minister of Transportation to Shimon Peres, who at that time was the Minister. My first official discussions were at Lod Airport, where I was given a complete analysis of the Japanese terrorist attack and the measures taken to avoid recurrence. My hosts were quite frank about the mistakes that had been made. I reviewed the system changes they had put into effect and considered them in the light of our recent experience. The major difference, of course, was the far greater number of passengers and flights in the United States.

We had dinner on our second night with Col. and Mrs. Prihar. Shula Prihar and Agatha had been friends in Washington when Colonel Prihar was Israel's air attaché; it was good to see them again. Mrs. Guy showed Agatha around while I worked, and then we went sightseeing in Tel Aviv, Masada, Sharm-el-shaik, and Jerusalem, where we visited the Holocaust Memorial, the markets, and many other sections of the city. From Jerusalem we proceeded to the Golan Heights, made famous in the recent war won by Israeli military prowess. At a kibbutz some residents told us how their daily lives were constantly threatened with hostile attack. We observed them working in the fields with their children, weapons close at hand. Our week ended with a dinner hosted by Minister Peres. Agatha and I both admired the high spirits of all the Israelis we met. Despite the ever-present threats to their very existence, they were determined to survive and prosper.

Stopping over in Rome, I again consulted with some of the security people at da Vinci Airport and was more favorably impressed than I had been on my last visit. Agatha and I walked Via Veneto and marveled at the prices, visited the catacombs, and felt glad to be in Rome. We called Gen. Gino Violante, our friend from Washington, where he had been air attaché. His wife, Mieta, picked us up and took us to their elegant home for a lively reunion. The next day I obtained an embassy car and we drove to Naples, then to Salerno via the Amalfi Drive—a repeat of our visit in the late 1950s, and one of the most scenic trips one could take anywhere. We returned to Washington the next day.

## Speeding Up Cargo Data

Robert Redding and his capable assistant, Harold Harriman, joined Transportation's Office of Environment, Safety, and Consumer Affairs in early 1973. Bob headed the Office of Facilitation. He was concerned with the development and transmission of data associated with the distribution of raw materials and finished products. Little progress had been made in processing the mountains of paperwork that impeded world trade, and the department put up with antiquated practices. But the recent rapid development of new problems accompanying the high-speed transport of more sophisticated commodities, chemicals, and electronics demanded improvement in the efficiency of data movement.

Bob leaped into the future by developing the Cargo Data Interchange System (CARDIS). The Office of Facilitation considered this system vital to the efficient handling of intermodal cargo and thought that the CARDIS approach would cure the old plague of excessive paperwork. CARDIS was still in its beginning stages when I took over the Office of Facilitation, and Bob, Hal, and I had continued to press hard in its development. By late 1974 tests had shown that CARDIS would speed up the flow of cargo data immeasurably, and we expected to have a working system in place soon for the transfer of data.

By using standard codes and message formats, CARDIS could deliver cargo data faster than the cargo could travel. In 1974 a fast ocean container ship could cross the Atlantic in three days or the Pacific in six and a half days. Yet it might take ten days to two weeks to get the necessary documentation to the port of arrival. Because of customs requirements, the cargo could not move until the data arrived, thus subjecting it to mounting costs, outright theft, and pilferage. In air shipments, the carriers could not possibly provide the advance arrival of essential information at the point of discharge of the goods. With CARDIS the information would be there ahead of the cargo, and the arrival could be anticipated and handled promptly. The system would link up with automated cargo data facilities such as the United Kingdom's London Airport Cargo Electronic Data System, thereby extending the usefulness of the network.

When CARDIS became fully operational, it was expected to reduce shipping costs and the chances of error and to increase cargo security. Bob's office worked with foreign governments and international trade organizations. The program was moved forward by close liaison among interested and knowledgeable officials in all the countries involved and frequent discussions of coding and other facilitation improvements, plus visits to key trade areas. We envisioned a worldwide CARDIS network that would benefit all trading nations.

I attended cargo data transmission conferences and tests in Hong Kong, Taiwan, Japan, the United Kingdom, and Canada. On the longest of these trips Agatha met me in Taipei. We called on Gen. Chiang Ching-kuo, who was to become president of the Republic of China the following year upon the death of his father. Most hospitable and warm in his welcome, Ching-kuo presented Agatha with a miniature pin of the Cloud and Banner medal the Republic of China had given me upon my departure in 1957. Agatha and I combined pleasure with business, seeing old friends, particularly Gen. I Fu En and his wife, Lillian. In Hong Kong there were fewer bargains than in the past, but its unique bustling atmosphere and the incomparable night view made the trip worthwhile. In Japan, while I met with facilitation experts, Agatha visited Bert Livingston in Tokyo and Arakawasan in Seijo Machi.

Over a period of months I watched the dramatic developments of the Watergate scandal. Its stench permeated the entire administration. The very foundation of our government was threatened, and only the application of sound judicial principles enabled it to survive. Watergate should have impressed all government servants with the importance of the rule of law and the dangers of disregarding it. Everyone was interested in Watergate because of the principles involved, but most government employees, including me, were not affected in the day-to-day discharge of our responsibilities.

After President Nixon's resignation, President Ford called for an intensive national effort to combat inflation. In response Secretary of Transportation Brinegar conducted a transportation industry conference on inflation in Los Angeles, involving leading representatives of government and transportation management, labor, and trade associations. It was universally agreed at the conference that the key contribution transportation could make to combating inflation was to increase productivity. I believed that the Office of Facilitation was doing its part to increase productivity in international trade; Bob, Hal, and our counterparts in Canada, England, Taiwan, and Japan were pushing as hard as they could, and the groundwork had been laid for increased efficiency and reduced costs in handling intermodal cargo.

I was named chairman for the final meetings of my three-year term with the Air Force Academy Board of Visitors. As always, the meetings were stimulating. We discussed one unusually controversial subject this time: the appointment of women as cadets. At first, the Superintendent and all the board members except me opposed the entry of women, as did many other prominent military people. One national figure expressed the absurd view that at some point in the future a female appointee might deny another Eisenhower the chance to attend West Point. Our lively discussion ended with the recognition that the participation of women in most walks of life was the wave of the future, and that they should be appointed to the Air Force Academy. The board took this position in its report.

On one of my visits to the Academy I was requested to meet with a group of black cadets. I indicated my pleasure with doing so, but expressed the hope that white cadets would not be excluded, since what I had to say would be for all cadets, black or white. I then met with such a mixed group of white and black cadets. For me, an important principle was involved: the old difference of opinion between separatists and integrationists. In many predominantly white colleges in the United States, blacks had banded together in so-called black student unions. I recall one of the Campus Unrest Commission hearings at Kent State University, during which a young man appearing as a witness had stated that as president of the Black Student Union he represented some 600 black students. A friend of Agatha's whose daughter was a Kent State student questioned whether the young man truly represented the views of all black students, adding that he certainly did not represent her daughter's views. I had read about black student unions and had seen a television documentary about blacks at a Michigan university, where relations between black and white students were violent. I had fought all my life for the integration of blacks into the mainstream of American life and was strongly opposed to condoning any sort of separatist grouping of black cadets at the Air Force Academy. I considered this arrangement divisive and inimical to good human relations in general, and particularly in the military. I knew that when the cadets graduated and went into the Air Force they would have to stand on their own feet without depending on a group of peers to help them solve their problems. The Academy aimed to develop leaders, not followers.

In January 1975 Jean Bosson, commercial counselor to the French embassy, and his assistant, Jean de Levizac, invited me to visit France to discuss transportation security, airport security, new transportation systems, and CARDIS. The State Department's attempts to involve the French in cooperative antiterrorism and security efforts over the past two and a half years had been notably unsuccessful, so I thought that this trip might present an opportunity for joint action in these important areas. The trip was to include discussions with civil aviation authorities, the French Secretary of Transportation, Air France, and France's Office of Facilitation. I took Agatha along at my personal expense, in spite of persistent efforts by the French to make her an official guest.

We departed Dulles in mid-March for Paris, where we were met by Etienne Dreyfous, a senior official of Air France. Etienne and I had worked together on facilitation projects in Canada and England. Upon arriving at Orly I discovered with some dismay that my luggage was missing. Apparently not even my position as Assistant Secretary of Transportation could save me from this all-too-common occurrence of commercial air travel. The French sent messages to the subsequent destinations of the plane and located my luggage in Athens. I purchased necessary items to tide me over until I was reunited with my personal articles in Toulouse; the high cost of these items in Paris compared to their price in the States was alarming.

I spent the following day in meetings while Agatha was escorted by Etienne's friend, Jill, to Pierre Balmain's, one of the first-line couturiers of Paris. That evening we went to see Josephine Baker in a musical. Every seat was taken, and some people were sitting on the steps in the aisles. The audience listened in rapt attention to a series of beautiful scenes about Miss Baker's life: the 17 children she had adopted and brought to her home in southern France; her activities during World War II, when she had engaged in marathon tours for the entertainment of Allied troops; and other scenes depicting the entertainer of legend. We were saddened to read a few days later that Miss Baker had collapsed onstage and died.

We traveled by train to Toulouse, where we had a close look at the interior of the Concorde and observed one landing and taking off. The airplane was so new at that time that when it landed or took off, all activity would cease and people would give all their attention to it. Oddly enough, a German test pilot had been assigned to escort us and provide the details of this remarkable aircraft. In Marseilles we were met by a delightful couple and their two young children, who took great pride in showing us the port and the World Trade Center, billed as a "living" example of facilitation in action. After three days on the Riviera we returned by train to Paris, where we rode the turbotrain and visited the factory where it had been built. Our trip was professionally profitable and we were royally treated, but I did not succeed in arranging cooperation between the United States and France in air security and antiterrorism. Our policies differed too widely from those of the French, who permitted more stringent personal searches and had far fewer flights.

Early in 1975 a TWA jetliner flew into the top of a Blue Ridge foothill on the approach to Dulles Airport. Ninety-two people were killed instantly. The severe reaction to this tragic crash was thoroughly understandable. For those concerned with civil aviation safety, especially those in the federal government, it had nightmarish elements. A crowded airliner on the approach to a federally operated airport serving the nation's capital had hit a mountain for no explicable reason other than human error—a collapse in communications or a confusion in procedures. Congress issued a critical report accusing the FAA of lagging in the safety area. The National Transportation Safety Board conducted the longest and most exhaustive hearings in its history, and Secretary Brinegar named me to head a task force to examine FAA's safety mission. The panel included distinguished educators, safety experts, industry experts, and two astronauts—Neil Armstrong and Michael Collins. Our report, containing numerous recommendations, went to William Coleman, who had replaced Claude Brinegar as Secretary of Transportation. It stressed the importance of details that would tighten flight procedures and the vital need for greater attention to human engineering factors. FAA moved strongly, changing its regulations to specify exactly when a plane might begin its descent during the landing approach and ordering the installation of ground proximity warning indicators, or "whoopers," on all scheduled airliners.

## Hazardous Materials and Saving Lives

Early in 1975 President Ford signed into law the Hazardous Materials Transportation Act, legislation that our department had been promoting for a long time. This law materially broadened the scope of the Secretary of Transportation's authority in the regulation of hazardous materials. Under it, our Office of Hazardous Materials could cite the Secretary as the authority for regulations, application of civil or criminal penalties, and other administrative procedures. Other changes related to the registration of shippers, restrictions on the transport of radioactive materials on passenger-carrying aircraft, and the qualification of container manufacturers. In a speech to regulators, shippers, and carriers, I stressed my conviction that the problems in the movement of hazardous materials stemmed not from a lack of regulations but from the lack of compliance with regulations that had long been in effect. Our investigations had revealed that most shipments checked in air terminals and elsewhere were in violation of some aspect of regulations. Too many people were clearly not equipped with a thorough knowledge and understanding of the requirements. Bill Burns's office expanded still further its educational program of shipper/carrier seminars, planning to disseminate new or revised information on the handling of hazardous materials as soon as it became available.

in the spring of 1975 Joe Caldwell accompanied me to the Fifth Symposium on Pipeline Research, organized by the American Gas Association and held in Houston. I discussed the recently amended Mineral Leasing Act, which required the examination of all pipelines and associated facilities on federal lands at least once a year and a report of any potential leaks or safety problems. The Secretary was required to report annually to the President, the Congress, the Secretary of the Interior, and the Interstate Commerce Commission on any explosions, danger of explosion, spillage, or danger of spillage on federal lands, with a summary of corrective action taken. Some management people asked why we had to be so tough about our regulations, pointing out the overall excellence of the pipeline safety record. I agreed that the record was good but said that there was room for improvement; the Secretary's goal was zero deaths and injuries.

Everyone in the gas industry agreed that most leaks on pipeline systems were caused by corrosion and that the major failures resulted from excavations or other outside forces. Our Office of Pipeline Safety regulations specifically detailed performance requirements for the protection of gas pipelines from both external and internal corrosion. To attack the outside forces problem, the office drafted and proposed the enactment of a model statute for the protection of underground pipelines and utilities. Laws relating to this protection were already on the books in a number of states and in the Los Angeles and Honolulu metropolitan areas. Michigan and New Mexico had enacted comparable laws, and several other states were considering such legislation.

Environmental impact statements, always controversial, repeatedly attracted public attention. Marty Convisser and I fought many battles with special interest groups. We were doing our job in accordance with the law as we saw it, and the special interests were equally conscientious in pursuing what they believed to be their entirely reasonable and honorable objectives. Sometimes we won, and sometimes we lost, but it was never dull. Special interest groups were usually passionately devoted to their cause, and the environmental groups opposing them were equally determined in their defense of the environment.

In the Washington area no construction project attracted as much attention as the building of Interstate Highway 66 (I-66). Our Office of Environmental Affairs made exhaustive efforts to give the project an even-handed evaluation. I studied the evaluation conscientiously and met with groups representing both sides of the controversy. In the end I recommended that I-66 not be built and sent the environmental impact statement to Secretary Coleman. This was one of the battles that we lost; Secretary Coleman reversed our recommendation, pointing out major actions incorporated into the construction that would mitigate its adverse effects on the environment. I-66 was built, and its considerable traffic now moves rapidly between Washington and Virginia.

I became deeply involved in advocating the 55-mile-per-hour speed limit from 1973 on, when Congress passed the measure to conserve fuel and alleviate the energy crisis. During its first year in operation, this law reduced annual highway fatalities from 55,000 to 46,000, thus saving more than 9,000 lives. Citing these figures, the Ford administration, the Department of Transportation, and the nation's safety councils successfully petitioned Congress to retain the reduced speed limit permanently. I appeared before Congress as the department witness on 55 on numerous occasions and before the Federal Highway Administration and the National Highway and Traffic Safety Administration as a supporting witness for budget hearings, and I made numerous speeches in all parts of the country. I sought the active support of the International Association of Chiefs of Police in enforcing the new speed limit.

More than half the highway deaths in the United States resulted from crashes in which alcohol was a factor—30,000 annually. (The single largest killer of people between the ages of 17 and 25 was the combination of motor vehicle and alcohol, sometimes mixed with drugs.) The department's Alcohol Countermeasures Program, carried out in partnership with states, municipalities, and concerned citizen organizations, focused national attention on the drunk driver problem and forced corrective actions. The goals were to identify the dangerous driver, increase the conviction rate for drunk drivers, and steer them into education and rehabilitation programs. We strongly recommended the use of safety belts and shoulder harnesses by all drivers and passengers in automobiles. We achieved a modest degree of success in mobilizing state efforts to improve driving safety, but much remained to be done. I slowed my own driving to 55 and below and trained myself to automatically fasten my safety belt upon entering my car.

## Looking Back before a Second Retirement

When I left the Department of Transportation in 1975, I was particularly pleased with our progress in the Civil Aviation Security Program. John Volpe had brought me to the department for the express purpose of ending the frequent hijackings to Cuba. That objective had been achieved, and I was proud of our success. Of course we had long since increased the scope of that objective in attempts to make airports and airlines safe from criminals, saboteurs, and terrorists. The nation had gone for two and a half years without a successful hijacking of a scheduled airliner from the domestic civil aviation fleet; for over one year not a single attempt had been made to take over a specific aircraft. Worldwide, 22 hijackings occurred in 1973 and 19 in 1974, but the 50 states were free of either a hijacking or an aircraft bombing. Skyjacking in the United States had become a thing of the past.

These results were not achieved overnight. From the peak year of 1969, when 40 airliners were hijacked to Cuba, we went through a three-year period of trial and error that involved a good deal of squabbling between government and the airline industry. When it finally did emerge in 1972, the Federal Civil Aviation Security Program embraced two concepts: an armed potential hijacker had to be kept off an airliner, and the security measures to do so had to be mandatory. These procedures included restricting the operating side of an air terminal with signs, gates, fences, and lights; the use of personnel identification; and most important, the screening of all passengers. The concept, quite simply, was interception. Whatever happened, we did not want it to happen on a crowded airline parked at the ramp, taxiing, or in flight.

This was no small assignment. These measures had to be applied to the half million people who flew commercially in the United States every day, with more aircraft departures than the rest of the free world combined. All passengers and their luggage on all scheduled flights were screened all the time. As a result, all attempts to seize airliners were stopped on the ground in 1974, and 2,663 passengers were denied boarding. In most instances they were barred from flight because of a weapon on their person or in their carry-on baggage. A few would-be comedians wondered out loud if the plane was going to Cuba. In all, screening detected and caused to be confiscated 2,450 guns; 14,928 explosives and ammunition rounds, including fireworks; 21,468 knives; and 26,864 other dangerous articles, not including the discarded weapons found in airport wastebaskets, towel bins, and potted palms—testimony to a last-minute loss of nerve.

The primary components of our security system were the highly visible armed police officers or guards, present at every boarding gate during the screening process. The second essential element was the metal detector, whose principal quarry was the concealed handgun. Firearms, most of them handguns, were involved in 115 of the 145 hijackings of U.S. commercial planes between 1961 and the end of 1972. Short of a hand search, security personnel depended on the detector to find guns and other weapons. The detector that we used measured anomalies in a magnetic field generated by the system. It was the same principle used in conventional land-mine and coin detectors and in geophysical prospecting. Although it was highly discriminating in the search for weapons, the metal detector had been declared safe for undeveloped film, magnetic tape, and even pace-makers. We regarded the X ray, which had become increasingly so-phisticated and effective, as the particular defense against the threat of bombs and sabotage. We employed it primarily to inspect carry-on luggage and enplaned baggage. From all indications, when public information was adequate, air travelers readily accepted X-ray inspec-tion of their carry-on items and baggage.

The Department of Transportation established this security shield because of the spiraling domestic crime rate and the international terrorist movement. Terrorism and its perpetrators, after all, are only a jet ride away from this country, if not in our very midst. Even though the Civil Aviation Security System effectively eliminated "transporta-tion to Cuba" hijackings, we are still vulnerable today to the machi-nations of terrorists, saboteurs, and deranged persons. By no means have we stamped out air piracy; we have simply arrested it at home. As long as these dangers exist—and there is no end in sight—all airline passengers and their luggage will continue to be screened.

I left the Department of Transportation with a civil service retire-ment after five years. Secretary Coleman, presiding at a warm farewell party held at the Fort McNair Officers' Club, spoke of my service in complimentary terms. I thanked my colleagues for the help and coop-eration I had received, which had enabled us to be successful. Secre-tary Coleman then presented me with the department's highest award, the Gold Medal for Achievement. I left the party feeling completely satisfied with the work I had done in the department and thankful it had gone so well. The work had been most rewarding, affording me a great variety of personal contacts. William Coleman had become an outstanding Secretary, brilliant in his analysis of problems; Agatha and I hoped to see him appointed to the Supreme Court. We were also grateful to James Beggs, the Deputy Secretary for part of my service in the department, and to June Liverman, my administrative assistant, who had faithfully supported both of us for five years.

On the way home from the party Agatha and I discussed the fact that I was now out of a regular, full-time job. She had always maintained that retirees must remain active, that the brain cells must be continually exercised to keep rigor mortis from setting in. As usual, I agreed with her wholeheartedly. I was aware that I could not survive on golf and duplicate bridge alone. I could have stayed on in the department as Assistant Secretary had I desired to do so, but I was looking forward to a change. Working as hard as I had done on a full-time basis for five years had been enough. Fortunately, before I retired, I had been invited to work in retirement part-time as a personal representative of the Secretary and a consultant on safety matters. I was happy to accept the invitation—it was like having my cake and eating it too.

**19.**

*Just as I had learned in World War II that I could
dramatically extend the range of our escort fighters by
cruising at reduced engine speed, Ryder Truck Lines,
which was operating its engines at reduced speed and
with smaller injectors, had increased its operating
efficiency about 75 percent.*

On a beautiful day in 1989 I left Andrews Air Force Base and drove to
Bolling Air Force Base. I traveled part of the way on the Beltway, the
eight-lane highway encircling Washington. Heavy traffic and the high
speed of the vehicles made it difficult for me to enter the freeway.
After getting into the stream of traffic and driving in one of the
outside lanes, a large, intimidating truck began tailgating me. I moved
to the right so the truck could pass, but I soon encountered the same
problem in my new lane. For several years I had been referred to as
"Mr. 55" throughout the United States—the Secretary of Transportation's spokesman on the 55-mile-per-hour speed limit to numerous
organizations throughout the country, and the recognized authority
on the subject both in and out of government. I could visualize the
ruinous publicity if I were arrested for speeding! On this day, however, by maintaining the speed limit I was violating a prime piece of
safety advice that I believed in and respected: it is much safer to travel
with the flow of the traffic. I increased my speed to 60 miles per hour
and moved to the extreme right lane, getting away from the speeding
trucks about to climb into the trunk of my car.

Fifty-five was a national program of great importance to which I devoted myself for more than seven years. I made scores of speeches to influential groups, participated in frequent television interviews, and championed the cause of 55 on an untold number of radio talk shows in the effort to win public support. Originally conceived as a program to conserve fuel and reduce our dependence on foreign oil-producing nations, it had the additional and even greater benefit of saving thousands of lives on the nation's highways each year.

In the early days of 55, the administration sought to win public support for conservation measures. Thus I would stress the virtues of reduced fuel consumption at 55 miles per hour as opposed to the 75- and 85-mile-per-hour speeds that were commonplace on our interstate highways. I spoke to highway safety groups in Indianapolis, Dayton, Cleveland, Charlotte, and Albuquerque. Because my speeches supported White House objectives, I was cordially received in all these cities and generously awarded with the seal of Indianapolis by Mayor Richard G. Lugar, the corporate seal of Cleveland by Mayor Ralph J. Perk, the key to Charlotte by Mayor John M. Belk, and the keys to Dayton and Albuquerque.

The bulk of my work on 55 came after I had left full-time work in the Department of Transportation and became a consultant. In 1976 I spoke to a committee of the American Trucking Associations (ATA). I opened my speech with a statement of thanks on behalf of Secretary Coleman to the chairman of the board, Lee Sollenbarger, for adopting formal and public industry positions urging carriers to self-enforce the 55 limit. As Robert Begeman of the Transport Insurance Company had said, "Slow them down and run them steady—it's your complete answer." I lauded ATA for having invested in more efficient equipment to save fuel and operating costs, rerating engines so power leveled off between 50 and 60 miles per hour. I suggested that the organization might also consider the need for a relatively tamper-proof road speed governor, then provided by Mack trucks and used by some carriers and intercity bus companies. Although such speed-cutting, fuel-saving equipment had initial costs, savings resulted in the long run. In the first full year of the reduced speed limit, 1974, truck accidents had decreased 18 percent, fatalities 21 percent, and injuries 24 percent; in 1975 the numbers had declined still further. Nevertheless, there was considerable room for improvement. Bob Begeman's extensive study showed that 30 percent of the trucks exceeded 60 miles per hour, and 60 percent exceeded 55. Because trucks were more visible and intimidating than cars, the public was increasingly less inclined to see truckers as knights of the road, and the trucking industry was interested in restoring a positive public image.

## Dislodging Truckers' Myths

It was not easy to dislodge the myth that slower speeds do not save fuel and lives. Several years later the Department of Transportation and members of the voluntary truck and bus fuel economy improvement program challenged 32 independent truckers to prove their contention that they could save more fuel at speeds higher than 55. In what was known as the Double Nickel Challenge, the competitors drove their own rigs and paid their own expenses, an indication of how strongly they believed they could operate efficiently at faster speeds. The test track at the Transportation Research Center at East Liberty, Ohio, was a $7\frac{1}{2}$-mile oval. Each driver drove six laps (45 miles) at 55, and then six laps at any other speed he thought would be more fuel-efficient. Each rig was equipped with special tanks and tachometers, and official observers rode with each entrant. A few of the drivers pulled empty trailers for the competition, but some simply stopped off at East Liberty while on a run and made the test with whatever cargo they happened to be carrying. Of course, both we and our competitors knew there were ways to beat 55; a trucker could drive in the wrong gear during the slower laps, for example, which burns more fuel. Even so, though we did not make a clean sweep of the Double Nickel Challenge, we did win 26 of the 32 tests. Fuel efficiency at 55 was as much as 27 percent better than at higher speeds. Through this test the department convincingly disproved the argument that "faster is cheaper." At the time too many truckers, some carriers, and many motorists believed this fallacy.

Many big carriers, such as Ryder Truck Lines, strictly enforced 55 with tachographs and road checks. Ryder was still profitable, refuting the myth that slower speeds would not cut maintenance costs. Just as I had learned in World War II that I could dramatically extend the range of our escort fighters by cruising at reduced engine speed, Ryder, which was operating its engines at reduced speed and with smaller injectors, had increased its operating efficiency about 75 percent. Donald Wilson, an industry maintenance expert, had told me that driving trucks at 55 prolonged tire, engine, and brake life; reduced drive-line maintenance; and resulted in fewer accidents. By the late 1970s the big rig operators had finally come to the conclusion that lower highway speeds would save wear and tear on engines, thereby reducing maintenance costs. Unfortunately, for their own reasons many truckers continue to menace automobile drivers by exceeding the speed limit.

Besides reducing maintenance costs, 55 saved lives. In the seven years following the passage of the Highway Safety Act in 1966, the highway fatality rate (deaths per miles traveled) had declined a fraction of a point each year, but the actual number of fatalities (people killed by motor vehicles) still climbed higher. With the adoption of the 55-mile-per-hour speed limit, the fatality rate plummeted, and the number of deaths dropped by a remarkable 16 percent. The reduced speed limit did more for highway safety than the seven years of effort and expense. Having taken to 55 as a temporary conservation measure in 1973, we not only decreased energy losses but also dramatically decreased the loss of lives. By 1978, however, the nation had slipped backward. As the memory of the oil embargo receded, so did respect for the speed limit, and the increase in speeds was causing a rise in the fatality count.

When I began working as a consultant for the Department of Transportation in April 1976, Judith Connor, my replacement as Assistant Secretary for Environment, Safety, and Consumer Affairs, had established a task force for the department's actions on 55. Its purpose was to exchange information, review and coordinate existing programs, and monitor enforcement and state compliance. John Barnum, the Deputy Secretary, directed implementation of a public support program. As an addressee for this program, I continued to report to the Secretary of Transportation. All my speeches were prepared by Robert Beasley, a long-time media expert and a veteran of the department's Public Affairs Office. It was a genuine pleasure to work with Bob. We traveled all over the country together; in 1976 I made 38 speeches, many of which were keyed to enforcement, in far-flung places, including Alaska.

In 1977 I presented the Governor of Massachusetts, Michael Dukakis, with an award for his state's enforcement efforts, and I met with Governors Ella Grasso, Ray Blanton, Cliff Finch, Joseph Teasdale, Raul Castro, Robert Straub, Thomas Judge, and Robert Ray to reinforce 55's contribution to energy conservation, its life-saving benefits, and the need for better enforcement and more effective state laws to punish violators. With a continued emphasis on legislation and enforcement, I spoke to diverse groups through 1978 and 1979. In 1980, reflecting a renewed interest in energy conservation, my speeches advocated car and van pooling and the use of bicycles. Many municipalities and organizations supported pooling, which was vitally effective in energy conservation.

## New Volunteer Involvements

With my new freedom from the responsibilities of full-time employment, I was able to pursue a great variety of extracurricular activities. Before my official retirement from the Department of Transportation, I had become aquainted with Robert Hendon, vice president and Washington representative of Consolidated Freightways, a West Coast—based transportation firm. When Bob learned of my impending retirement he asked me whether I was interested in becoming a member of the board of the Manhattan Life Insurance Company, on which he had served for several years. He discussed the possibility with Thomas Lovejoy, Jr., the chairman of the board, and Donald Fordyce, the president of the company. They invited me to lunch, discussed the prospects with me, and the day after my retirement from Transportation I attended my first board meeting in New York. There I was introduced as the newest member, with a seat at the foot of the long table in the boardroom. Everyone was most cordial, and I was highly impressed with the caliber of the other members.

Born in Lovejoy, Georgia, Chairman Lovejoy was a gentleman of the old school, quiet spoken, and always considerate of the feelings of other people. Achieving business success at Manhattan Life, he had witnessed the fulfillment of a long-time ambition—the company's installation on the New York Stock Exchange. He never forgot the importance of people-to-people relationships, and his attitude and demeanor had a beneficial effect upon all the board members. His attention to duty was directed not only to the business, but also to the welfare of his employees. Tom retired as chairman of the board during the early years of my service as a board member, turning the reins of leadership over to Donald Fordyce. Tom died shortly after his retirement. He was sorely missed.

Tom's son, Thomas E. Lovejoy III, served as chairman of the Executive Committee for several years. Young Tom, as many affectionately called him, is Agatha's close friend and mine. In addition to retaining a close and important association with Manhattan, he is now Assistant Secretary for External Affairs at the Smithsonian Institution. Tommy actively participated in board discussions, and his advice was always valuable. A talented individual, he applies his philosophy of life toward the betterment of all people and things that he touches.

I served on the board of Manhattan Life for 10 years. At first I was assigned to the Insurance Committee. Later I served on the Executive Committee, and prior to my retirement in 1985 I chaired the Human Resources Committee. In the latter position I was concerned with the company's social responsibility and matters pertaining to the training and administration of personnel. I supported the company's open-door policy, which enabled management to pay close attention to the individual problems of employees.

In the spring of 1977 Harold Brown, the Secretary of Defense, invited me to be a member of the soon-to-be-formed Presidential Commission on Military Compensation. Once I determined that I could fit this new responsibility into my already busy schedule, I was happy to serve. The executive order creating the commission, issued on 27 June, called for recommendations on how the military compensation system could best be structured to serve the national interest. If changes in the current system were recommended, the commission would estimate their costs and propose an implementation plan and timetable.

Meetings, public hearings, and field trips to American military installations all over the world were scheduled to help the commission arrive at its recommendations. With the exception of Gen. William DuPuy and me, all the commissioners were civilians and needed to be educated on the nature of military life. Throughout our deliberations, I repeatedly stressed the need to recognize the special demands of that life, which set the armed forces apart from society at large. The commissioners accompanying me on the field trip to Germany came to understand the particular situation of the military people stationed at Ramstein, Hanau, Kitzingen, and Mannheim. With the dollar-mark exchange rate of 1977, these personnel were essentially restricted to base living, unable to afford German civilian economy quarters or any form of entertainment off base.

In his appearance before the commission, John C. Stetson, the Secretary of the Air Force, spoke eloquently on behalf of the existing system:

> The Air Force and other military services are unique callings. The demands we place on our military men and women are unlike those of any other country. Our worldwide interests and commitments place heavy burdens and responsibilities on their shoulders. They must be prepared to live anywhere, fight anywhere, and maintain high morale and combat efficiency under frequently adverse and uncomfortable conditions. They accept abridgment of freedom of speech, political and organizational activity, and control over living and working conditions. These are all part of the very personal price our military people pay. Yet all of this must be done in the light of—and comparison to—a civilian sector that is considerably different. We ask military people to be highly disciplined when society places a heavy premium on individual freedom, to maintain a steady and acute sense of purpose when some in society question the value of our institutions and debate our national goals. In short, we ask them to surrender elements of their freedom in order to serve and defend a society that has the highest degree of liberty and independence in the world. And, I might add, a society with the highest standard of living and an unmatched quality of life. Implicit in this concept of military service must be long-term security and a system of institutional supports for the serviceman and his family which are beyond the level of compensation commonly offered in the private, industrial sector.

These paramount considerations were stressed by both military and civilian leaders. The Joint Chiefs of Staff and the Secretaries of the Army, Navy, and Air Force strongly recommended retaining the 20-year retirement option at approximately current levels. Two other flag officers, both former deputy assistant defense secretaries for military personnel policy, recommended retention of the current system for retirement, with added incentives for longer military careers.

In spite of these admonitions, the commission's report did not recognize the extraordinary demands imposed upon military personnel and instead recommended changes in the retirement system to reduce costs:

> We view the current system as being out of balance with most other retirement systems and an unfair burden on American taxpayers. . . . We

find no compelling evidence that the calling to a military career is sufficiently unique to justify the current system. Likewise, we are not persuaded that the military is so special and different as to invalidate comparisons with other retirement systems. Finally, in view of the many years
prior to 1945 when the military functioned without the current system,
. . . we reject the notion that the current system is a fundamental under-
pinning of the military way of life.

It was my cynical view that some of the members of the commission,
far from forming their own impartial views as a result of our study,
had set about to achieve results dictated to them by senior administrators in the Office of Management and Budget. Their recommendations advocated eliminating the 20-year retirement and adopting
the 30-year plan of the civil service, under which retirees qualified for
benefits after the age of 55. These changes would have drastically
reduced the total lifetime value to the backbone of the career military
force—those who served 20 years or more—unless they served the
full 30 years. For example, under the existing system, the lifetime
value of pay to an officer who served 20 years and retired as a lieutenant colonel was $400,000, while under the recommended system he
would have received only $274,000. These changes would have
made a military career so unattractive that the services would have
found it impossible, in an all-volunteer environment, to maintain a
career force of the required size and quality.

Three "supplementary views" were included in the commission's
report. Mine, which could more accurately be described as a dissent,
was long and detailed. It opposed most of the report's recommendations. I did agree with the commission in its rejection of a salary
system for the military, but I objected to the notion that there was no
significant difference between military and civilian life. The chairman
of the commission, Charles J. Zwick, called me to say I was being
unfair to the other commissioners and suggested that I withdraw my
statement. I replied that I understood the military quite well and felt
obliged to provide a true expression of my views. My minority opinion remained part of the report.

Fortunately, the commission report died a natural death because
no sponsor could be found for legislation based on its provisions. It is
still my firm opinion that eliminating the 20-year retirement would
have created a disastrous blow to morale that would have been most
difficult for the services to absorb. Under a concept that equated

military life with that of the civil servant, it would have instituted the questionable practice of taking dollars out of the serviceman's pocket in the name of budgetary savings.

## The Battle Monuments Commission

On 27 November 1978 President Jimmy Carter appointed me to the American Battle Monuments Commission. Established by Congress in 1923, the commission directed a worldwide program for commemorating the achievements and sacrifices of the men and women of our armed services who had given their lives for their country. My father had served on the commission from 1953 to 1961, and I was aware of its importance. Shortly after my appointment I received a cordial letter from Gen. Mark Clark, the commission chairman, welcoming me and providing current information. In 1978 the commission administered 23 cemetery memorials and 11 separate monuments in 10 foreign countries, and three memorials on U.S. soil. General Clark told me of his past visits to the cemeteries in Europe, North Africa, and the Philippines and most of the separate monuments, describing them as awe-inspiring and fitting tributes.

At a get-acquainted meeting in Washington on 11 April 1979, General Clark expressed his desire that new members have the opportunity to visit some of the cemeteries as soon as travel funds became available. My overall impression, however, was one of an extremely austere operation, one that barely permitted adequate maintenance by a small and greatly overworked overseas staff. Apparently their work was a labor of love.

On 5 September 1979 Agatha and I departed for Rome on commission business with Gen. and Mrs. Louis Wilson. Unfortunately, Agatha's bag never appeared at da Vinci airport, and she was reduced to living for seven days in the clothes she had worn out of Washington, washing them each night and learning that all of us carry far too much clothing with us when we travel. We were reimbursed for the loss, but Agatha lost some personal articles that could not be replaced.

We visited the Sicily-Rome American Cemetery at the north edge of Nettuno and the port area of Anzio. Anzio had been the site of critical air and ground battles in the winter of 1944, ending the

German occupation of Italy and leading to the fall of Rome to the Allies in June 1944. One of my fighter squadrons, the 99th, had distinguished itself by shooting down 16 German fighters in two days of combat during the air battles over Anzio. The American dead were commemorated on the marble walls of the cemetery chapel, where the names of 3,094 missing soldiers were engraved. The names of some men from my fighter units were listed among the missing. The beauty of the cemetery is beyond my ability to describe adequately: the monument itself, the landscape design, the symmetrical patterns of the paths, and the shining cleanliness of the headstones affect one with a profound sense of peacefulness. The next day we inspected the Florence cemetery and drove to Pisa, where we visited the Leaning Tower and shared dinner with the resident American Battle Monuments Commission people. The quality of the maintenance in Florence equaled anything we had seen the day before in Rome. In both places I was impressed by the dedication and skill of the people who maintained the cemeteries.

In my last act of support for the 55-mile-per-hour speed limit, I served on a committee assembled by the National Research Council in the early 1980s to evaluate the benefits, costs, and law-enforcement aspects of lowered highway speeds. The panel was chaired by Dr. Alan A. Altshuler, dean of the Graduate School of Public Administration, New York University. His job was not easy. The committee members were all authorities in their own fields, and each seemed to have his mind made up about the problems under discussion. My own ideas were fixed, and I was pleasantly surprised that I agreed wholeheartedly with the final report submitted to Congress.

There proved to be substantial agreement among the committee members on the consequences of 55 in the first year after the law's enactment. Not all the 9,100 fewer fatalities in 1974 could be attributed to the lowered speed limit, but the magnitude of the decline appeared to be far greater than could be explained by reduced travel, improved vehicles, better highways, and more efficient medical services. Toll roads with accurate travel records demonstrated a larger decline in fatalities than could be expected based merely on the decline in travel. Many states had evaluated their speed and fatality records and concluded that much of the safety improvement had resulted from 55. Although the average speed driven on rural interstate highways had increased from 57.6 miles per hour in 1974 to

59.1 in 1983, it was still far below 65, the average rural interstate speed in 1973. Most important, the distribution of highway speeds was much narrower than it had been before 55 became the law, and the reduced variation in speed enhanced safety. The committee also agreed on the energy savings attributable to 55, finding that the chief penalty of the lowered limit was additional travel time for passenger vehicles, especially on rural interstates. Balancing all the factors, the committee concluded that 55 should be retained on almost all the nation's highways.

The committee members differed on how speeds should be set on rural interstates. Some believed that 55 should be retained without exception; others argued that changes could be made as part of a broader safety improvement strategy, which would encourage states to enact other measures such as mandatory safety-belt use. Essentially the committee recommended no specific steps, stating its belief that Congress, being aware of the substantial benefits of 55 and the risks associated with major modifications, was the body best suited to resolve major regional differences in public needs and attitudes and the concern about growing public noncompliance.

I believed that 55 should have been retained and enforced, but I realized that this position was not substantially different from that taken in the report. Under any and all circumstances, Congress would have to act on the matter. On the whole I was completely satisfied with the study, and I said farewell to the committee with great admiration for the manner in which Dr. Altshuler had discharged his responsibilities.

★  ★  ★  **Free Time**

# 20.

*Our lives became much less structured after my work with the Department of Transportation and the presidential commissions wound down. Agatha and I stayed busy, but now we were busy out of choice, without any unwanted demands. We still traveled, but only when we wanted to travel to a specific place.*

In late 1975 Agatha felt the need to develop some family solidarity. We had spent so much time out of the country that we had missed seeing family members regularly over the years. Now that we would not be moving about as much, we decided that the tradition of the Scott family Christmas should be renewed. Everyone had enjoyed the big family parties of former years, and it seemed clear that all that was required to bring them back was the initiative of a truly interested family member. On the first of the new year Agatha wrote to all the members of our families inviting them to spend Christmas with us in December 1976. We were pleased with the immediate and enthusiastic response. Over the months before the family assembled, she planned a party that would be fun for everybody, regardless of age.

After lengthy and elaborate preparations, the big day finally arrived. Agatha addressed the assembled clan after dinner on Christmas Eve:

What a Christmas for us! It had taken us a long time to get you to celebrate the Holiday at our house. You don't know how happy you have made us by coming—thanks for your royal presence. While we have so

399

many of the family together, we want to say thanks for all the nice things
you have done for us along the way. We hope you forgive us, too, for any
thoughtless things we have done to you. It was great fun for me to grow
up with Edith, Viv, Herman, and Mil. Ben adored Nora and she him (at
first, I was a bit jealous of their relationship). To our family each one
brought the one he and she loved. And so we grew and grew and grew.
Now we are many, each leading a different kind of life but held together by
the love we have for each other.

The party turned out to be a success far beyond our expectations. it
lasted until a little before four o'clock Christmas morning, and even
then nobody wanted to leave. Agatha's dedication to the concept of
family unity was the basis for the enjoyment of all who participated.

Family reunions aside, our lives became much less structured after
my work with the Department of Transportation and the presidential
commissions wound down. We stayed busy, but now we were busy
out of choice, without any unwanted demands. We still traveled, but
only when we wanted to travel to a specific place. When we were
home I arose at an early hour, prepared breakfast, and frequently
went out to play golf at Andrews Air Force Base. I enjoyed playing
with just about anyone who was available, particularly retirees I had
known from years before, but also young airmen from whom I
learned much about the current Air Force. I also continued playing
duplicate bridge. It seemed that all the nationally known players
came to Washington tournaments. It was a thrill playing opposite
some of the players, whose exploits I had frequently read about.
Many of them were congenial; others would never let you forget they
were the best of the best.

While I played golf and bridge, Agatha took upholstery classes
from Jean Bagley, the talented wife of a naval officer, and repaired
our living-room and dining-room chairs. I frequently attended late
afternoon lectures at the Cosmos Club as a resident member of the
Washington Institute of Foreign Affairs. Limited to the membership,
the meetings were strictly off the record. They dealt with current
affairs and featured authoritative speakers, usually officials deeply
concerned with the problems under discussion. The lectures covered
such diverse subjects as Nicaragua, South Africa, Panama, NATO,
Indochina, and the Middle East. Agatha and I also attended a "Fix It"
evening class in Arlington. I learned that the most valuable attribute
of a fix-it person is the attitude that you can and will fix any ap-

pliance or device. We repaired several old steam irons and some other items that had been gathering dust in our apartment. Also in Arlington, we attended a Red Cross cardiovascular pulmonary resuscitation course. We both got certificates, but I hope no one ever chokes while eating in my presence; understanding the Heimlich maneuver and doing it properly under real emergency conditions are two different things.

## Political Involvements

Agatha volunteered to work for Jimmy Carter in 1976 and 1980 at the Democratic Party National Headquarters in downtown Washington. She later worked in Walter Mondale's campaign in 1983 and 1984. When we encountered Mary Margaret Whipple, a member of the Arlington County Board of Supervisors, at a lecture at the Arlington County Library, Agatha inquired how one could become a delegate to the Democratic National Convention. Ms. Whipple explained the process and suggested that both of us run for the position. I was reluctant at first, but Agatha persuaded me to try and agreed to be my campaign manager. She prepared hand-out sheets for me and helped me buttonhole people and get them to commit themselves to my candidacy. I ran in Arlington and, along with many other people, won the privilege of running for district delegate in Fairfax County; for the first time in my life, I was elected to a political position. Before going to the state convention in Norfolk, however, I learned that I had no chance whatsoever to be a national delegate. Only one delegate would be chosen from Arlington County, and the voting had been structured in such a way that a new arrival to the Arlington political process could never have been selected. This came as something of a disappointment; Agatha and I had taken considerable trouble to play the game, and I should have been told much earlier that I had no chance to be a national delegate. In spite of our disappointment with the delegate selection process, we continued to register voters and serve as election officials. We were continually shocked by the relatively small number of citizens who exercised their privilege to vote.

Separately, Agatha and I both contributed to the campaign of State Senator Douglas Wilder, who was running for Lieutenant Governor of Virginia. I received a gracious personal letter from Senator Wilder thanking me for my contribution; when Agatha later received a form-letter response, she pointed out that because the contributions had been her idea in the first place, she should have been the one to get the personal letter. After Senator Wilder won the election he sent us invitations to the inauguration. We were particularly proud of Doug Wilder. He had removed many barriers and made Virginia a better state. We were also proud of Virginia for having elected him on the basis of his ability and not on the basis of his race. The state had clearly catapulted itself into the progressive ranks by simultaneously electing a black man as Lieutenant Governor and a woman as At-torney General.

In 1972 Agatha and I attended national meetings of the Retired Officers Association. I spoke at the convention in Anaheim, Califor-nia, and reported on the status of the Commission on Military Com-pensation at a local dinner meeting. I continued to accept many invitations to speak at seminars on the terrorist threat and possible guards against that threat, should attacks be launched against our embassies abroad or installations within the continental limits of the United States. At the Patterson School of Diplomacy in Lexington, Kentucky, we met young people who were interested in jobs with the federal government. We traveled to the Air Force Academy in Col-orado Springs, where I received a tribute from the Falcon Foundation, which offers a limited number of highly motivated young people an opportunity to attend the Academy by providing them with scholar-ships at preparatory schools especially selected for this purpose. The tribute consisted of a presentation titled "Benjamin O. Davis, Jr., Aviation Pioneer: A Salute from the Falcon Foundation." Narrated by Gen. Alton Slay, former commander of the Air Force Systems Com-mand and a classmate of mine at the Combat Crew Training School at Nellis Air Force Base in 1953, the story was depicted in a large album with photographs of me and the many personalities I had known over the years. The foundation also commissioned an artist to paint my portrait for display at the Academy.

## Travels for Pleasure and for Recognition

Agatha and I had visited Honolulu several times on official trips to the Far East, but could never stay as long as we wanted. Now that we had the time, we made two trips there solely for pleasure. Lottie and Bill Waddell, friends of ours going back to the late 1930s at Tuskegee Institute, now lived in Honolulu. We called them when we arrived in Oahu, and from that moment on our activities did not cease for the entire 10 days we spent there. On the first day we met a Minnesota family and their friends, who had traveled to Hawaii to attend the wedding of their son to a Hawaiian girl. Hundreds of people, friends of the bride and groom, had attended the wedding reception, held aboard a ship anchored in the harbor. Enough food had been prepared for the reception to supply a succession of parties that took place for days after the wedding. At the one such party we attended, the air was one of unrestrained gaiety, exceeded only by the cordiality and friendliness of all the guests toward one another. No one, except possibly us, seemed surprised that a young man of Swedish descent was marrying a Hawaiian girl of obviously mixed blood. We gained the distinct impression that life in Hawaii was lived differently from the life we had known elsewhere in the States. Mixed marriages were common in Hawaii and apparently as successful as other marriages.

Lottie's daughter, Kay, was a professor at the University of Hawaii and a young lady with a fascinating lifestyle. She seemed completely happy and unconcerned about the troubles that worried most people, young or old. She was married to a young Japanese who was aspiring to be an artist. Kay was close to finishing her dissertation and getting her doctorate. In addition to continuing her teaching at the University of Hawaii, she was interested in another career in television and other forms of communications. Though Kay had been born in Alabama, she retained none of the qualities of a mainlander and had assumed much of the understanding and attitudes of a citizen of the world. She was a remarkable person—a scholar, teacher, poet, and lover of beauty in all its myriad forms. Her daughter, Karla, was a lovely child with all the colors of Hawaii in her face and sunbeams in her hair.

Lottie had some interesting friends. Agatha and Lottie took a ride up in the mountains far above Honolulu, from which Waikiki was visible. They stopped in front of a magnificent house that Agatha had admired, and Lottie remarked that it was the home of friends we were going to visit. We met this couple later and spent many hours with them playing bridge. The lady of the house was Japanese, and she had inherited the property from her brother, a prominent, wealthy, Hawaiian-Japanese doctor. Apparently her whole family had been deeply hurt by her marriage to an American man of color, and there had been no communication between her and her relatives for many years. Terminally ill, the doctor wrote to his sister and asked that she come to see him, saying that he had some important matters to discuss. When she visited, he told her with considerable emotion of his great regret over the rift that existed in the family. He was proud of the success she had made of her life and said he wanted her to be his sole heir because she had demonstrated conclusively that she was the only member of their family who could be depended upon to preserve the value of his large estate. The home was elaborately furnished in oriental style; having lived in Japan, we appreciated the quality of the many Japanese artifacts. All in all, we had a glorious visit to Hawaii, thanks to the beauty of the islands, the graciousness of the people, and the hospitality of our good friends, the Waddells.

A month after we had attended the Falcon Foundation meeting in Colorado Springs, we accepted an invitation from the Air Force Sergeants Association to Langley Air Force Base, where I was inducted into the Order of the Sword. It had always been clear to me that the Air Force could achieve no success without the willing and eager support of the thousands of enlisted people who hold in their hands the difference between victory and defeat. At any moment critical roles might be played by the line chief, who sees to it that aircraft are combat ready; the people in armament, communications, or supply; or the many others whose efforts are largely unsung. At Langley I was addressed by representatives of these people, whose contributions to the U.S. Air Force I considered to be of the highest order. Robert D. Gaylor, Chief Master Sergeant of the Air Force, said, "Our paths first crossed at Korat, Thailand, in 1967 when you visited our Wing as Commander, 13AF. As I sat in your audience, I was initially impressed by your love for the Air Force and concern for your fellow man. Those patterns were most obvious in your recent service as a member of the Pay Commission [Commission on Military Compensation] where you continually displayed the courage to speak out on behalf of all service members." Donald L. Harlow, a former Chief Master Sergeant of the Air Force, also spoke: "The courage of your convictions, steadfastness, and integrity exhibited while serving as a member of the Blue Ribbon Commission [Commission on Military Compensation] endeared you to the hearts of enlisted men and women of the United States Air Force throughout the world. On many issues which could prove detrimental to the morale and welfare of the enlisted corps of the Armed Services, you stood alone in opposition. However, as always, you stood tall with head unbowed." I was deeply grateful to the association for their recognition; no honor could have meant more to me.

I was also gratified to have a visit from Ed Gleed, who informed me that the Tuskegee Airmen, Inc., were going to present me with their prestigious Distinguished Achievement Award for my "efforts in breaking the race barrier in the once segregated skies of the U.S. military." An article in the national publication of the Tuskegee Airmen told of the part I had played over the years, helping to open the doors of West Point and the skies of the Air Force to black men and women. The article concluded that my presence among the black airmen who trained at Tuskegee and fought in World War II had "improved the quality of life for all Americans." I greatly appreciated the tribute, but I would have added that the outstanding men under my command had made it easy for me to achieve excellence, and that without their hard work and dedication I could have accomplished nothing worthwhile.

Shortly after Colonel Gleed's visit, I received a letter from Roy A. Anderson, chairman of the board of the Lockheed Corporation. Mr. Anderson informed me that he was serving as chairman of the Tuskegee Airmen Distinguished Achievement Award dinner, to be given in my honor at the Beverly Hilton Hotel in Los Angeles. He expressed his desire to expand the base of support for the Tuskegee Airmen Scholarship Fund and asked that I send a list of people who might want to participate in that effort. I provided the list and thanked Mr. Anderson for his participation in the worthwhile efforts of the Airmen.

Agatha and I greatly enjoyed our visit to Los Angeles to receive the award. The role I had played as commander of the 99th Fighter Squadron, the 332d Fighter Group, and the 477th Bombardment Group had not been easy, primarily because of the segregation that had then weighed so heavily on the lives of all black officers and airmen. The very nature of segregation was demeaning, and its effect upon its victims was deadening. I had found it absolutely necessary to compound the troubles of black officers and airmen by asking that they perform better than their contemporaries in comparable white Air Force units. The eventual result of these demands was recognition throughout the Air Force of superior achievement, and in the minds

of at least some of those under my command my actions were justified. Others did not fully understand my rigorous style, but years later
I received acknowledgments that the greater demands placed on our
people turned out to be beneficial to them. The black airmen of
Tuskegee are today viewed with the respect they earned, and they are
held in high regard throughout the military services.

## Museums and Lectures

In 1982 Agatha and I became deeply involved with the Smithsonian's
National Air and Space Museum. Curators Von Hardesty and Domi-
nick Pisano, realizing that the museum had not taken sufficient note
of the participation of blacks in aviation, asked us to provide information and consult with them in creating the Black Wings exhibit. We
participated in numerous conferences and provided detailed information, photographs, and other memorabilia. At Von's request, I narrated a script for the exhibit. Col. Bill Thompson, my armament officer
in the early days of the 99th, provided numerous photographs, background information, and other help. Agatha offered her valuable
insight into events that occurred at Tuskegee Army Air Field.

The Black Wings exhibit filled a substantial void in the Air and
Space Museum's collection. Agatha was interested to learn how it
was being received by the general public. Armed with a tape recorder,
she interviewed local people, people from other parts of the United
States, and foreigners at the museum. Not surprisingly, she discovered
that before visiting the exhibit, most people had not known that
blacks had participated in combat flying operations during World War
II. After Black Wings became a permanent part of the museum, a
traveling exhibit was designed and constructed so that it could be
used in various parts of the country. It was much in demand.

As a result of this collaboration with the museum, I became a
member of the committee that selected the winners of the newly
created National Air and Space Museum Trophy for outstanding
achievements in aerospace science and technology. Awards were
given for current and past accomplishment. Recently the trophy was
awarded to Richard Rutan and Jeana Yeager for their historic, nine-
day, nonstop, unrefueled flight around the world; and John Steiner,

leader of the Boeing team that developed the 727 airliner. A year later we attended the reception commemorating the installation of the Rutan-Yeager aircraft, *Voyager,* in the museum. I was honored to receive an invitation to present the Lindbergh Lecture at the museum on the 60th anniversary of Charles Lindbergh's 1927 flight from Long Island to Paris. I enjoyed preparing for the lecture and learned much more about Lindbergh than I had known before. My lecture pointed out how much this young American had contributed to the United States in achieving his near miracle—not only in the development of aviation, but also in his approach to life itself.

Agatha and I often attended lectures, accepting the invitation of the Secretary of the Smithsonian Institution and the chairman of Doubleday & Company to the annual Frank Nelson Doubleday Lectures. Some of the most memorable were "Arts, Letters, and Americans" by Studs Terkel; "Roots" by Alex Haley; "America on Stage" by Theodore S. Chapin and David Bishop; and the Washington premiere of "Huey Long," a film by Ken Burns. We will never forget "An Evening of Classic Jazz" with the Louisiana Repertory Jazz Ensemble of New Orleans, led by Frederick Starr, president of Oberlin College. Dr. Starr demonstrated his versatility on many different instruments, and the audience was thrilled by Louisiana's great contribution to American music. We also attended lectures on health-related issues at the National Institutes of Health, Montgomery College, and Arlington Hospital. At the National Archives we heard presentations on the Constitution, and from time to time we would go to programs at the Library of Congress. We also saw plays at Arena Stage, visited Washington's art museums, and frequently attended functions of the Sino-American Cultural Society, where we could catch up with our many Chinese friends.

Rather inadvertently, Agatha became involved in an issue of aviation safety while sitting innocently at home in our den, overlooking the Potomac. Having lived on air bases for a number of years, she was accustomed to the sound of planes flying over. On this day, however, what she described as a "tremendous roar" enveloped the room, and when she looked up, her view of the Potomac and all of Washington was blocked by a portion of an airplane's fuselage. All she could see was a small part of the side of the plane. Our apartment is on the ninth floor, and the airplane was well below and wide of the normal flight pattern. The newspapers reported the incident and the concern it had caused workers in the USA Today building, across the street from our apartment and much farther away from the path of the plane than we. It had also caused considerable alarm among our fellow tenants. Agatha reported the incident in writing to the FAA. It was investigated by two officials, one from FAA's Flight Standards Office and the other from the National Transportation Safety Board. The pilots' statements that they had not been where Agatha said they were was not borne out by the testimony from people who saw the airplane from the USA Today building. No airplanes have flown close to our apartment in recent years; now, when they go by our building, they stay over the Potomac.

In 1981 I received a cordial letter from Dr. Arthur Jefferson, the general superintendent of schools in Detroit, informing me that the Detroit Board of Education was planning to build five vocational/ technical centers for 11th- and 12th-grade students. He wrote, "The approval by the Board of Education to proceed with the development of the vocational/technical centers is a giant stride toward meeting the needs of a large number of young men and women who elect to enter the world of work upon the completion of high school as well as those who will continue their formal education. The centers will be committed to the delivery of quality vocational education programs and services that will prepare students to be competitive in the skilled job market." One of the centers, focusing on aerospace studies, was to be named the Benjamin Oliver Davis, Jr., Vocational/ Technical Center for, Dr. Jefferson wrote, the "outstanding contributions in the Air Force and the impact which you had on the many young men and women who followed you."

Upon my arrival in Detroit for the dedication of the Davis Center, I was met by Dr. Elmore Kennedy, who commanded one of my units during World War II, along with other members of the Detroit chapter of the Tuskegee Airmen. It was a pleasure to see them, and I especially appreciated having dinner and chatting with Elmore. I always had a strong feeling of gratification upon seeing the outstanding successes attained by so many of my wartime comrades. At the dedication, I spoke to a large audience and attended a reception given by the Tuskegee Airmen. It was a memorable opportunity to meet old friends and see the resources the new center would offer to Detroit's young people.

## Return to Alabama

I made four trips to Alabama during the 1980s, the first to attend the dedication of an Alabama National Guard Armory on the outskirts of Tuskegee. The armory was named for both my father and me: Fort Benjamin O. Davis, Sr., and Fort Benjamin O. Davis, Jr. After military honors to me, Dr. Luther H. Foster, president of Tuskegee Institute, spoke of the contributions my father and I had made to the Institute, and Mayor Johnny L. Ford presented me with the key to the city of Tuskegee. A new friendliness existed between blacks and whites in the city; it was encouraging to see that the spirit of democracy had taken hold, removing the hostility that had poisoned the atmosphere of 40 years earlier. An effective black mayor had been elected for all the people. I accepted with thanks the honor accorded my father and me by the state of Alabama, the city of Tuskegee, and the Institute. I spent the afternoon traveling around the area with Agatha's and my friend Laly Washington. Laly took me first to the Veterans Hospital to see our close mutual friend Rose Green, and we reminisced with Rose and other friends whom I had not seen in many years.

Agatha and I traveled to Maxwell Air Force Base in May 1986 to attend an Air Command and Staff College graduation project entitled "Gathering of Eagles." A letter from Maj. Julian D. Allen, the project officer, explained that the project was designed to develop an interest in aviation history within his class. No government funds were involved, and all expenses of the nonprofit endeavor would be covered through the sale of a limited-edition lithograph. An original painting would depict each aviator honored by the Gathering, his aircraft, and the spirit of manned flight he represented. Eighteen aviators met at Maxwell to sign the lithographs and be honored at a graduation dinner. For Agatha and me it was a privilege to spend some time in the company of the students, gain some perspective on the current Air Force and its people, and learn of the changes that had taken place since my retirement in 1970.

We were picked up by an Air Force Learjet at Andrews and flown to Maxwell, where we were met by Gen. Frank Willis, the commandant of the Air Command and Staff College; Mrs. Willis; our escort officer, Maj. Theodore Mercer; and his wife, Mikey. Ted Mercer had a background in missiles; upon graduation he would be reassigned to the Pentagon. Mikey worked as a flight attendant for United Airlines.

We would see a lot of the Mercers during our visit, and they made us feel very much at home.

The first evening we went to dinner at a large, popular restaurant on the outskirts of Montgomery. Seated near some of the other Eagles and their wives, we immediately found ourselves a part of the cordial group we would be with the next few days. I knew Paul Tibbets, who piloted the *Enola Gay* and dropped the first atomic bomb on Japan; Francis ("Gabby") Gabreski, who had shot down more enemy aircraft in aerial combat than any other living American ace from World War II and Korea; and Robert Scott, World War II ace, fighter group commander, and author of *God Is My Co-Pilot*, a book about flying combat in the Pacific theater. We were introduced to General Harris, a pioneer U.S. Air Service test pilot and veteran of the first American flight across the Alps; Clyde East, also a World War II ace, who had flown reconnaissance missions during the Cuban missile crisis; and Rudolf ("Pitz") Opitz, a German test pilot for the first operational rocket-powered flight.

Interspersed with the monumental chore of signing some 1,600 lithographs, we were interviewed by local and national media representatives. Meanwhile, our wives took bus tours of historic Montgomery, the first capital of the Confederacy; and Selma and the route of the Montgomery-Selma civil rights march. The Montgomery chapter of the Air Force Association held a luncheon for all the aviators, their wives, and official guests of the Air Command and Staff College. The members of the Air Force Association contribute greatly to the Air Force in all its efforts, and in Montgomery, as in other chapters, they represented the leadership of the community. Agatha and I could not help contrasting this visit to Maxwell with our visits of earlier days and noting the changes that had taken place since 1950. It was hard to find anything in common between the inhumane treatment of those days and the warmth of the local people at the Gathering.

The graduation dinner and dance, a colorful, formal affair with a military motif, was held at the Montgomery Civic Center. After dinner each aviator was introduced in a short film clip, showing why he had been selected to participate. Foreign aviators were especially welcomed and honored: Capt. Hans H. Wind, the top-ranking Finnish ace, with 75 victories; and Air Vice Marshal James E. ("Johnnie") Johnson, the top-scoring ace in the British Commonwealth during

World War II, with 38 victories. The audience took special notice of the accomplishments of Bobbie Trout, a pioneer woman aviator of the 1920s and 1930s, and two winners of the Medal of Honor, Col. William R. Lawley and Chief Warrant Officer Michael J. Novosel. All of us were similarly recognized: Comdr. Alexander Vraciu, the U.S. Navy's ranking ace, with 19 victories; Lt. Col. Roger C. Locher, with three victories in Vietnam, who evaded the enemy for 23 days after being shot down; and Col. Joseph W. Kittinger, Jr., holder of balloon and parachute altitude and distance records and a Vietnam prisoner of war credited with downing one MIG. The audience reserved its loudest applause for Rear Adm. Alan B. Shepard, Jr., one of the original seven U.S. astronauts, the first American in space, and the fifth man on the moon.

After the last scheduled event of the Gathering, we took a prearranged drive to Tuskegee Institute, which the Mercers had never visited, and tried in vain to find Tuskegee Army Air Field. All the buildings had been removed, and only the runways remained. We did find Tuskegee's railroad station at Chehaw, which I had last seen when the 99th Fighter Squadron boarded a troop train there in April 1943. The station was in shambles. Seeing it brought back unpleasant memories of segregated railroad cars, the condescending attitudes of Chehaw employees, and the degrading treatment blacks received there. I particularly recalled the quaint practice of assigning Lower 13, a drawing room on a Pullman car, to certain black officials so they would not encounter the full effects of segregation experienced by less privileged blacks. As we drove through Chehaw, we saw a political candidate for state office making a campaign speech from a restored and politically decorated railroad car. But my thoughts kept drifting back to the harsh treatment reserved for blacks by the ruling class of the South in the 1930s.

After driving around to see the area's landmarks, we visited a number of old friends, among them Chief Anderson, who had contributed so much to the early progress of blacks in aviation. We then drove through the Institute campus, toured the George Washington Carver Museum, and looked at the buildings and other places that were so familiar to Agatha and me. We were a little disappointed in the overall appearance of the campus; its upkeep was not at the high standard we remembered. We attempted to call on Reverend Newman, who had rented us a house when we really needed one, and left a note at the door. Some days later we received a letter from Mrs. Newman telling us that Reverend Newman had died and thanking us for remembering them. We drove by "the block," a local commercial section, and saw the house we had lived in when we were stationed at Tuskegee Institute. On the way back to Maxwell we passed the house Tuskegee Institute had built for my family when my father took us there from Washington in 1920. Early the next morning we said our goodbyes and departed for Andrews. It had been an exhilarating and nostalgic five days.

I returned to Maxwell a few months later to appear with three other aviators in a program called "Air Power: Living History." Gen. Frank Willis, whom I had met at the Gathering of Eagles, explained that hearing about our experiences would give the class an uncommon perspective on tactical air combat by means of teaching interviews. The other guests were Col. Walker ("Bud") Mahurin, Col. Joseph Jackson, and Col. Leo Thorsness. I had known Bud Mahurin in the early 1950s when I had been stationed in the Pentagon. He had an impressive combat record: 21 victories in Europe during World War II, one in the Pacific, and three and a half during the Korean War. He had also spent 16 months in solitary confinement as a prisoner of war in Korea. Colonel Jackson, a fighter pilot in the Korean War, had been awarded the Distinguished Flying Cross. In 1967 he had earned the Congressional Medal of Honor as the Da Nang Air Base detachment commander while flying a C-123, the only Air Force airlift pilot to receive this honor. Colonel Thorsness won the Congressional Medal of Honor while flying a mission to North Vietnam in a two-seat F-105 "wild weasel," designed to protect other American attack aircraft from surface-to-air missiles and antiaircraft artillery. Considering the great concentration of defensive weapons in the Hanoi area, the inherent nature of the "wild weasel" mission made it especially dangerous. Shot down and captured 11 days later, Colonel Thorsness had spent almost six years in captivity.

My area was close air support during World War II. I answered questions about the characteristics of the P-40, the P-47, and the P-51; the differences in their utilization by my fighter units in close air support operations; ground attack operations on targets in Sicily; air coverage of the Salerno and Anzio landings, with particular attention to the attack of ground targets at Anzio and support of the beach-head; attacks on enemy radar in preparation for the invasion of southern France; the use of the P-51 in long-range bomber escort missions over Europe; and the differences between my command of conventional fighter squadrons in World War II and my command of an F-86 jet fighter wing in Korea. Finally, the subject of blacks in the Air Force before, during, and after World War II was raised. I discussed the problems of segregation and the contributions black airmen had made during the war, making it possible for the Air Force to integrate blacks into white Air Force units. It was stimulating to participate in discussions with modern-day Air Force student officers.

I visited Huntsville, Alabama, several months later to be inducted into the Alabama Aviation Hall of Fame along with Edward Stinson, Dr. Wernher von Braun (deceased), and Robert Hudgens. I enjoyed meeting the cordial people of Huntsville and listening to the frank, informative remarks of the guest speaker, astronaut Henry Hartsfield. A special bonus was seeing an old friend, Gen. John Dyas, a former Hall of Fame inductee who had retired from the Air Force and was now living in Mobile. Johnny and I had been assigned to Ramstein Air Base in Germany together. Cols. Herbert Carter and Chuck Dryden, who had served with me in the 99th more than 40 years before, also attended the ceremony.

## More Tributes

In February 1987 John C. Spooner, vice president and director of human relations of the Harris Bank of Chicago, invited me to participate in the bank's annual Black History Month. I strongly believe that black history should be considered an integral part of American history, and not treated as a subject apart. I wanted, however, to support the bank's effort. Mr. Spooner gave me some compelling incentives to participate, pointing out that their main objective was to plant "good seeds" in the hearts and minds of their 4,000 employees, of whom 22 percent were black. The bank had developed a booklet depicting the history of the Tuskegee airmen to give their employees an example of how obstacles can be overcome and goals achieved, even in the most hostile of social environments. It stressed the accomplishments of the airmen against the odds and the resistance they faced, and informed bank employees of a chapter in U.S. history that they might not have been exposed to in the past. Prepared with generous assistance from

Col. Bill Thompson's extensive collection of photographs and other memorabilia, the booklet was by far the best publication of its kind I had seen. The bank also invited wartime members of the 332d Fighter Group from all parts of the country to Chicago as their guests and developed a photographic display on black aviation, which was open to the general public. As I requested, the bank also made a generous contribution to the Tuskegee Airmen Scholarship Fund. I was delighted to see the airmen who attended the event and a party given by the Chicago chapter of the Tuskegee Airmen. Felix Kirkpatrick, who had been an active fighter pilot in the 332d during World War II, was the chapter president.

In September 1987 the Office of Air Force History published *Makers of the United States Air Force,* edited by John L. Frisbee. The book's preface states:

> Realizing that it takes more than a handful of leaders to ensure the creation, growth, and continuing success of the Air Force, the [Air Force Historical] Foundation decided to produce an anthology in which it identified twelve unique individuals whose careers provide penetrating and valuable insights into those major elements that give new meaning to the definition of leadership. After much reflection, twelve outstanding leaders—Hoyt Vandenberg, Nathan Twining, George Kenney, Bernard Schriever, Frank Andrews, Benjamin Davis, Harold George, William Kepner, Elwood Quesada, Benjamin Foulois, Hugh Knerr, and Robbie Risner—were selected for inclusion in this anthology. While it was recognized that many other individuals also merit special note for their distinguished Air Force accomplishments, it was decided that the careers of the above-mentioned twelve general officers best represented a cross-section of the Air Force leadership and the unique problems they faced during the last half century. In both peace and war they faced challenges that brought out the best in each of them, and their accomplishments, encompassing everything from combat operations to high command, have produced some of the major milestones in the history of military aviation.

I was deeply honored to be included in this study and named as one of this prominent group of men. The chapter about me, written by the distinguished Air Force historian Dr. Alan L. Gropman, emphasizes the participation of blacks in the Army Air Corps and World War II and their integration into the mainstream of the Air Force. It concludes with the following paragraph: "General Benjamin O. Davis, Jr., can claim a larger measure of credit for inaugurating this critical reform [integration] than can any other person. None of his many achievements holds for him the satisfaction of moving the United States Air Force to racial integration. For that pioneering accomplishment, America stands in his debt." In response to this tribute, I can only express my boundless gratitude for the efforts of the black men and women of the Air Force, who were the key players in the great drama that finally made integration attractive to Air Force leaders.

# ★ ★ ★    West Point Revisited

**21.**

*Agatha and I spent hours in the Academy's Directorate of Admissions office. Our session was open, unreserved, and frank. We discussed changes in curriculum, the attitude toward minorities, the treatment of cadets, leave, athletics, cars, and uniforms. The service academies had become far more democratic than they had been in my day.*

In 1987, more than 50 years after I had left the U.S. Military Academy, Agatha and I decided to visit West Point, compare it with the Academy we had known when I was a cadet, and collect material from its archives for this autobiography. During those five decades many changes had taken place at West Point, in the United States, in its people, and in us. We had followed activities at the Point through television, newspapers, and magazine articles, in addition to conversations with the cadets, officers, and families we had met through the years. We had also received useful written material from the Academy. Nevertheless, I wanted to get the flavor of West Point in the 1980s, see for myself the changes that had taken place, talk with some of the officials and cadets, and spend several days learning firsthand many things I could not possibly discover in any other way.

In May 1987 I wrote a letter to the Superintendent requesting permission to visit the archives, see the Academy's physical plant, and learn the current philosophy of cadet education. We asked to stay at the Visiting Officers Quarters and spend time with the Academy's public affairs staff, who could help us in our investigation. After the dates of June 1 to 7 were suggested, I contacted the archivist and sent a list of the materials we would like to review.

We looked forward to seven educational and memory-filled days. We drove north from Arlington through New Jersey to Route 9W, which took us into West Point. On the way we reminisced about my four years there, the Saturdays we had spent together, and just how much they had meant to me. The drive was beautiful, especially Palisades Parkway; it was an unparalleled treat to see all the brilliant colors of nature in full bloom. On many a Friday when I was a cadet, Agatha had driven from New Haven to New York City, spent the night with Vivienne, and on Saturday crossed the Hudson River by ferry to 9W, which in the early 1930s was a two-lane road. It was easy to drive to West Point now compared to then.

As we neared Highland Falls, adjacent to the Academy, we knew we would soon be approaching Thayer Gate, the south entrance to the post. Highland Falls had grown. It still looked like a small town, only more sprawling. Outside the gate, what was once a Catholic school had been purchased by the government, and one of the buildings was the new Visitors' Information Center. As we drove through the gate to Thayer Road, we felt the impact of being once more on the West Point grounds. On our way to the Public Affairs Office, we passed by many of the regal Gothic buildings I remembered so well. When I had been at West Point there were only 1,400 cadets, but by 1987 enrollment had increased to 4,400. The construction of new buildings to accommodate this increase had radically altered the appearance of the Academy. Some of the new buildings encroached upon the Plain, and as a result the Academy had lost much of its graceful beauty and looked more crowded than I remembered it.

We could tell immediately that we would have a pleasant and profitable few days when we found Albert Konecny waiting outside the Public Affairs Office to greet us. A senior civilian in the office, Mr. Konecny had worked at West Point for several years and knew about almost everything we wanted to learn during our visit. He welcomed us cordially and offered us his office's parking space while we were at the Academy. No other spaces were available in the cramped and overcrowded headquarters area, so we greatly appreciated his thoughtfulness.

Mr. Konecny took us to the Public Affairs Office, where we met Col. John B. Yeagley, the public affairs officer. After a few words about our mission, Colonel Yeagley gave us an interesting briefing about the life and activities of West Point in 1987. While we were engaged in this lively session, Lt. Gen. David Palmer, the Superintendent, came in to greet us and ask if the itinerary that had been prepared was satisfactory. We could ask for little more; a full schedule had been made out for each day of our visit. General Palmer, a historian, was a charming, down-to-earth, relaxed gentleman. Before he left our meeting, he invited us to have lunch in his quarters on Wednesday.

Just before we left Colonel Yeagley's office, Maj. Richard Sutton of the Equal Opportunity Branch of the Directorate of Admissions arrived and invited us to a briefing at the Admissions Office the next afternoon. Mr. Konecny rode with us en route to Newburgh, where we were going to stay, and immediately commenced his tour-guide routine. He was obviously eager to reacquaint us with the old buildings and how they and the grounds had been altered to accommodate the necessary enlargements of the physical plant.

## Retrospective Thoughts

The first half-day of our visit had thus been a rip-roaring success. We left the post and drove to Newburgh to the Morale, Welfare, and Recreation Center of the Stewart Army Subpost, which some of my golf buddies had recommended as a desirable place to stay. In 1972 Gen. Charles Bonesteel, my boss in Korea as commander in chief, United Nations Command, had asked me to be a member of the board of trustees of the Association of Graduates. Attending a meeting of the board at that time, I stayed at the Thayer Hotel—owned by the government, run by a contractor, and open for use by the public. I found it to be a great disappointment; surely, accommodations at Stewart had to be better.

After my 1972 visit I had received a letter from the Superintendent at that time, Lt. Gen. William A. Knowland:

> The number of our Black cadets [has] continued to increase, and I am interested in providing for them here at the Academy some visual evidence of the military heritage they have received from their forebears in the Armed Forces. Among the exploits of units, the service of the 9th and 10th Cavalries in the Indian Wars and at San Juan Hill comes readily to

mind, while in the area of individual careers, yours is of exceptional distinction. I believe that if we could display a portrait of you in a place commonly frequented by cadets, such as Grant Hall, it would represent a source of both satisfaction and inspiration for these young men. By encouraging pride in past achievements, it could instill the determination to live up to a great tradition and convey a sense of belonging by right to the military profession. I find that many of our Black cadets are well aware of their heritage, but I believe public recognition of it would provide a welcome reinforcement. These considerations lead me to ask you to consent to sit for a portrait which would be painted by a leading portraitist and displayed at West Point. The West Point Fund Advisory Committee has endorsed the project wholeheartedly and the fund will defray all expenses. . . . I look forward to a favorable reply with the conviction that the completion and display of the portrait will represent a satisfying distinct service to West Point.

I replied as follows:

Dear Bill:

I wrote you yesterday indicating my pleasure to accept the honor you did me by suggesting the display of a portrait of me at West Point and agreeing to everything in your letter. Unfortunately, after more mature consideration I have changed my mind and prefer not to have the portrait made and displayed under the concept described in your letter.

There are several schools of thought on the utilization of black servicemen in the Armed Forces. As you know, we went through the separate unit segregated phase into a phase in which the black serviceman was simply another serviceman who was treated and employed without regard to his race. Now, we seem to be in a rather fluid state in which some black people desire to emphasize their race and seek out separate treatment in various forms. I still belong to the school that would treat all servicemen alike in every respect and in no way take official notice of their race. I recognize the fact that many people disagree with this position, but I would extend it beyond the Armed Forces to include indiscriminate treatment of all citizens regardless of race.

Having the views that I have, I think it would be inconsistent for me to have my portrait displayed as "a source of both satisfaction and inspiration" for black cadets, the reason simply being that there is a strong implication of the existence of a separate group in the Corps of Cadets. To some this concept is unimportant; to me it is most important because it is something I have lived with for a very long time.

The letter I wrote to you yesterday expressed my gratitude to you for your kind offer, and I repeat it in this letter.

The drive to Stewart was picturesque. The base, however, was deserted and dreary, and although the people who ran the temporary officers' quarters welcomed us cordially and were quite helpful, the quarters themselves were a disaster. We had to share a bathroom with the occupant of the adjoining room and, unaware of how the locks worked, we failed to unlock the door to his bedroom. At 4:00 A.M. there was a loud knocking on our door; our neighbor wanted to use the toilet. The desk clerk came running and explained how the locks were supposed to be operated. We knew then that this was not the place for us and decided to move as soon as we could find a better place to stay.

Early the next morning we drove to the Point to make our scheduled tour with Mr. Konecny. Agatha was eager to see my room; the sinks, where the meeting to silence me had taken place; classrooms; recreation rooms; the enlarged dining hall; and places we never got to see in the 1930s. Of course we also wanted to see the library, where we had spent so many hours on the cold, rainy, or snowy days when she visited me.

We went by the archives to meet the staff and make arrangements to do daily research. Marie Capps, acting archivist, was a veritable walking encyclopedia on the Academy, eager to help us all she could with our book. We spent many happy hours talking with her, asking questions, and finding material pertaining to my days as a cadet. Her husband, Col. Jack L. Capps, was a professor and the head of the Department of English. She had lived on the post for many years, and her son, a West Pointer, had had a black roommate.

## A New Spirit of Democracy

That afternoon we spent hours in the Directorate of Admissions office. We were received by Col. Pierce A. Rushton, Jr., the director of admissions; Major Sutton; and an impressive young captain who recruited male and female black students from many integrated and segregated high schools all over the nation. Our session was open, unreserved, and frank. Agatha had brought a long list of questions, and she was as skilled as a professional journalist in her investigations. We discussed changes in curriculum, the attitude toward minorities, the treatment of cadets, leave, athletics, cars, and uniforms. These and other changes had been brought about by President Truman's bold and far-reaching 1948 executive order mandating the desegregation of the armed forces and equal opportunity for all its members; courageous civil and human rights actions by President Johnson, who increased the authorized strength of the Corps of Cadets to 4,400; and President Nixon's opening of the academies to qualified women. As a result, the service academies had become far more democratic than they had been in my day.

Many important changes had been brought about by the Department of Defense, some of them stemming from scandals over honor violations, such as the case of James Pelosi. Cadet dissatisfaction had led to more humane regulations, and the treatment of all minorities had improved. The curriculum had been modernized and expanded to offer many previously unavailable majors and elective subjects. Largely as a result of these changes, interest in the military academies had surged. Young men and women were attracted by the prospect of receiving a free and excellent education with $6,500 a year pay; free room, board, and medical and dental care; a bachelor's degree; and upon graduation, a commission as a second lieutenant with annual pay of $18,000. In return they assumed the obligation to serve their country for five years after graduation. Whatever the reasons for the changes, they seemed to appeal to the general population, and the academies were having no trouble meeting their recruiting objectives. In 1984–85, about 12,644 applicants sought admission to West Point, of whom 2,736 qualified for admission, 1,935 were offered admission, and 1,432 were enrolled.

The treatment of black officers and soldiers has always been a serious problem in all the military services. Even today some people believe the desegregation of the military remains incomplete, if not in law, at least in the attitude and behavior of many of its members. Agatha and I discussed this subject in detail at our meeting in the Admissions Office. She reminded us that it is a myth that white people have to study black people and black people have to study white people for us to understand one another. She maintained that all people come into the world the same way and leave the same way, and that we all share the same essential goals and aspirations. She believed that 40 years of equal opportunity and courses to teach people to be kind and civil to others should have been enough. Given the limited progress that has been made in the fight against racism, however, she strongly supported equal opportunity and affirmative action, which recognizes that blacks in the United States are disadvantaged from birth and require treatment that will enable them to compete on an equal basis.

Although we have laws mandating equal opportunity, they have in no way produced their intended results, nor have the federal Equal Employment Opportunity Commission and other governmental agencies. Even well-qualified and overqualified blacks continue to be denied jobs on the basis of their race. Laws and regulations do represent progress, but all too often the final decision is a personal choice by a prejudiced employer. For the same reason, active recruitment of minorities and women continues to be needed. Far from representing an unhealthy emphasis on race and gender over qualifications, such programs will remain necessary in the foreseeable future to overcome obstacles and provide at least some progress toward equal opportunity.

By 1987 West Point had already devoted considerable attention to the enrollment of minority students and women. An applicant could still be nominated by a member of Congress, the President, Vice President, or someone in the military services, but the race, nationality, and religion of the nominee were not asked on the nomination forms. As part of West Point's recruiting and admissions program, special information packets for minorities and women were distributed. In 1986 a memorandum from the equal admissions officer stated that "the military's long range goal is to have the Corps' minority population proportional to that of the national population." At the time of our visit, however, recent progress toward that goal had slowed. We learned that the admissions staff were trying hard to reach more qualified minority high school juniors and seniors through visits to schools all over the United States and by obtaining help from West Point graduates.

Our discussion group agreed that much remains to be done to bring minorities into the mainstream of American life. Many Americans believe that all the progress in this area that is needed has already been accomplished, but the fact is that minority groups retain a sense of stigma, of being separate and unequal, living apart with marked feelings of hostility. The movement forward to eliminate this unsatisfactory condition was measurably slowed during the 1980s, and America is sorely in need of a renewed effort to eliminate racist attitudes.

One symptom of these persistent attitudes is the nomenclature applied to Greek Americans, Italian Americans, Irish Americans, black Americans, and other ethnic groups. Some black Americans, Rev. Jesse Jackson among them, have suggested that blacks be called African Americans. As President Theodore Roosevelt remarked some decades ago, Americanism is diminished by this kind of divisive nomenclature. We are all simply Americans. Differentiations created by extensive statistical studies for no obvious purpose except to prove the superiority of a particular group are not helpful, and surely the unnecessary labeling of people by race, religion, or ethnicity does nothing to bring the many diverse groups of American society together. Sandra Day O'Connor is probably tired of hearing that she is the first woman appointee to the Supreme Court, and I do not find it complimentary to me or to the nation to be called "the first black West Point graduate in this century."

In 1976 women were admitted to all the military academies for the first time. They were not allowed to be married or pregnant or to have children to support. Otherwise, except for height and weight, the entrance requirements for women were the same as those for men, and all benefits and pay were the same. Women sometimes wore skirts, but their uniforms in other respects were similar to the men's. Plebe women could date only plebe men. As yearlings they could date anyone except plebes. Some jewelry was authorized to be worn with some uniforms; clear nail polish was permitted. The barracks where they lived were also occupied by male cadets, and each room for males or females had two or three cadets living in it. Short hair was preferred for women; it was not permitted to extend below the bottom edge of the collar. Athletics, just as important for women as they were for men, continued to be strongly emphasized in the 1980s, as they had been in the 1930s. Every cadet had to compete in intramural or intercollegiate sports, some of which were practiced only by women.

Great changes had taken place in leave policies at West Point. I had taken my first Christmas leave about 18 months after I had entered the Academy, furlough the summer of 1934, and Christmas leave in 1934 and 1935. Modern cadets all have three summer vacations of one month each, as well as Christmas leave each year, including plebe year.

Only first classmen were allowed to keep cars at West Point. The cadets of 1936 were not even allowed to sit in a parked car. I was skinned by Capt. Clyde Eddleman for sitting in a car with Agatha near Michie Stadium, costing me 6 demerits and 10 punishment tours, for which I had to walk the area for 10 hours on Wednesdays and Saturdays. Captain Eddleman later became Vice Chief of Staff of the Army. I was also skinned by Gen. Omar Bradley for riding in Agatha's car on a portion of a road near Michie Stadium, where we were not supposed to be. This little ride cost me 3 demerits.

In my day poor grades had meant a cadet would be found and dismissed, although he could be allowed to return the next school year and drop down to the class below. Some cadets would spend five years at the Academy before graduating. Today some cadets who have not made good grades during the school year are allowed to go to summer school and, if they pass, to continue with their class. In the 1930s all cadets took the same courses, but now, in addition to required subjects, there is a large number of electives.

Washington Hall, the mess hall, had been greatly enlarged to serve about 4,400 cadets each day. No change had taken place in the seating at meals; it was still 10 cadets to a table, with family-style service. In 1987 plebes were expected to attend all weekday meals, and upperclassmen had a choice of a full or continental breakfast. In the 1930s the allowance for rations had been $.60 per day; today it is $3.80. This allowance constitutes a major benefit, especially considering the high cost of food and the fact that the benefit is not taxable. A so-called poop deck is used by the Superintendent, the commandant, the dean, or the officer of the day. Dignitaries and official guests are also invited to eat there. When I was a plebe and my father visited me at the Point, the two of us were permitted to have our meals on the poop deck. The mess hall is quite colorful, decorated with portraits of all the former Superintendents and the flags of all the states, the District of Columbia, and Puerto Rico.

Cadets live by the honor code, and it is expected that as officers they will continue to observe its principles. The code at West Point is quite simple: "A cadet will not lie, cheat, or steal, nor tolerate those who do." All cadets are carefully indoctrinated in the meaning of the code, so there is complete confidence that they will not violate it in any way. Anyone disregarding any element of the honor system is reported to the Cadet Honor Committee. If found guilty of an honor offense, a cadet could be dismissed, tried by court-martial, or required to resign from the Academy in disgrace.

In 1973 the Honor Committee voted to do away with silencing, which included requiring the silenced cadet to eat and room alone. (It interested me that the silencing imposed upon me did not include eating alone, although several cadets avoided sitting at a mess hall table to which I was assigned.) The commandant's office redefined the practice of forcing plebes to brace—that is, standing at exaggerated attention—as hazing. It also changed some of its regulations and modified many rules. In 1973 the courts ruled that mandatory attendance at chapel violated the Constitution and that such attendance must no longer be required. I had marched to chapel every Sunday for four years.

## A Place in West Point History

Before we left our marathon session with the well-informed people at Admissions, we had covered a great deal of *West Point Today,* the information manual published by the Academy. We were grateful for all the help they had given us, considerably improving our understanding of the new West Point. Our next stop was the library and the archives to learn more about what had happened from 1932 to 1936. To get into the building we had to walk through a metal detector and sign in. At the desk Agatha asked whether they had any books, magazines, or newspapers with any information about Benjamin O. Davis, Jr. The man at the desk checked and found some cards in the files. One of them read "Davis, Benjamin Oliver, Jr., 1912–1970." We were momentarily puzzled by the "1970," which could only mean that I had died in that year. Agatha suggested that a mistake had been made, pointing out that Benjamin O. Davis, Jr., was alive, well, and at that very moment standing in front of the librarian. Obviously, because my father had died in 1970, the date had been put on my card by mistake. I asked that the 1970 be taken off the card, and we all had a big laugh when the librarian said, "I have to get permission before I can change it."

The archives were unbelievably orderly and jam-packed with history. Mrs. Capps took us into a room where she had piled up books, magazines, orders books, and articles on a huge table. We were able to spend days reading about and reliving my cadet days. Each day we visited the archives we had long chats with Mrs. Capps, who had answers to all our questions. She loved West Point, had spent many years learning about it and, most important to us, was kind enough to share her knowledge. Meeting and spending time with her was one of the highlights of our visit, and after we left we took advantage of her offer to write when we needed more information.

Our next stop was the Thayer Hotel. To our surprise, it had been recently renovated and now had 170 rooms, so we were glad to make a reservation and stay there for the remainder of our visit. Besides being a better place to stay, the Thayer was also more convenient to West Point than Newburgh.

After spending the rest of the morning with Mr. Konecny, we joined Superintendent and Mrs. Palmer for lunch in their quarters. Their home was impressive, filled with handsome antiques and inhabited by two warm, friendly, and cordial people. We felt that we had known them for a long time. After lunch General Palmer walked us to his office, where we were treated to a historian's perspective on his position as Superintendent. The office itself was a museum, full of all kinds of military memorabilia. In another room portraits of the past Superintendents hung on all four walls.

We spent the next two days doing research at the archives. We could have spent much more time there, but the library was closed on weekends, so we spent Saturday seeing the U.S. Military Academy Museum and the Visitors Center. In the Visitors Center, an exhibit entitled "The Great Train of Tradition" comprised an entire wall of pictures of outstanding West Point cadets from 1819 to 1950. Two men were included from the class of 1936: William C. Westmoreland, "Chief of Staff, Army, Commander, Forces Viet Nam, and Superintendent"; and Benjamin O. Davis, Jr., "World War hero, helped integrate Air Force."

The next day we left for the long drive home. Agatha asked me how I had enjoyed my return to the Point. My answer was, "It was the best week I ever spent at West Point."

# ★ ★ ★ Index